Mark L. Howe Charles J. Brainerd
Valerie F. Reyna
Editors

Development of Long-Term Retention

With 27 Illustrations

Springer-Verlag
New York Berlin Heidelberg London Paris
Tokyo Hong Kong Barcelona Budapest

Mark L. Howe
Department of Psychology
Memorial University
St. John's, Newfoundland
Canada A1B 3X9

Charles J. Brainerd
Department of Educational Psychology
University of Arizona
Tucson, AZ 85721
USA

Valerie F. Reyna
Department of Educational Psychology
University of Arizona
Tucson, AZ 85721
USA

Library of Congress Cataloging-in-Publication Data
Development of long-term retention / edited by Mark L. Howe, Charles J. Brainerd, and Valerie F. Reyna.
p. cm.
Includes bibliographical references and index.

ISBN-13: 978-1-4612-7702-6 e-ISBN-13: 978-1-4612-2868-4
DOI:10.1007/ 978-1-4612-2868-4

1. Memory in children. I. Howe, Mark L. II. Brainerd, Charles J. III. Reyna, Valerie F., 1955-
[DNLM: 1. Retention (Psychology) – in infancy & childhood. WS 105.5.M2 D489]
BF723.M4D48 1992
155.4'13122 – dc20 91-5157

Printed on acid-free paper.

Softcover reprint of the hardcover 1st edition 1992

Production managed by Bill Imbornoni; manufacturing supervised by Jacqui Ashri.
Typeset by Best-Set Typesetter, Ltd., Chaiwan, Hong Kong.

9 8 7 6 5 4 3 2 1

Preface

For a number of decades now the study of children's memory development, with few exceptions, has been synonymous with the development of processes that lead to the initial encoding and immediate retention of information. Although there is little doubt that the study of such acquisition processes is central to understanding memory development, the long-term retention of previously encoded information represents at least as important a component of children's memory. Indeed, as both students of memory development and educators, our interest is in the maintenance and utilization of knowledge over considerable periods of time, not just in the immediate (e.g., classroom) context. Clearly, then, without an understanding of how recently acquired information is maintained in memory over extended periods of time, our theories of long-term memory development remain incomplete at best.

Although children's forgetting and reminiscence was a topic of inquiry early in this century, it is only recently, due in part to the current controversy concerning the reliability of children's eyewitness testimony, that the study of long-term retention has resurfaced in the scientific literature. The purpose of this volume is to draw together some of the principals involved in this resurgence to summarize their recent research programs, present new and previously unpublished findings from their labs, and outline the issues they believe are important in the study of children's long-term retention. In so doing, we hope to underscore the importance of examining ontogenetic changes in long-term retention processes in their own right. We also hope that this volume acts as a catalyst, encouraging others to get involved in this often neglected area of study and participate in the formalization of a more extended theory of memory development in childhood.

The authors of the chapters in this volume grapple with a number of key issues in long-term retention, including the extent to which changes in what is remembered are the result of alterations of the memories themselves in storage as well as alterations in how such memories are retrieved, how memories can be inoculated against forgetting, and how memories that are apparently gone can be reinstated. The chapters are organized into three sections. The first section deals with fundamental issues in retention development, namely forgetting and memory reactivation in infancy (Rovee-Collier & Shyi, Chapter 1), formal modeling of storage and retrieval contributions to forgetting and reminiscence in childhood and early adulthood (Howe, Kelland, Bryant-Brown, & Clark, Chapter 2), and the relationship between the type of information retained (verbatim or gist) and reasoning (Reyna, Chapter 3). The second section deals with more pragmatic concerns, namely children's retention of naturalistic events, including visits to the doctor (Ornstein, Gordon, & Baker-Ward, Chapter 4), the influence of misinformation on recollection (Loftus, Hoffman, & Wagenaar, Chapter 5; Zaragoza, Dahlgren, & Muench, Chapter 6), and the role of suggestibility in event retention (Toglia, Ross, Ceci, & Hembrooke, Chapter 7). In the final section, Howe, O'Sullivan, and Marche (Chapter 8) provide an integrative overview of the issues raised in the various chapters, ones that are critical to charting the developmental course of changes in children's long-term retention.

We are pleased with the contributions of the authors to this volume and are gratified that the chapters represent a robust blend of theoretical development, methodological/analytical innovation, and empirical data. Although there are at least as many questions raised as there are answered, it is hoped that the vibrant discussion of issues in this volume will stimulate further basic and applied research on the development of long-term retention. With interest in the maintenance of children's memories rekindled, perhaps a more complete theory of the development of children's memory will be forthcoming.

Acknowledgment. Preparation of this volume was facilitated by a research grant from the Natural Sciences and Engineering Research Council of Canada (OGP0003334) to Mark L. Howe.

Mark L. Howe
Charles J. Brainerd
Valerie F. Reyna

Contents

Contributors

LYNNE E. BAKER-WARD, PHD
Department of Psychology, North Carolina State University, Raleigh, NC 27695-7801, USA

LYNN BRYANT-BROWN
Department of Psychology, Memorial University, St. John's, Newfoundland, A1B 3X9, Canada

STEPHEN J. CECI, PHD
Human Development and Family Studies, Cornell University, Ithaca, NY 14853, USA

SANDRA L. CLARK
Department of Psychology, Memorial University, St. John's, Newfoundland, A1B 3X9, Canada

DONNA DAHLGREN
Department of Psychology, Kent State University, Kent, OH 44242, USA

BETTY N. GORDON, PHD
Department of Psychology, University of North Carolina, Chapel Hill, NC 27599-3270, USA

HELENE HEMBROOKE
Department of Psychology, State University of New York at Binghamton, Binghamton, NY 13901, USA

HUNTER G. HOFFMAN
Department of Psychology, University of Washington, Seattle, WA 98195, USA

Mark L. Howe, PhD
Department of Psychology, Memorial University, St. John's, Newfoundland, A1B 3X9, Canada

Andrea Kelland
Faculty of Education, Memorial University, St. John's, Newfoundland, A1B 3X8, Canada

Elizabeth F. Loftus, PhD
Department of Psychology, University of Washington, Seattle, WA 98195, USA

Tammy A. Marche
Department of Psychology, Memorial University, St. John's, Newfoundland, A1B 3X9, Canada

Jean Muench
Department of Psychology, Kent State University, Kent, OH 44242, USA

Peter A. Ornstein, PhD
Department of Psychology, University of North Carolina, Chapel Hill, NC 27599-3270, USA

Julia T. O'Sullivan, PhD
Faculty of Education, Memorial University, St. John's, Newfoundland, A1B 3X8, Canada

Valerie F. Reyna, PhD
Department of Educational Psychology, University of Arizona, Tucson, AZ 85721, USA

Carolyn Rovee-Collier, PhD
Department of Psychology, Busch Campus, Rutgers University, New Brunswick, NJ 08903, USA

David F. Ross, PhD
Department of Psychology, Boise State University, Boise, ID 83715, USA

C.-W. Gary Shyi
Department of Psychology, Busch Campus, Rutgers University, New Brunswick, NJ 08903, USA

Michael P. Toglia, PhD
Department of Psychology, State University of New York, College at Cortland, Cortland, NY 13045, USA

WILLEM A. WAGENAAR, PHD
Vakgroep Functieleer, Leiden University, Postbus 9509, 2300 RA Leiden, Netherlands

MARIA S. ZARAGOZA, PHD
Department of Psychology, Kent State University, Kent, OH 44242, USA

Part I
Fundamental Aspects of Retention

1
A Functional and Cognitive Analysis of Infant Long-Term Retention

CAROLYN ROVEE-COLLIER and C.-W. GARY SHYI

Introduction

It is widely thought that the brain of the young infant is not sufficiently developed to store and maintain memories over the long term. The hippocampus, for example, which plays a major role in memory storage and retrieval in adults, is believed to be incompletely functional until the eighth or ninth postnatal month (Bachvalier & Mishkin, 1984; Nadel, Willner, & Kurz, 1985; Nadel & Zola-Morgan, 1984; Schacter & Moscovitch, 1984). Cited in support of this belief is the large body of data that has been gathered over the last two decades via procedures that exploit the young infant's robust visual response to novel stimuli. This research has consistently obtained evidence of retention on the order of a few seconds or minutes at most (Fagan, 1984; Olson & Strauss, 1984; Sherman, 1985; Werner & Perlmutter, 1979; but see Fagan, 1973).

In a seminal chapter on the ontogeny of infant learning and memory in 1976, Campbell and Coulter observed:

> The ontogeny of memory is clearly a neglected area of study. To our knowledge, there are no experiments on long-term retention in human infants . . . (p. 136). Our best estimates [of retention over long intervals] come from retrospective studies of early childhood memories. . . . We cannot overemphasize the differences between these indices of long-term memory in man and those used to study memory in the developing rat. The human is asked to recall events of early childhood in the absence of any stimuli associated with that era. The rat, on the other hand, is returned to a highly distinctive setting and asked to reproduce a specific response. If these same procedures were used with man, it seems quite likely that evidence for long-term memory would appear much earlier. (pp. 144–145)

Coincidentally, our first study of infant retention, published the same year, followed the approach advocated by Campbell and Coulter. In that study, we reported near-perfect 24-hr retention on the part of 3-month-olds (Rovee & Fagen, 1976). In subsequent studies with 2- and 3-month-olds, we used operant learning procedures (Rovee & Rovee, 1969) to characterize the forgetting function and specificity of a newly acquired memory over retention intervals of 1 to 14 days (Fagen, Rovee, & Kaplan, 1976; Gekoski & Fagen, 1984; Rovee-Collier & Sullivan, 1980; Sullivan, Rovee-Collier, & Tynes, 1979; Vander Linde, 1982) and of a reactivated memory over retention intervals of 14 to 28 days (Davis & Rovee-Collier, 1983; Fagen & Rovee-Collier, 1983; Fagen, Yengo, Rovee-Collier, & Enright, 1981; Rovee-Collier, Enright, Lucas, Fagen, & Gekoski, 1981; Rovee-Collier & Hayne, 1987; Rovee-Collier, Patterson, & Hayne, 1985; Rovee-Collier, Sullivan, Enright, Lucas, & Fagen, 1980; Sullivan, 1982; Vander Linde, 1982).

Recently, our research has taken two different courses. First, we have explored factors that influence the duration and specificity of long-term retention, including *age* (Boller, Rovee-Collier, Borovsky, O'Connor, & Shyi, 1990; Fagen & Ohr, 1986; Greco, Rovee-Collier, Hayne, Griesler, & Earley, 1986; Hayne, 1988; Hayne, Greco, Earley, Griesler, & Rovee-Collier, 1986; Hill, Borovsky, & Rovee-Collier, 1988; Rovee-Collier, Earley, & Stafford, 1989; Timmons, 1990), *the number of reminders* (Hayne, 1988), *the time course of memory retrieval* (Boller et al., 1990; Borza & Rovee-Collier, 1989; Fagen & Rovee-Collier, 1983; Greco & Rovee-Collier, 1988; Greco et al., 1986; Hayne, 1988), *the amount of training* (Enright, Rovee-Collier, Fagen, & Caniglia, 1983; Ohr, Fagen, Rovee-Collier, Hayne, & Vander Linde, 1989; Vander Linde, Morrongiello, & Rovee-Collier, 1985), and *the training and testing context* (Amabile & Rovee-Collier, 1991; Borovsky & Rovee-Collier, 1990; Butler & Rovee-Collier, 1989; Rovee-Collier & DuFault, 1991; Hayne, Rovee-Collier, & Borza, 1991; Mast, Fagen, Rovee-Collier, & Sullivan, 1980; Rovee-Collier, Griesler, & Earley, 1985; Shields & Rovee-Collier, 1992). Second, we have used the simple-forgetting and reactivation paradigms as tools to study *perception* (Rovee-Collier, Schechter, Shyi, & Shields, 1992; Shyi, 1990), *categorization* (Fagen, Morrongiello, Rovee-Collier, & Gekoski, 1984; Greco, Hayne, & Rovee-Collier, 1990; Hayne, Rovee-Collier, & Perris, 1987; Shields & Rovee-Collier, 1992), and *memory modification* (Boller & Rovee-Collier, 1992; Borza & Rovee-Collier, 1989; Greco et al., 1990; Greco & Rovee-Collier, 1988).

In addition to conclusions about long-term retention early in development, we believe that our findings offer some general insights into the fundaments of memory processing per se (for reviews, see Rovee-Collier, 1991, and Rovee-Collier & Hayne, 1987). In this chapter, we will focus on the specificity of newly acquired and reactivated memories, the time-dependent nature of memory retrieval, contextual constraints on memory retrieval, the effect of multiple reminders on long-term retention, and the modification of early memories. Although the bulk of evidence will come from studies of 3-month-olds, we will also refer to relevant evidence from studies of linguistically competent subjects.

Review of the Literature

Only a few studies of long-term retention other than our own have been conducted with infants during the first half-year of life. A particularly impressive demonstration of retention of auditory information during the newborn period was provided by DeCasper and his students (DeCasper & Fifer, 1980; DeCasper & Spence, 1986; Fifer, 1980), who studied the retention of auditory information to which infants had been prenatally exposed. In these studies, infants fitted with headphones produced access to a stereophonic tape recording of a particular voice or passage by sucking at a high and stable rate on a nonnutritive nipple. Infants approximately 33 hr old not only increased responding reinforced by the prenatally audible maternal voice relative to that reinforced by an unfamiliar female's voice but also discriminated a recording of a particular passage that the mother had read aloud daily during her last trimester of pregnancy from a novel test passage recorded by the mother. Postnatal auditory experience did not contribute to these preferences (DeCasper & Prescott, 1984). Although the primary focus of this research was on prenatal learning, long-term retention was clearly prerequisite for infants' postnatal discriminations.

The only other report of long-term retention in the first half-year involved a classical conditioning procedure. Little, Lipsitt, and Rovee-Collier (1984) trained independent groups of 10-, 20-, and 30-day-old infants to blink to a tone (the conditional stimulus [CS]) in anticipation of a corneal air puff (the unconditional stimulus [UCS]) and assessed their retention 10 days later. At each age, groups of infants were trained with either an optimal CS-UCS interval (1,500 ms) or a CS-UCS interval too brief to permit associative learning at this age (500 ms). The conditioning performance of groups trained for the first time at each age served as a maturational standard against which to compare the Session-2 retention of subjects trained 10 days earlier. At all ages, responding of infants in the 1,500-ms but not in the 500-ms groups was greater during testing than during training and was also greater than the performance of corresponding maturational control groups. In addition, long-term retention by infants trained at 30 days was superior to that of infants trained at 10.

Our studies of long-term retention have involved an operant conditioning procedure ("mobile conjugate reinforcement"). This procedure is not effective with infants less than 4 to 6 weeks of age (Rovee-Collier & Gekoski, 1979). The remainder of the chapter will focus on this research.

Training Procedure and Retention Measures

Rationale

Because very young infants lack a verbal response by which to inform us of what they remember about an event, we provide them with a motoric one. To this end, we teach infants an operant response, a foot kick, that is reinforced by the movement of a particular mobile, the visual characteristics of which constitute the cue. Infants then "tell" us whether or not the visual information that is displayed on a test mobile 24 hr later is a retrieval cue for the training memory (i.e., is represented in the newly acquired memory) by whether or not they produce the learned response. If they do, then we infer that the visual information is represented in the memory; if they do not respond, then we infer that it was not encoded. In effect, the specific characteristics of the test mobile are used to probe the memory contents active at the time of testing. If infants respond to the cues on a given test mobile after 24 hr but not after a longer delay, then we infer that the information was encoded but subsequently forgotten.

By manipulating the information on the test mobile and gradually increasing the interval between training and testing, we can determine the rates at which different kinds of memory attributes are forgotten. In addition to the visual information that is displayed directly on the mobile components, we often vary the characteristics of the context or setting in which learning occurs, such as the colors and/or patterns on a cloth liner that is draped around the infants' cribs or playpens, a particular place in the room, or a particular room in the infant's home.

Training Procedure

All studies are conducted in the infants' homes. For 2- and 3-month-olds, each session consists of a 9-min reinforcement phase (acquisition) that is preceded and followed by a 3-min nonreinforcement phase. During reinforcement phases, the mobile is linked to the infant's ankle by a ribbon (Figure 1.1a), allowing the infant to control both the frequency and the intensity of mobile movement by the frequency and vigor of kicking ("conjugate reinforcement"). We emphasize that the *movement* of the mobile and not merely its visual presence is the reinforcement. Infants trained in this procedure learn rapidly, usually doubling or tripling their baseline level of responding within a few minutes. This increase in responding is due solely to the introduction of the contingency and not to behavioral arousal (Rovee-Collier & Fagen, 1981). During nonreinforcement phases, the ankle ribbon is attached to an "empty" mobile stand so that the infant can see the mobile but cannot move it. For 6-month-olds, the experimental arrangement is the same except that infants are trained and tested in their playpens, and each phase is shorter by one-third (Figure 1.1b).

The initial 3-min nonreinforcement period of Session 1 is a *baseline phase* during which the infant's operant level of responding prior to training is measured. The 3-min nonreinforcement period at the end of acquisition in Session 2 is an *immediate retention test phase* for the infant's performance after no delay, when forgetting should be minimal. At the

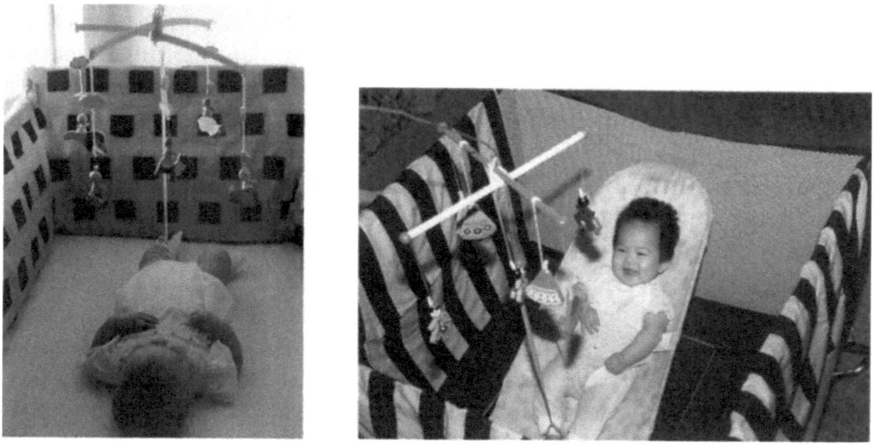

(a) (b)

FIGURE 1.1. The experimental arrangement during training for 3-month-olds (a) and 6-month-olds (b).

end of the specified retention interval, we return for another, identical session. This time, the initial 3-min nonreinforcement period serves as a *long-term retention test phase*. This retention test phase is procedurally identical both to the immediate retention test phase that followed the conclusion of training after no delay and to the original baseline phase—the mobile is *not* connected to the infant's ankle. Because retention is only assessed during nonreinforcement phases, test performance does not reflect savings but only a relatively "pure" memory component, i.e., what the infant brings into the session from what he or she had previously learned.

Measures of Long-Term Retention

Forgetting and retention are operationally defined in terms of an individual infant's performance during the long-term test relative to the performance of that same infant at the end of training (the immediate retention test) and prior to training (the baseline phase), respectively. The *retention ratio* indexes the extent to which the infant continues to respond during the long-term test as he/she did during the immediate retention test at the end of training, after no delay. If the infant responds at the same high rate during the long-term test as during the immediate test, then retention is "perfect," and the retention ratio is 1.00 (100%). The less the infant kicks during the long-term retention test relative to the immediate retention test, the lower the retention ratio, and the greater the extent of forgetting. A mean retention ratio significantly less than 1.00 confirms that a significant amount of forgetting has taken place.

Even if infants exhibit a significant degree of forgetting, they may still remember some of what they originally encoded. To determine whether the extent of forgetting during the long-term test is partial or complete, a *baseline ratio* is obtained by dividing the infant's kick rate during the long-term test by the infant's kick rate during the baseline phase. Individual baseline ratios of 1.50 or greater indicate that the infant is responding during the test at the rate previously required to meet the learning criterion—a conservative measure of retention. Mean baseline ratios significantly greater than 1.00 indicate that responding during the long-term retention test still significantly exceeds the rate at which infants had responded prior to originally learning the task. If infants respond at the same rate as they did prior to training (i.e., a baseline ratio of 1.00), however, then they are treating the mobile as novel, and we infer that forgetting is "complete." The 9-min reacquisition phase is introduced following the long-term retention test in the final session to ensure that poor test performance is not a result of poor motivation or illness on that particular test day.

All data points are contributed by independent groups of infants tested only once. We rarely ask, however, whether our test groups differ from one another. Groups may not have differed, for example, yet some or all may have remembered, or some or all may have forgotten. Instead, we seek a yes/no answer to the question of whether any given test group exhibits retention. To obtain this answer, we use *t* tests to compare each group's mean baseline and retention ratio with a theoretical baseline and retention ratio of 1.00 (no retention or perfect retention, respectively).

Long-Term Retention Paradigms

Simple-Forgetting Paradigm

Our standard paradigm for studying the long-term retention of a newly acquired memory involves 2 consecutive days of training followed by an immediate retention test after no delay and then by a long-term retention test after a specified interval has elapsed. In various studies, this interval has ranged from 1 to 42 days. We emphasize that long-term retention is always measured during the nonreinforcement period at the outset of a temporally distant session.

As Campbell and Coulter (1976) had envisioned, this procedure yields strong evidence of long-term retention. At 3 months, retention is excellent for several days following training and then gradually declines until forgetting is complete 13 days later (Sullivan et al., 1979). As shown in Figure 1.2, the forgetting function is steeper at 2 months (Greco et al., 1986) and shallower at 6 (Hill et al., 1988). Increasing either the duration of a single session or the number of sessions significantly prolongs retention (Ohr et al., 1989; Vander Linde et al., 1985).

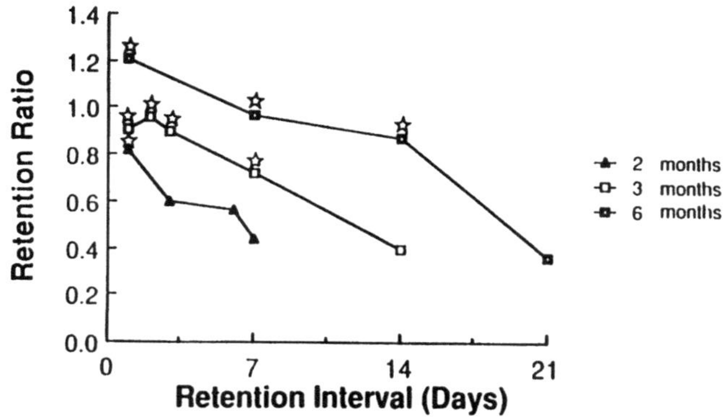

FIGURE 1.2. Retention ratios of independent groups of 2-, 3-, and 6-month-olds who were trained for two sessions and tested after retention intervals of 1 to 21 days in the simple-forgetting paradigm. Stars indicate significant retention (*M* baseline ratio significantly >1.00). (From "Continuity in Infant Memory Development" by W.L. Hill, D. Borovsky, and C. Rovee-Collier, 1988. *Developmental Psychobiology*, *21*, pp. 43–62. Copyright 1988 by John Wiley & Sons. Reprinted by permission.)

Reactivation Paradigm

Tulving (1972, 1983) distinguished between memories that are inaccessible and those that are unavailable. Spear (1973) hypothesized that a reminder or reactivation stimulus primes or recycles the forgotten (or dormant) memory, making it more accessible during the actual retention test. If a memory that has been forgotten can be retrieved at a later time, then we conclude that it was only inaccessible rather than permanently unavailable for retrieval. The memory reactivation paradigm, described by Spear (1973), has been used with animals (Greenfield & Riccio, 1972; Spear & Parsons, 1976), grade-school children (Hoving & Choi, 1972; Hoving, Coates, Bertucci, & Riccio, 1972), and human infants (Rovee-Collier et al., 1980; Sullivan, 1982; for review, see Rovee-Collier & Hayne, 1987) to recover forgotten memories.

Our standard memory reactivation paradigm involves (a) allowing sufficient time to elapse since training for simple forgetting of the newly acquired training memory to occur, (b) exposing the infant to some cue (a reminder) that was presumably represented in the newly acquired memory, and (c) testing at some point after the reminder (usually 24 h) to determine whether or not the memory has been recovered. If the reminder is sufficient and presented within a given time-window since training (Greco et al., 1986; Hayne, 1988), then the memory will be reactivated, or *primed*, and will be expressed under appropriate conditions during the long-term retention test. The rate at which the memory

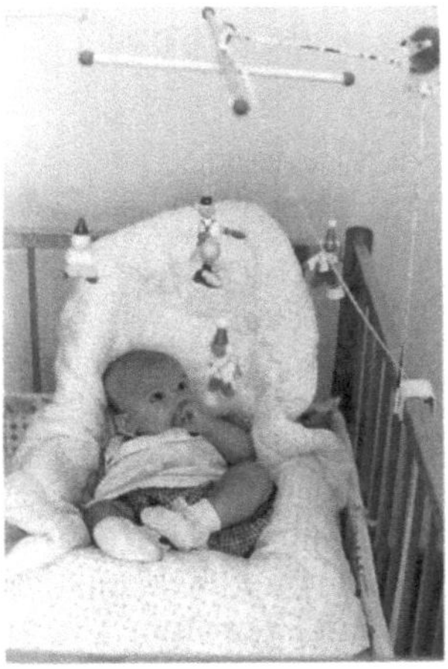

FIGURE 1.3. The experimental arrangement during a reactivation treatment, administered in a 2-month-old's own crib, without a distinctive crib liner.

(or a particular type of memory attribute) is recovered can be determined by testing at different intervals after the reminder presentation. In effect, the reminder is simply a retrieval cue that is presented in advance of the long-term retention test (Spear, 1978). Critical control groups include infants with prior training who receive no reminder (no-reactivation control group) and infants without prior training who receive the reminder (reactivation control group) (see also Campbell & Jaynes, 1966).

We expose infants to the reminder only briefly—for 3 min at 2 and 3 months and 2 min at 6 months. In the past, our reminders have included exposure to noncontingent mobile movement (e.g., Rovee-Collier et al., 1980), returning infants to the distinctive context in which training occurred (Rovee-Collier, Griesler, et al., 1985), or both (Butler & Rovee-Collier, 1989; Hayne, 1988; Hill et al., 1988). Although 2- and 3-month-olds are trained in a supine position, we usually present the mobile reminder while they are in an infant seat (Figure 1.3) in order to minimize their activity (Sullivan, 1982) and hence the possibility of either adventitious reinforcement or, conversely, detection that the mobile movement is response-noncontingent; we obtain the same result if the reminder is presented when infants are supine (Fagen & Rovee-Collier, 1983).

An effective reminder alleviates forgetting such that infants respond during the long-term retention test at the same high rate that they had displayed when tested immediately following the conclusion of training days or weeks earlier. In contrast, infants who receive no interpolated reminder and infants who receive a reminder without prior training respond at their baseline rate.

Figure 1.4 shows the forgettting function of the newly acquired memory as well as the reforgetting function of the reactivated memory. The same reforgetting function is obtained whether the reminder is administered 2

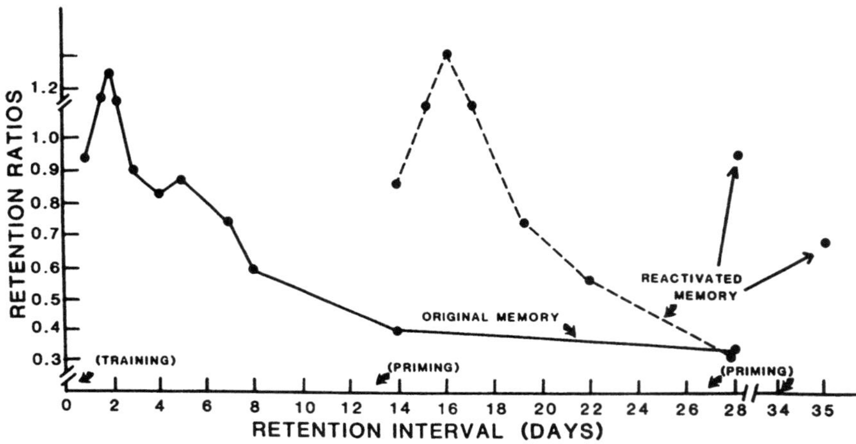

FIGURE 1.4. The simple forgetting function of a newly acquired memory (solid line) and the reforgetting function of a reactivated memory (dashed line) for independent groups of 3-month-olds. A single reminder ("priming") was presented on either day 13, 27, or 34. (Redrawn from "Reactivation of Infant Memory" by C.K. Rovee-Collier, M.W. Sullivan, M. Enright, D. Lucas, and J.W. Fagen, 1980, *Science*, *208*, pp. 1159–1161. Copyright 1980 by the American Association for the Advancement of Science. Adapted by permission.)

weeks after the conclusion of training (Rovee-Collier et al., 1980), as shown here, or 3 weeks after (Hayne, 1990). These data reveal that the memory is restored to its original level by a single reminder and that it remains accessible as a potential influence on behavior for the same period as it had following original training. Also shown is the effect of a single reactivation treatment administered either 27 or 34 days after the end of training. The reminder significantly alleviated forgetting after a retention interval of 4 weeks but not after 5 (Greco et al., 1986). Thus, there is a limit to the effectiveness of a single reactivation treatment. This is likely to vary with the type of reminder, the parameters of the task, the age of the infant, and possibly the time since the memory has been forgotten.

The Specificity of Infants' Memories

Specificity of Memory at 2 and 3 Months

At both 2 and 3 months, infants discriminate a novel test mobile from the original training mobile after 24 hr. If different numbers of novel mobile objects are substituted for familiar ones during a retention test 24 hr after training, such that some infants are tested with a mobile containing four original objects and one new object, others are tested with a mobile containing three original objects and two new ones, etc., 24-hr retention is not only impaired (Fagen et al., 1976) but is completely disrupted if the test mobile contains more than just a single substitution (Hayne et al., 1986). Because 24-hr retention is otherwise perfect, this result indicates that infants as young as 2 months have not forgotten the task and have discriminated the test mobile from the training mobile they last saw 24 hr earlier.

These data clearly challenge the conclusion of Kagan (1979, 1984; Kagan & Hamburg, 1981) that infants less than 8 or 9 months of age cannot maintain the representation of their own mother "on the stage of memory" for longer than a few minutes. According to Kagan, infants show stranger distress and cry if they detect a discrepancy between the visual characteristics of the mother and those of a stranger. He argues that infants do not cry before the eighth postnatal month when a stranger enters a room after the mother has left because at younger ages they cannot retain a visual image of their mother in her physical absence.

As the interval between training and testing increases, 3-month-olds increasingly generalize to novel test mobiles (Rovee-Collier & Sullivan, 1980), suggesting the progressive forgetting of the specific details of the training mobile. Despite this, however, a novel mobile is not an effective reminder once the newly acquired memory has been forgotten (Enright, 1981). More striking is the finding that if the reminder mobile contains more than a single novel object, it is ineffective in alleviating forgetting (Rovee-Collier, Patterson, et al., 1985). Prefamiliarization with the new objects that are substituted into the reminder mobile does not alter this result.

Fagen et al. (1981) used a classic behavioral contrast paradigm to teach infants a discrimination between two block mobiles that differed in the colors and patterns they displayed. During acquisition, mobiles were presented successively for 2 min each, and responding in the presence of both was conjugately reinforced. During discrimination training, reinforcement was withdrawn in the presence of one of the mobiles (S−) but was maintained in the presence of the other (S+). This procedure produces a characteristic decrease in responding to S− and an increase in responding to S+ even though S+ had not been associated with an increase in reinforcement. After a 3-week retention interval, when forgetting was complete, a brief exposure to S+ reactivated the full discrimination: Infants once more responded to S+ but not to S−. In contrast, a brief exposure to S− was no more effective than no reminder at all—it did not restore responding to S+. Interpretation of the latter negative finding is tempered by evidence that nonmoving mobiles in general are not effective reminders at 3 months, even if presented for twice as long as a moving one. Because the S− had been initially reinforced during acquisition, however, reactivation of the discrimination by S+ suggests a strong *recency effect* for the significance of the S− memory component. We have also obtained strong recency effects in studies of memory modification (Boller et al., 1990; Borza & Rovee-Collier, 1989; Greco & Rovee-Collier, 1988), discussed below.

Although long-term retention is highly specific to the cues encountered during training, if infants receive category training with a novel mobile in each of two consecutive sessions, then they will respond to another novel mobile during a 24-hr retention test, and a novel mobile will be an effective reminder once forgetting is complete (Fagen et al., 1984; Greco et al., 1990). In a study of artificial categories, for example, Hayne et al. (1987) trained 3-month-olds with a series of yellow-block mobiles that had a felt character (*A* or *2*) affixed on all sides of each block (see, e.g., Figure 1.19a). All of the objects on a single mobile displayed the same character in the same color (red, black, blue, green, purple). Infants trained for 3 consecutive days with the same mobile (e.g., red *A*s) discriminated a change in either color (e.g., red *A*s to green *A*s), shape (e.g., red *A*s to red *2*s), or both (e.g., red *A*s to green *2*s) during a 24-hr generalization test. When infants were assigned to either an *A* or a *2* category and were trained with a discriminably different mobile from the assigned category on each of the 3 days (e.g., red *A*, green *A*, black *A*), they transferred responding to another novel category exemplar (e.g., blue *A*) during the retention test 24 hr later, but they did not respond to an exemplar from the other category (e.g., blue *2*). Likewise, once their forgetting was complete, a novel category exemplar (e.g., purple *A*) was an effective reminder, but a novel member of the other category (e.g., purple *2*) was not. Thus even following category training, the cues for retrieval are highly specific to the category cues encountered during original training.

Specificity of Memory at 6 Months

The cues required to retrieve infants' memories are even more specific to the original training situation at 6 months that at 3. Six-month-olds, for example, discriminate a novel test mobile for 2 weeks—the same duration that they remember the task (Boller et al., 1990; Hill et al., 1988). Also at 6 months, we have observed a similar but more complex example of retrieval specificity. In a recently completed dissertation, Timmons (1990) trained infants to move a mobile suspended over the playpen, or to turn on a music box affixed to the front of the playpen, by either arm-pulling or foot-kicking—a paired-associates task. Infants were trained in a distinctive context for 2 days with one cue-response pair and, 3 days later, were trained with the other cue-response pair in the same context. Three days after training on the second task, infants were tested with each of the cues in the same context to see what response they would emit. Figure 1.5 shows the data from infants tested with the mobile

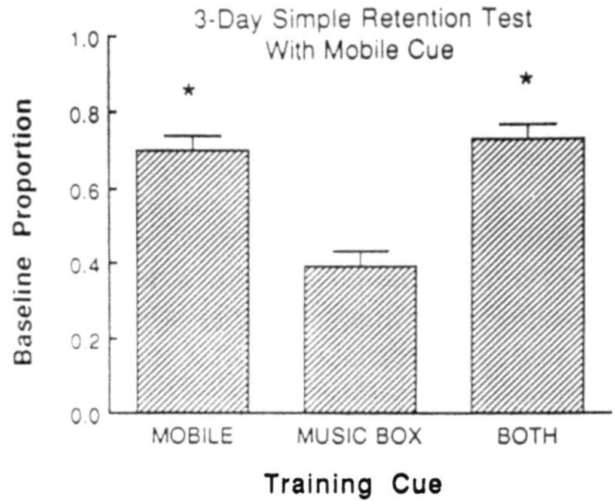

FIGURE 1.5. Retention of a specific cue-response association by 6-month-olds previously trained both to move a mobile and to operate a music box by arm-pulling or foot-kicking and tested with the mobile 3 days after learning the second cue-response pair (right column). Control groups (left and middle column) were tested with the mobile after training on only one task. (Redrawn from *Interactions of Independent Memories in Six-Month-Old Infants* by C.R. Timmons, 1990, Unpublished Doctoral Dissertation, Rutgers University, New Brunswick, NJ. Copyright 1990 by C.R. Timmons. Adapted by permission.)

cue. As expected, infants trained only to operate the music box did not perform the mobile-appropriate response (middle column), whereas infants trained only to move the mobile did (left column). Despite training on both tasks (right column), however, infants' responding was highly specific to the training cue: They produced the cue-appropriate response, whatever it was, even if their most recent training was with the other cue-response pair.

Three weeks after identical training on both tasks, when both tasks had been forgotten, Timmons presented either the mobile or the music box as a reminder in a reactivation paradigm and tested all infants with the mobile 24 hr later. As expected, infants reminded with the mobile exhibited the mobile-appropriate response during the 3-week retention test with the mobile (Figure 1.6). Infants reminded with the music box, however, also exhibited the mobile-appropriate response during the mobile retention test! Because these infants had not been reminded with the mobile, and because the mobile memory had been forgotten at the time of the reminder, Timmons concluded that the music box reactivated its corresponding memory attributes, which, in turn, reactivated the memory attributes representing the mobile that had been encountered in that same context, thereby enabling the mobile-specific response to be performed. These data are among the first to illustrate associative networks (Anderson, 1976; Anderson & Bower, 1973). Despite their

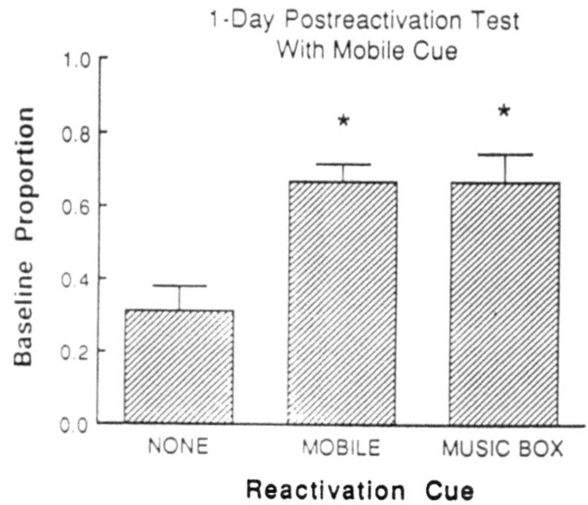

FIGURE 1.6. Retention of an otherwise forgotten cue-response association by 6-month-olds trained 3 weeks earlier both to move a mobile and to operate a music box by arm-pulling or foot-kicking and tested with the mobile 1 day after a reactivation treatment with the music box. (Redrawn from *Interactions of Independent Memories in Six-Month-Old Infants* by C.R. Timmons, 1990, Unpublished Doctoral Dissertation, Rutgers University, New Brunswick, NJ. Copyright 1990 by C.R. Timmons. Adapted by permission.)

linkage, presumably via the common training context, the specific cue-response components within each of these memories remained intact. These data are consistent with findings from free-recall studies of older children, which indicate that the probability that item-specific information will be retrieved is enhanced if the item has been linked with other features in a tightly structured associative network. In such an instance, activation of one or more of these other features will, in turn, activate the target item (for review, see Bjorklund, 1987). Such retrieval is highly organized but need not be strategic (see also Perlmutter, 1984).

Additional evidence of the specificity of infants' memories has been obtained from studies of contextual change, discussed below. Taken together, these findings provide clear evidence that young infants' memories are not generalized and undifferentiated as many developmental psychologists have claimed (Nelson, 1986; Olson & Strauss, 1984).

The Time-Dependent Nature of Memory Retrieval

Developmental Changes

Our finding that memory retrieval is time-locked at 3 months was surprising (Fagen & Rovee-Collier, 1983). Figure 1.7 presents the retention

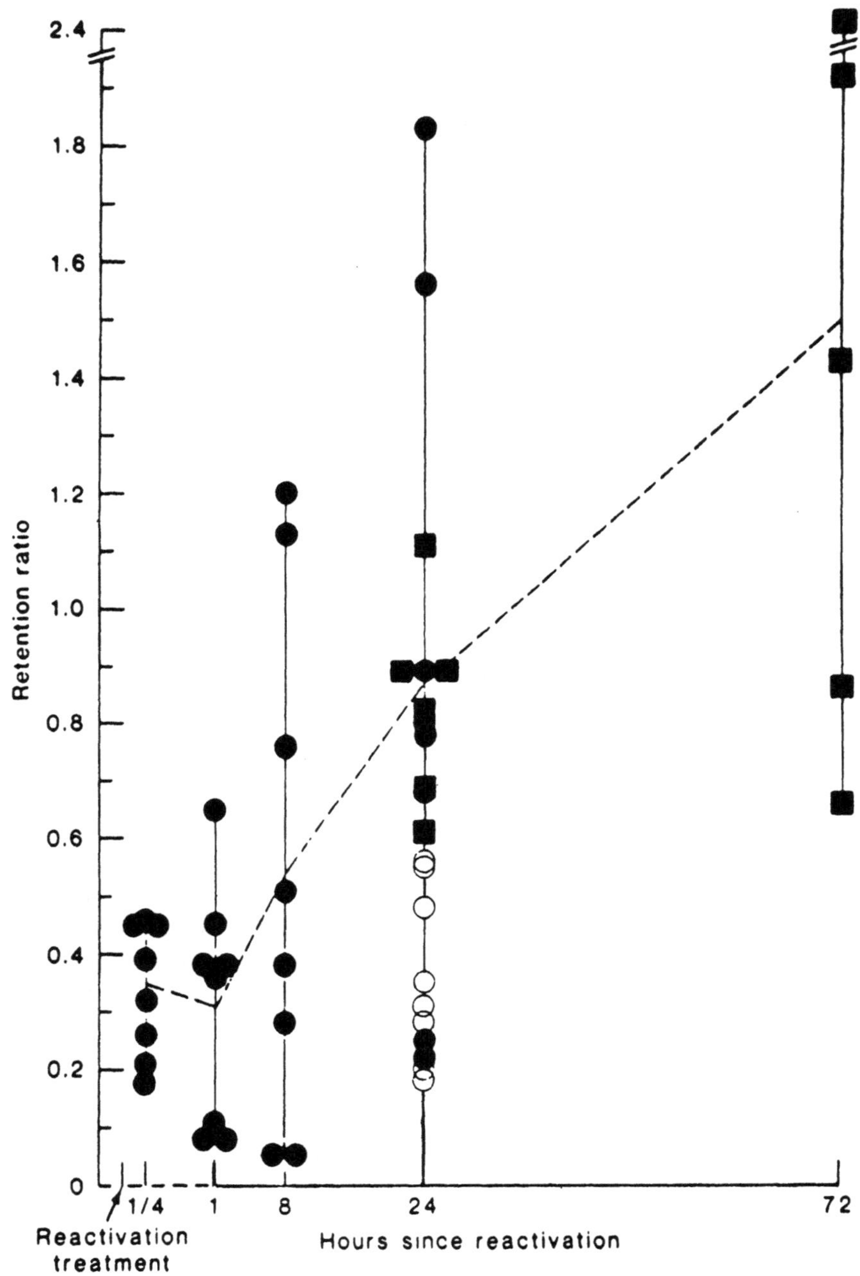

FIGURE 1.7. Individual retention ratios of independent groups of 3-month-olds tested at different points in time following a reactivation treatment that occurred 13 days following the conclusion of training (filled circles and squares) and of a no-reactivation control group tested on day 14 (open circles). (From "Memory Retrieval: A Time-Locked Process in Infancy" by J.W. Fagen and C. Rovee-Collier, 1983, *Science*, *222*, pp. 1349–1351. Copyright 1983 by American Association for the Advancement of Science. Reprinted by permission.)

ratios of independent groups of infants tested only once at different intervals following a reminder presented 13 days after the conclusion of training. The open circles represent subjects in control groups who received no reminder. Fifteen minutes and even an hour after the reactivation treatment, 3-month-olds showed no evidence of remembering. Eight hours later, some infants remembered better, and 24 hr later, retention was perfect. The longer the time infants in the 8-hr test group napped between the reminder and the test, the higher were their retention ratios ($n = 8$, $r = .75$). As can be seen, performance continued to improve for 72 hr following the reminder—a significant hypermnesia effect identical to that which occurs following original training (Rovee-Collier et al., 1981). It is difficult to conceptualize of physiological processes other than hormonal actions that endure for such extended periods and that could mediate such a protracted phenomenon.

Boller et al. (1990) have obtained similar evidence of time-dependent memory retrieval at 6 months. Like younger infants, 6-month-olds exhibit no evidence that their memory has been reactivated immediately following the reminder presentation. After a 1-hr delay, however, their test performance is significantly above baseline, and after 4 hr, their retention appears to have peaked (Figure 1.8), declining significantly thereafter.

The increase in the rate of retrieval from 3 to 6 months is striking (Figure 1.9). These findings are consistent with reports that information is processed more rapidly with age during both infancy (Hunter & Ames, 1988; Rose, 1981, 1983; Rose, Gottfried, Melloy-Carminar, & Bridger, 1982) and childhood (Kail, 1986; Thompson & Massaro, 1989), and that semantic memory is accessed more readily by older than younger children (Bjorklund, 1987). Because the speed of memory retrieval increases so rapidly between 3 and 6 months, we think it may be difficult to obtain evidence of time-dependent retrieval in older infants, much less in children and adults, whose networks of language-based associations must surely facilitate and speed retrieval.

Retrograde Amnesia

Anterograde and retrograde amnesia are among the few phenomena illustrating time-dependent memory retrieval in linguistically competent subjects. In most of these studies, the amnesia was caused by amnestic agents such as a blow to the head, electroconvulsive shock, or the onset of Korsakoff's syndrome. Fagen and colleagues (Fagen, Ohr, Fleckenstein, & Ribner, 1985; Fagen, Ohr, Singer, & Klein, 1989; Ohr, Fleckenstein, Fagen, Klein, & Pioli, 1990) reported that infants who displayed negative affect after a reinforcement shift exhibit a similar retrograde amnesia effect. Fagen et al. (1985) trained 3-month-olds for 2 days to produce movement in a 10-object mobile by kicking. Four minutes into acquisition during Session 3, however, they shifted the

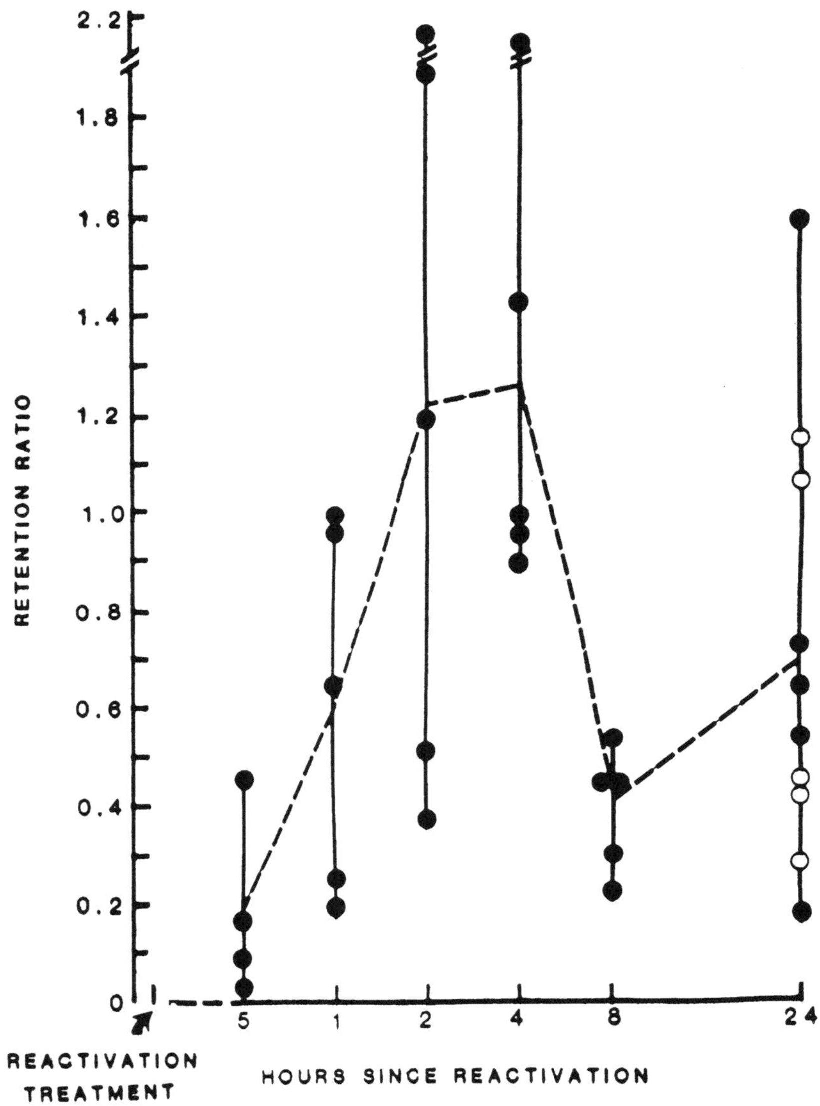

FIGURE 1.8. Individual retention ratios of independent groups of 6-month-olds tested at different points in time following a reactivation treatment presented 20 days following the conclusion of training and of a no-reactivation control group tested on day 20. Data from a 24-hr replication test group (open circles) are also shown. (From "Developmental Changes in the Time-Dependent Nature of Memory Retrieval" by K. Boller, C. Rovee-Collier, D. Borovsky, J. O'Connor, and G. Shyi, 1990, *Developmental Psychology*, *26*, 770–779. Copyright 1990 by the American Psychological Association. Reprinted by permission.)

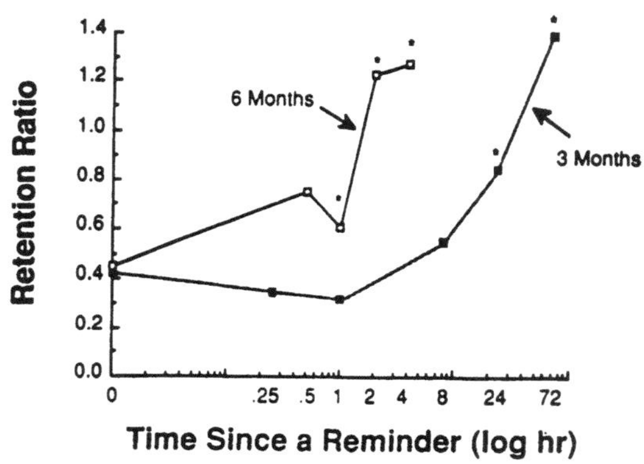

FIGURE 1.9. The time required for retention to peak following a reactivation treatment presented to independent groups of 3- and 6-month-olds. Asterisks indicate significant retention (i.e., *M* baseline ratio significantly >1.00). (From "Developmental Changes in the Time-Dependent Nature of Memory Retrieval" by K. Boller, C. Rovee-Collier, D. Borovsky, J. O'Connor, and G. Shyi, 1990, *Developmental Psychology*, *26*, 770–779. Copyright 1990 by the American Psychological Association. Reprinted by permission.)

reinforcer to a 2-object mobile. This shift typically produces crying in approximately 50% of the infants. Although all infants exhibited excellent retention 1 day after the shift, only those who did not cry exhibited retention after 7 days; those who cried exhibited none! This result was independent of which mobile (10-object or 2-object) was used during the 7-day test.

When Fagen et al. (1989) repeated this procedure but allowed either 0, 2, 5, 15 or 30 min to elapse prior to the shift from the 10- to the 2-object mobile, they observed a significant linear increase in 1-week retention on the part of criers as a function of the delay interval preceding the shift. As before, infants in all delay groups who did not cry when shifted to the 2-object mobile exhibited significant 1-week retention; of the infants who cried, however, only those in the 30-min delay group exhibited retention after 1 week (Figure 1.10). Fagen et al. interpreted this retrograde amnesia effect as a retrieval deficit resulting from a change in the internal (affective) context between training and testing. This interpretation is consistent with findings that changes in the internal context can impair memory retrieval (Boller et al., 1990; Eich, 1989; Overton, 1982; Spear, 1973). Figure 1.8, for example, showed that 6-month-olds tested 8 hr after a reminder exhibited significantly poorer retention than infants tested either 4 hr earlier or 16 hr later. We think that this impairment resulted from changes in internal cues associated with circadian rhythms or other periodicities (e.g., feeding, sleeping) between the clock hours of original encoding and testing.

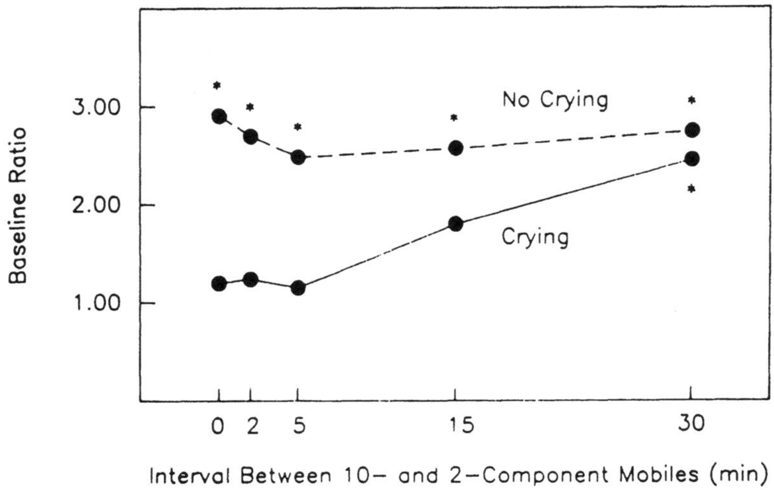

FIGURE 1.10. One-week retention of independent groups of 3-month-olds who either did (solid line) or did not (dashed line) cry in response to a shift from a 10- to a 2-object mobile as a function of the time intervening between training with the 10-object mobile and presentation of the 2-object mobile. Asterisks indicate significant retention. (From "Crying and Retrograde Amnesia in Infants" by J.W. Fagen, P.S. Ohr, J.M. Singer, and S.J. Klein, 1989, *Infant Behavior and Development*, *12*, pp. 13–24. Copyright 1989 by Ablex Publishing Corporation. Reprinted by permission.)

Different Types of Memory Attributes

We have obtained evidence that different types of memory attributes are forgotten and retrieved at different rates (Rovee-Collier & Sullivan, 1980; see also Atkinson & Shiffrin, 1968, and Spear, 1978). Infants discriminated a novel test mobile after a 1-day delay but, over time, responding increasingly generalized. After 3 days, they responded as vigorously to a novel test mobile as to their original one (Figure 1.11). This finding suggested that memory attributes corresponding to the specific details of the training mobile are forgotten more rapidly than those corresponding to its more general features (Rovee-Collier & Sullivan, 1980). Similar findings have been obtained in other studies of 3-month-olds (Ohr et al., 1990) as well as in studies of adults tested in verbal-learning paradigms (Ceraso, 1987; Hasher & Griffin, 1978) and animals (Riccio, Richardson, & Ebner, 1984; Spear, 1978).

We also have found evidence that attributes that have been forgotten for longer periods take longer to be retrieved. Despite the failure of a novel mobile to serve as an effective reminder, for example, 3-month-olds readily generalize responding to a novel test mobile 24 hr following an

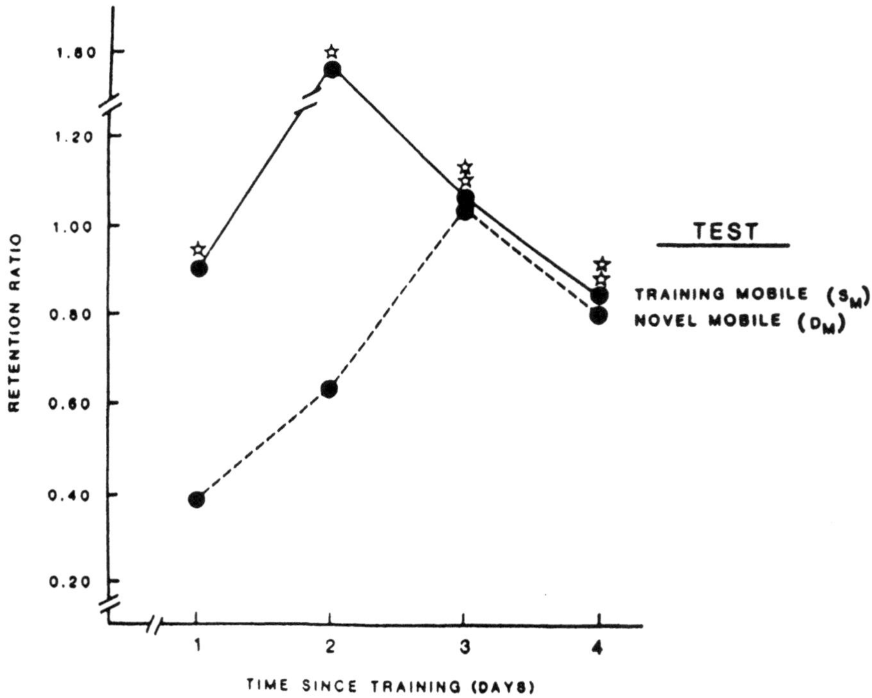

FIGURE 1.11. Retention to independent groups of 3-month-olds tested with either the same mobile (S_m) or one different (D_m) from the mobile with which they had been trained either 1, 2, 3, or 4 days earlier. (From "Reactivation of Infant Memory: Implications for Cognitive Development" by C. Rovee-Collier and H. Hayne in *Advances in Child Development and Behavior*, vol. 20, pp. 185–238, edited by H.W. Reese, 1987, New York: Academic Press. Copyright 1987 by Academic Press. Reprinted by permission.)

appropriate reminder just as they had generalized responding to a novel test mobile 3 days and longer after original training (Enright, 1981). We hypothesized that if the attributes in the original memory representation that had been forgotten last were still relatively more accessible than those that had been forgotten first, then infants' generalization 1 day after a reminder may have resulted because the memory attributes corresponding to the general features of the mobile (forgotten last) were recovered more rapidly than the attibutes corresponding to the specific details of the mobile (forgotten first).

On this basis, we hypothesized that infants might discriminate a novel test mobile if the delay between the reminder and the longer-term retention test were longer. The "last-out, first-in" hypothesis was confirmed (Rovee-Collier & Hayne, 1987). Independent groups of infants *generalized* responding to a novel test mobile 1 day after the reminder

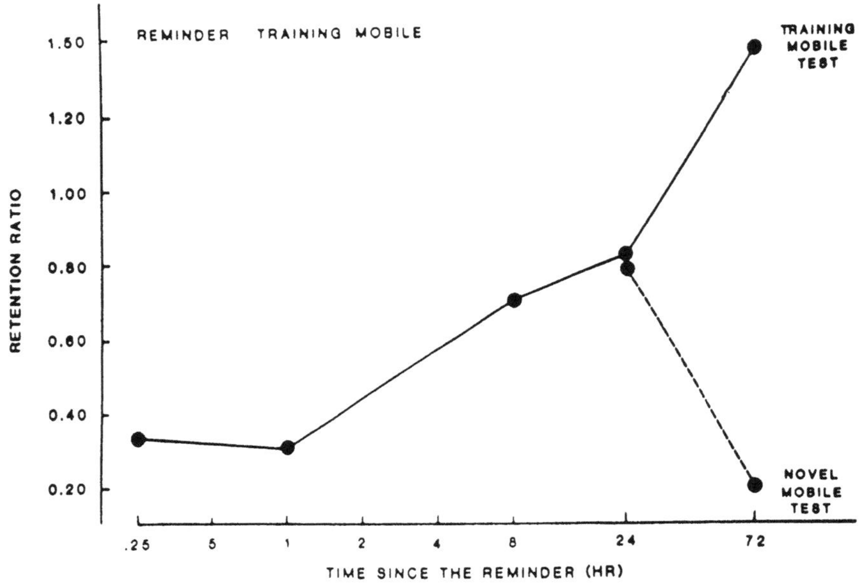

FIGURE 1.12. The recovery of general and specific attributes of a forgotten memory as revealed in the test performance of independent groups of 3-month-olds at different points in time following a reactivation treatment administered 13 days after the conclusion of training. Infants were tested with either the original training mobile (solid line) or a novel one (dashed line). Infants exhibited excellent retention of both test mobiles 24 hr after the reactivation treatment but responded only to the original mobile 72 hr afterward. (From "Reactivation of Infant Memory: Implications for Cognitive Development" by C. Rovee-Collier and H. Hayne in *Advances in Child Development and Behavior*, vol. 20, pp. 185–238, edited by H.W. Reese, 1987, New York: Academic Press. Copyright 1987 by Academic Press. Reprinted by permission.)

but *discriminated* a novel test mobile 3 days after the reminder—a delay after which retention of the original mobile was excellent (Figure 1.12).

This analysis is consistent with the conclusion reached by Johnson and her colleagues in their recent studies on adults' memories for perceived versus imagined autobiographical events (Johnson, Foley, Suengas, & Raye, 1988; Suengas & Johnson, 1988). Their evidence similarly suggests that memories for complex events comprise several partially independent qualities (Johnson, 1983; Johnson & Raye, 1981) and that these memory characteristics differ not only in their contents and susceptibility to retrieval but also in their accessibility over time. Although the memory attributes we have proposed do not correspond exactly to the memory qualities that these investigators had in mind (e.g., clarity, sensory and perceptual qualities, emotional qualities, etc.), the shared view is that various aspects of the memory of a (complex) event may be forgotten and retrieved at different rates.

We think it likely that the time-dependent course of memory retrieval contributes to infantile amnesia. If a memory is subject to modification at the time of retrieval, for example, and the content of the active memory differs at different points in time (see also Atkinson & Shiffrin, 1968), then a memory would be differentially modified depending upon when particular memory attributes attained an active state. In addition, because a given retrieval cue can indirectly activate memories with which the directly activated memory is associated (Timmons, 1990), there is opportunity for the indirectly activated memories to be modified as well. On the other hand, a distinctive and unique training context appears to buffer the memory against generalized retrieval and therefore could restrict the pool of indirect activated memories to those encoded in that context. Training, reminding, and testing infants in a unique and highly distinctive context, for example, completely eliminates generalization both 24 hr after original training (Butler & Rovee-Collier, 1989) and 24 hr after a reminder (Rovee-Collier & Hayne, 1987). Contextual constraints on memory retrieval are discussed below.

Contextual Constraints on Long-Term Retention

A common finding in research with both animals and human adults is that greater similarity between the contexts of training and testing leads to better retention (Cohen, 1985; Eich, 1989; Overton, 1982; Spear, 1978; Tulving & Thomson, 1973). Conversely, naturally occurring change in contextual cues with time passage has been invoked as a major source of long-term forgetting (e.g., Bower, 1981; Estes, 1950; Miller & Schachtman, 1985). Campbell and Spear (1972) proposed that the changing perception of physical contextual cues by a rapidly developing organism might also contribute substantially to infantile amnesia. Riccio et al. (1984), however, argued that contextual information is not likely to account for forgetting after long intervals because it is forgotten more rapidly than other attributes represented in the memory of an event. As support for this argument, they cited evidence that (a) the disrupting effect of a change in context is greatest closest to the time of the original event, and that (b) test performance in an altered context improves as the retention interval increases and, presumably, the training context is forgotten. The contribution of time-based changes in environmental contextual cues to adult forgetting has similarly been challenged, leading Crowder (1985) to conclude that "... conceptual drift is more an article of faith than it is an operational concept" (p. 33).

In a study with infants, Rovee-Collier, Griesler, et al. (1985) found that changing the distinctive surround in which the mobile task had been

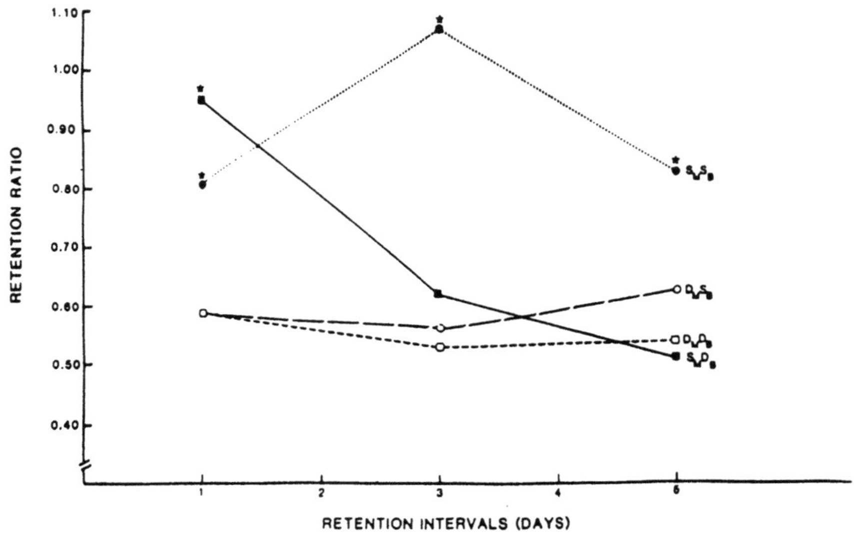

FIGURE 1.13. Retention of independent groups of 3-month-olds tested 1, 3, or 5 days following the conclusion of training as a function of the similarity of the training and test mobiles and contexts (crib liner or bumper). Infants were tested in the presence of the same mobile and same bumper (S_MS_B), the same mobile and a different bumper (S_MD_B), a different mobile and the same bumper (D_MS_B), or a different mobile and a different bumper (D_MD_B). Stars indicate significant retention (i.e., *M* baseline ratio significantly >1.00). (From "Contextual Gating of Memory Retrieval" by J. Butler and C. Rovee-Collier, 1989, *Developmental Psychobiology*, *22*, pp. 533–552. Copyright 1989 by John Wiley & Sons. Reprinted by permission.)

learned impaired retention during testing 7 days later. Moreover, merely replacing infants in the highly distinctive training context per se, with no mobile present, was an effective reminder for the forgotten memory 2 weeks after the conclusion of training. These data confirmed that information about the environmental context was, in fact, encoded in the memory representation of the training episode by infants as young as 3 months.

To determine how context information interacted with the nominal cue (the mobile), we trained infants in the standard paradigm but changed either the cue or the context, both, or neither during a retention test administered to independent groups either 1, 3, or 5 days following the conclusion of training (Butler & Rovee-Collier, 1989). Although Riccio et al. (1984) predicted that a contextual change would most disrupt retention closest in time to training and least after longer delays, we found a different pattern at 3 months. Changing the context only 1 day after training had no effect on retention—a finding we replicated. After longer delays, however, when retention in the original context was still perfect, infants exhibited no retention whatsoever in an altered context (Figure 1.13). Likewise, the effectiveness of the original mobile as a reminder was significantly impaired if the reactivation context was altered.

In the preceding study, infants were trained and tested in a unique and highly distinctive context and exhibited no retention after any delay if the mobile was changed, either in a simple-forgetting (Figure 1.13) or a reactivation paradigm. This result differs from that typically obtained when 3-month-olds are trained and tested in their own, unlined cribs—a context that is not unique to the training episode (Ohr et al., 1990; Rovee-Collier & Sullivan, 1980). Recall that under the latter circumstances, infants discriminated a novel test mobile shortly after training (e.g., 1 day) but, as the retention interval increased, they progressively generalized to a novel test mobile; after 3 days, they responded at the same high rate whether the test mobile was novel or not (see Figure 1.11).

In all of the preceding studies, we have assumed that as long as the infant remembers the specific details of the original training mobile, he/she will discriminate a novel test mobile, that is, it will not cue retrieval of the training memory. Once they have forgotten the details of the training mobile, the general features of the novel test mobile that correspond to the general features of the training mobile become effective retrieval cues for the training memory. Because the paradoxical increase in responding to a novel test cue after longer delays is eliminated by training in a unique and highly distinctive context, we have concluded that the distinctive context must be a retrieval cue for the specific details of the training mobile which, once active, permit the infants to discriminate a novel test mobile after intervals when they otherwise would not (Butler & Rovee-Collier, 1989).

We have found it useful to conceptualize of memory retrieval as a process by which detection of effective retrieval cues results in the successive opening and closing of a series of attention gates. The initial gate is at the level of the context, and the final gate is at the level of the nominal stimulus that signals the contingency. With a change in either the context or the cue, the appropriate retrieval cues will fail to be detected, and the corresponding attention gates will fail to open. As a result, attention will fail to "flow" to the next set of cues, and the memory retrieval process will be aborted at that point. This metaphor was modeled after an attention-gating model of retrieval from visual short-term memory (Reeves & Sperling, 1986).

In the preceding studies (Butler & Rovee-Collier, 1989; Rovee-Collier, Griesler, et al., 1985), the context was created by draping a distinctively colored and patterned liner about the infant's crib or playpen. As a natural analogue of this manipulation, we have trained and tested 3-month-olds in their home cribs but reminded them with the training mobile in the infant seat placed in a location that was *familiar* (in the kitchen or elsewhere in the bedroom) but *different* from where they were trained. The otherwise effective reminder was not effective unless infants were exposed to it where they were trained. When we draped a highly distinctive liner over a portacrib placed in their bedrooms during training and tested them 1 day later in the kitchen in the same liner-draped portacrib, their retention was perfect, as when we had changed their crib liners 1 day after training. But when we trained infants in the liner-draped portacrib and *reminded* them in the kitchen in the same, liner-draped portacrib, the reminder did not work (Hayne et al., 1991).

The considerable degree of contextual specificity required to reactivate a memory is underscored by the fact that when we trained and tested infants in their liner-draped crib and reminded them in a liner-draped portacrib placed in exactly the same location where their own crib had stood, the reminder did not work (Rovee-Collier & Hayne, 1987). A portacrib is lower than a regular crib, perhaps offering a different view of the room; alternatively, infants may "know" if they are in their crib or not.

Recently, we have obtained evidence that a unique and highly distinctive training context can facilitate retention in infants as it does in normal adults (Eich, 1985; Smith, Glenberg, & Bjork, 1978) and Korsakoff amnesics (Winocur & Kinsbourne, 1978). Following category training for 3 days with a series of discriminably different yellow-block mobiles in a highly distinctive context, for example, 3-month-olds will transfer responding to yet another novel yellow-block mobile in that same context 14 days later—a delay after which infants trained identically but not in a highly distinctive context exhibit complete forgetting. In addition, a unique and distinctive training context is prerequisite for multiple reminders to be effective at 3 months (Hayne, 1988).

Developmental Changes

Infants' long-term retention is even more strongly determined by contextual information at 6 months than at 3. Although 6-month-olds remember the details of their training mobile for as long as they remember the task and do not generalize to a novel test mobile after any delay whether the context is unique or not (Boller et al., 1990; Hill et al., 1988), they exhibit no reactivation effect 24 hr after a reminder unless training, reminding, and testing take place in a setting that is unique to the training episode (Boller et al., 1990). In addition, despite evidence that they remember the details of their training mobile for 2 weeks, they stare at it "blankly" and appear not to recognize it just 1 day after training if the test context is different. (Recall that at 3 months, a contextual change had *no* effect on test performance after a 1-day delay; see Figure 1.13.)

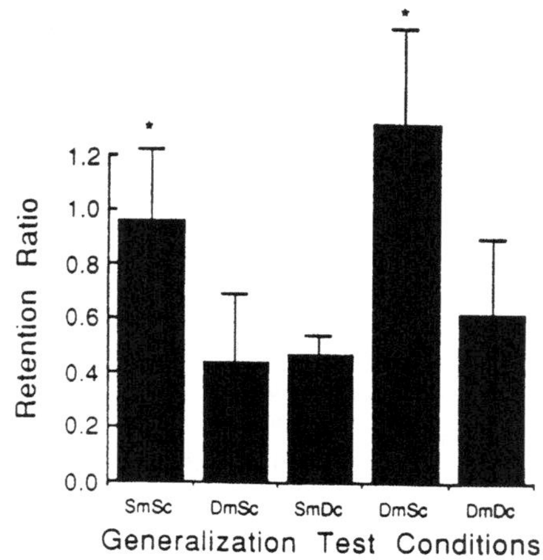

FIGURE 1.14. The effect of training 6-month-olds with the same or a perceptibly different mobile in the same context on each of 2 days on 24-hr retention in the same or a different test context. (From "Long-Term Memory for Context-Specific Category Information at Six Months" by P. Shields and C. Rovee-Collier, 1992, *Child Development*, *63*, 175–214. Copyright 1992 by The Society for Research in Child Development. Reprinted by permission.)

The disruption of long-term retention by a novel test context can be overcome by variable-contextual training (Smith, 1982), but the effectiveness of this procedure diminishes with age. Rovee-Collier and DuFault (1991), for example, trained 3-month-olds in a different context on each of 2 days and tested them 3 days later in yet another novel context. Following variable-contextual training, the retention impairment otherwise incurred by a novel test context both after a 3-day delay (e.g., see Figure 1.13) and 2 weeks later, at the time of reminding, were completely eliminated. At 6 months, however, variable-contextual training eliminated the disrupting effect of a novel test context on retention 1 day after training (Amabile & Rovee-Collier, 1991), but it did not affect performance in a reactivation paradigm. The original mobile was still completely ineffective in alleviating forgetting 3 weeks after training if it was presented in a novel context.

The specificity of infants' memory representation of their training context at 6 months is also independent of the status of the training cue. Shields and Rovee-Collier (1992), for example, trained 6-month-olds with a different mobile on each of 2 days in the same context and tested them with another different mobile 1 day later in either the original training context or in a different one. Variable-cue training eliminated the disruption in 24-hr retention otherwise incurred by a novel test mobile, but it had no effect on the disruption incurred after the same delay by a different test context (Figure 1.14). Exactly the same pattern was seen

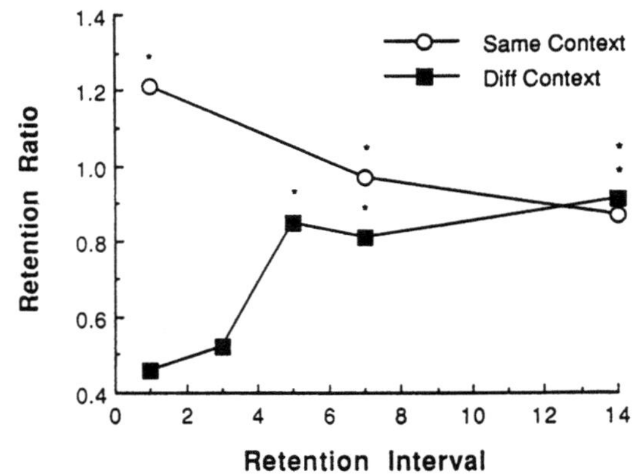

FIGURE 1.15. Retention of independent groups of 6-month-olds tested with the training mobile in the presence of a different playpen liner (Diff Context) after retention intervals of 1, 3, 5, 7, or 14 days or in the presence of the original liner (Same Context) after intervals of 1, 7, or 14 days. Asterisks indicate significant retention during the long-term test (i.e., *M* baseline ratio significantly > 1.00). (From "Contextual Constraints on Memory Retrieval at 6 Months" by D.B. Borovsky and C. Rovee-Collier, 1990, *Child Development*, *61*, 1569–1583. Copyright 1990 by the Society for Research in Child Development. Reprinted by permission.)

both when these same cue-context combinations were presented as reminders 3 weeks after training and when they were presented during a transfer test 1 day following an effective reminder.

In view of the greater reliance on contextual information for memory retrieval at 6 months, it seems paradoxical that their forgetting function for contextual information in the newly acquired memory is relatively steep, as Riccio et al. (1984) predicted. The effect of an altered context on retention is greatest immediately after training and disappears within 5 to 7 days (Figure 1.15). Despite this, an otherwise effective reminder will not reactivate the forgotten memory 20 days after training if it is presented in a different context (Borovsky & Rovee-Collier, 1990). This phenomenon mirrors that described earlier (see Figure 1.11) when 3-month-olds were trained and tested in a relatively nondistinctive context with a novel mobile after different delays (Rovee-Collier & Sullivan, 1980). Even though these infants had generalized to a novel test mobile after delays of 3 days and longer, a novel mobile could not reactivate the forgotten memory 14 days after training (Butler & Rovee-Collier, 1989; Enright, 1981; Rovee-Collier, Patterson, et al., 1985).

The Role of Specific Contextual Attributes

The specificity with which particular types of contextual attributes constrain memory retrieval at 6 months is also surprising. The work by

Treisman and her colleagues on feature-integration theory has provided some useful insights into this issue. According to Treisman (1988), visual information processing can be divided into two distinct stages defined by the engagement of selective attention. In the first stage, *preattentive processing*, features of various dimensions (e.g., color, shape, size, orientation, etc.) of an array of visual stimuli can be registered in parallel over a large spatial area. In the second stage, *attentive processing*, attention is directed to each stimulus location so that the (free-floating) features belonging to the same object can be properly conjoined to ensure accurate object identification.

During the past decade, Treisman and her colleagues have accrued a significant amount of data to support this theory: (a) a feature-defined target can be searched in parallel (the "pop-out" effect), unaffected by the display size, but a conjunction-defined target must be searched serially (Treisman & Gelade, 1980; Treisman, Sykes, & Gelade, 1977); (b) feature differences among texture elements lead to fast and easy texture segmentation, but conjunction differences do not (Treisman & Gelade, 1980; Treisman & Paterson, 1984); (c) when attention is distracted or overloaded, an illusory conjunction among features may be formed (Treisman & Schmidt, 1982); and (d) illusory conjunctions are not limited to elementary features—emergent features, for example, can sometimes be erroneously conjoined with other features (Treisman & Paterson, 1984; Treisman & Souther, 1985; for review, see Treisman, 1988).

Motivated by Treisman's ideas and findings, Rovee-Collier et al. (1992) examined whether alterations of either a single dimension of the visual information of the context (figure shape, figure color, background (Dannemiller & Braun, 1988) would disrupt 6-month-olds' retention. They trained infants for 2 days in the presence of a distinct playpen liner and tested 1 day later, when a contextual change is most disruptive (Borovsky & Rovee-Collier, 1990). Retention was unaffected when the shape of the figure was changed from squares to triangles, but it was eliminated when the shape was changed from squares to either circles or stripes, and vice versa. Retention was also unaffected by a change in figure color only (background color and shape held constant), but a change in background color only (figure color and shape held constant) disrupted retention. The latter result suggests that the disruption of retention when the figure/ground chromatic relation is reversed can be attributed to the change in background color (see also Dannemiller & Braun, 1988).

Surprisingly, when the figures were stripped from the liner (Fig. 1.16, F) at the time of testing, leaving it "blank," infants' retention was excellent, but the blank liner was not an effective reminder 3 weeks later, when forgetting was complete. This and other evidence (Boller et al., 1990; Hayne, 1988; Rovee-Collier & Hayne, 1987) suggest that more

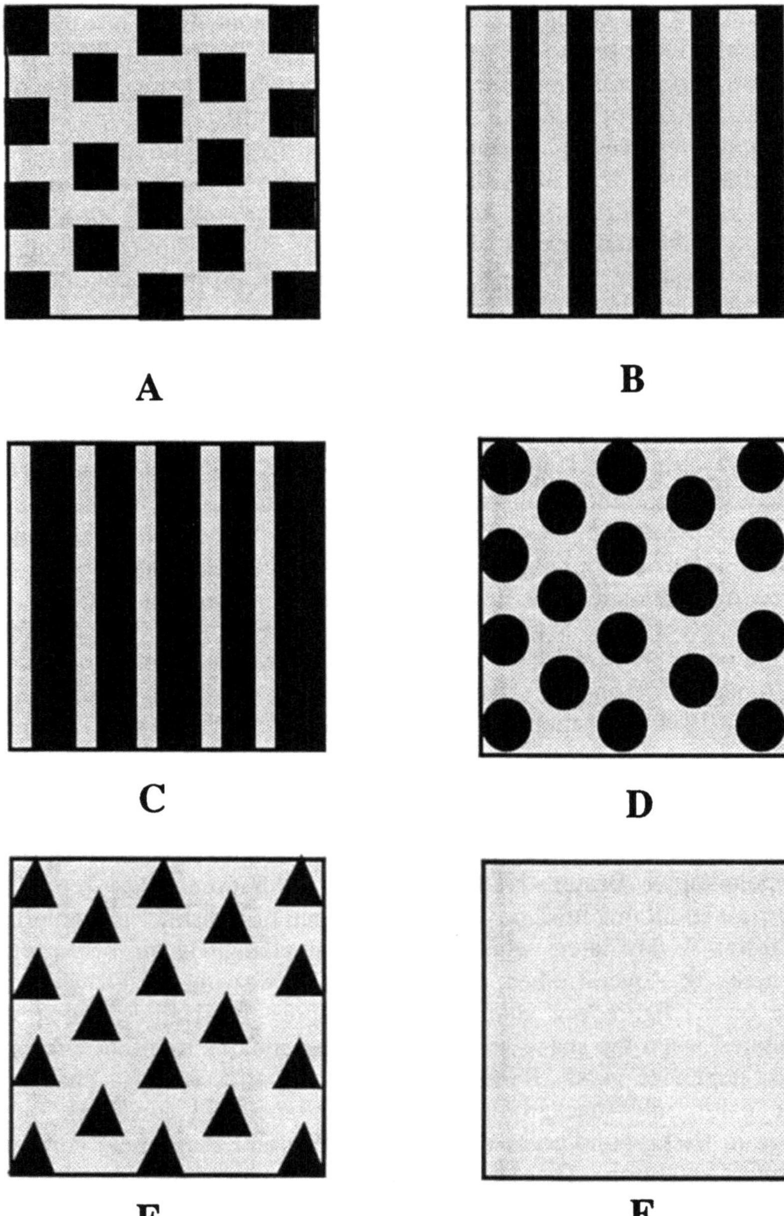

FIGURE 1.16. The training and test patterns used to study the specificity of encoding for contextual attributes at 6 months (see also Figure 1.1b).

contextual support may be required to recover a memory once all of its components have become inaccessible than to retrieve a newly acquired memory with components that are still highly accessible as, for example, 24 hr after training.

When the patterned training liner was removed altogether from the sides of the playpen during testing, permitting infants visual access to a different but familiar surround (the surrounding room), their retention was completely disrupted. As before, infants simply stared at the training mobile, appearing not to recognize it. Thus, the critical aspect of the altered context in the preceding studies was not its novelty but whether or not it was represented in the memory of training (see also Borovsky & Rovee-Collier, 1990; Hayne et al., 1991; Rovee-Collier, Patterson, et al., 1985).

Because retention was perfect when the figures were removed from the cloth liner but no retention was displayed when the liner was removed altogether, we conjecture that the detection of distractors in a test context acts in a manner similar to the absence of contextual retrieval cues to prevent the first attention gate from opening, thereby precluding recognition of the mobile at 6 months. Barring the detection of distractors, however, detection of the common background color permits the attention gate to open sufficiently for retrieval to occur (see Butler & Rovee-Collier, 1989, for discussion).

Because all components of the context in the Rovee-Collier et al. (1992) study were not equally effective in cuing retrieval (see also Hayne et al., 1987), and no single critical feature (Treisman & Gelade, 1980) was prerequisite for retrieval, we conclude that infants did not perceive the cue-context (mobile-liner) combination holistically. The finding that a contextual change after 1 day did not affect retention at 3 months (Butler & Rovee-Collier, 1989) is further support for this interpretation. This conclusion should not, however, be taken as an argument against the commonly held view that perceptual development proceeds from the perception of similarity structure to the perception of dimensional structure. In studies of children's perceptual development, the predominant mode of perception has been assessed within a *single* object by examining whether children could selectively attend to various stimulus dimensions (e.g., color, shape, orientation, etc.) that comprised the objects as the basis for their responses required by a given task. Our data merely suggest that the cue (mobile) and the context (liner) are treated as distinct and separate entities by infants as young as 3 months.

The studies discussed so far indicate that 6-month-old infants are able to detect and encode local information in their environment and that its alteration can disrupt retention. It is not clear, however, if 6-month-olds are equally sensitive to changes of global, configurational information in their environment.

Configurational versus Component Processing

There has been ample evidence suggesting that young infants can detect the change of configuration of visual pattern (see Dodwell, Humphrey, & Muir, 1987, for review). Milewski (1979), for example, reported that a 3-month-old could detect the change when a linear arrangement of three dots was shifted to a triangular arrangement. More recently, Ghim and Eimas (1988) showed that 3- to 4-month-old infants process both global (configurational) information and local (component) information in a visual pattern; moreover, the infants exhibit a preference for processing global information—a *global precedence effect* (Navon, 1977; Pomerantz, 1983). Dineen and Meyer (1980) have also reported that 6-month-olds are sensitive both to changes in the configuration of a visual pattern and to changes in the elements that comprise the pattern. Even if infants are capable of extracting both configurational and component information in a visual stimulus when explicitly asked to do so in a laboratory setting, these findings do not directly speak to the question of whether or not 6-month-olds extract this same type of information from the setting in which learning takes place and use it later to constrain retrieval.

To address this question, Shyi (1990) trained 6-month-olds with one of three yellow playpen liners that differed in the configurational or component information they displayed (green stripes, green squares aligned in columns like stripes, or green squares in a grid pattern), and examined the consequences of testing infants 1 day later with one of the other liners. Infants trained in the presence of green stripes and tested in the presence of green squares aligned in columns showed significant (albeit not perfect) retention—a result that was replicated. The opposite arrangement and all other training-test changes, however, were discriminated after 1 day. That is, retention was eliminated by all other changes in the testing context. These findings suggest that (a) 6-month-olds encode both global, configurational information and local, component information, and (b) global, configurational information may be processed faster, and thus may be available earlier, than the local, component information (Kinchla & Wolfe, 1979; Miller, 1981).

The preceding studies, considered jointly, have led us to view the context as a critical source of retrieval cues for infants as young as 3 months. Contextual information appears to protect the memory from retrieval in inappropriate locations, where it might be extinguished or modified, and after delays at which younger infants would otherwise generalize responding to an ambiguous or fuzzy cue. By 6 months, contextual information exerts even stronger control over memory retrieval. These findings refute claims that the brains of infants younger than 8 to 9 months are functionally too immature to encode and maintain information about the place where learning occurs (Diamond, 1991; Nadel et al., 1985; Nadel & Zola-Morgan, 1984; Schacter & Moscovitch,

1984). Apparently, prelocomotor infants learn what happens in what place substantially before they learn the spatial relations between those places or how to get from one place to another (see also Richardson, Riccio, & McKenney, 1988). This conclusion is consistent with recent evidence that 8-month-olds can acquire information about the location of objects in a search task (Baillargeon & Graber, 1988). We propose that contextual information may be even more important to memory retrieval for human infants than for children (West & Stanovich, 1978) or adults (Crowder, 1985; Crowder & Greene, 1987). In this regard, Duchek's (1984) finding that reinstatement of the original *semantic* context has a greater facilitating effect on retrieval by younger than by older adults is also relevant.

The Effect of Multiple Reminders on Long-Term Retention

Tulving (1972, 1983) proposed a dual-storage memory system consisting of episodic memory for the storage of time- and context-dependent memories and semantic memory for the storage of general information and knowledge that is independent of the time and place of encoding. Although he originally viewed episodic memory as the first system to develop ontogenetically, this position has been reversed (Bachvalier & Mishkin, 1984; Schacter & Moscovitch, 1984; Tulving, 1985). Alternatively, episodic and semantic memory may not constitute altogether different memory systems but merely may define opposite poles of a single continuum of memory (see also Kintsch, 1974). The finding that a once-reactivated memory and a newly acquired memory are forgotten at identical rates fanned our interest in this latter alternative. We hypothesized that repeatedly reactivating a memory might strengthen it and progressively flatten its reforgetting function such that, at some point, the memory would be accessed so rapidly after very long retention intervals that it would correspond to Tulving's characterization of semantic memory.

This hypothesis was pursued in a dissertation by Hayne (1988). She exposed 3-month-olds to one, two, or three reminders and tested their retention at different intervals following the final reminder presentation. As expected, infants who received one reminder 20 days after original training exhibited complete forgetting of the reactivated memory after 7 days. Infants who received two reminders, however, still exhibited near-perfect retention 2 weeks later, whether the second reminder was presented 2, 3, or 4 weeks after the time of training (Figure 1.17). For infants in the 4-week group, this constituted a retention interval of *6 weeks* following the conclusion of original training. The highly facilitating effect of a second reminder was not due to the increase in the total

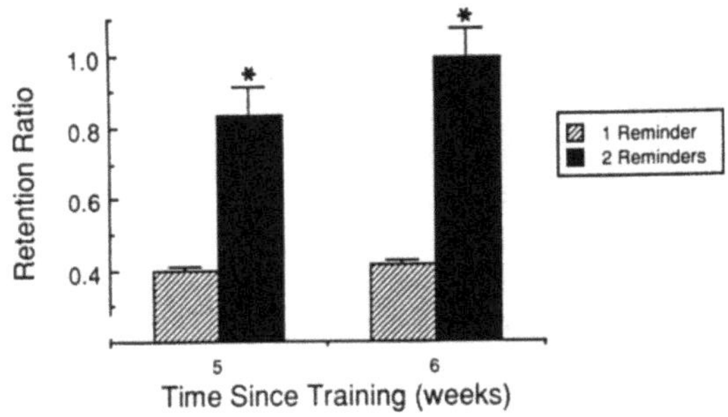

FIGURE 1.17. Long-term retention exhibited by independent groups of 3-month-olds tested 2 weeks after receiving either one or two reminders. Asterisks indicate significant retention (*M* baseline ratio significantly >1.00). (From *The Effect of Multiple Reminders on Long-Term Retention in Human Infants* by H. Hayne, 1988. Unpublished Doctoral Dissertation, Rutgers University, New Brunswick, NJ. Copyright 1988 by H. Hayne. Reprinted by permission.)

amount of time that a reminder was exposed. Infants who received a single 6-min reminder 20 days after training exhibited no retention after 1 week.

The facilitating effect of retrieval on subsequent retention also has been reported in studies using verbal materials with adults. McDaniel and Masson (1985), for example, compared the effects of a number of initial retrieval tasks (e.g., cued-recall with different types of cues, two-alternative forced-choice recognition test, and a second encoding task) on performance during a later cued-recall test. Their results suggest that initial retrieval experiences facilitate later recall so long as they produce elaboration of an existing memory representation, which, in turn, increases the variability of encoded information. As a result, the memory can be accessed by more than a single route. A similar account has been proposed for hypermnesia effects observed after repeated testing (Payne, 1986; Roediger & Payne, 1982).

Surprisingly, when Hayne (1988) presented three reminders (on Days 6, 13, and 20 after original training), they were only as effective as a single reminder (Figure 1.18). Because infants exhibited perfect retention 24 hr after their third reminder, an extinction account of this effect was precluded. Because infants who had received two reminders in the preceding study had exhibited perfect retention 2 weeks after a second reminder and reminders were always presented 1 week apart, the twice-reactivated memory was already highly accessible at the time infants in the present study received their third reminder on Day 20. Hayne concluded, therefore, that the highly accessible twice-reactivated memory was retrieved and modified prior to the time that she administered the long-term retention test a week later. Because training, reminding, and

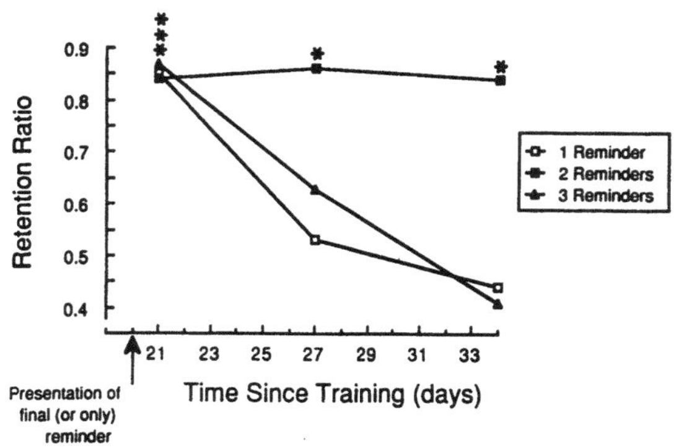

FIGURE 1.18. Long-term retention exhibited by independent groups of 3-month-olds receiving either one (Day 20), two (Days 13 and 20), or three (Days 6, 13, and 20) reminders and tested 1, 7, or 14 days after the final reminder (i.e., 21, 27, or 34 days following the conclusion of training, respectively). Asterisks indicate significant retention during the long-term test (*M* baseline ratio significantly >1.00). (From *The Effect of Multiple Reminders on Long-Term Retention in Human Infants* by H. Hayne, 1988. Unpublished Doctoral Dissertation, Rutgers University, New Brunswick, NJ. Copyright 1988 by H. Hayne. Reprinted by permission.)

testing had occurred in a highly distinctive context, which typically protects a newly acquired memory against retrieval in a generalized context by a generalized cue, we suspect that a twice-reactivated memory may be organized differently or contain fewer specific details of cue or context than a newly acquired or a once-reactivated memory. Recent data from studies of animal learning and memory, for example, suggest that the organization of memory attributes of a learned event changes over time (Gisquet-Verrier, Dekeyne, & Alexinsky, 1989). These possibilities, however, remain to be explored in future research, as does the question of whether allowing the memory to be completely forgotten before the presentation of a third reminder would alter this result. Unfortunately, Hayne could not pursue the latter question within the framework of her procedure: Once infants begin to roll from their backs to their stomachs, at approximately 17 weeks (the age of her oldest infants at the time of testing), they cannot be tested in the original supine training position.

Support for Hayne's conclusion comes from studies of rehearsal in adults. Like rehearsal, a reminder increases the accessibility of input already in memory and returns it to an active state (or to short-term memory), where it is maintained (for review, see Johnson, 1980). Although researchers typically report an advantage of maintenance rehearsal for delayed recognition but not recall (e.g., Craik & Watkins, 1973; Woodward, Bjork, & Jongeward, 1973), others have reported an advantage for delayed recall as well (e.g., Baddeley, 1978; Dark &

Loftus, 1976; Modigliani, 1976). Of particular relevance to Hayne's finding is Neisser's (1967) suggestion that rehearsal is more than the simple "invigoration" of an old memory but, rather, provides an opportunity for the formation of new associations. This suggestion is similar to Kintsch's (1974) proposal that retrieval information complements stored information at the time of retrieval, Bjork's (1975) proposal that the act of retrieval per se may alter the level of processing of stored information (Craik & Lockhart, 1972), Tulving's (1983) proposal that a retrieval cue and stored information interact ("ecphory"), and Loftus's proposal that either an original memory is recoded by new information present at the time of retrieval (Loftus, 1979, 1981; Loftus, Miller, & Burns, 1978) or a new memory is created at that time (Loftus & Hoffman, 1989).

Additional support for the memory modification hypothesis comes from recent findings with 3-month-olds, discussed below, that presentation of a memory prime *before* a newly acquired memory is initially forgotten prolongs retention of the most recently encountered cue but also alters retention of the original memory (Boller & Rovee-Collier, 1992; Greco & Rovee-Collier, 1988).

From the preceding data, we conclude that how long an event is remembered and what is remembered depend on how many times the memory has been retrieved, the status of the memory at the time it is accessed, and the context in which retrieval occurs. Because different components of either directly or indirectly activated memories can be strengthened or weakened and their contents can be modified by new information that is encountered at the time of retrieval, it would be virtually impossible to determine whether the original memory representation is retained permanently or is eventually lost. A similar point has been made by Squire (1987).

Modification of Infants' Memories

Memory modification following encoding has been studied in both animals and humans primarily with respect to the phenomenon of consolidation, retroactive interference, and the administration of amnestic or memory-enhancing agents. The general conclusion from both cognitive and neuropsychological research is that processing of an event continues for a period of time after the actual event is over, during which time the memory can be modulated (McGaugh & Dawson, 1971; Squire, 1987). Recent research with roots in traditional interference theory has focused on the modification of eyewitness testimony by postevent information (Ceci, Toglia, & Ross, 1987; Loftus, 1979, 1981; Loftus et al., 1978).

Postevent Information and Memory Modification

The postevent information procedure was originally used by Loftus and her colleagues to investigate whether postevent information pertinent to a prior event can be integrated into the event and thus alter its memory representation (Loftus, 1979, 1981; Loftus et al., 1978). Their procedure typically involved first presenting the subjects with a series of slides depicting an event such as an automobile accident. Subjects were then provided with additional information about the witnessed event, such as a narrative or questionnaire. The experimental group received misleading information about some nonfocal aspect of the scene, for example, a "stop" sign was described as a "yield" sign in the narrative, whereas a control group received no misleading information about those same items. Subjects in both groups were later given a two-alternative forced-choice recognition test in which they had to choose between the original item depicted in the slides and the misleading item more recently mentioned in the narrative. The general finding is that the experimental group performs significantly worse than the control group.

Loftus and her colleagues proposed that the information initially represented in the memory of the event was overwritten or replaced by the more recent misleading information. The more general implications of their findings are that memory traces are not permanent (Howe & Brainerd, 1989; Loftus & Loftus, 1980) and that the testimony of eyewitnesses may not always be reliable because their memories may be distorted by information encountered subsequently (see also Loftus et al., this volume; Schooler, Gerhard, & Loftus, 1987).

Not all researchers have agreed with Loftus and her colleagues' conclusions. Bekerian and Bowers (1983) and Christiaansen and Ochalek (1983), for example, have argued that the original memory was not permanently lost but was merely rendered inaccessible or nonretrievable by the postevent information. McCloskey and Zaragoza (1985), for example, argued that Loftus' test procedure of asking subjects to choose between the original and the misleading item was inappropriate for assessing the effects of misleading information on original memory. They proposed instead that subjects be asked to choose between the original and a third, never-mentioned novel item. Only if the control group outperformed the experimental group under these conditions could conclusions be drawn about the alteration or mutation of the original memory. Using the modified recognition test procedure, however, McCloskey and Zaragoza found no differences between the two groups. They have also obtained null results using a more stringent recall test (Zaragoza, McCloskey, & Jamis, 1987).

Questions such as whether misleading postevent information or any pertinent subsequent information can indeed be integrated into the memory for an original event, and if so, in what form the integration is

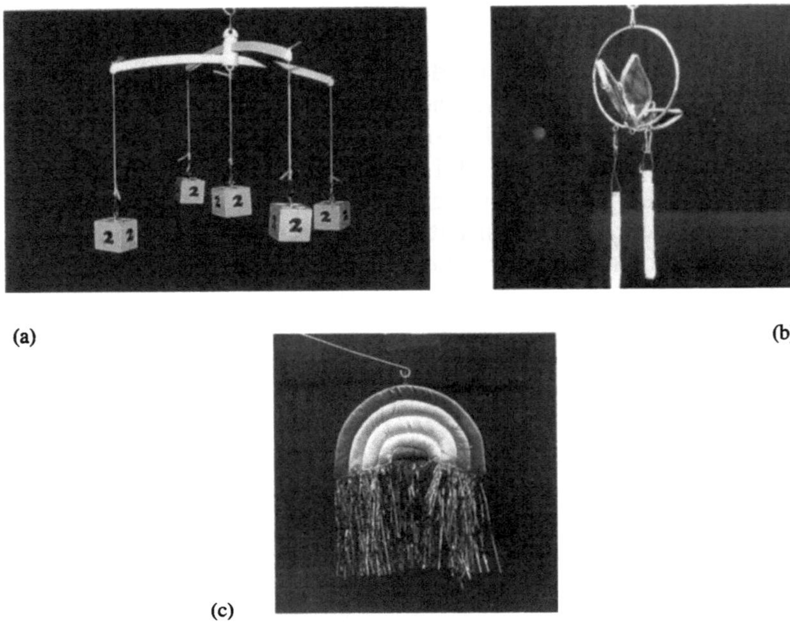

FIGURE 1.19. Objects used in studies of categorization and memory modification at 3 months: (a) a yellow-block mobile training exemplar; (b) the muted butterfly wind-chimes constructed of metal and colored glass; (c) the multicolored, quilted-satin rainbow pillow.

achieved, are still open. Recently, for example, Loftus and Hoffman (1989) have suggested that either memory blends or new memories are created by information encountered subsequent to a witnessed event. As McCloskey and Zaragoza (1985) noted, however, no satisfactory answers can be cultivated until notions such as integration can be explicitly and meaningfully specified. Our most recent research with infants has attempted to address this issue.

Memory Modification in Young Infants

In a series of studies with 3- and 6-month-olds, we have explored how new information modifies or is integrated with old memories. Greco et al. (1990) reported that when a highly physically dissimilar object (butterfly in Figure 1.19b) was suspended motionless over infants' cribs for 3 min immediately following category training with a series of discriminably different yellow-block mobiles (Figure 1.19a), 3-month-old infants transferred responding to the object 24 hr later if and only if they had been trained for 3 days in a unique and highly distinctive context and had also viewed the motionless butterfly in that same, unique context. During the transfer test the distinctive context was not present to mediate responding. When infants were trained and exposed to the motionless butterfly immediately afterward in a context that was neither highly distinctive nor unique, the object did not cue retrieval during the 24-hr transfer test. Thus, mere temporal contiguity between the butterfly and the training blocks alone cannot account for this result.

We have obtained a similar result when the butterfly context was introduced only in the third session during training and when the butterfly was exposed; as before, the context was not present at the time of testing. These data suggest that the memory of a specific prior episode was retrieved during the 24-hr test. Apparently, the context acts as a catalyst that integrates or associates the butterfly with the prior training memory; once represented in the prior training memory, however, butterfly can cue retrieval on its own, without the context.

Although encountering physically dissimilar objects in a common context can result in their joint association, common functional information can also override physical dissimilarity as a basis for association. Infants were trained and tested without a unique or highly distinctive crib liner and, immediately afterward, were allowed to passively view the highly physically dissimilar butterfly in motion—a function that it shared with the yellow-block training mobiles. Not only did the stationary butterfly cue retrieval of the training memory during a transfer test 24 hr later but also it was an effective reminder for that training memory 2 weeks later! In contrast, butterfly was *not* an effective retrieval cue either 24 hr after training or as a reminder if it was motionless during the postevent exposure immediately following training. As in the case of the common context, the common function (motion) apparently served as a catalyst that integrated the butterfly with the training memory. During testing, infants responded even though the catalyst (the motion) was absent. Exposure to additional postevent information that either decreased or increased the functional similarity between butterfly and the category exemplars encountered during training correspondingly shifted the effectiveness of the butterfly as a retrieval cue in both a simple-forgetting and a reminder paradigm (Greco et al., 1990).

We emphasize that infants were *never directly trained* to respond to the physically dissimilar object but only viewed it passively, and that it was always motionless at the time of testing. These conditions refute claims that younger infants can exhibit long-term retention only if a conditioned response is directly associated with a stimulus that is physically present and elicits the response at the time of testing (Gopnik & Meltzoff, 1987; Mandler, 1984; Schacter & Moscovitch, 1984).

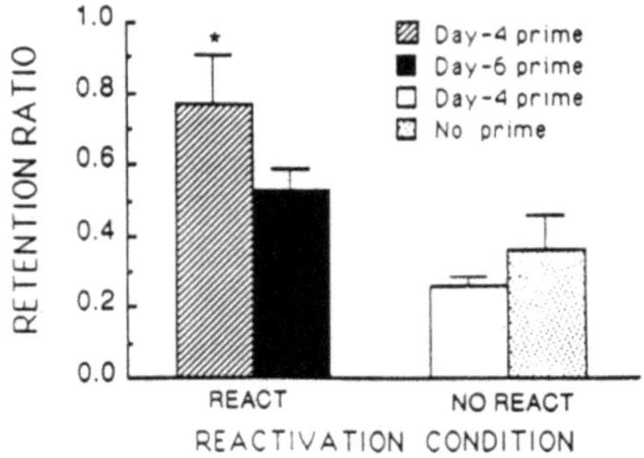

FIGURE 1.20. Retention of independent groups of 3-month-olds tested 24 hr following the presentation of the butterfly as a reminder. Infants had initially been passively exposed to the butterfly in motion either inside (4 days) or outside (6 days) the time window for memory modification by postevent information. (From "Postevent Bonding: The Time Window for the Malleability of Infant Memory" by C. Greco and C. Rovee-Collier, 1988, presented at the meeting of the International Conference on Infant Studies, Washington, DC. Copyright 1988 by C. Greco and C. Rovee-Collier. Reprinted by permission.)

Time Window for Memory Modification

We have found that integration with the prior training memory can occur by passive exposure to the moving object within a 4-day time window at 3 months (Greco & Rovee-Collier, 1988). If the object is viewed in motion within 4 days after the conclusion of training, then it is an effective retrieval cue 24 hr later, and it also is an effective reminder for the forgotten training memory 3 weeks later. In contrast, if the object is passively viewed in motion outside of this time window (for example, 6 days after training), then it does not cue retrieval after any delay in either a simple-forgetting or a reactivation paradigm (Figure 1.20).

Not only does exposure to the highly physically dissimilar but functionally similar object within a 4-day time window result in its association with the training memory of the yellow-block mobiles, but also its retention is influenced by when in the time window the exposure occurs. Figure 1.21 presents the forgetting function obtained when infants are tested with the physically dissimilar object (butterfly) after viewing it immediately after training. They exhibit no retention of the object 7 days later. Also shown is the forgetting function for the object when its initial exposure has been delayed until the end of the time window—4 days after training. Under these circumstances, infants now remember the object for at least 10 days after its initial exposure—14 days after the conclusion of training. Because the training memory was already in an active state at the time of the immediate exposure but had to be retrieved

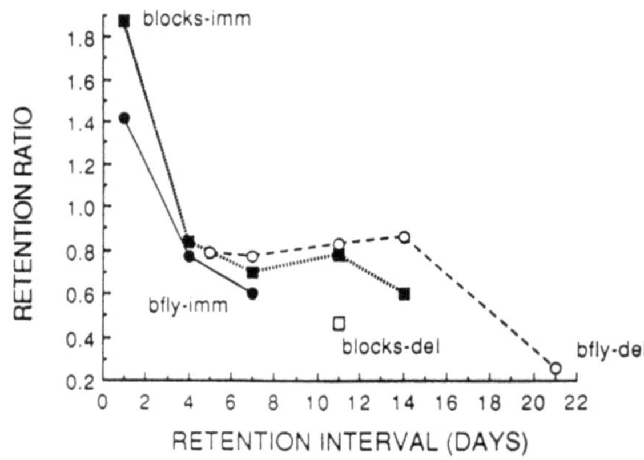

FIGURE 1.21. The forgetting functions for the butterfly and a novel yellow-block mobile following either the immediate or delayed postevent exposure of the butterfly in motion. Note that retention of the butterfly was extended (dashed line) when its exposure was delayed until 4 days after the conclusion of category training with a series of yellow-block mobiles. Retention by infants tested with a novel yellow-block mobile 11 days after the conclusion of training and 7 days after the delayed exposure to the butterfly was not significantly above baseline. (From "Postevent Bonding: The Time Window for the Malleability of Infant Memory" by C. Greco and C. Rovee-Collier, 1988, presented at the meeting of the International Conference on Infant Studies, Washington, DC. Copyright 1988 by C. Greco and C. Rovee-Collier, Reprinted by permission.)

to an active state at the time of the delayed exposure, we conclude that retrieval per se acted in a manner analogous to rehearsal, prolonging retention (see preceding section).

The retention advantage associated with passive exposure to the butterfly at the end of the time window is offset by an impairment in retention for a novel member of the yellow-block training series. Although infants originally remembered a yellow-block mobile for 11 days—longer than they remembered the butterfly when it was exposed immediately following training, they exhibited absolutely no retention of a yellow-block mobile 11 days after training when the passive exposure to the butterfly was delayed until the end of the time window (Figure 1.21). Thus, modification of the training memory by the introduction of a new component at the time it was retrieved appears to have weakened one of the original components of the memory. This strong recency effect is particularly remarkable given that infants had been explicitly trained with yellow-block mobiles for 3 days but had never been trained with the butterfly, only passively viewing it in motion for 3 min. These data strongly suggest that the ease with which early memories can be updated following variable training may be a major source of the infantile amnesia phenomenon.

The latter possibility is heightened by our observation that infants' subsequent classification of the butterfly as a category member was not based merely on their recognition of having viewed it before (Greco et al., 1990). Infants who had been exposed to the moving butterfly following category training also transferred responding to another highly physically dissimilar stimulus (rainbow in Figure 1.19c) that they had *never* previously encountered. In contrast, infants who had not been exposed to the moving butterfly immediately after training did not transfer responding to the rainbow during the 24-hr transfer test. These data suggest that infants as young as 3 months represent information in a conceptual format; integrating the butterfly with the category-training memory was not specific to butterfly but increased the breadth of the training category. This result is consistent with findings from adult research that increasing the variability among encountered exemplars expands the range of novel items classified as category members (Flannagan, Fried, & Holyoak, 1986; Fried & Holyoak, 1984). It also suggests that infants as young as 3 months may have the ability to respond analogically in new situations on the basis of information acquired in the past. Having encountered one highly physically dissimilar object (butterfly) that was functionally similar to the training mobiles, infants may have hypothesized that another highly physically dissimilar object (rainbow) suspended over their cribs might also function in the same way and produced the learned response in an attempt to *make* it move.

In the preceding studies, infants were trained with a perceptibly different mobile in each session. Variable-cue training is not, however, prerequisite for the integration of postevent information with a previously encoded memory. Recall that when infants are trained with the same mobile in each of two sessions (AA), a novel mobile (B) does not cue retrieval after a 24-hr delay; when infants are trained with a different mobile in each session (AB), however, yet another novel mobile (C) does cue retrieval (Fagen et al., 1984; Hill et al., 1988; Shields & Rovee-Collier, 1992; Figure 1.22, top left panel). Recently, we trained 3-month-olds with the same mobile for two sessions (AA) and then passively exposed them to a novel mobile (B), moving noncontingently, for 3 min after the completion of training (Borza & Rovee-Collier, 1989). During a 24-hr retention test, both mobile B *and* the previously unseen mobile C cued retrieval of the training memory (Figure 1.22, bottom panel), just as in the butterfly/rainbow studies described above. Also as before, temporal contiguity alone could not account for this result: When mobile B remained stationary during its postevent exposure, neither it nor mobile C was an effective retrieval cue 24 hr later (Figure 1.22, top right panel). Thus, 3-month-olds had to be exposed to information that the two physically dissimilar mobiles were *functionally* similar in order for post-event information about the physically dissimilar mobile to be intergrated with their prior memory of training.

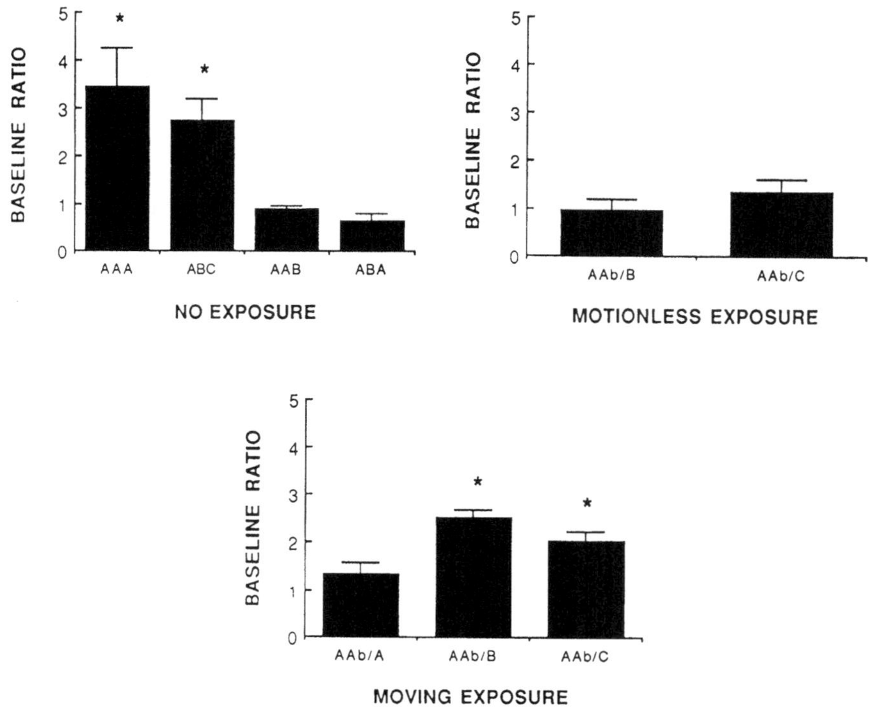

FIGURE 1.22. Retention at 3 months during a 24-hr test with a stationary mobile in Session 3. Top left panel: No-exposure control groups trained and tested with either the same mobile (AAA) or a novel one (ABC) in each session, trained with the same mobile and tested with a novel mobile (AAB), trained with a novel one on each day and tested with the original mobile (ABA). Top right panel: Motionless-exposure groups trained with the same mobile and exposed to a novel, motionless mobile (b) immediately following the end of Session 2 and tested with the exposed mobile (B) or another novel one (C). Bottom panel: Moving-exposure groups trained with the same mobile and exposed to a novel noncontingently moving mobile (b) immediately afterward and tested with either the exposed mobile (B) or another novel one (C). Asterisks indicate significant retention during the 24-hr test (*M* baseline ratio significantly >1.00). (From "Memory Modification in 3-Month-Olds" by M. Borza and C. Rovee-Collier, 1989, presented at the meeting of the International Society for Developmental Psychobiology, San Francisco, CA. Copyright 1989 by M. Borza and C. Rovee-Collier. Reprinted by permission.)

The finding that infants again completely transferred responding to a discriminably different mobile that they had never previously encountered (C) suggests that the brief exposure to mobile B in Session 2 altered their memory of training with mobile A to produce a variable-cue training effect (group ABC in Figure 1.22, top left panel) and that their excellent performance during the 24-hr test was based on retrieval of this altered,

Session-2 memory token. The phenomenon can also be obtained, but with less robust transfer, if the initial postevent exposure to mobile B, moving noncontingently, does not occur until 1 day after the conclusion of training. No effect is seen, however, if the initial postevent exposure is delayed by 2 days. Unlike the butterfly studies in which infants were explicitly trained with a physically different mobile on each of three sessions, the modification observed after constant training is limited to the newly acquired memory. Neither mobile B nor mobile C is an effective reminder in a reactivation paradigm.

Postevent information also affects the retention of contextual information at 6 months. Boller and Rovee-Collier (1992) briefly exposed infants to a novel context for 2 min following the conclusion of training in a constant context and tested them with the original mobile in the post-event context or in one not previously encountered 24 hr later, when even the slightest contextual change typically disrupts retention at 6 months (Borovsky & Rovee-Collier, 1990; Rovee-Collier et al., 1992; Shyi, 1990). During the ensuing retention test, infants not only responded vigorously in the context to which they had been exposed immediately following the conclusion of Session 2 but also they responded in the completely novel context. The same effect was obtained whether the mobile was present (moving or nonmoving) or absent during the postevent exposure to context B. As at 3 months, however, the effect is relatively transient and limited to the newly acquired memory. Following passive exposure to the original mobile, moving noncontingently, in a novel context, the original mobile was not an effective reminder if presented in that same context during a reactivation treatment 3 weeks later. The latter finding is consistent with the finding, described earlier, that for 6-month-olds who have been explicitly trained in a different context in each session, the original mobile is not an effective reminder 3 weeks later in another novel context (Amabile & Rovee-Collier, 1991).

Thus, passive exposure to a perceptibly different cue or context following constant training can achieve a result similar to that obtained by explicit variable training with a series of different cues or contexts, but the effect appears to be short-lived and restricted to the newly acquired memory. Conceivably, different parameters of training or exposure would strengthen the long-term effect.

General Discussion

The preceding demonstrations of long-term retention in infants as young as 2 to 3 months of age have necessitated a dramatic revision of the prevailing view of the course of normal memory development during the first year of life. Very young infants are clearly endowed with neuroanatomical structures that can support the encoding, storage, and retrieval of memories over very long intervals. In addition, our findings on memory specificity, the time-dependent nature of memory retrieval, multiple reminders, memory modification and its time window, the role of functional information in categorization, and on the contextual determinants of memory retrieval at 3 and 6 months are unique.

The specificity of a reminder with respect both to its details and the context within which it is encountered suggests that infantile amnesia may also result, at least in part, from either real or perceived contextual changes that are increasingly likely to occur as a simple function of time passage. This specificity appears to buffer against the possibility that memories will be retrieved in inappropriate situations where they might either "misguide" behavior or become inappropriately modified (e.g., a predictive relation could lose its predictive value). Additionally, the requirement that retrieval cues be context-specific relieves immature organisms with a poorly developed inhibitory system of the need to withhold responding in an inappropriate context by severely constraining the probability that retrieval will be instantiated in the first place. In effect, the response constraints are contained in the structure of the environment at a time when central inhibitory mechanisms are not fully functional. This same factor, however, reduces the probability of retrieval after very long intervals.

The encoding and use of contextual information has been described both as a hippocampal function (Nadel et al., 1985; Nadel & Zola-Morgan, 1984) and as a defining characteristic of episodic or declarative memory (Squire, 1986, 1987), neither of which are presumed to be implicated in memory processing by infants less than 8 or 9 months of age (see also Bachvalier & Mishkin, 1984; Schacter & Moscovitch, 1984). Because the adult brain mechanisms that process place information are presumably not functional at this point in development, additional research will be required to reveal just how this information is processed, and what happens to the centers that are responsible for its processing later in development. Alternatively, researchers may conclude that the relevant adult structures mature earlier than previously thought.

We think that the temporal course of attribute accessibility in newly acquired and reactivated memories as well as the time window within which infants sample previous memories and integrate new information with them are also important keys to the understanding of infantile amnesia. Because infants' memories are so readily modified and this modification may weaken earlier and/or unused components of the original memory, the original memory may eventually become unavailable for retrieval. The findings from our research are consistent with proposals that memory traces are mutable (Brainerd, Reyna, Howe, & Kingma, 1990; Howe & Brainerd, 1989; Loftus & Loftus, 1980) and, at a minimum, indicate that both storage factors and retrieval factors must be considered in any adequate account of infant long-term retention.

A similar conclusion has been reached concerning accounts of the development of long-term retention in childhood (Brainerd et al., 1990; Howe & Brainerd, 1989; Howe & Hunter, 1986). Howe and Brainerd (1989) have proposed a comprehensive model of the development of long-term retention that assumes that performance on long-term retention tests is a direct function of the strength of the memory trace. The latter refers to the degree to which the elements comprising a trace are integrated. In their formulation, storage corresponds to early stages of integration in which elements of a memory trace are integrated or "glued" into a trace structure, and retrieval corresponds to later stages of integration in which the trace structure is configured so that the memory trace will be activated in the presence of sufficient retrieval cues. Retention failure could be caused either by disintegration of the configuration of the trace structure that renders retrieval cues ineffective even though the trace is still intact, or by disintegration of the trace structure itself such that the memory trace becomes indistinguishable from the background noise (see also Brainerd et al., 1990; Howe et al., this volume). Although there are a number of obvious correspondences between our data and the trace-integrity model, its adequacy in describing long-term retention early in infancy cannot be evaluated at this point in our knowledge.

Although our procedures were modeled after procedures used to study long-term retention in animals, our results are consistent with findings that have been obtained in radically different tasks with human children and adults. In addition to raising more questions about early memory development, we think that our data have a number of fundamental cognitive implications for all organisms who share common underlying neural mechanisms, including children and adults as well as animals.

Acknowledgments. The research reported here has been supported by grant nos. MH32307 and MH00902 from the National Institute of Mental Health to the first author. We are deeply grateful to the many colleagues and students who have made important contributions to this research program over the years including, most recently, Harlene Hayne, Carolyn Greco, Margaret Borza, Kimberly Boller, Dianne Borovsky, Judy Butler, Pamela Shields, Robin Timmons, Toni Amabile, and Deborah DuFault.

References

Amabile, T.A., & Rovee-Collier, C. (1991). Contextual variation and memory retrieval at six months. *Child Development*, *62*, 1155–1166.

Anderson, J.R. (1976). *Language, memory, and thought*. Hillsdale, NJ: Erlbaum.

Anderson, J.R., & Bower, G.H. (1973). *Human associative memory*. Washington: Winston and Sons.

Atkinson, R.C., & Shiffrin, R.M. (1968). Human memory: A proposed system and its control processes. In K.W. Spence & J.T. Spence (Eds.), *The psychology of learning and motivation* (Vol. 2, pp. 89–195). New York: Academic.

Bachvalier, J., & Mishkin, M. (1984). An early and a late developing system for learning and retention in infant monkeys. *Behavioral Neuroscience, 98*, 770–778.

Baddeley, A.D. (1978). The trouble with levels: A reexamination of Craik and Lockhart's framework for memory research. *Psychological Review, 85*, 139–152.

Baillargeon, R., & Graber, M. (1988). Evidence of location memory in 8-month-old infants in a nonsearch AB task. *Developmental Psychology, 24*, 502–511.

Bekerian, D.A., & Bowers, J.M. (1983). Eyewitness testimony: Were we misled? *Journal of Experimental Psychology: Learning, Memory, and Cognition, 9*, 139–145.

Bjork, R.A. (1975). Retrieval as a memory modifier: An interpretation of negative recency and related phenomenon. In R.L. Solso (Ed.), *Information processing and cognition: The Loyola symposium* (pp. 123–144). Hillsdale, NJ: Erlbaum.

Bjorklund, D.F. (1987). How age changes in knowledge base contribute to the development of children's memory: An interpretive review. *Developmental Review, 7*, 93–130.

Boller, K., & Rovee-Collier, C. (1992). Contextual coding and recoding of infant memory. *Journal of Experimental Child Psychology, 52*, 1–23.

Boller, K., Rovee-Collier, C., Borovsky, D., O'Connor, J., & Shyi, G. (1990). Developmental changes in the time-dependent nature of memory retrieval. *Developmental Psychology, 26*, 770–779.

Borovsky, D.B., & Rovee-Collier, C. (1990). Contextual constraints on memory retrieval at 6 months. *Child Development, 61*, 1569–1583.

Borza, M., & Rovee-Collier, C. (1989, October). *Memory modification in 3-month-olds*. Paper presented at the meeting of the International Society for Developmental Psychobiology, San Francisco, CA.

Bower, G.H. (1981). Mood and memory. *American Psychologist, 36*, 129–148.

Brainerd, C.J., Reyna, V.F., Howe, M.L., & Kingma, J. (1990). Development of forgetting and reminiscence. *Monographs of the Society for Research in Child Development, 55* (3–4, serial No. 222).

Butler, J., & Rovee-Collier, C. (1989). Contextual gating of memory retrieval. *Developmental Psychobiology, 22*, 533–552.

Campbell, B.A., & Coulter, X. (1976). Neural and psychological processes underlying the development of learning and memory. In T.J. Tighe & R.N. Leaton (Eds.), *Habituation* (pp. 129–157). Hillsdale, NJ: Erlbaum.

Campbell, B.A., & Jaynes, J. (1966). Reinstatement. *Psychological Review, 73*, 478–480.

Campbell, B.A., & Spear, N.E. (1972). Ontogeny of memory. *Psychological Review, 79*, 215–236.

Ceci, S.J., Toglia, M.P., & Ross, D.F. (Eds.) (1987). *Children's eyewitness memory*. New York: Springer-Verlag.

Ceraso, J. (1987). On generic memory. In D.S. Gorfein & R.R. Hoffman (Eds.), *Memory and learning* (pp. 319–327). Hillsdale, NJ: Erlbaum.

Christiaansen, R.E., & Ochalek, K. (1983). Editing misleading information from memory: Evidence for the coexistence of original and postevent information, *Memory & Cognition, 11*, 467–475.

Cohen, R.L. (1985). On the generality of the laws of memory. In L.-G. Nilsson & T. Archer (Eds.), *Perspectives on learning and memory* (pp. 247–277). Hillsdale, NJ: Erlbaum.
Craik, F.I.M., & Lockhart, R.S. (1972). Levels of processing: A framework for memory research. *Journal of Verbal Learning and Verbal Behavior, 11*, 671–684.
Craik, F.I.M., & Watkins, M.J. (1973). The role of rehearsal in short-term memory. *Journal of Verbal Learning and Verbal Behavior, 12*, 599–607.
Crowder, R.L. (1985). Basic theoretical concepts in human learning and cognition. In L.-G. Nilsson & T. Archer (Eds.), *Perspectives on learning and memory* (pp. 19–37). Hillsdale, NJ: Erlbaum.
Crowder, R.L., & Greene, R.L. (1987). The context of remembering: Comments on the chapters by Glenberg, Gorfein, and Wickens. In D.S. Gorfein & R.R. Hoffman (Eds.), *Memory and learning* (pp. 191–199). Hillsdale, NJ: Erlbaum.
Dannemiller, J.L., & Braun, A. (1988). The perception of chromatic figure/ground relationships in 5-month-olds. *Infant Behavior and Development, 11*, 31–42.
Dark, V.J., & Loftus, G.R. (1976). The role of rehearsal in long-term memory performance. *Journal of Verbal Learning and Verbal Behavior, 15*, 479–490.
Davis, J., & Rovee-Collier, C.K. (1983). Alleviated forgetting of a learned contingency in 8-week-old infants. *Developmental Psychology, 19*, 353–365.
DeCasper, A.J., & Fifer, W.P. (1980). Of human bonding: Newborns prefer their mothers' voices. *Science, 208*, 1174–1176.
DeCasper, A.J., & Prescott, P.A. (1984). Human newborns' perception of male voices: Preference, discrimination, and reinforcing value. *Developmental Psychobiology, 17*, 481–491.
DeCasper, A.J., & Spence, M.J. (1986). Prenatal maternal speech influences newborns' perception of speech sounds. *Infant Behavior and Development, 9*, 133–150.
Diamond, A. (Ed.) (1991). *The development and neural bases of higher cognitive functions. Annals of the New York Academy of Sciences, 608.*
Dineen, J.T., & Meyer, W.J. (1980). Developmental changes in visual orienting behavior to featural versus structural information in the human infant. *Developmental Psychobiology, 13*, 123–130.
Dodwell, P.C., Humphrey, G.K., & Muir, D.W. (1987). Shape and pattern perception. In P. Salapatek & L. Cohen (Eds.), *Handbook of infant perception* (Vol. 2, pp. 1–77). New York: Academic Press.
Duchek, J.M. (1984). Encoding and retrieval differences between young and old: The impact of attentional capacity usage. *Developmental Psychology, 20*, 1173–1180.
Eich, J.E. (1985). Context, memory, and integrated item/context imagery. *Journal of Experimental Psychology: Learning, Memory, and Cognition, 11*, 764–770.
Eich, J.E. (1989). Theoretical issues in state dependent memory. In H.L. Roediger & F.I.M. Craik (Eds.), *Varieties of memory and consciousness: Essays in honour of Endel Tulving* (pp. 43–57). Hillsdale, NJ: Erlbaum.
Enright, M.K. (1981). *A comparison of newly acquired and reactivated memories of three-month-old infants.* Unpublished doctoral dissertation, Rutgers University, New Brunswick, NJ.

Enright, M.K., Rovee-Collier, C., Fagen, J.W., & Caniglia, K. (1983). The effects of distributed training on retention of operant conditioning in human infants. *Journal of Experimental Child Psychology*, *36*, 209–225.

Estes, W.K. (1950). Toward a statistical theory of learning. *Psychological Review*, *57*, 94–107.

Fagan, J.F. (1973). Infants' delayed recognition memory and forgetting. *Journal of Experimental Child Psychology*, *16*, 424–450.

Fagan, J.F. (1984). Infant memory: History, current trends, relations to cognitive psychology. In M. Moscovitch (Ed.), *Advances in the study of communication and affect, Vol. 9: Infant memory* (pp. 1–27). New York: Plenum.

Fagen, J.W., Morrongiello, B.A., Rovee-Collier, C., & Gekoski, M.J. (1984). Expectancies and memory retrieval in 3-month-old infants. *Child Development*, *54*, 394–403.

Fagen, J.W., & Ohr, P.S. (1986, April). *Learning and memory from three to eleven months: A longitudinal study*. Paper presented at the meeting of the International Conference on Infant Studies, Los Angeles, CA.

Fagen, J.W., Ohr, P.S., Fleckenstein, L.K., & Ribner, D.R. (1985). The effect of crying on long-term memory in infancy. *Child Development*, *56*, 1584–1592.

Fagen, J.W., Ohr, P.S., Singer, J.M., & Klein, S.J. (1989). Crying and retrograde amnesia in infants. *Infant Behavior and Development*, *12*, 13–24.

Fagen, J.W., Rovee, C.K., & Kaplan, M.G. (1976). Psychophysical scaling of stimulus similarity in 3-month-old infants and adults. *Journal of Experimental Child Psychology*, *22*, 272–281.

Fagen, J.W., & Rovee-Collier, C. (1983). Memory retrieval: A time-locked process in infancy. *Science*, *222*, 1349–1351.

Fagen, J.W., Yengo, L.A., Rovee-Collier, C., & Enright, M.K. (1981). Reactivation of a visual discrimination in early infancy. *Developmental Psychology*, *17*, 266–274.

Fifer, W.P. (1980). *Early attachment: Maternal voice preference in one- and three-day-old infants*. Unpublished doctoral dissertation, University of North Carolina-Greensboro, Greensboro, NC.

Flannagan, M.J., Fried, L.S., & Holyoak, K.J. (1986). Distributional expectations and the induction of category structure. *Journal of Experimental Psychology: Learning, Memory, and Cognition*, *12*, 241–256.

Fried, L.S., & Holyoak, K.J. (1984). Induction of category distributions: A framework for classification learning. *Journal of Experimental Psychology: Learning, Memory, and Cognition*, *10*, 234–257.

Gekoski, M.J., & Fagen J.W. (1984). Noncontingent stimulation, stimulus familiarization, and subsequent learning in young infants. *Child Development*, *55*, 226–233.

Ghim, H.R., & Eimas, P.D. (1988). Global and local processing by 3- and 4-month-old infants. *Perception & Psychophysics*, *43*, 165–171.

Gisquet-Verrier, P., Dekeyne, A., & Alexinsky, T. (1989). Differential effects of several retrieval cues over time: Evidence for time-dependent reorganization of memory. *Animal Learning and Behavior*, *17*, 394–408.

Gopnik, A., & Meltzoff, A. (1987). The development of categorization in the second year and its relation to other cognitive and linguistic development. *Child Development*, *58*, 1523–1531.

Greco, C., Hayne, H., & Rovee-Collier, C. (1990). The roles of function, reminding, and variability in categorization by 3-month-old infants. *Journal of Experimental Psychology: Learning, Memory, and Cognition*, *16*, 617–633.

Greco, C., & Rovee-Collier, C. (1988, April). *Postevent bonding: The time window for the malleability of infant memory*. Paper presented at the meeting of the International Conference on Infant Studies, Washington, DC.

Greco, C., Rovee-Collier, C., Hayne, H., Griesler, P., & Earley, L. (1986). Ontogeny of early event memory: I. Forgetting and retrieval by 2- and 3-month-olds. *Infant Behavior and Development*, *9*, 441–460.

Greenfield, H., & Riccio, D.C. (1972). Conditioned reinstatement in rats: Effects of exposure distribution and cues. *Psychological Reports*, *31*, 79–83.

Hasher, L., & Griffin, M.J. (1978). Reconstructive and reproductive processes in memory. *Journal of Experimental Psychology: Human Learning and Memory*, *4*, 318–330.

Hayne, H. (1988). *The effect of multiple reminders on long-term retention in human infants*. Unpublished doctoral dissertation, Rutgers University, New Brunswick, NJ.

Hayne, H. (1990). The effect of multiple reminders on long-term retention in human infants. *Developmental Psychobiology*, *23*, 453–477.

Hayne, H., Greco, C., Earley, L., Griesler, P., & Rovee-Collier, C. (1986). Ontogeny of early event memory: II. Encoding and retrieval by 2- and 3-month-olds. *Infant Behavior and Development*, *9*, 461–472.

Hayne, H., Rovee-Collier, C., & Borza, M. (1991). Infant memory for place information. *Memory & Cognition*, *19*, 378–386.

Hayne, H., Rovee-Collier, C., & Perris, E.E. (1987). Categorization and memory retrieval by 3-month-olds. *Child Development*, *58*, 750–767.

Hill, W.L., Borovsky, D., & Rovee-Collier, C. (1988). Continuities in infant memory development. *Development Psychobiology*, *21*, 43–62.

Hoving, K.L., & Choi, K. (1972). Some necessary conditions for producing reinstatement effects in children. *Developmental Psychology*, *6*, 214–217.

Hoving, K.L., Coates, L., Bertucci, M., & Riccio, D.C. (1972). Reinstatement effects in children. *Developmental Psychology*, *6*, 426–429.

Howe, M.L., & Brainerd, C.J. (1989). Development of children's long-term retention. *Developmental Review*, *9*, 301–340.

Howe, M.L., & Hunter, M.A. (1986). Long-term memory in adulthood: An examination of the development of storage and retrieval processes at acquisition and retention. *Developmental Review*, *6*, 334–364.

Hunter, M.A., & Ames, E. (1988). A multifactor model of infant preferences for novel and familiar stimuli. In C. Rovee-Collier & L.P. Lipsitt (Eds.), *Advances in infancy research* (Vol. 5, pp. 69–95). Norwood, NJ: Ablex.

Johnson, M.K. (1983). A multiple-entry, modular memory system. In G.H. Bower (Ed.), *The psychology of learning and motivation: Advances in research and theory* (Vol. 17, pp. 81–123). New York: Academic.

Johnson, M.K., Foley, M.A., Suengas, A.G., & Raye, C.L. (1988). Phenomenal characteristics of memories for perceived and imagined autobiographical events. *Journal of Experimental Psychology: General*, *117*, 371–376.

Johnson, M.K., & Raye, C.L. (1981). Reality monitoring. *Psychological Review*, *88*, 67–85.

Johnson, R.E. (1980). Memory-based rehearsal. In G.H. Bower (Ed.), *The psychology of learning and motivation* (Vol. 14, pp. 263–307). New York: Academic.

Kagan, J. (1979). Growing by leaps: The form of early cognitive development. *The Sciences*, *19*, 8–12.

Kagan, J. (1984). *The nature of the child.* New York: Basic Books.

Kagan, J., & Hamburg, M. (1981). The enhancement of memory in the first year. *Journal of Genetic Psychology*, *138*, 3–14.

Kail, R. (1986). Sources of age differences in speed of processing. *Child Development*, *57*, 969–987.

Kinchla, R.A., & Wolfe, J.M. (1979). The order of visual processing: "Top-down," "bottom-up," or "middle-out." *Perception & Psychophysics*, *25*, 225–231.

Kintsch, W. (1974). *The representation of meaning in memory.* Hillsdale, NJ: Erlbaum.

Little, A.H., Lipsitt, L.P., & Rovee-Collier, C. (1984). Classical conditioning and retention of the infant's eyelid response: Effects of age and interstimulus interval. *Journal of Experimental Child Psychology*, *37*, 512–524.

Loftus, E.F. (1979). *Eyewitness testimony*. Cambridge, MA: Harvard University Press.

Loftus, E.F. (1981). Mentalmorphosis: Alterations in memory produced by the mental bonding of new information to old. In J. Long & A. Baddeley (Eds.), *Attention and performance IX* (pp. 417–434). Hillsdale, NJ: Erlbaum.

Loftus, E.F., & Hoffman, H.G. (1989). Misinformation and memory: The creation of new memory. *Journal of Experimental Psychology: General*, *118*, 100–104.

Loftus, E.F., & Loftus, G.R. (1980). On the permanence of stored information in the human brain. *American Psychologist*, *35*, 409–420.

Loftus, E.F., Miller, D.G., & Burns, H.J. (1978). Semantic integration of verbal information into visual memory. *Journal of Experimental Psychology: Human Learning and Memory*, *4*, 19–31.

Mandler, J.M. (1984). Representation and recall in infancy. In M. Moscovitch (Ed.), *Advances in the study of affect and communication, Vol. 9: Infant memory* (pp. 75–101). New York: Plenum.

Mast, V.K., Fagen, J.W., Rovee-Collier, C., & Sullivan, M.W. (1980). Immediate and long-term memory for reinforcement context: The development of learned expectancies in early infancy. *Child Development*, *51*, 700–707.

McCloskey, M., & Zaragoza, M. (1985). Misleading postevent information and memory for events: Arguments and evidence against memory impairment hypotheses. *Journal of Experimental Psychology: General*, *114*, 1–16.

McDaniel, M.A., & Masson, M.E.J. (1985). Altering memory representations through retrieval. *Journal of Experimental Psychology: Learning, Memory, and Cognition*, *11*, 371–385.

McGaugh, J.L., & Dawson, R.G. (1971). Modification of memory storage processes. In W.K. Honig & P.H.R. James (Eds.), *Animal memory* (pp. 215–242). New York: Academic.

Milewski, A.E. (1979). Visual discrimination and detection of configurational invariance in 3-month infants. *Developmental Psychology*, *15*, 357–363.

Miller, J. (1981). Global precedence in attention and decision. *Journal of Experimental Psychology: Human Perception and Performance*, *7*, 1161–1174.

Miller, R.R., & Schactman, T.R. (1985). The several roles of context at the time of retrieval. In P.D. Balsam & A. Tomie (Eds.), Context and learning (pp. 167–194). Hillsdale, NJ: Erlbaum.

Modigliani, V. (1976). Effects on a later recall by delaying initial recall. *Journal of Experimental Psychology: Human Learning and Memory*, *2*, 609–622.

Nadel, L., Willner, J., & Kurz, E.M. (1985). Cognitive maps and environmental context. In P.D. Balsam & A. Tomie (Eds.), *Context and learning* (pp. 385–406). Hillsdale, NJ: Erlbaum.

Nadel, L., & Zola-Morgan, S. (1984). Infantile amnesia: A neurobiological perspective. In M. Moscovitch (Ed.), *Advances in the study of communication and affect, Vol. 9: Infant memory* (pp. 145–172). New York: Plenum.

Navon, D. (1977). Forest before trees: The precedence of global features in visual perception. *Cognitive Psychology*, *9*, 353–383.

Neisser, U. (1967). *Cognitive psychology*. New York: Appleton.

Nelson, K. (1986, April). *Remembering: A functional developmental perspective*. Paper presented at the G. Stanley Hall Symposium, Williams College, Williamstown, MA.

Ohr, P., Fagen, J. W., Rovee-Collier, C., Hayne, H., & Vander Linde, E. (1989). Amount of training and retention by infants. *Developmental Psychobiology*, *22*, 69–80.

Ohr, P., Fleckenstein, L.K., Fagen, J.W., Klein, S.J., & Pioli, L.M. (1990). Crying-produced forgetting in infants: A contextual analysis. *Infant Behavior and Development*, *13*, 305–320.

Olson, G.M., & Strauss, M.S. (1984). The development of infant memory. In M. Moscovitch (Ed.), *Advances in the study of communication and affect, Vol. 9: Infant memory* (pp. 29–48). New York: Plenum.

Overton, D.A. (1982). Memory retrieval failures produced by changes in drug state. In R.L. Isaacson & N.E. Spear (Eds.), *The expression of knowledge* (pp. 113–139). New York: Plenum.

Payne, D.G. (1986). Hypermnesia for pictures and words: Testing the recall level hypothesis. *Journal of Experimental Psychology: Learning, Memory, and Cognition*, *12*, 16–29.

Perlmutter, M. (1984). Continuities and discontinuities in early human memory paradigm, processes, and performance. In R. Kail & N.E. Spear (Eds.), *Comparative perspectives on the development of memory* (pp. 253–284). Hillsdale, NJ: Erlbaum.

Pomerantz, J.R. (1983). Global and local precedence: Selective attention in form and motion perception. *Journal of Experimental Psychology: General*, *112*, 516–540.

Reeves, A., & Sperling, G. (1986). Attention gating in short-term visual memory. *Psychological Review*, *93*, 180–206.

Riccio, D.C., Richardson, R., & Ebner, D.L. (1984). Memory retrieval deficits based upon altered contextual cues: A paradox. *Psychological Bulletin*, *96*, 152–165.

Richardson, R., Riccio, D.C., & McKenney, M. (1988). Stimulus attributes of reactivated memory: Alleviation of ontogenetic forgetting in rats is context specific. *Developmental Psychobiology*, *21*, 135–143.

Roediger, H.L., & Payne, D.G. (1982). Hypermnesia: The role of repeated testing. *Journal of Experimental Psychology: Learning, Memory, and Cognition*, *8*, 66–72.
Rose, S.A. (1981). Developmental changes in infants' retention of visual stimuli. *Child Development*, *52*, 227–233.
Rose, S.A. (1983). Differential rates of visual information processing in fullterm and preterm infants. *Child Development*, *54*, 1189–1198.
Rose, S.A., Gottfried, A.W., Melloy-Carminar, P., & Bridger, W.H. (1982). Familiarity and novelty preferences in infant recognition memory: Implications for information processing. *Developmental Psychology*, *18*, 704–713.
Rovee, C.K., & Fagen, J.W. (1976). Extended conditioning and 24-hr retention in infants. *Journal of Experimental Child Psychology*, *21*, 1–11.
Rovee, C.K., & Rovee, D.T. (1969). Conjugate reinforcement of infant exploratory behavior. *Journal of Experimental Child Psychology*, *8*, 33–39.
Rovee-Collier, C. (1991). The "memory system" of prelinguistic infants. In A. Diamond (Ed.), *The development and neural bases of higher cognitive functions. Annals of the New York Academy of Sciences*, *608*, 517–542.
Rovee-Collier, C., & DuFault, D. (1991). Multiple contexts and memory retrieval at 3 months. *Developmental Psychobiology*, *24*, 39–49.
Rovee-Collier, C., Earley, L., & Stafford, S. (1989). Ontogeny of early event memory: III. Attentional determinants of retrieval at 2 and 3 months. *Infant Behavior and Development*, *12*, 147–161.
Rovee-Collier, C.K., Enright, M.K., Lucas, D., Fagen, J.W., & Gekoski, M.J. (1981). The forgetting of newly acquired and reactivated memories of 3-month-old infants. *Infant Behavior and Development*, *4*, 317–331.
Rovee-Collier, C.K., & Fagen, J.W. (1981). The retrieval of memory in early infancy. In L.P. Lipsitt (Ed.), *Advances in infancy research* (Vol. 1, pp. 225–254). Norwood, NJ: Ablex.
Rovee-Collier, C.K., & Gekoski, M.J. (1979). The economics of infancy: A review of conjugate reinforcement. In H.W. Reese & L.P. Lipsitt (Eds.), *Advances in child development and research* (Vol. 13, pp. 195–255). New York: Academic.
Rovee-Collier, C.K., Griesler, P.C., & Earley, L.A. (1985). Contextual determinants of retrieval in three-month-old infants. *Learning and Motivation*, *16*, 139–157.
Rovee-Collier, C., & Hayne, H. (1987). Reactivation of infant memory: Implications for cognitive development. In H.W. Reese (Ed.), *Advances in child development and behavior* (Vol. 20, pp. 185–238). New York: Academic.
Rovee-Collier, C., Patterson, J., & Hayne, H. (1985). Specificity in the reactivation of infant memory. *Developmental Psychobiology*, *18*, 559–574.
Rovee-Collier, C., Schechter, A., Shyi, G.C.-W., & Shields, P. (1992). Perceptual identification of contextual attributes and infant memory retrieval. *Developmental Psychology*, *28* (2).
Rovee-Collier, C.K., & Sullivan, M.W. (1980). Organization of infant memory. *Journal of Experimental Psychology: Human Learning and Memory*, *6*, 798–807.
Rovee-Collier, C.K., Sullivan, M.W., Enright, M., Lucas, D., & Fagen, J.W. (1980). Reactivation of infant memory. *Science*, *208*, 1159–1161.

Schacter, D.L., & Moscovitch, M. (1984). Infants, amnesics, and dissociable memory systems. In M. Moscovitch (Ed.), *Advances in the study of communication and affect. Vol. 9: Infant memory* (pp. 173–216). New York: Plenum.

Schooler J.W., Gerhard, D., & Loftus, E.F. (1987). Qualities of the unreal. *Journal of Experimental Psychology: Learning, Memory, and Cognition, 12*, 171–181.

Sherman, T. (1985). Categorization skills in infants. *Child Development, 56*, 1561–1573.

Shields, P., & Rovee-Collier, C. (1992). Long-term memory for context-specific category information at six months. *Child Development, 63*, 175–214.

Shyi, G.C.-W. (1990). *The effects of configuration and component information on retrieval at 6 months*. Paper presented at the meeting of the Eastern Psychological Association, Philadelphia, PA.

Smith, S.M. (1982). Enhancement of recall using multiple environmental contexts during learning. *Memory & Cognition, 10*, 405–412.

Smith, S.M., Glenberg, A., & Bjork, R.A. (1978). Environmental context and human memory. *Memory & Cognition, 6*, 342–353.

Spear, N.E. (1973). Retrieval of memories in animals. *Psychological Review, 80*, 163–194.

Spear, N.E. (1978). *The processing of memories: Forgetting and retention*. Hillsdale, NJ: Erlbaum.

Spear, N.E., & Parsons, P.J. (1976). Analysis of a reactivation treatment: Ontogenetic determinants of alleviated forgetting. In D.L. Medin, W.A. Roberts, & R.T. Davis (Eds.), *Processes of animal memory* (pp. 135–165). Hillsdale, NJ: Erlbaum.

Squire, L.R. (1986). Mechanisms of memory. *Science, 232*, 1612–1619.

Squire, L.R. (1987). *Memory and brain*. New York: Oxford University Press.

Suengas, A.G., & Johnson, M.K. (1988). Qualitative effects of rehearsal on memories for perceived and imagined complex events. *Journal of Experimental Psychology: General, 117*, 377–389.

Sullivan, M.W. (1982). Reactivation: Priming forgotten memories in human infants. *Child Development, 57*, 100–104.

Sullivan, M.W., Rovee-Collier, C.K., & Tynes, D.M. (1979). A conditioning analysis of infant long-term memory. *Child Development, 50*, 152–162.

Thompson, L.A., & Massaro, D.W. (1989). Before you see it, you see its parts: Evidence for feature encoding and integration in preschool children and adults. *Cognitive Psychology, 21*, 334–362.

Timmons, C.R. (1990). *Interactions of independent memories in six-month-old infants*. Unpublished doctoral dissertation, Rutgers University, New Brunswick, NJ.

Treisman, A. (1988). Features and objects: The 14th Bartlett memorial lecture. *Quarterly Journal of Experimental Psychology, 40A*, 201–237.

Treisman, A., & Gelade, G. (1980). A feature-integration theory of attention. *Cognitive Psychology, 12*, 97–136.

Treisman, A., & Paterson, R. (1984). Emergent features, attention and object perception. *Journal of Experimental Psychology: Human Perception and Performance, 10*, 12–31.

Treisman, A., & Schmidt, H. (1982). Illusory conjunctions in the perception of objects. *Cognitive Psychology*, *14*, 107–141.

Treisman, A., & Souther, J. (1985). Search asymmetry: A diagnostic for preattentive processing of separable features. *Journal of Experimental Psychology: General*, *114*, 285–310.

Treisman, A., Sykes, M., & Gelade, G. (1977). Selective attention and stimulus integration. In S. Dornic (Ed.), *Attention and performance V* (pp. 333–362). Hillsdale, NJ: Erlbaum.

Tulving, E. (1972). Episodic and semantic memory. In E. Tulving & W. Donaldson (Eds.), *Organization of memory* (pp. 381–403). New York: Academic.

Tulving, E. (1983). *Elements of episodic memory*. New York: Oxford University Press.

Tulving, E. (1985). How many memory systems are there? *American Psychologist*, *40*, 385–398.

Tulving, E., & Thomson, D.M. (1973). Encoding specificity and retrieval processes in episodic memory. *Psychological Review*, *80*, 352–372.

Vander Linde, E. (1982). *The effects of training factors on acquisition and retention in early infancy*. Unpublished doctoral dissertation, Rutgers University, New Brunswick, NJ.

Vander Linde, E., Morrongiello, B.A., & Rovee-Collier, C. (1985). Determinants of retention in 8-week-old infants. *Developmental Psychology*, *21*, 601–613.

Werner, J.S., & Perlmutter, M. (1979). Development of visual memory in infants. In H.W. Reese & L.P. Lipsitt (Eds.), *Advances in child development and behavior* (Vol. 14, pp. 1–56). New York: Academic.

West, R.F., & Stanovich, K.E. (1978). Automatic contextual facilitation in readers of three ages. *Child Development*, *49*, 717–727.

Winocur, G., & Kinsbourne, M. (1978). Contextual cuing as an aid to Korsakoff amnesics. *Neuropsychologia*, *16*, 671–682.

Woodward, A.E., Jr., Bjork, R.A., & Jongeward, R.H., Jr. (1973). Recall and recognition as a function of primary rehearsal. *Journal of Verbal Learning and Verbal Behavior*, *12*, 608–617.

Zaragoza, M., McCloskey, M., & Jamis, M. (1987). Misleading postevent information and recall of the original event: Further evidence against the memory impairment hypotheses. *Journal of Experimental Psychology: Learning, Memory, and Cognition*, *13*, 36–44.

2
Measuring the Development of Children's Amnesia and Hypermnesia

Mark L. Howe, Andrea Kelland, Lynn Bryant-Brown, and Sandra L. Clark

The study of memory development in childhood has, for the most part, focused on processes involved in the initial acquisition of information, with considerably less attention having been directed at understanding the ontogeny of long-term retention processes. The paucity of research on this latter topic may be due to a general failure in the past to identify significant age trends in children's long-term retention (for recent reviews, see Brainerd, Kingma, & Howe, 1985; Howe & Brainerd, 1989). When reliable age differences have been observed, they tend to be small in absolute magnitude (Fajnsztejn-Pollack, 1973; Hasher & Thomas, 1973; Kagan, Klein, Haith, & Morrison, 1973; Lehman, Mikesell, & Doherty, 1985; Morrison, Haith, & Kagan, 1980; Nelson, 1971; Rogoff, Newcombe, & Kagan, 1974; Sophian & Perlmutter, 1980; Wagner, 1978; Wickelgren, 1975).

Recently, however, reviewers have suggested that a number of variables exist that may obscure developmental trends in long-term retention (Brainerd et al., 1985; Brainerd, Reyna, Howe, & Kingma, 1990; Howe & Brainerd, 1989; Howe & Hunter, 1986). Examples of these variables include failures to control levels of learning across items and subjects, as well as failures to adequately separate factors that depress performance on long-term retention tests (forgetting) from factors that enhance performance on long-term retention tests (reminiscence). In this chapter, we examine the impact of these variables on children's long-term retention performance. Our experiments concern the development of storage and retrieval properties of four constituents of long-term retention, namely, amnesia, hypermnesia, forgetting, and reminiscence. We begin by defining these four concepts and evaluating what is known about them empirically. Along the way, we discuss various methodological and measurement issues critical to evaluating the development of retention. Finally, we provide an overview of a recently developed (mathematical) implementation of these constructs (Howe & Brainerd, 1989) and use this model to analyze the data from two experiments.

Definitions

In a standard long-term retention experiment, children of different ages are initially given single or multiple opportunities to study some to-be-remembered information. Children are subsequently administered a test of retention of this material and performance is evaluated by comparing the number of items retained on the last acquisition trial to the same performance statistic on the retention test or, in multitrial retention experiments, by also comparing the number of items retained on the first retention test with the same statistic on subsequent test trials.

Performance on tests such as these can be described using two aggregate variables (amnesia and hypermnesia), each of which are composed of two other variables (forgetting and reminiscence) that refer to the behavior of individual items. *Amnesia* refers to a net decrease, and *hypermnesia* refers to a net increase, in recall across increasing retention intervals or test trials. *Forgetting* is the inability to recall a previously recallable item, whereas *reminiscence*[1] is the ability to recall a previously unrecallable item.

In terms of our long-term retention paradigm, global performance can be of two types. First, if amnesia has occurred (i.e., subjects forget more than they reminisce), children will have recalled fewer items during the retention test than at the end of the acquisition test, or across retention test trials. Second, if hypermnesia has occurred (i.e., reminiscence exceeds forgetting), then children's net recall levels will have improved over the retention interval(s) or as a function of multiple testing opportunities during the retention test itself. In general, retention performance is determined by some function that takes both forgetting and reminiscence into account. Because retention performance depends directly on the relationship between the amount of forgetting and the amount of reminiscence, it

---

[1] The term *reminiscence*, as used here, requires some clarification. First, our use of this term incorporates what Howe and Brainerd (1989) referred to as test-induced (redintegrative) processes that lead to increments in performance. What they called "restorage" we shall subsequently be calling "storage-based reminiscence," and what they termed "retrieval relearning" we will subsequently refer to as "retrieval-based reminiscence." Second, the usual sense of the term *reminiscence* refers to "the remembering again of the forgotten without relearning" (Ballard, 1913, p. v). Contrary to this, however, we consider reminiscence to be a special (test-induced) case of relearning in which information that is in various stages of integrity in memory becomes better integrated (a form of relearning), leading to better recall, simply as a function of processes that operate on test trials (this process is described in more detail later in this chapter). Finally, it is also important to distinguish what we mean by relearning from the more classic interpretation, namely, that relearning involves the re-presentation of information as in the popular "savings" paradigm. In our use of reminiscence-as-relearning we refer strictly to those processes that occur as a function of testing opportunities, not additional study opportunities.

could turn out that when these two influences are effectively isolated Age × Retention interactions will emerge (also see Howe & Brainerd, 1989).

Empirical and Conceptual Issues

As already noted, with the exception of a few recent studies (Brainerd et al., 1985, 1990; Howe, 1987, 1991), research on children's amnesia has produced few findings of developmental interest. Although a number of factors have probably contributed to this "nonfinding" (see Howe & Brainerd, 1989), one of the most important reasons may have been that age differences in forgetting were offset by the presence of opposing developmental changes in reminiscence.

In the literature on long-term retention in adults, reliable hypermnesic effects have been observed using pictures (e.g., Erdelyi & Stein, 1981; Shapiro & Erdelyi, 1974; Yarmey, 1976), words (e.g., Madigan, 1976; Runquist, 1983), Socratic stimuli (e.g., Erdelyi, Buschke, & Finkelstein, 1977), semantic and phonemic encoding tasks (e.g., McDaniel & Masson, 1985), orthographic, phonological, and semantic operations on words (e.g., Belmore, 1981; Roediger, Payne, Gillespie, & Lean, 1982), faces (e.g., Deffenbacher, Carr, & Leu, 1981), and eyewitnessed events (e.g., Eugenio, Buckout, Kostes, & Ellison, 1982; Scrivner & Safer, 1988). Such effects tend to occur regardless of the way in which memory is tested, having been observed using forced-choice recall (e.g., Erdelyi et al., 1977), cued recall (e.g., Runquist, 1983), recognition (e.g., Deffenbacher et al., 1981), and free recall (e.g., Madigan, 1976).

Considerably less research has been conducted on children's hypermnesia and the studies that do exist have produced conflicting results (see review in Howe & Brainerd, 1989). For example, early, poorly controlled studies appeared to indicate that quantitative improvements occurred at retention as a function of successive recall attempts (e.g., Ballard, 1913; Piaget & Inhelder, 1973, pp. 47–48). In addition, Ballard (1913) observed that the amount of hypermnesia was directly related to chronological age such that *younger* children exhibited greater hypermnesia than older children. Hypermnesia has also been obtained using a paired-associate learning procedure. For example, Vertes (1931/32) found that older children forget less than younger children following a 1-day interval and that average recall scores improved by 10% on a 1-week retention test over a 1-day test. Unlike Ballard, Vertes found that recall improvements on the 1-week test were restricted to *older* children and that younger children's recall scores continued to decline.

Like this early work, recent research on reconstructive memory (e.g., Paris & Lindauer, 1977), eyewitness memory (e.g., Ceci, Toglia, & Ross, 1987), and the effects of test trials (e.g., Richardson, 1985) on long-term retention have shown that improvements in children's recollection do occur. However, the existence and direction of any developmental interaction remains unclear. For example, like adults, children's hypermnesia is greater for concrete than abstract material (Shaw, 1985, cited in Richardson, 1985) and children's accuracy of recollection of details of a filmed robbery tends to improve across repeated recall attempts (Dent & Stevenson, 1979). Although neither of these studies reported the presence of a developmental interaction, Paris (1978) has shown that grade 6 children performed better on tests of long-term retention than grade 2 children and, like the other studies, both grade 2 and grade 6 children showed significant reminiscence across long-term retention tests. However, the source of the developmental interaction in overall performance was an age-related decline in the number of items forgotten, not in the number of new words produced. In contrast to these findings, Brainerd and Reyna (1988a, Exp. 2) found that, whereas amnesia and forgetting tended to decrease with age, hypermnesia and reminiscence tended to increase. Unfortunately, the results of this latter study are inconclusive because (a) the analytical procedure (conditional probabilities) used to dissever amnesia/forgetting and hypermnesia/reminiscence fails to address the critical issues involved in the development of independent measures of the components of long-term retention (see measurement discussion below), and (b) their study provided no leverage on the key theoretical issue of the extent to which children's retention performance is controlled by changes in what is in storage, how it is retrieved, or both (see discussion below and Howe & Brainerd, 1989).

In view of the relative uncertainty concerning the direction of any developmental interaction, it would seem important to develop procedures that effectively isolate the different contributions of forgetting and reminiscence that determine global amnesic or hypermnesic performance on tests of long-term retention. To do this effectively, three issues must be addressed: (a) equating levels of initial learning, (b) factoring forgetting from reminiscence, and (c) distinguishing changes in the availability of information in memory (storage mediated conditions of retention) and changes in the accessibility of information in memory (retrieval mediated conditions of retention).

The levels-of-learning problem is an old one in research on retention and is of particular concern in developmental studies (see Howe & Brainerd, 1989). Briefly, when a fixed number of acquisition trials are administered, easier items will be better learned than harder items and older children will (on average) have learned more items than younger children. Such discrepancies tend to increase as the number of initial acquisition trials decrease. What this implies is that amnesia and hypermnesia may simply reflect unmeasured variations in original learning. Worse, the appearance and disappearance of hypermnesia across various studies may simply reflect the combined effects of differences in number of acquisition trials and ease of item acquisition.

Developmentally, if we assume that forgetting varies inversely with the initial level of learning whereas reminiscence varies positively, and that forgetting decreases with age whereas reminiscence increases with age in childhood, the frequently reported absence of an Age × Retention interaction would be observed despite its obvious presence. The solution to this problem is to require all participants to reach a stringent acquisition criterion (e.g., two or three consecutive errorless recall trials). Because learning curves are negatively accelerated, item and age differences in initial levels of memorization should be minimized as acquisition trials progress.[2]

The above considerations lead to another conclusion, namely, that we must provide direct and independent measures of both the forgetting and reminiscence components of long-term retention performance. This measurement question is further complicated by the need to determine whether changes in retention are due to alterations in the memory trace itself (a change in what is stored), changes in the accessibility of the trace (changes in the retrievability of the trace), or both. Specifically, if items are initially memorized to some strict criterion at acquisition, then it is reasonable to assume that they have been stored in memory and are in a state of high retrievability on immediate test trials. (Note that these assumptions can be evaluated more formally by applying Markov models to the acquisition data, see Footnote 2.) Consequently, forgetting and reminiscence on subsequent tests (days, weeks, or months following acquisition) of long-term retention can be due to changes in availability (storage-based processes), changes in accessibility (retrieval-based processes), or both. Although hypotheses about changes of the accessibility type are common in the literature on long-term retention, the concept of changes of the availability type is perhaps novel and warrants some discussion.

The typical view of forgetting (and reminiscence on test trials) is that it is a pure retrieval phenomenon (e.g., see comments by Chechile, 1987, and Loftus & Loftus, 1980). In general, the argument is that once information has been stored in long-term memory it is no longer labile

---

[2] An additional analytical refinement can be used to control both item and age effects in criterion designs, namely, the fitting of Markov models to the acquisition data (e.g., Howe & Hunter, 1986). Because these models deliver independent measures of storage and retrieval at the end of the acquisition phase, these measures can be used to "adjust" the retention data for any residual item and age differences attributable to either underlearning or overlearning that may have been present at the termination of acquisition (also see Howe & Brainerd, 1989). As it turns out, the magnitude of this correction factor is usually very small, requiring only minimal adjustments to the retention data, when a two- or three-trial criterion is used during the acquisition phase.

and becomes permanent. Forgetting is simply a matter of retrieval, not storage, failure and when the appropriate (retrieval) conditions pertain, information will once again become accessible.

More recently, the view that retention processes can also be mediated by changes in the availability of information in storage has been revived. For example, changes in recollection may be the result of a special case of retroactive interference, namely, trace substitution (e.g., Loftus & Loftus, 1980) or destructive updating (e.g., Loftus, 1983). Here, failures in recollection are due to the replacement or addition of previously encoded information with more recently encoded information. Reminiscence in this case may result from some process akin to redintegration (e.g., Horowitz & Prytulak, 1969).

Although the idea that forgetting and reminiscence can result from changes in what is in storage may appear novel, it has actually been around for some time (e.g., Allen, Mahler, & Estes, 1969; Shepard & Chang, 1963). Recently, the notion that long-term storage is not a permanent repository and that memory traces are mutable is at the core of a number of theories including search of associative memory (SAM) (Raaijmakers & Shiffrin, 1981), the composite holographic associative recall model (CHARM) (Eich, 1982) and the theory of distributed associative memory (TODAM) (Murdock, 1982), the set of parallel distributed processing models (e.g., McClelland & Rumelhart, 1985), and neural models of memory (e.g., Greenough & Bailey, 1988). As Tulving (1984) points out, a distinctive characteristic of memory traces (engrams) is their mutability: "Functional properties of engrams change over time. *Recoding* is the generic name of related operations and processes that take place after the encoding of the original event and thereby bring about changes in the engram" (p. 230). In fact, there is clear evidence that failures at retention can be mediated by storage-based losses from long-term memory (e.g., Chechile, 1987; Chechile & Ehrensbeck, 1983).

It would seem reasonable, therefore, to suggest that both storage and retrieval processes play a role in the development of children's long-term retention, just as they do at acquisition. Because we do not believe that performance at acquisition is mediated by a static long-term storage system (e.g., incoming information is encoded and integrated into continuously updated knowledge structures, see Bjorklund, 1987), neither should we believe that long-term retention is mediated by anything other than a dynamic storage medium. As Paris and Lindauer (1977) pointed out over a decade ago, "An adequate model of memory must not assume that the input to a memory store is retrieved intact. . . . Memory is not a repository for experiences that are encoded and recalled one time; rather, meaningful material is subject to continuous reorganization in memory" (p. 52). Thus, the answer to the question of whether changes in long-term retention performance can be mediated by alterations of what is in storage seems to be yes, by most accounts. The question of theoretical interest today, then, is the extent to which, and under what conditions, changes in storage versus changes in retrieval are responsible for observed increases and decreases in children's long-term retention performance at different ages.

To investigate this and other questions concerning the development of long-term retention more thoroughly, it may be useful to reconceptualize the constructs of storage and retrieval. For example, as Howe and Brainerd (1989) point out, although storage and retrieval can be viewed as two different memory processes, it may be that they simply represent different aspects of a single memory process. The assumption that storage and retrieval processes operate in unison is common in a number of recent theories of memory, particularly those of the encoding specificity variety (e.g., Ackerman, 1985, 1987). If, as supposed in many memory models, long-term memory traces consist of well-encoded feature sets, then it is possible that the accuracy of recollection is directly related to the featural integrity and richness of the trace. Storage-based and retrieval-based forgetting could represent different stages in the process of trace *disintegration* in which the bonds that unite features of the trace erode. Here, retrieval failures might be associated with early stages of trace erosion and storage failures might be associated with later stages. Reminiscence, then, is simply the reinstatement of the trace to greater levels of integrity through the mechanism of *redintegration*. This latter hypothesis should not be altogether unfamiliar as it figures prominently in recent theories of working memory (e.g., Brainerd & Kingma, 1985) and in theories that invoke the notion of reconstructive processing (e.g., Piaget & Inhelder, 1973). Because it would be premature to rule out the possibility that both storage and retrieval processes contribute to long-term retention performance, it is important to provide measures of these components of forgetting and reminiscence when analyzing retention data.

Partitioning Components of Long-Term Retention Performance

One solution to the problem of measuring the different theoretical processes (storage and retrieval) that characterize forgetting and reminiscence is to develop a mathematical model of retention performance. The most recent model of this sort is Howe and Brainerd's (1989) *trace-integrity model*. At a theoretical level, both forgetting and reminiscence are represented along a single (trace integrity) continuum in which the critical component is variation in the "strength" of the bonds that unite features to form a memory trace. (Note that the word *strength* is used here metaphorically and can refer to any mechanism that serves to bind primitive elements together to form a memory trace including the number of connections between nodes, concentration levels of the "glue" that holds features together, and so on.)

First, consider the idea of *forgetting as disintegration*. Rather than viewing storage-based and retrieval-based forgetting as arising from different mechanisms (e.g., trace destruction and poor external cue support, respectively), the trace-integrity approach regards both as manifestations of the degree of trace disintegration. That is, as interfeatural bonds loosen during the retention interval, trace discriminability (from the background noise of other, more intact traces) decreases. Initial levels of disintegration result in traces being recalled on some occasions but not others. Most would agree that such *imperfect recall* is diagnostic of retrieval problems, and, hence, is referred to as *retrieval-based forgetting* in the trace-integrity framework. Subsequent levels of disintegration result in traces fading so severely that they can never be discriminated against the background noise of other traces. Many would agree that such *zero recall* is indicative of dramatic changes of what was originally in storage, and, hence, is referred to as *storage-based forgetting* in the trace-integrity framework. It is important to note, however, that unlike the trace destruction view of storage failure common in the literature, a central postulate of the trace-integrity theory is that traces that have fallen below the zero-recall threshold can still retain some level of integrity, one that can be potentially reactivated on tests of long-term retention.

Next, consider the mechanism underlying trace reactivation, namely, *reminiscence as redintegration*. Redintegration is a process in which the activation of some of the trace's features spreads to other features in the trace (Horowitz & Prytulak, 1969), producing a net increase in the trace's level of integration. It is this reminiscence-as-redintegration mechanism that is exploited in the trace-integrity theory to explain spontaneous recovery on tests of long-term retention without restudying the item. Thus, *retrieval-based reminiscence* refers to redintegration of traces that have faded to the level of imperfect recall, and *storage-based reminiscence* refers to redintegration of traces that have faded to the zero recall level.

At a mathematical level, this model is derived mainly from our prior work using Markov models of forgetting (Brainerd et al., 1985; Howe & Hunter, 1986). In such models, previously learned items are, as a result of processes operating during the retention interval, either perfectly recallable (i.e., no forgetting), recallable with some probability that is less than 1 but greater than 0 (retrieval failures), or not recallable (storage failures) at the time of the retention test. By relaxing the strong stage-like properties of these models, as well as the Markov assumption, such changes can be viewed as occurring in a continuous rather than a discrete fashion (consistent with certain memory models [e.g., encoding specificity] as well as our own assumption that storage and retrieval demarcate different ends of a continuum rather than different and distinct processes). In this way, both positive (hypermnesia/reminiscence) and

TABLE 2.1. Theoretical definitions of the retention model's parameters.

Process and parameter	Theoretical definition
Forgetting	
S	The probability of storage failure.
R	For information that is in storage (or that subsequently undergoes storage-based reminiscence), the probability of retrieval failure.
Reminiscence	
a	For information not in storage, the probability of storage-based reminiscence on any trial.
r_1	The probability that stored (or storage-based reminisced) information is successfully recalled following a success on the immediately preceding trial.
r_2	The probability that stored (or storage-based reminisced) information is successfully recalled following successes on the two immediately preceding trials.
r_3	The probability that stored (or storage-based reminisced) information is successfully recalled following successes on the three immediately preceding trials.
f_1	The probability that stored (or storage-based reminisced) information is successfully recalled following an error on the immediately preceding trial.
f_2	The probability that stored (or storage-based reminisced) information is successfully recalled following errors on the two immediately preceding trials.
f_3	The probability that stored (or storage-based reminisced) information is successfully recalled following errors on the three immediately preceding trials.

negative (amnesia/forgetting) changes that occur across the retention interval and across the retention tests themselves can be easily represented (for more details, see Howe & Brainerd, 1989).

Actually, the present model is a hybrid of the Markov models and the repeated-recall models used by Kail, Wilkinson, and their associates (Kail & Leonard, 1986; Wilkinson & Koestler, 1983). This new model applies to retention paradigms in which subjects initially memorize material to a criterion of two or three errorless passes through the list. Retention is subsequently tested using a series of four test trials without further study opportunities. The partitioning of forgetting and reminiscence factors is accomplished by defining a stochastic model over an outcome space that consists of 16 unique combinations of incorrect (E) and correct (C) responses (i.e., CCCC, CCCE, . . . , EEEC, EEEE). Theoretical interpretations of the parameters in this model are summarized in Table 2.1 and the relevant probability expressions for each of the 16 possible outcomes in the data space are provided in Table 2.2.

As can be seen from these tables, forgetting is measured by two parameters (S and R) and reminiscence is measured by seven parameters (a, r_1, r_2, r_3, f_1, f_2, and f_3). In terms of forgetting, the parameter S gives

TABLE 2.2. The retention model's theoretical expressions for the 16 probabilities in the empirical outcome space.

Outcome probability	Theoretical expression
p (CCCC)	$(1 - S)(1 - R)r_1r_2r_3$
p (CCCE)	$(1 - S)(1 - R)r_1r_2(1 - r_3)$
p (CCEC)	$(1 - S)(1 - R)r_1(1 - r_2)f_1$
p (CECC)	$(1 - S)(1 - R)(1 - r_1)f_1r_1$
p (ECCC)	$Sa(1 - R)r_1r_2 + (1 - S)Rf_1r_1r_2$
p (CCEE)	$(1 - S)(1 - R)r_1(1 - r_2)(1 - f_1)$
p (CECE)	$(1 - S)(1 - R)(1 - r_1)f_1(1 - r_1)$
p (ECCE)	$Sa(1 - R)r_1(1 - r_2) + (1 - S)Rf_1r_1(1 - r_2)$
p (CEEC)	$(1 - S)(1 - R)(1 - r_1)(1 - f_1)f_2$
p (ECEC)	$Sa(1 - R)(1 - r_1)f_1 + (1 - S)Rf_1(1 - r_1)f_1$
p (EECC)	$S(1 - a)a(1 - R)r_1 + SaRf_1r_1 + (1 - S)R(1 - f_1)f_2r_1$
p (CEEE)	$(1 - S)(1 - R)(1 - r_1)(1 - f_1)(1 - f_2)$
p (ECEE)	$Sa(1 - R)(1 - r_1)(1 - f_1) + (1 - S)Rf_1(1 - r_1)(1 - f_1)$
p (EECE)	$S(1 - a)a(1 - R)(1 - r_1) + SaRf_1(1 - r_1) + (1 - S)R$ $(1 - f_1)f_2(1 - r_1)$
p (EEEC)	$S(1 - a)^2a(1 - R) + S(1 - a)aRf_1 + SaR(1 - f_1)f_2 + (1 - S)R$ $(1 - f_1)(1 - f_2)f_3$
p (EEEE)	$S(1 - a)^3 + S(1 - a)^2aR + S(1 - a)aR(1 - f_1) + SaR(1 - f_1)$ $(1 - f_2) + (1 - S)R(1 - f_1)(1 - f_2)(1 - f_3)$

Note. C = correct response and E = incorrect response.

the unconditional probability that an item is unavailable for recall following the retention interval. As the likelihood of a correct response is zero, we identify S as a storage failure parameter.[3] That is, regardless of one's preferred metaphor (e.g., trace disintegration, trace substitution, overwriting, decay, etc.), S refers to forgetting that is due to alterations in the memory trace itself. Simple item availability, of course, does not guarantee that it can be accessed on a test trial. The parameter R, therefore, is associated with problems in accessing traces that are available in memory. Specifically, the retrieval failure parameter R is the conditional probability that an item that is available for recall, either on Trial 1 $(1 - S)$ or on subsequent trials (a), is inaccessible.

The parameter a is a measure of storage-based reminiscence and refers to the conditional probability that an item that was unavailable following

[3] It should be emphasized here that storage-based forgetting, as measured by the parameter S, refers not only to the first test trial but also to all other test trials in which (a) storage failure occurred during the retention interval and (b) storage-based reminiscence has not occurred. Specifically, the probability of storage failure can be computed for each trial [i.e., $T_1 = S$, $T_2 = S(1 - a)$, $T_3 = S(1 - a)^2$, and $T_4 = S(1 - a)^3$] and across all trials [$S + S(1 - a) + S(1 - a)^2 + S(1 - a)^3$]. However, because storage-based forgetting is not equated with trace absence in our theory, permitting the possibility of a test-induced storage-based reminiscence effect, it could be legitimately argued that Trial 1 is actually the purest measure of storage-based forgetting.

the retention interval (with probability S) is subsequently redintegrated to a level above the zero-recall threshold. It is important to recall that the notion of trace availability in this model is not an all-or-none matter (as in the classic "trace absence" view of storage loss), but rather, is a matter of degree of trace disintegration. Thus, it is entirely possible that a trace can be unavailable for recall at the beginning of the retention session but can be subsequently "fleshed out" through redintegrative processes that reestablish its integrity against the background of other traces in storage.

Reminiscence that occurs through the reestablishment of retrieval processes is measured by two sets of parameters, the *success-contingent retrieval-based reminiscence parameters* (the r_i) and the *error-contingent retrieval-based reminiscence parameters* (the f_i). These parameters represent conditional probabilities that track an item's retrieval history across the retention session and apply only after the first test trial. Specifically, the success-contingent retrieval parameters (r_1, r_2, and r_3) measure the probability of two, three, and four consecutive successes, respectively, across the four retention test trials. The error-contingent retrieval parameters (f_1, f_2, and f_3) measure the probability of a success given one, two, and three immediately preceding errors, respectively, across the four retention test trials. Retrieval-based reminiscence can be evaluated by simply comparing the values of the r_i and f_i to the initial probability of item retrievability ($1 - R$). That is, if the r_i are larger than $1 - R$ then success-contingent retrieval occurs on retention tests. Similarly, if the f_i are larger than R then error-contingent retrieval occurs on retention tests.

Two additional points merit attention. First, the r_i and the f_i provide information on the relative importance of successes and errors in reestablishing trace accessibility (for a discussion of the importance of this issue see Howe & Brainerd, 1989, and Richardson, 1985). Second, the parameters r_i, f_i, and a provide independent measures of whether hypermnesia during the retention test is due to changes in the trace itself (storage-based reminiscence), changes in trace accessibility (retrieval-based reminiscence), or both. Overall, then, this model provides a mathematical factoring procedure that accomplishes the dual goal of partitioning forgetting and reminiscence contributions to global (amnesia and hypermnesia) retention performance and determines the storage and retrieval loci of these effects. We now turn to a series of experiments designed to assess the utility of this procedure in determining the nature of the development of children's long-term retention skills.

Experiments 1 and 2

The purpose of these two experiments was to examine developmental differences in forgetting and reminiscence across two age levels, namely, grades 2 and 5 (Experiment 1) and grade 8 and college (Experiment 2). It has been argued that pictures engender greater levels of hypermnesia than words and that modality manipulations are more powerful than semantic manipulations (although rarely have pictures and words and related and unrelated materials been directly compared in the same experiment). To test this directly, we had different groups of subjects memorize clusters (consisting of three concepts) of unrelated pictures, related pictures, unrelated words, or related words.

Second, we wanted to assess the effects of timing of retention tests (each of which consisted of four test trials) and the impact of an initial retention test on a subsequent retention test. This was accomplished by having two overlapping sets of retention intervals. For half of the subjects, an initial retention test was administered 2 days following acquisition and a second test 2 weeks later or 16 days since acquisition. For the other half of the subjects, an initial retention test was administered 16′ days following acquisition (the prime will be used throughout to differentiate it from the other subjects' second retention test) and a second test 2 weeks later or 30 days since acquisition. By using this design we can evaluate the effects of (a) time of the initial retention test (2 days vs. 16′ days), (b) time of the first retention test on performance on a second test of retention administered following the same 2-week interval (16 days and 30 days), and (c) the potential abatement of forgetting over the first 16 days due to the administration of a previous test of retention (16 days vs. 16′ days). Thus, both Experiments 1 and 2 involved a six-factor long-term retention design: 2 (Age: either grade 2 vs. 5, or grade 8 vs. college) × 2 (Modality: picture vs. word) × 2 (Semantic: unrelated vs. related) × 2 (Retention Sequence: 2- and 16-day vs. 16′- and 30-day) × 2 (Retention Test: first vs. second) × 4 (Trial: 1 through 4) where the first four factors were between subjects and the last two factors were within subjects.

Because of the similarity of the two experiments, we report them together. We begin by outlining the general method and then describe the results of the two experiments separately.

General Methodology

Subjects

The subjects in Experiment 1 were 160 (80 males and 80 females) grade 2 students (mean age = 7 years, 5 months; standard deviation [SD] = 4 months) and 160 (80 males and 80 females) grade 5 students (mean age = 10 years, 4 months; SD = 4 months). The subjects in Experiment 2 were 120 (60 males and 60 females) grade 8 students (mean age = 13 years, 6 months; SD = 4 months) and 120 (60 males and 60 females) college students (mean age = 19 years, 8 months; SD = 2 years, 6 months).

Grade-school children's permission to participate was secured via a letter of parental consent. The college students were paid for their participation.

Lists and Procedure

During the acquisition phase, students in Experiment 1 memorized a 6-cluster list and students in Experiment 2 memorized a 14-cluster list. Each cluster consisted of three concrete concepts drawn from the Snodgrass and Vanderwart (1980) norms and cross-checked with both the Battig and Montague (1969) and Toglia and Battig (1978) norms for high typicality, familiarity, concreteness, and pictureability. Four lists were constructed from this pool, two in which items within a cluster were drawn from different categories (the unrelated picture and word lists) and two in which the items within a cluster were drawn from the same category (the related picture and word lists). One concept was designated the cue term (the same term was used for all lists) and the remaining two terms were designated the targets. (Note that by using a cued-recall procedure we had more rigorous control over the stimulus used to generate children's recall at retention.) Subjects were randomly assigned to the four list conditions except that an equal number of males and females from each age group participate in each condition.

All of the subjects were tested individually using a standard study-test procedure in which items were presented at a 5-sec rate. Relevant controls were employed in order to avoid serial position and short-term memory effects (items were presented in random order and at least three items intervened between study and test trials for any given item). Guessing was encouraged and subjects were told that if they could only remember one of the response items to be sure to give that one. During the initial study trial, the experimenter verbalized the name of the items in order to ensure that (a) no ambiguity existed with labeling the pictures and (b) no differences existed in naming the words. A response was scored as correct (at least for the purposes of determining when criterion learning had occurred) if the subject recalled the remaining two cluster items upon presentation of the cue. Subjects were required to reach an acquisition criterion of three consecutive test trials without an error.

Following criterion, subjects were randomly assigned (keeping the male/female ratio approximately constant) to either the 2- and 16-day retention sequence or the 16′- and 30-day retention sequence. All of the subjects were retested using a cued-recall procedure. Each subject was given standard paced-recall instructions and was then administered a sequence of four test trials without further study opportunities. The same controls as used above were again employed, and cues were presented at the same 5-sec rate.

Experiment 1: Results and Discussion

First, all of the analyses were based on recall of the entire cluster (the procedure used to define a correct response for the purposes of criterion learning). The reason for this was that analyses of recall of the individual targets revealed that partial recall (i.e., recalling one but not the other target term) was the exception, not the rule. That is, subjects recalled both targets given the cue or they recalled neither target. When a separate series of analyses was conducted on the individual responses, the same pattern of results emerged as when recall of the entire cluster was analyzed. This was true for both the acquisition and retention data, and held for both experiments reported in this chapter. This finding is consistent with previous research in the adult literature using this cluster technique (Howe, 1985) and is consistent with the general theoretical position that memory units tend to be flexible in size and can contain a number of elements (e.g., Anderson, 1980) depending on task demands. Given the above rationale, and because our interest is in the recall of the entire memory unit, results for both experiments will be reported in terms of memory for the entire cluster.

The results begin with a brief statement summarizing the findings at acquisition. Following this, the retention data are analyzed both in a summary fashion and then using the trace integrity model. All of the results were significant at the $p<.01$ level.

Summary Findings

Consistent with previous research, analysis of variance and post-hoc tests of the acquisition data showed that both the semantic and modality manipulations facilitated children's performance across acquisition trials and that, in general, older children were better memorizers than younger children. Global performance on long-term retention tests was evaluated using a 2 (Grade) × 2 (Semantic) × 2 (Modality) × 2 (Retention Sequence) × 2 (Retention Test) × 4 (Trial) analysis of variance. Three main effects were obtained: (a) semantic $F(1, 304) = 356.39$, where performance was better for related ($M = 5.41$) than unrelated ($M = 3.18$) clusters, (b) retention sequence $F(1, 304) = 62.52$, where performance was better for the earlier sequence (2- and 16-day, $M = 4.76$) than the later sequence (16′- and 30-day, $M = 3.83$), and (c) trial $F(3, 912) = 37.95$, where post-hoc tests showed that performance on Trial 1 was inferior to performance on Trials 3 and 4, and that performance on Trial 2 was inferior to performance on Trial 4. One first-order interaction was observed, Retention Test × Retention Sequence $F(1, 304) = 37.50$. Post-hoc tests indicated that performance was superior on the 2- and 16-day than the 16′- and 30-day sequence, with no differences between

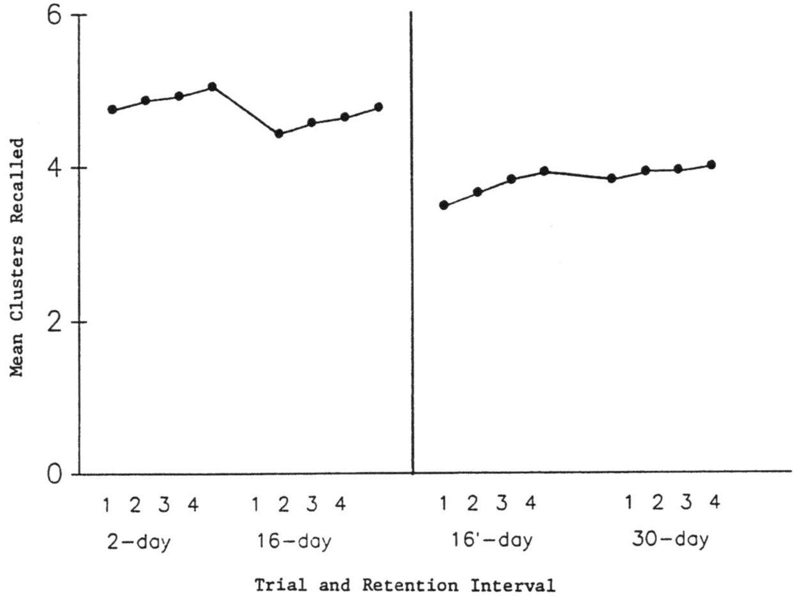

FIGURE 2.1. Mean number of clusters recalled (collapsed across age and list conditions) for each test trial across the different retention test sequences in Experiment 1.

2 and 16 days, but significant differences between 16′ and 30 days. Finally, a second-order interaction was obtained [Retention Test × Retention Sequence × Trial $F(3, 912) = 3.96$] and is shown in Figure 2.1. Post-hoc analysis of this interaction showed that (a) performance improved across test trials (hypermnesia) more dramatically for the 2- (all trials different except for Trials 1 vs. 2) and 16- (all trials different) day sequence than for the 16′- (all trials different) and 30- (where only Trial 1 was different than Trial 4) day sequence, (b) performance was poorer on the 16′–30 day sequence than the 2–16 day sequence, and (c) performance did not deteriorate over the 2-week retention interval for the 16′–30 day sequence but did decline over the same interval for the 2–16 day sequence (amnesia).

It would appear that children's long-term retention performance is sensitive to when retention is tested and to semantic factors. Importantly, regardless of when retention was tested, performance improved across test trials within a retention session. Finally, unlike the modality and developmental differences observed at acquisition, no picture-word or age differences were observed in global performance measures at retention. However, as shown in the next section, when a more sensitive factoring procedure is used, both modality and age contribute to retention.

Model-Based Findings

Prior to using the trace-integrity model's parameters to determine the locus of these effects, it is necessary to establish that the model provides a reasonable account of the sample data. Goodness of fit was evaluated using standard likelihood-ratio procedures (see Howe & Brainerd, 1989, Eqs. 1 and 2) and the results of these tests are given in Table 2.3 for Experiment 1. As can be seen in the third column, while two null hypothesis rejections were obtained at $p<.05$, given the number of comparisons, such an outcome would be expected by chance alone. Moreover, because not one null hypothesis rejection was obtained at $p<.01$, we can conclude that the model provided an acceptable account of the long-term retention data. The numerical values of the model's parameters are presented in Table 2.4.

Because the model's parameters are identifiable (see Howe & Brainerd, 1989), they can be used to make inferences about the underlying processes involved in retention. To effect these inferences, a standard three-step likelihood-ratio procedure was used to conduct hypothesis testing (see Brainerd, Howe, & Kingma 1982). First, an *experimentwise* test was performed. Like the omnibus *F* test, this test evaluates the null hypothesis that the numerical values of the parameters did not vary between conditions in this experiment as a whole. The results of this test showed that this hypothesis could be rejected [χ^2 (279) = 1429.41].

The second step involved a series of *conditionwise* tests. Like the *t* test, this test evaluates the null hypothesis that the numerical values of the parameters did not vary between specific pairs of conditions. In this experiment, a total of 88 χ^2 (9) conditionwise tests were used to localize the source of the experimentwise difference, 16 for each of the potential developmental effects, picture-word effects, semantic effects, and Retention Test 1 (T_1) versus Retention Test 2 (T_2) effects. An additional series of eight conditionwise tests were used to evaluate each the remaining effects, namely, the effect of a preceding test of retention on 16-day performance (16 vs. 16′), the effects of the timing of T_1 (2- vs. 16′-day), and the effects of the timing of T_2 (16- vs. 30-day). The results of these analyses are given in Table 2.5.

The final step involved the use of *parameterwise* tests. Each of these tests evaluates the null hypothesis that a specific parameter has the same value for two conditions. Because these tests are tedious and space-consuming to report, it customary to provide an overview of the significant effects only. Given the large number of parameterwise tests involved in this experiment, only a summary of reliable differences is provided in the following three subsections.

TABLE 2.3. Goodness-of-fit assessment of the long-term retention model for Experiment 1.

Grade and list condition	$-2lnL_9$	$-2lnL_{15}$	χ^2 (6)
	Grade 2		
Unrelated pictures			
2-days	396.88	384.31	12.57
16-days	389.04	387.38	1.66
16′-days	357.28	347.97	9.31
30-days	341.99	333.62	8.37
Related pictures			
2-days	46.62	46.57	0.05
16-days	101.27	98.79	2.48
16′-days	174.49	174.06	0.43
30-days	130.97	130.31	0.66
Unrelated words			
2-days	323.82	320.45	3.37
16-days	294.97	280.60	14.37
16′-days	265.99	249.67	16.32
30-days	291.06	282.74	8.32
Related words			
2-days	31.92	31.87	0.05
16-days	105.03	104.10	0.93
16′-days	309.39	304.12	5.27
30-days	228.61	222.83	5.78
	Grade 5		
Unrelated pictures			
2-days	345.37	345.21	0.16
16-days	379.43	375.16	4.27
16′-days	400.04	392.71	7.33
30-days	369.00	365.57	3.43
Related pictures			
2-days	39.62	39.57	0.05
16-days	54.74	52.11	2.63
16′-days	191.70	181.50	10.20
30-days	102.84	93.01	9.83
Unrelated words			
2-days	304.96	301.58	3.38
16-days	357.48	352.59	4.89
16′-days	351.95	344.65	7.30
30-days	290.96	284.64	6.32
Related words			
2-days	56.03	55.96	0.07
16-days	168.72	159.72	9.00
16′-days	220.32	215.96	4.36
30-days	173.07	172.98	0.09

Note. To demonstrate goodness of fit, the value in the third column must not exceed 16.81 ($p < .01$).

TABLE 2.4. Estimates of the retention model's theoretical parameters for Experiment 1.

Grade and list condition	S	R	a	r_1	r_2	r_3	f_1	f_2	f_3
Grade 2									
Unrelated pictures									
2-days	.25	.14	.22	.86	.93	.99	.48	.10	.34
16-days	.44	.00	.11	.83	.95	.98	.79	.50	.34
16′-days	.65	.00	.08	.87	.93	1.0	.55	.34	.41
30-days	.54	.11	.05	.87	.94	1.0	.59	.00	.31
Related pictures									
2-days	.03	.01	.03	1.0	1.0	1.0	.95	.00	.00
16-days	.05	.01	.10	.98	.99	1.0	.67	.00	.00
16′-days	.14	.02	.10	.99	1.0	.98	.96	.97	.15
30-days	.08	.04	.00	.98	1.0	1.0	.66	.97	.00
Unrelated words									
2-days	.27	.17	.02	.93	1.0	.96	.62	.39	.35
16-days	.39	.12	.03	.96	.96	1.0	.67	.31	.46
16′-days	.60	.24	.02	.96	.95	1.0	.33	.22	.12
30-days	.61	.03	.03	.85	.95	.97	.85	.00	.96
Related words									
2-days	.01	.01	.00	1.0	1.0	1.0	.70	.00	.29
16-days	.03	.04	.00	.99	.99	1.0	.86	.39	.10
16′-days	.12	.21	.00	.95	.99	.97	.32	.51	.13
30-days	.16	.05	.01	.94	.99	1.0	.55	.39	.63
Grade 5									
Unrelated pictures									
2-days	.22	.15	.02	.90	.97	.99	.43	.46	.41
16-days	.31	.18	.10	.89	.97	1.0	.47	.37	.00
16′-days	.29	.33	.00	.78	.96	.96	.44	.27	.19
30-days	.37	.19	.00	.92	.89	.94	.70	.48	.24
Related pictures									
2-days	.01	.03	.00	1.0	1.0	1.0	.69	.00	.00
16-days	.03	.00	.09	.98	1.0	1.0	.68	.15	.00
16′-days	.11	.06	.08	.98	.99	1.0	.60	.82	.23
30-days	.07	.02	.00	.98	1.0	1.0	.66	.95	.00
Unrelated words									
2-days	.30	.10	.09	.92	1.0	.97	.61	.28	.41
16-days	.31	.17	.10	.89	.97	.97	.27	.20	.13
16′-days	.58	.20	.08	.87	.96	1.0	.62	.10	.46
30-days	.36	.27	.00	.89	.96	.98	.25	.00	.07
Related words									
2-days	.03	.03	.00	1.0	1.0	1.0	.68	.00	.00
16-days	.09	.01	.12	.96	.99	1.0	.60	.00	.00
16′-days	.11	.12	.00	.96	.99	1.0	.60	.00	.19
30-days	.18	.03	.00	.99	.99	.99	.68	.01	.04

TABLE 2.5. Conditionwise tests for Experiment 1.

Effect	2-day	16-day	16′-day	30-day
Developmental effects				
Unrelated pictures	22.48	26.60	24.70	27.37
Related pictures	ns	ns	ns	ns
Unrelated words	ns	23.45	30.38	25.60
Related words	32.90	29.11	25.87	ns
Picture-word effects				
Grade 2 unrelated	42.27	21.94	ns	ns
related	ns	ns	54.63	27.06
Grade 5 unrelated	ns	ns	22.56	28.86
related	ns	ns	22.48	23.76
Semantic effects				
Grade 2 pictures	256.25	191.94	213.91	214.51
words	307.00	196.74	124.09	121.54
Grade 5 pictures	210.81	203.71	182.84	171.76
words	186.53	137.53	129.83	94.99

	Unrelated pictures	Related pictures	Unrelated words	Related words
T_1 vs. T_2 effects				
Grade 2				
2 vs. 16 days	32.01	ns	21.98	63.28
16′ vs. 30 days	22.65	ns	25.53	22.65
Grade 5				
2 vs. 16 days	ns	ns	27.66	33.33
16′ vs. 30 days	32.94	ns	21.88	ns
16 vs. 16′ effects				
Grade 2	28.01	ns	32.90	110.85
Grade 5	29.59	47.73	22.38	39.05
T_1 (2 vs. 16′) effects				
Grade 2	82.88	38.03	65.66	258.97
Grade 5	35.79	59.20	41.35	45.42
T_2 (16 vs. 30) effects				
Grade 2	21.95	21.83	34.88	67.84
Grade 5	35.85	22.05	22.50	56.40

Note. Values are χ^2 (9) statistics that are significant at $p < .01$ (21.67); ns = not significant.

Developmental Effects

Age differences in forgetting were confined to the unrelated lists. Younger children exhibited more storage failures than older children, with these differences being larger for unrelated pictures (all comparisons except the 2-day test, with an average numerical difference across intervals of .17) than unrelated words (only the 30-day comparison was significant, and the average numerical difference across intervals was .09). Older children were more prone to retrieval failures for unrelated pictures (16- and 16′-day tests) and unrelated words (30-day test). Again, the average numerical magnitude of this difference across intervals tended to be larger for unrelated pictures (.15) than unrelated words (.05). The only instance in which this trend was reversed was for unrelated words on the 16′-day test. A striking result, from a theoretical perspective, was that, regardless of age, the average storage failure rate (.27 and .21 for grades 2 and 5, respectively) was greater than the average retrieval failure rate (.08 and .12 for grades 2 and 5, respectively).

Two differences were obtained at storage-based reminiscence, one favoring the younger children (unrelated pictures, 2-day test) and one favoring the older children (related words, 16-day test). These effects can be better appreciated by examining the probability of storage-based reminiscence on any test trial (a) and the cumulative probability that storage-based reminiscence occurred on one of the test trials [$a + a(1 - a) + a(1 - a)^2 + a(1 - a)^3$]. Collapsing across factors, it is clear that the average and cumulative storage-based reminiscence rates for grade 2 (.05 and .19, respectively) and grade 5 students (.04 and .16, respectively) did not differ.

Concerning retrieval-based reminiscence, all of the differences were confined to the error-contingent retrieval parameters; however, no consistent developmental trends emerged. Specifically, error-contingent retrieval sometimes favored younger children (f_1: unrelated pictures, 16- and 16′-day, unrelated words, 16- and 30-day, related pictures, 16-day; f_2: unrelated words, 16′-day, related words, 16-, 16′-, and 30-day; and f_3: unrelated words, 30-day) and at other times favored older children (f_1: unrelated words, 16′-day, related words, 16′-day; and f_2: unrelated pictures, 2- and 30-day).

The absence of developmental differences in retrieval-based reminiscence was also reflected in the averaged success- and error-contingent retrieval statistics. That is, no differences were observed in the average rate of success-contingent retrieval for either the grade 2 ($1 - R = .92$, $r_1 = .94$, $r_2 = .97$, and $r_3 = .99$) or grade 5 students ($1 - R = .88$, $r_1 = .93$, $r_2 = .98$, and $r_3 = .99$). Similarly, although error-contingent retrieval tended to decline across trials, developmental differences between grade 2 ($R = .08$, $f_1 = .66$, $f_2 = .32$, and $f_3 = .29$) and grade 5 students ($R = .12$, $f_1 = .56$, $f_2 = .26$, and $f_3 = .15$) were absent.

To summarize, developmental differences in long-term retention were due primarily to forgetting, not reminiscence. More important, developmental differences in forgetting were confined to unrelated materials, tended to be more prominent with pictures than words, and were localized at storage for younger children and at retrieval for older children.

Modality and Semantic Effects

Overall, semantic effects were larger than modality effects, particularly at forgetting. Forgetting differences due to the modality manipulation, although few (only 5 differences out of 16 comparisons), generally favored pictures over words. For grade 2 children, words were subject to more storage-based forgetting (related 30-day) and retrieval-based forgetting (unrelated and related 16′-day) than pictures. For grade 5, the greater forgetting of words than pictures was confined to storage failures (unrelated 16′-day and related 30-day).

In contrast, each of the 16 comparisons used to evaluate semantic effects revealed a significant difference in forgetting. In each case, these differences favored related over unrelated clusters, with the overriding form of forgetting for the unrelated clusters being storage failures. For both grade 2 and 5 children, more storage failures were observed for unrelated than related clusters for each comparison. Although the average storage failure rate did not differ as a function of the picture- (.28 and .18 for grades 2 and 5, respectively) word (.28 and .25 for grades 2 and 5, respectively) manipulation, it was clearly larger for unrelated (.47 and .35 for grades 2 and 5, respectively) than related (.08 for both grades 2 and 5) clusters. In terms of retrieval failures, grade 2 children experienced more retrieval failures for unrelated than related pictures and words, but these differences were confined to the 2-day retention test. For the grade 5 children, more retrieval failures were observed for unrelated than related pictures (all comparisons) and for the 16- and 30-day tests for words. Finally, regardless of age, the average storage failure rate was higher than the average retrieval failure rate.

Regardless of age, storage-based reminiscence rates were higher for pictures than for words (2- and 16-day tests for unrelated clusters and 16- and 16′-day tests for related clusters, grade 2; 16′-day for the related clusters, grade 5). Interestingly, although this modest picture advantage would be anticipated from the adult literature (see Payne, 1987), it is usually attributed to changes in retrieval, not storage, factors. As we will see below, the largest contributor to pictorial hypermnesia in this experiment was storage-based, not retrieval-based, reminiscence.

The only storage-based reminiscence difference that emerged as a result of the semantic manipulation was one that favored unrelated pictures on the 2-day test for grade 2 students. However, interpretation of this finding is complicated by ceiling recall levels in the related picture condition (leaving little room for improvement). The average and cumulative storage-based reminiscence rates for the grade 2 children showed that pictures (.09 and .31, respectively) were more easily redintegrated than words (.02 and .06, respectively) and that unrelated clusters (.08 and .26, respectively) were better redintegrated than related clusters (.03 and .12, respectively). For grade 5 children, on the other hand, these average and cumulative rates were not reactive to the picture- (.04 and .14, respectively) word (.05 and .18, respectively) manipulation or to whether the clusters were unrelated (.05 and .18, respectively) or related (.04 and .14, respectively).

No differences were observed for the grade 2 students on success-contingent retrieval-based reminiscence, but grade 5 children found this form of retrieval easier (as measured by r_1) for related than unrelated pictures (16′-day test) and words (30-day test). At a global level, no differences in success-contingent retrieval were observed as a function of modality or semantic manipulations for the younger children, but significant increases were observed across trials as a function of the semantic manipulation (but not modality) for the grade 5 children. Here, success-contingent retrieval increased across the first three trials for the unrelated (.80, .88, .96, and .98, respectively) but not the related clusters (.96, .99, 1.0, and 1.0, respectively).

Differences in error-contingent retrieval-based reminiscence did not consistently favor pictures (f_1: unrelated 16′-day, related 2- and 16′-day; f_2: unrelated 16-day, related 16′- and 30-day) or words (f_1: unrelated 2- and 30-day, related 16-day; f_2: unrelated 2-day; f_3: related 30-day) for grade 2, but did for grade 5 (f_1: unrelated 16- and 30-day; f_2: unrelated 30-day and related 16′- and 30-day). Similarly, for the semantic manipulation, differences did not consistently favor related (f_1: pictures 2- and 16′-day; f_2: pictures 16′- and 30-day, words 16′- and 30-day) over unrelated (f_1: words 30-day; f_2: pictures 16-day) clusters for grade 2 or grade 5 (unrelated better—f_2: pictures 2- and 16-day, words 2- and 16-day; related better—f_1: pictures 2-day, words 16- and 30-day; f_2: pictures 16′- and 30-day). For both grades, average error-contingent retrieval declined across trials.

To summarize, changes in performance due to modality and semantic factors were again controlled primarily by forgetting and not reminiscence. More important, differences in forgetting were greater for the semantic than the modality manipulation, and storage failures were more likely than retrieval failures. Reminiscence differences that did emerge indicated that neither storage nor retrieval failures were permanent, with improvements in recall across retention test trials (hypermnesia) being controlled by storage-based and, to a lesser extent, success-contingent retrieval-based, reminiscence.

Test and Time Effects

Test/Retest Effects

To begin, we consider the effects of repeated testing both for the early (2- vs. 16-days) and late (16′- vs. 30-days) sequences. Overall, forgetting differences depended on age and timing of the sequence, with average differences in forgetting being larger for grade 2 than 5. For the early sequence, no forgetting differences were obtained for the grade 5 students, but younger children experienced more storage failures on the 16- than 2-day test for unrelated clusters. These same children exhibited more retrieval-based forgetting on the 2- than 16-day test for unrelated pictures.

For the later retention sequence, grade 5 students exhibited more forgetting on the 16′- than 30-day tests, where these differences were confined to the unrelated clusters (more retrieval failures on the unrelated picture list and more storage failures on the unrelated word list). For grade 2 children, more storage-based forgetting occurred on the 16′- than 30-day test for unrelated pictures, more retrieval-based forgetting on the 16′- than 30-day test for the word lists (both unrelated and related), and more retrieval failures on the 30- than 16′-day test for unrelated pictures. Thus, more forgetting tended to occur on the later than earlier retention test sequence, the dominant mode of forgetting was storage failures, younger children forget more than older children particularly on the early retention test sequence, and more forgetting occurred at 16 days, regardless of whether it was the first or second test in the sequence (see subsequent comparison of 16- vs. 16′-day tests).

Differences in storage-based reminiscence were confined to the early test sequence, where more reminiscence occurred at 2- than 16-days for the younger children (unrelated pictures). For grade 5, more reminiscence occurred at 16- than 2-days (related words). Although average rates did not differ reliably with age or time of the test sequence (grade 2 early sequence, .07, late sequence, .04; grade 5 early sequence, .07, late sequence, .02), the cumulative storage-based reminiscence probability was higher on the earlier (grade 2, .24; grade 5, .23) than the later test sequence (grade 2, .14; grade 5, .08).

Few differences were obtained for success-contingent retrieval-based reminiscence (one for the younger children—better on 16′- than 30-days for unrelated words as measured by r_1; and one for grade 5—better on 30- than 16′-days for unrelated pictures as measured by r_1). No differences were obtained in average success-contingent retrieval as a function of age, materials, and time of the retention test sequence.

Differences in error-contingent retrieval-based reminiscence did not consistently favor one time interval over another. Younger children were better at 16- than 2-days (unrelated pictures, f_1 and f_2; related words, f_2), on 16′- than 30-days (unrelated pictures, f_2; related pictures, f_1), and better on 30- than 16′-days (unrelated and related words, f_1 and f_3). Older children were better at 2- than 16-days (unrelated words, f_1), on 16′- than 30-days (unrelated words, f_1), and on 30- than 16′-days (unrelated pictures, f_1 and f_2). As before, the general trend was for error-contingent retrieval to decline across trials, but no differences in the average rate of this statistic were obtained as a function of age, materials, or time of the retention test sequence.

Time of Test

Next, consider the timing of T_1 (2- vs. 16′-day) and T_2 (16- vs. 30-day). Regardless of age, forgetting differences were more pronounced on T_1

than T_2. At T_1, there were more storage failures (all lists) than retrieval failures (related words only) for grade 2 at 16′- than 2-days, with only one difference showing more retrieval failures at 2- than 16′-days (unrelated pictorial clusters). For grade 5, there were no differences between the number of storage failures (unrelated words and related pictures and words) and retrieval failures (unrelated pictures and words and related words) and all of the differences showed more forgetting at 16′- than 2-days. In addition, differences in the average magnitude of storage and retrieval failure rates were larger at 16′-days (.38 and .12, respectively, for grade 2; .27 and .18, respectively, for grade 5) than at 2-days (.14 and .08, respectively, for both grade 2 and 5 children).

At T_2, there were more storage failures (unrelated pictures and words and related words) than retrieval failures (unrelated pictures only) for grade 2 at 30- than 16-days. For grade 5, there was only one storage failure difference (related words) and one retrieval failure difference (unrelated words), with both differences showing more forgetting at 30- than 16-days. Like T_1, differences in the average magnitude of storage and retrieval failure rates at T_2 were larger on the later test (30-days—.35 and .06, respectively, for grade 2; .25 and .13, respectively, for grade 5) than the earlier test (16-days—.23 and .04, respectively, for grade 2; .19 and .09, respectively, for grade 5).

Differences in storage-based reminiscence were again small in absolute terms. At T_1, the only difference occurred for grade 2 (unrelated pictures, 2- > 16′-days). At T_2, four storage-based reminiscence differences were obtained, one for grade 2 (related pictures) and three for grade 5 (unrelated pictures and words and related words), each of which favored 16- over 30-days. Average and cumulative storage-based reminiscence rates did not differ across grades at T_1 (.06 and .22, respectively, for grade 2 and .04 and .14, respectively, for grade 5) or at T_2 (.04 and .15, respectively, for grade 2 and .05 and .17, respectively, for grade 5).

Differences in success-contingent retrieval-based reminiscence were observed for grade 5 at T_1 (unrelated pictures, 2- > 16′-days on r_1) and grade 2 at T_2 (unrelated words, 16- > 30-days on r_1). No differences existed across trials as a function of age, materials, or T_1 versus T_2. No consistent differences in error-contingent retrieval-based reminiscence were obtained at T_1 for grade 2 (favoring 2- over 16′-day for words [f_1, unrelated and related] and favoring 16′- over 2-days for related pictures and words [f_2]) or grade 5 (favoring 16′- over 2-days for related pictures [f_2]). Similarly, at T_2, differences were obtained on all lists for grade 2, two of which were observed for unrelated materials and favored 16- over 30-days (pictures, f_1 and f_2, and words, f_2), and two of which pertained to related materials and favored 30- over 16-days (pictures, f_2, and words, f_3). For grade 5, these differences were confined to pictorial lists and favored 30- over 16-days for both the unrelated (f_1) and related pictures (f_2). Although error-contingent retrieval declined across trials, no differences in the average rate of this statistic were obtained as a function of age, materials, or T_1 versus T_2.

Test versus No-Test Effects

Finally, consider differences in 16-day performance as a function of whether a preceding test of retention had been administered (16- vs. 16′-days). Here, regardless of age, more forgetting was observed at 16′- than 16-days except for the related pictorial clusters. For grade 2, storage failures (unrelated pictures and words and related words) occurred more frequently than retrieval failures (word lists only). For grade 5, the opposite pattern emerged. Here, storage failures occurred only on the unrelated word list and retrieval failures on both the unrelated picture and related word lists. The average rate of storage failure was higher than retrieval failure at 16′-days (.38 and .12, respectively, for grade 2; .27 and .18, respectively, for grade 5) and 16-days (.23 and .04, respectively, for grade 2; .19 and .09, respectively, for grade 5).

Differences in storage-based reminiscence were observed only for grade 5 children, and was greater for 16- than 16′-days for the unrelated picture and related word lists. The only age difference in average or cumulative storage-based reminiscence was that these values were higher for grade 5 on 16-day (.10 and .34, respectively) than 16′-day (.04 and .16, respectively), whereas no differences were observed for grade 2. Differences in success-contingent retrieval-based reminiscence were obtained only for grade 5 (with r_1 being larger at 16- than 16′-days for the unrelated picture list). No differences in average success-contingent retrieval were obtained across trials. Last, differences in error-contingent retrieval-based reminiscence favored 16- over 16′-days for grade 2 (unrelated pictures and words and related pictures, f_1), but favored 16′- over 16-days for grade 5 (unrelated words, f_1, and related pictures, f_2). Although error-contingent retrieval declined across trials, no differences in the average rate of this statistic were obtained as a function of age, materials, or 16- versus 16′-days.

Summary

The effects of testing and timing were generally larger in terms of forgetting than reminiscence, with the former effects being larger for younger than older children. The effects of repeated testing on forgetting varied with age such that differences were confined to the later test sequence for the older children, but were obtained at both the early and late sequence for the younger subjects. More forgetting was observed on the first retention test than on the second, indicating that one effect of a preceding test is to attenuate forgetting on a subsequent test *regardless of the timing of these tests*. This latter effect is more pronounced when performance at 16 days is considered with (16) than without (16′) a preceding test of retention. Here, less forgetting occurred when a preceding test had been administered than when it had not. Interestingly, more storage-based reminiscence was observed at 16 days when a preceding test had been administered, but these effects were confined to the older children.

Summary of Results for Experiment 1

Overall, the results of Experiment 1 indicate that the majority of differences in elementary school children's retention are controlled by forgetting rather than reminiscence processes. In addition, the findings are generally consistent with the theoretical proposals in the trace-integrity model outlined earlier. First, in terms of forgetting, the results consistently showed that regardless of age, storage failures were more common than retrieval failures. Although younger children tended, on average, to forget more than older children, forgetting rates for both age groups were controlled more by semantic factors than by presentation modality. Here, as predicted, more forgetting occurred with unrelated than related items. Apparently, semantically related material is more resistant to forgetting than unrelated material. In a similar vein, forgetting increased as the length of the retention interval increased and was attenuated following a 2-week interval by the presentation of an earlier test of retention, *regardless of when this first test was administered*. Specifically (a) more forgetting occurred on the first test of retention than on the second regardless of the timing of these tests and (b) less forgetting occurred at 16 days when a preceding test had been administered (at 2 days) than when it had not.

Second, reminiscence effects clearly contributed to performance increments across retention test trials. Here, the results indicated that hypermnesia was controlled by storage-based reminiscence and, to a lesser extent, success-contingent retrieval-based reminiscence. Contrary to trace-absence views of storage failure, storage-based reminiscence contributed to trace recovery, although differences favoring related over unrelated materials were obscured by ceiling effects. The interesting thing to note here is that consistent with the trace-integrity theory, storage-based reminiscence was evident with unrelated items as well, indicating that redintegration processes are not strictly confined to semantically integrated materials (see Howe & Brainerd, 1989). In terms of modality effects, hypermnesia as measured by storage-based reminiscence was, on average, no more likely with pictures than words, although in those cases where such effects did emerge, they tended to favor pictures. Storage-based reminiscence rates also tended to be higher on earlier retention tests, particularly for the older children. Although success-contingent retrieval-based reminiscence tended to be constant across most of the factors in this experiment, it is important to note that these rates were consistently high. That is, once an item had been successfully retrieved, it tended to remain highly retrievable.

Finally, few differences were observed in error-contingent retrieval-based reminiscence. The main result here was that regardless of the manipulation under consideration, error-contingent retrieval *declined* across test trials. This result, in conjunction with the observed increase in cumulative storage-based reminiscence rates, indicates that reminiscence is primarily controlled by storage factors, with the probability of retrieval-based reminiscence following an error decreasing steadily across retention test trials.

Experiment 2: Results and Discussion

Summary Findings

The pattern of results at acquisition was similar to that obtained in Experiment 1, was consistent with previous research, and showed that both the semantic and modality manipulations facilitated students' performance across acquisition trials and that, in general, college subjects were better memorizers than grade 8 children. Global performance on long-term retention tests was evaluated using a 2 (Grade) × 2 (Semantic) × 2 (Modality) × 2 (Retention Sequence) × 2 (Retention Test) × 4 (Trial) analysis of variance. Three main effects were obtained: (a) semantic $F(1, 224) = 72.52$, where performance was better for related ($M = 11.77$) than unrelated ($M = 9.05$) clusters; (b) retention sequence $F(1, 224) = 138.52$, where performance was better for the earlier sequence (2- and 16-day, $M = 12.29$) than the later sequence (16′- and 30-day, $M = 8.53$); and (c) trial $F(3, 672) = 132.48$, where post-hoc tests showed that performance differed between all of the trials except between Trials 3 and 4.

Three first-order interactions were observed: (a) Semantic × Retention Sequence $F(1, 224) = 14.75$, where post-hoc tests showed that performance was poorest for unrelated clusters on 16′- and 30-day tests, with no differences between the other conditions; (b) Retention Test × Retention Sequence $F(1, 224) = 106.18$, where post-hoc tests revealed that all differences were significant with performance being ordered (from best to worst): 2-day > 16-day > 16′day > 30-day; and (c) Semantic × Trial $F(3, 672) = 5.37$, where post-hoc tests showed that although performance improved across all trials except Trials 3 versus 4 for the unrelated clusters, performance improvement was confined to Trials 1 versus 2 for the related clusters.

Two second-order interactions were obtained: (a) Grade × Retention Test × Retention Sequence $F(1, 224) = 18.70$ (shown in Figure 2.2), where post-hoc tests showed that although performance was better on

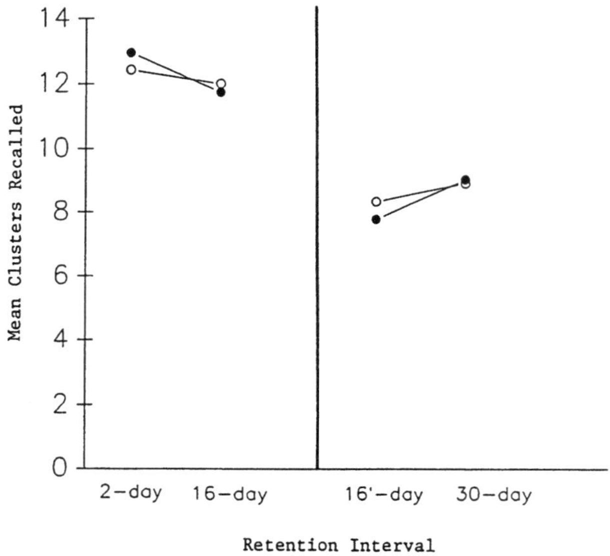

FIGURE 2.2. Mean number of clusters recalled for grade 8 (open circles) and college students (solid circles) at each of the retention test sequences in Experiment 2.

earlier (2- and 16-day) than later (16′- and 30-day) retention tests for all subjects, college students were better than grade 8 children on the 2-day test, and whereas performance declined between 2- and 16-days (and more so for the college than grade 8 students), average performance improved between the 16′- and 30-day tests; and (b) Retention Test × Retention Sequence × Trial $F(3, 672) = 12.11$. As in Experiment 1, post-hoc tests indicated that performance was superior on the 2- and 16-day than the 16′- and 30-day sequence, with no differences between 2 and 16 days, but significant differences between 16′ and 30 days.

Finally, a fourth-order Semantic × Modality × Retention Test × Retention Sequence × Trial interaction $F(3, 672) = 4.41$ emerged and is shown in Figure 2.3. Post-hoc analysis of *performance differences between retention intervals* showed that (a) performance on the 2- and 16-day tests was superior to that on the 16′- and 30-day tests, (b) performance *declined* between the last trial of the 2-day tests and the first trial of the 16-day tests, and (c) performance *improved* between the initial trials of the 16′-day test and the later trials of the 30-day test.

Additional post-hoc analyses of this five-way interaction were conducted to assess *performance differences at each retention interval* using a series of four lower order Modality × Semantic × Trial analyses of variance, one for each retention interval (2-, 16-, 16′-, and 30-day tests). The main results from these analyses were that at each of the retention intervals there was (a) a main effect for the semantic factor [$Fs(1, 116) =$

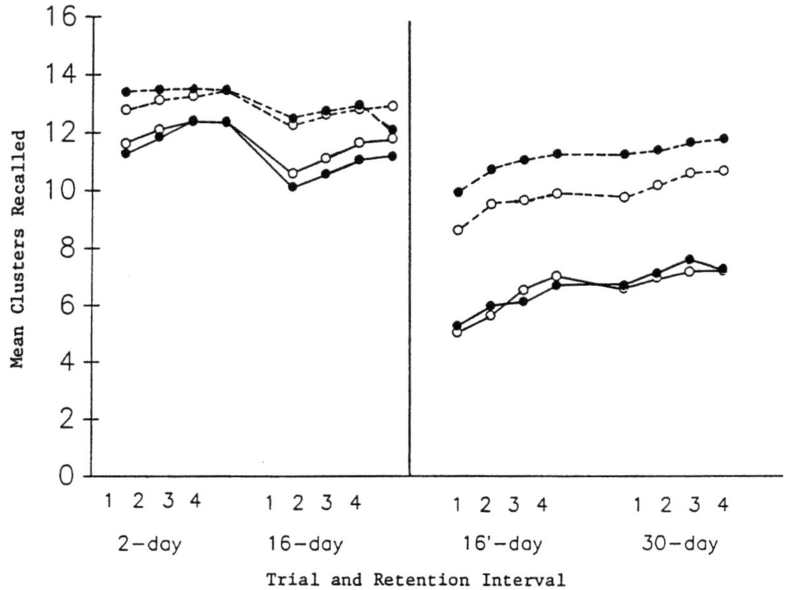

FIGURE 2.3. Mean number of clusters recalled (collapsed across age) for pictures (closed circles) and words (open circles) that were either unrelated (solid line) or related (dashed line) for each test trial across the different retention test sequences in Experiment 2.

18.35 to 57.63] where related clusters were better recalled than unrelated clusters, and (b) a main effect for trial [*F*s(3, 348) = 20.56 to 29.77] where post-hoc tests indicated that performance improved significantly between Trials 1 and 2 and Trials 2 and 3 for all retention intervals, and between Trials 3 and 4 for the 16′-day interval only. Finally, for the 2-day interval only, a first-order Semantic × Trial interaction [$F(3, 348) = 6.29$] and a second-order Semantic × Modality × Trial interaction [$F(3, 348) = 3.15$] emerged. Post-hoc analysis of the three-way interaction showed that the locus of this effect was confined to Trial 1 where differences between pictures and words occurred for the related clusters only.

In summary, then, it would appear that children's long-term retention performance is sensitive to exactly when retention is tested and to semantic factors. Importantly, regardless of when retention was tested, performance improved across test trials within a retention session (barring ceiling effects). Finally, unlike the large modality and developmental differences observed at acquisition, few picture-word, and no age differences, were observed in global performance measures at retention. However, as shown in the next section, when a more sensitive factoring is used, both modality and age are important in long-term retention.

Model-Based Findings

Goodness-of-fit statistics are given in Table 2.6 for Experiment 2. As before, the model provided an excellent fit to the long-term retention data. The numerical values of the model's parameters are presented in Table 2.7.

The experimentwise test was significant, χ^2 (279) = 1,801.36. As before, 88 χ^2 (9) conditionwise tests were used to localize the source of the experimentwise difference. The results of these analyses are given in Table 2.8 and a summary of reliable parameterwise differences is provided below.

Developmental Effects

Age differences in forgetting were generally confined to later retention tests, where the direction of the age differences varied with presentation modality. For pictures, grade 8 children exhibited more storage failures than college students on the unrelated list (16- and 30-day) and more retrieval failures on the related list (16-day). The only difference favoring grade 8 was a lower probability of retrieval failure on the unrelated list on the 16-day test. For words, college students showed more storage failures than grade 8 students (unrelated list, 16-day, and related list, 16′- and 30-day), but the younger students exhibited more retrieval failures (related list, 30-day). As in Experiment 1, regardless of age, the average storage failure rate (.21 and .22 for grade 8 and college, respectively) was greater than the retrieval failure rate (.11 and .10 for grade 8 and college, respectively).

Only three differences, favoring college over grade 8, were obtained in storage-based reminiscence (2- and 16-day test for related pictures and 2-day test for related words). Average and cumulative storage-based reminiscence rates were greater for college (.09 and .31, respectively) than grade 8 (.05 and .19, respectively). All of the retrieval-based reminiscence differences were confined to retrieval following errors. Here, no consistent developmental trends emerged on picture lists (grade 8 better than college on the unrelated list 16-day, all f_i, and on the related list 2-day, f_1; college better than grade 8 on the related list 16-day, f_1, and on 30-day, f_2), but college students were superior to grade 8 on word lists (unrelated 16-day f_2 and f_3, related 2-day f_1, 16-day f_1 and f_3, 16′-day f_1 and f_3, and 30-day f_1 and f_2). Average success- and error-contingent retrieval-based reminiscence statistics did not differ developmentally, although error-contingent retrieval declined steadily across trials.

To summarize, developmental differences were more prominent at forgetting than at reminiscence. In terms of forgetting, grade 8 children exhibited more forgetting of pictures, whereas college students tended to forget more words. Again, the overriding form of forgetting was storage

TABLE 2.6. Goodness-of-fit assessment of the long-term retention model for Experiment 2.

Grade and list condition	$-2lnL_9$	$-2lnL_{15}$	χ^2 (6)
	Grade 8		
Unrelated pictures			
2-days	436.60	433.69	2.91
16-days	436.64	427.59	9.05
16′-days	560.14	558.95	1.19
30-days	572.66	564.56	8.10
Related pictures			
2-days	131.05	131.01	0.04
16-days	276.04	275.31	0.73
16′-days	407.81	402.60	5.21
30-days	319.98	319.84	0.14
Unrelated words			
2-days	386.99	379.89	7.10
16-days	349.90	344.58	5.32
16′-days	593.68	583.84	9.84
30-days	481.82	469.85	11.97
Related words			
2-days	198.32	195.60	2.72
16-days	279.21	274.61	4.60
16′-days	447.64	439.98	7.66
30-days	458.56	446.92	11.64
	College		
Unrelated pictures			
2-days	442.47	432.97	9.50
16-days	616.37	611.83	4.54
16′-days	540.43	538.33	2.10
30-days	426.70	423.80	2.90
Related pictures			
2-days	76.05	65.35	10.70
16-days	185.88	181.53	4.35
16′-days	493.75	488.02	5.73
30-days	304.49	301.05	3.44
Unrelated words			
2-days	320.34	308.47	11.87
16-days	500.39	496.59	3.80
16′-days	597.67	586.43	11.24
30-days	436.70	428.39	8.31
Related words			
2-days	146.14	145.23	0.91
16-days	237.83	233.24	4.59
16′-days	574.96	562.68	12.28
30-days	414.77	413.22	1.55

Note. To demonstrate goodness of fit, the value in the third column must not exceed 16.81 ($p < .01$).

TABLE 2.7. Estimates of the retention model's theoretical parameters for Experiment 2.

Grade and list condition	S	R	a	r_1	r_2	r_3	f_1	f_2	f_3
Grade 8									
Unrelated pictures									
2-days	.10	.13	.13	.98	.98	.98	.53	.56	.00
16-days	.23	.00	.14	.95	.99	1.0	.80	.50	.61
16′-days	.60	.14	.04	.93	.94	.98	.81	.49	.57
30-days	.52	.12	.05	.91	.96	.98	.54	.40	.05
Related pictures									
2-days	.05	.02	.00	1.0	1.0	1.0	.48	.51	.10
16-days	.00	.14	.00	.99	.99	1.0	.35	.10	.00
16′-days	.13	.13	.14	.97	1.0	.99	.40	.00	.10
30-days	.14	.04	.03	.96	1.0	1.0	.50	.34	.12
Unrelated words									
2-days	.10	.11	.07	.96	.99	.99	.65	.39	.20
16-days	.13	.07	.08	.98	.99	.99	.75	.25	.19
16′-days	.54	.19	.05	.90	.98	1.0	.58	.55	.25
30-days	.46	.19	.02	.96	.98	.99	.56	.40	.26
Related words									
2-days	.06	.05	.00	1.0	1.0	1.0	.30	.39	.30
16-days	.00	.13	.00	.99	1.0	1.0	.28	.19	.00
16′-days	.13	.20	.11	.98	.98	1.0	.40	.02	.00
30-days	.10	.17	.00	.94	.99	1.0	.56	.22	.00
College									
Unrelated pictures									
2-days	.07	.11	.04	.93	.99	.98	.67	.67	.21
16-days	.08	.25	.05	.89	.97	.98	.49	.26	.03
16′-days	.50	.15	.02	.92	.97	1.0	.66	.51	.28
30-days	.41	.09	.00	.96	.99	1.0	.52	.54	.10
Related pictures									
2-days	.01	.01	.36	1.0	1.0	1.0	.00	.49	.00
16-days	.06	.02	.25	1.0	1.0	1.0	.59	.00	.00
16′-days	.13	.14	.10	.97	.99	1.0	.42	.12	.23
30-days	.17	.07	.00	.99	1.0	1.0	.41	.77	.00
Unrelated words									
2-days	.08	.06	.00	.96	1.0	.99	.67	.78	.10
16-days	.26	.05	.14	.95	.99	.99	.70	.85	.51
16′-days	.52	.27	.02	.92	.97	.98	.67	.64	.30
30-days	.45	.11	.00	.96	1.0	1.0	.70	.63	.33
Related words									
2-days	.06	.00	.31	1.0	1.0	1.0	1.0	.39	.60
16-days	.06	.06	.00	.99	1.0	1.0	.80	.33	.50
16′-days	.38	.13	.06	.96	.97	.97	.71	.00	.52
30-days	.33	.03	.05	.97	.99	1.0	.75	.87	.36

TABLE 2.8. Conditionwise tests for Experiment 2.

Effect	2-day	16-day	16′-day	30-day
Developmental effects				
Unrelated pictures	ns	42.32	ns	34.53
Related pictures	44.86	22.36	ns	37.71
Unrelated words	ns	34.96	ns	ns
Related words	21.94	23.56	38.00	63.48
Picture-word effects				
Grade 8 unrelated	ns	23.23	21.89	ns
related	ns	ns	ns	33.35
College unrelated	ns	36.27	ns	ns
related	47.43	25.42	37.85	38.77
Semantic effects				
Grade 8 pictures	72.15	61.88	217.92	186.51
words	42.97	33.03	161.92	142.07
College pictures	188.13	184.41	102.55	82.91
words	50.79	82.34	59.05	36.76

	Unrelated pictures	Related pictures	Unrelated words	Related words
T_1 vs. T_2 effects				
Grade 8				
2 vs. 16 days	29.68	29.76	ns	ns
16′ vs. 30 days	22.38	24.53	ns	24.11
College				
2 vs. 16 days	41.91	73.97	63.41	32.08
16′ vs. 30 days	25.66	42.49	38.32	33.24
16 vs. 16′ effects				
Grade 8	207.07	37.32	253.07	55.26
College	127.96	142.96	139.18	191.91
T_1 (2 vs. 16′) effects				
Grade 8	302.18	106.59	246.79	84.17
College	260.81	354.05	336.96	344.85
T_2 (16 vs. 30) effects				
Grade 8	151.23	31.87	192.68	56.92
College	105.16	84.05	102.53	118.78

Note. Values are χ^2 (9) statistics that are significant at $p < .01$ (21.67); ns = not significant.

failures. Finally, storage-based reminiscence was greater for related than unrelated materials, with cumulative rates being larger for college students.

Modality and Semantic Effects

As in Experiment 1, semantic effects were generally larger than modality effects, particularly in terms of forgetting. The few forgetting differences due to modality tended to favor pictures over words, at least for college students. Differences for grade 8 were mixed (more retrieval-based forgetting on the 30-day test for related words than pictures, but more storage-based forgetting on the unrelated 16-day test for pictures than words). For college students, the only case in which pictures were forgotten more frequently than words was on the 16-day unrelated list (greater retrieval failures). All other differences revealed more storage failures for words than pictures (unrelated 16-day, related 16′- and 30-day).

Tests of the effects due to the semantic manipulation revealed differences favoring the related over unrelated clusters, the single exception occurring for grade 8 (pictures, 16-day test, more retrieval failures for the related than unrelated list). Regardless of age, storage failures were more common than retrieval failures for all pairwise comparisons with two exceptions for grade 8 (pictures, 2-day, where the differences were confined to retrieval failures and words, 2-day, where no differences were obtained) and four for college (pictures, 2- and 16-day, where the differences were confined to retrieval failures, words, 2-day, where no differences were obtained, and words, 16′-day, where additional differences were observed in retrieval failures). For grade 8, the average storage failure rate did not differ as a function of the picture- (.22) word (.19) manipulation, but it was clearly larger for the unrelated (.34) than related (.08) clusters. For college students, average storage failure rates varied as a function of both modality and semantic manipulations (.27 and .09 for the unrelated and related pictures, respectively, and .33 and .21 for the unrelated and related words, respectively).

Only one storage-based reminiscence difference was observed as a function of modality (college, related pictures better than words at 16-days), and differences due to the semantic manipulation were confined to grade 8 (favoring unrelated pictures on the 2- and 16-day tests and favoring related pictures on the later 16′-day test). Again, interpretation of this finding is complicated by ceiling effects. The average and cumulative rates for grade 8 showed no differences for pictures (.07 and .24, respectively) and words (.04 and .24, respectively) and modest differences between unrelated (.08 and .26, respectively) and related clusters (.04 and .14, respectively). For college students, related pictures exhibited more storage-based reminiscence than unrelated pictures (2- and 16-days), but unrelated words were better than related words (16-days). The average and cumulative rates were not reactive to the picture- (.11 and .32, respectively) word (.08 and .27, respectively) manipulation, but did depend on whether the clusters were unrelated (.04 and .14, respectively) or related (.14 and .45, respectively).

Concerning retrieval-based reminiscence, differences were confined to error-contingent retrieval and consistently favored pictures over words for grade 8 (f_1: unrelated 16′-day, related 2-day; f_2: unrelated 16-day), but favored words over pictures for college students (unrelated 16-day, all f_i; f_1: related 2-, 16-, 16′-, and 30-day; f_3: 2- and 30-day). In terms of the semantic manipulation, differences consistently favored unrelated over related clusters for grade 8 (pictures 16- and 16′-day, all f_i; words 2- and 16-day f_1 and 16′-day f_2) and for college (pictures 2-day f_1 and 16′-day f_1 and f_2; words 2-, 16-, and 16′-day f_2). The only difference favoring related over unrelated clusters was for the college word list on the 2-day test (f_1 and f_3). Finally, regardless of age, the average probability of error-contingent retrieval declined across trials.

To summarize, changes in performance were controlled primarily by forgetting and not reminiscence. More important, differences in forgetting were greater for the semantic than the modality manipulation, and storage failures were more likely than retrieval failures. Reminiscence differences that did emerge indicated that neither storage nor retrieval failures were permanent, with improvements in recall across retention test trials (hypermnesia) being controlled by storage-based reminiscence and success-contingent retrieval-based reminiscence.

Test and Time Effects

Test/Retest Effects

Overall, forgetting differences depended on age and timing of the sequence, with average differences being larger for college than grade 8. For the early sequence, forgetting differences were obtained only for picture lists for grade 8 (more storage failure at 16- than 2-days for unrelated pictures; more retrieval failure at 2- than 16-days for unrelated pictures and at 16- than 2-days for related pictures) and only for unrelated lists for college (more storage failure at 16- than 2-days for unrelated words; more retrieval failure at 16- than 2-days for unrelated pictures). For the later retention sequence, no differences in forgetting were observed for grade 8 students, whereas for college students, differences were confined to retrieval failures on word lists (16′- > 30-days for both related and unrelated). Once again, average rates of forgetting tended to be larger for the later sequence than the earlier sequence, particularly for storage (grade 8 students .09 and .33 for early and late, respectively; college .09 and .36 for early and late, respectively) than for retrieval failures (grade 8 students .08 and .15 for early and late, respectively; college students .07 and .13 for early and late, respectively) with no differences in these averages across age.

Differences in storage-based reminiscence were restricted to related lists in the later sequence for grade 8 (16′- > 30-days for related pictures and words), but occurred both early and late for college (2- > 16-days for related pictures and words, 16- > 2-days for unrelated words; 16′- > 30-days for related pictures). Although the average and cumulative rates did not differ as a function of sequence timing for grade 8 (.06 and .21, respectively, for both early and late sequences), they tended to be larger for the early (.15 and .45, respectively) than the late sequence (.03 and .12, respectively) for the college students.

All retrieval-based reminiscence differences were confined to errors, but did not consistently favor one time interval over another. Grade 8 children were better at 16- than 2-days on unrelated pictures (f_1 and f_3) but were better at 2- than 16-days on related pictures (f_2). These same children were better on 16′- than 30-days on unrelated pictures (f_1 and f_3), but were better on 30- than 16′-days on related pictures (f_2). College students were better on 2- than 16-days on unrelated pictures (f_1 and f_2), related pictures (f_2), and related words (f_1), but were better on 16- than 2-days on related pictures (f_1) and unrelated words (f_3). They were also better at 16′- than 30-days on unrelated pictures (f_1), but better on 30- than 16′-days on related pictures (f_2) and words (f_2). As before, although error-contingent retrieval declined across trials, no differences in the average rate of this statistic were obtained as a function of age, materials, or time of the retention test sequence.

Time of Test

For grade 8 at T_1, more storage failures were observed on 16′- than 2-days for unrelated lists (both pictures and words) and more retrieval failures on related lists (both pictures and words). For college students at T_1, more storage failures were observed on 16′- than 2-days (all lists) and more retrieval failures were observed on all but the unrelated picture list. Differences in the average magnitude of storage and retrieval failures were larger at 16′-days (.35 and .17, respectively, for grade 8; .38 and .17, respectively, for college) than at 2-days (.08 for both, grade 8; .06 and .05, respectively, for college).

At T_2, there were more storage failures (unrelated pictures and words and related pictures) than retrieval failures (unrelated pictures and words) for grade 8 at 30- than 16-days. For college, there were more storage failures at 30- than 16-days (all lists) and one retrieval failure favoring 16- over 30-days (unrelated words). Like T_1, differences in the average magnitude of storage and retrieval failure rates at T_2 were larger on the later test (at 30-days—.31 and .13, respectively, for grade 8; .34 and .08, respectively, for college) than the earlier test (16-days—.09 and .08, respectively, grade 8; .10 and .12, respectively, for college).

Differences in storage-based reminiscence were again small in absolute terms. At T_1, only one difference was obtained for grade 8 (related pictures, 16′- > 2-days) and two for college (related pictures and words, 2- > 16′-days). At T_2, no differences were obtained for grade 8 but two were found for college (related pictures and unrelated words), each of which favored 16- over 30-days. Average and cumulative rates did not differ across age at T_1 (.07 and .25, respectively, for grade 8, and .12 and

.36, respectively, for college) or at T_2 (.05 and .17, respectively, for grade 8 and .06 and .20, respectively, for college).

Differences in error-contingent retrieval-based reminiscence were obtained at T_1 for grade 8 favoring 2- over 16′-day for related pictures and words (f_2), favoring 16′- over 2-days for unrelated pictures (f_1 and f_3), and for college favoring 2- over 16′-days for related pictures (f_2) and words (f_1 and f_2) and for 16′- over 2-days for related pictures (f_1). At T_2, differences for grade 8 were obtained on unrelated pictures (f_1 and f_3) and words (f_1) favoring 16- over 30-days and for college on unrelated words (f_2) favoring 16- over 30-days and for 30- over 16-days on unrelated pictures (f_2) and related pictures (f_2) and words (f_2). Although error-contingent retrieval declined across trials, no differences in the average rate of this statistic were obtained as a function of age, materials, or T_1 versus T_2.

Test versus No-Test Effects

Regardless of age, more forgetting was observed at 16′- than 16-days. For grade 8, storage failures (all lists) occurred more frequently than retrieval failures (unrelated lists only). For college, storage failures occurred on three lists (unrelated pictures and words and related words) and retrieval failures on two lists (related pictures and unrelated words). The average rate of storage failure was higher than that for retrieval failure at 16′-days (.35 and .17, respectively, for grade 8, and .38 and .17, respectively, for college) but not at 16-days (.09 and .08, respectively, for grade 8, and .10 and .12, respectively, for college). These rates did not vary with age.

Three storage-based reminiscence differences were observed for grade 8, one favoring 16- over 16′-days (unrelated pictures) and the others favoring 16′- over 16-days (related lists). For college, two differences were obtained, both of which favored 16- over 16′-days (related pictures and unrelated words). The only age difference in average or cumulative rates was higher values for college on 16-day (.11 and .37, respectively) than 16′-day (.05 and .19, respectively), whereas no differences were obtained for grade 8. The only differences in success-contingent retrieval-based reminiscence were obtained at 16′-day for both ages where average rates were better on r_1 (.95 and .94, respectively, for grade 8 and college) than on Trial 1 ($1 - R = .83$ for both grade 8 and college). No systematic differences in error-contingent retrieval-based reminiscence were obtained for grade 8 (unrelated words only, with one difference favoring 16- over 16′-days, f_1, and one favoring 16′- over 16-days, f_2) or for college (with some differences favoring 16- over 16′-days, related pictures f_1, unrelated words f_2, and related words f_2; and others favoring 16′- over 16-days, unrelated pictures, f_1 and f_2). Although error-contingent retrieval declined across trials, no differences in the average rate of this statistic were obtained as a function of age, materials, or 16- versus 16′-days.

Summary

The effects of testing and timing were generally larger in terms of forgetting than reminiscence, although this difference was not as pronounced as in Experiment 1. Regardless of age, the effects of repeated testing on forgetting were larger on the later than the earlier sequence. Storage-based reminiscence rates were higher on the later sequence for grade 8 students, but tended to be higher on the early sequences for college subjects. More forgetting was observed on the first retention test than on the second indicating that one effect of a preceding test is to ameliorate forgetting on a subsequent test *regardless of the timing of these tests*. This latter effect was more evident when performance at 16 days is considered with (16-days) and without (16′-days) a preceding test of retention. Here, less forgetting occurred when a preceding test had been administered than when it had not. Interestingly, more storage-based reminiscence was observed at 16 days when a preceding test had been administered, but these effects were confined to college students.

Summary of Results for Experiment 2

Overall, these results again indicate that differences in retention were primarily controlled by forgetting, not by reminiscence processes. Specifically, regardless of age, storage failures were more common than retrieval failures, and the magnitude of these effects did not differ with age. As in Experiment 1, forgetting in both age groups was more responsive to semantic factors than presentation modality, with more forgetting for unrelated than related items. As before, forgetting increased with the length of the retention interval and was attenuated following a 2-week interval by the presentation of an earlier test of retention, *regardless of when this first test was administered*. More forgetting occurred on the first test of retention than on the second retention test regardless of the timing of these tests, and less forgetting occurred at 16 days when a preceding test had been administered (at 2 days) than when no test preceded the 16-day test.

Again, hypermnesia was controlled by both storage-based and, to a lesser extent, success-contingent retrieval-based, reminiscence. Storage-based reminiscence contributed to trace recovery for both related and unrelated materials and pictures and words, and tended to be higher on earlier retention tests. Success-contingent retrieval-based reminiscence tended to be constant across most of the factors in this experiment and was consistently high. Finally, the main results for error-contingent retrieval were again that regardless of the manipulation under consideration, this form of reminiscence *declined* across test trials.

General Discussion

In contrast to the robust developmental changes that are routinely observed in children's acquisition abilities, few researchers, until recently, have concerned themselves with similar developments in long-term retention skills. It is now clear that previous reports in which developmental changes in retention were absent are subject to stages-of-learning confounds and failures to use sensitive measurement techniques. Because of these past inadequacies, current theorizing about memory development in childhood has been restricted to processes governing the initial memorization of information, leaving our understanding of the ontogeny of retention processes at a primitive level.

Our objective in this chapter has been to change this state of affairs by (a) eliminating stages-of-learning confounds through imposing a common learning criterion that ensured (mathematically) equivalent levels of information acquisition, and (b) decomposing retention data into processes responsible for performance erosion over the retention interval (storage- and retrieval-based forgetting) and processes that reinstate performance during the retention tests (storage- and retrieval-based reminiscence). In addition, we examined the impact of two sets of factors: (a) variables (modality and semantic) whose effects, although known to positively affect acquisition performance, are unclear at retention; and (b) variables (time and number of retention sessions) whose effects are said to enhance retention performance.

At a global level, the critical findings that emerged from this research were that regardless of the variables under consideration, (a) developmental differences at retention were dominated by shifts in forgetting, not reminiscence, and (b) storage processes (both forgetting and reminiscence) were as important, if not more important, than retrieval processes at retention. This latter finding is particularly critical because (a) theories of children's acquisition stress the importance of changes in *retrieval* processes as the primary contributor to the development of long-term memory (e.g., Howe, Brainerd, & Kingma, 1985), and (b) many current theorists hold that retention levels are controlled primarily by changes in the *retrievability* of information that is still in storage. With regard to the first point, it may be the case that the development of acquisition and retention components of long-term memory are governed by different rules (also see Brainerd et al., 1985; Howe & Brainerd, 1989; Howe & Hunter, 1986). If this is so, then it is particularly important to expand research efforts on the development of retention processes.

With regard to the second point, our results suggest that, consistent with some theorists (e.g., Chechile, 1987; Loftus & Loftus, 1980), retention performance is also mediated by changes that take place in the availability of information in storage (both in terms of information erosion and reinstatement). In the remainder of this chapter, we discuss these findings along with the questions concerning the role of forgetting and reminiscence processes in the development of long-term retention, and we interpret these findings in terms of the trace-integrity model.

Forgetting: The Contribution of Storage and Retrieval Failures

As indicated above, from a theoretical standpoint, perhaps the most important finding to emerge at forgetting was the robust pattern of storage failures. The grand mean across experiments for storage failures (.27, .21, .21, and .22, for grades 2, 5, 8, and college, respectively) exceeded that for retrieval failures (.08, .12, .11, and .10, for grades 2, 5, 8, and college, respectively). Given the apparent generality of this pattern it would appear that theorists who view forgetting as arising solely from failures to access stored information need to revise this position to include the important role that failures in trace availability play in determining amnesia across the retention interval.

In terms of developmental differences in storage and retrieval failures, the data clearly showed the presence of distinct trends for young elementary schoolers (Experiment 1), but few consistent differences for older students (Experiment 2). Specifically, relative to grade 5 children, grade 2 students experienced more storage failures. On the other hand, relative to grade 2 children, grade 5 students experienced more retrieval failures. Because acquisition levels were equated in this study, this difference cannot be attributed to younger children having more poorly encoded traces at acquisition than older children. Rather, these results are consistent with the general notion that differences in young children's amnesia rates are due to differences in processes that mediate the stability of memory traces in storage.

In Experiment 2, developmental differences in storage and retrieval failure rates were generally confined to later tests of retention and were more responsive to the modality manipulation than in Experiment 1. Specifically, few systematic differences emerged between grade 8 and college students, with both age groups experiencing relatively more storage or retrieval failures than the other depending on whether pictures (grade 8 worse than college) or words (college worse than grade 8) were being recalled.

Another important set of findings at forgetting concerns the relative contribution of storage and retrieval failures arising from modality and semantic manipulations. Although both of these factors have positive effects at acquisition, semantic factors were considerably more important at forgetting than modality, regardless of age. When differences did emerge for the modality manipulation they tended to favor pictures over words, regardless of age, and were not systematically related to type of forgetting. For the semantic manipulation, on the other hand, differences uniformly favored the related clusters, with the primary form of forgetting of unrelated clusters in all of the experiments being storage failures. Thus, regardless of age, forgetting was attenuated by the presence of features that bind elements of a trace together.

Finally, consider the effects of the timing and number of retention tests on forgetting. Here, regardless of which experiment is under consideration, more forgetting occurred on later retention tests (at the 16′-/30-day retention tests) than on early retention tests. In both experiments, forgetting differences as a function of the timing of the test were due principally to storage failures. Moreover, the effects of the first retention test upon the second depended on the timing of the former test. Specifically, if the first test occurred at 2 days, additional forgetting was observed at 16 days, whereas if the first test occurred at 16′ days, little forgetting occurred at 30 days. Thus, timing of the first test is important in determining the amount of forgetting on a second test, at least across a 2-week interval.

This effect was also seen in comparisons of retention after a 16-day interval when a preceding test had, or had not, been administered. Here, considerably more forgetting occurred in the absence of a prior (2-day) test of retention. Interestingly, the source of this forgetting varied with age in Experiment 1 such that for grade 2, the differences occurred primarily in storage failures and for grade 5 these differences occurred at retrieval. No differences in forgetting loci were observed in Experiment 2. Overall, then, the impact of a prior test of retention is to attenuate the rate of forgetting. This finding is consistent with previous evidence (e.g., Richardson, 1985) and also tells us that the loci of forgetting differences due to the timing and number of tests varies with age for young elementary schoolers, but tends to stabilize in older children and adults.

These trends in forgetting are important because they underscore the fact that amnesia is comprised of both storage and retrieval failures. Clearly, the forgetting-as-retrieval-failure scenario must be revised. Our findings clearly show that amnesia is dominated at all ages by forgetting-as-storage-failure. Importantly, contrary to the traditional view that storage failure means trace absence, our data showed that storage failures were not permanent and that traces could be reinstated even when they fell below the zero-recall threshold! As will be seen in the next section, storage-based reminiscence was one of the chief contributors to the hypermnesia observed across test trials at retention. Such results, although inconsistent with trace-absence metaphors, are consistent with the featural disintegration interpretation of storage-based forgetting (Howe & Brainerd, 1989). Rather than assuming trace absence, this hypothesis views storage failure as an extreme case of trace disintegration, a process that results in the loss of trace integrity reducing discriminability of that trace against the background of more intact traces. More importantly, because loss of integrity is a gradual, not an all-or-none, process, traces can be redintegrated on retention tests. It is this latter process that mediates the phenomenon of storage-based reminiscence. The advantage of this proposal lies not only in the fact that it unifies storage-related and retrieval-related forgetting within a single framework, but, more importantly, it views forgetting and reminiscence as the result of a single underlying mechanism, namely, the "integrity" of bonds that unite primitive elements to form a cohesive memory trace.

Reminiscence: The Contribution of Storage and Retrieval

A common finding in studies of long-term retention is that as test trials proceed, performance levels recover, sometimes to near acquisition levels. This hypermnesic phenomenon, although well documented, is not clearly understood. To better understand this phenomenon, the model used here partitioned hypermnesia during the retention phase into two primary components, namely, storage-based reminiscence and retrieval-based reminiscence following test trial successes and errors. Using this partitioning, several interesting findings emerged.

First, consistent with the disintegration/redintegration hypothesis, storage-based reminiscence contributed significantly to trace recovery *regardless of age*. Second, whereas retrieval-based reminiscence following a success was either constant across trials or tended to increase between the first and subsequent test trials, retrieval-based reminiscence following an error declined across retention test trials. Unlike forgetting, storage-based and retrieval-based reminiscence contributions to hypermnesia were generally unreactive to differences in age, modality, or semantic factors. Apparently, contrary to findings in the adult literature, hypermnesia in a cued recall context is no more prominent when presentation modality is varied than when semantic cohesion is manipulated (although clearly this conclusion must be tempered by the presence of ceiling effects in some comparisons). Moreover, storage-based and retrieval-based reminiscence did not vary consistently with the number or timing of retention tests. Rather, hypermnesia effects tend to be some constant of multiple testing opportunities. Thus, it would appear that (a) developmental gains in long-term retention are controlled primarily by alterations in forgetting rates, not reminiscence, and (b) hypermnesia occurs simply as a function of opportunities to recall.

General Implications and Conclusions

A comprehensive theory of memory development must include axioms pertaining to processes that govern both the acquisition of memory traces and the retention of those traces over time. Although it is still somewhat premature to articulate a complete theory, the findings that have emerged here represent a promising step forward. Equally important, the findings demonstrate the utility of translating theoretical memory constructs into measurable quantities (parameters) embedded within a model of the process under study. Although other models containing different parameter configurations will almost certainly be developed, the important point to bear in mind is that it is through the use of such modeling techniques that the operational precision required to advance theory is obtained.

At a general level, perhaps the single most important result to emerge from this study concerns the finding that amnesia involved both storage failures and retrieval failures, and that hypermnesia involves both storage-based and (success-contingent) retrieval-based reminiscence. It can be argued, therefore, that the debate concerning whether amnesia and hypermnesia are by-products of changes in the availability of the memory trace or of changes in trace accessibility is now a pseudoissue in the study of long-term retention. Clearly, attention should be focused on measuring the relative contribution of each of these changes to performance across a variety of conditions, retention intervals, and ages. In addition, what is needed is a theory that treats storage and retrieval as different aspects of a single process. In line with current feature-based accounts of memory representation, the disintegration/redintegration metaphor developed by Howe and Brainerd (1989) serves as a good organizing principle. The advantage of this hypothesis lies not only in the fact that it views storage and retrieval as different components of a single process, but also in that it serves to integrate the literatures on amnesia and hypermnesia. Specifically, both amnesia and hypermnesia can be treated as two different components (disintegration and redintegration, respectively) of a single mechanism, degree of trace integrity.

Another advantage is that the hypothesis makes contact with general theories of memory development including knowledge-base models (e.g., Bjorklund, 1987) and working memory models (e.g., Brainerd & Kingma, 1985; Brainerd & Reyna, 1988b). For example, in line with Bjorklund's knowledge-base theory, the present study found that the presence of semantic features retarded disintegration (less storage-based forgetting). However, presentation of a cue did not tend to redintegrate these traces more than other, unrelated materials, although these effects must be cautiously interpreted due to ceiling effects. And, like the findings from working-memory analyses, the best fitting explanation of the entire data pattern was one in which it was assumed that (a) the bonds that tie features together into a trace gradually erode over long periods of time, and (b) traces can be redintegrated by reconstructive-processing operations that are activated on retention tests.

Acknowledgments. Preparation of this chapter and the research reported herein were supported by grant OGP0003334 to the first author from the Natural Sciences and Engineering Research Council of Canada. Portions of this research were presented at the Biennial Meeting of the Society for Research in Child Development, Kansas City, Missouri, April, 1989.

References

Ackerman, B.P. (1985). Children's retrieval deficit. In C.J. Brainerd & M.Pressley (Eds.), *Basic processes in memory development: Progress in cognitive development research* (pp. 1–46). New York: Springer-Verlag.

Ackerman, B.P. (1987). Descriptions: A model of nonstrategic memory development. In H.W.Reese (Ed.), *Advances in child development and behavior* (Vol. 20, pp. 143–183). New York: Academic Press.

Allen, G.A., Mahler, W.A., & Estes, W.K. (1969). Effects of recall tests on long-term retention of paired associates. *Journal of Verbal Learning and Verbal Behavior*, *8*, 463–470.

Anderson, J.R. (1980). Concepts, propositions, and schemata: What are the cognitive units? *Nebraska Symposium of Motivation*, *28*, 121–162.

Ballard, P.B. (1913). Obliviscence and reminiscence. *British Journal of Psychology Monograph Supplements*, *1*, 1–82.

Battig, W.F., & Montague, W.E. (1969). Category norms for verbal items in 56 categories: A replication and extension of the Connecticut category norms. *Journal of Experimental Psychology Monograph*, *80*(3, Pt. 2).

Belmore, S.M. (1981). Imagery and semantic elaboration in hypermnesia for words. *Journal of Experimental Psychology: Human Learning and Memory*, *7*, 191–203.

Bjorklund, D.F. (1987). How age changes in knowledge base contribute to the development of children's memory: An interpretive review. *Developmental Review*, *7*, 93–130.

Brainerd, C.J., Howe, M.L., & Kingma, J. (1982). An identifiable model of two-stage learning. *Journal of Mathematical Psychology*, *26*, 263–293.

Brainerd, C.J., & Kingma, J. (1985). On the independence of short-term memory and working memory in cognitive development. *Cognitive Psychology*, *17*, 210–247.

Brainerd, C.J., Kingma, J., & Howe, M.L. (1985). On the development of forgetting. *Child Development*, *56*, 1103–1119.

Brainerd, C.J., & Reyna, V. F. (1988a). *Development of retention: Amnesia, hypermnesia, forgetting, and reminiscence.* Unpublished manuscript, University of Arizona.

Brainerd, C.J., & Reyna, V. F. (1988b). Generic resources, reconstructive processing, and children's mental arithmetic. *Developmental Psychology*, *24*, 324–334.

Brainerd, C.J., Reyna, V. F., Howe, M.L., & Kingma, J. (1990). Development of forgetting and reminiscence. *Monographs of the Society for Research in Child Development*, *55*(3–4, Serial No. 222).

Ceci, S.J., Toglia, M.P., & Ross, D.F. (Eds.). (1987). *Children's eyewitness memory*. New York: Springer-Verlag.

Chechile, R.A. (1987). Trace susceptibility theory. *Journal of Experimental Psychology: General, 116*, 203–222.

Chechile, R.A., & Ehrensbeck, K. (1983). Long-term storage losses: A dilemma for multistore models. *Journal of General Psychology, 109*, 15–30.

Deffenbacher, K. A., Carr, T.H., & Leu, J.R. (1981). Memory for words, pictures, and faces: Retroactive interference, forgetting, and reminiscence. *Journal of Experimental Psychology: Human Learning and Memory, 7*, 299–305.

Dent, H.R., & Stevenson, G.M. (1979). An experimental study of the effectiveness of different techniques of questioning child witnesses. *British Journal of Social and Clinical Psychology, 18*, 41–51.

Eich, J.M. (1982). A composite holographic associative recall model. *Psychological Review, 89*, 627–661.

Erdelyi, M., Buschke, H., & Finkelstein, S. (1977). Hypermnesia for Socratic stimuli: The growth of recall for an internally generated memory list abstracted from a series of riddles. *Memory & Cognition, 5*, 283–286.

Erdelyi, M., & Stein, J. (1981). Recognition hypermnesia: The growth of recognition memory (d′) over time with repeated testing. *Cognition, 9*, 23–33.

Eugenio, P., Buckout, R., Kostes, S., & Ellison, K. (1982). Hypermnesia in the eyewitness to a crime. *Bulletin of the Psychonomic Society, 19*, 83–86.

Fajnsztejn-Pollack, G. (1973). A developmental study of decay rate in long-term memory. *Journal of Experimental Child Psychology, 16*, 225–235.

Greenough, W.T., & Bailey, C.H. (1988). The anatomy of a memory: Convergence of results across a variety of tests. *Trends in Neuroscience, 11*, 142–147.

Hasher, L., & Thomas, H. (1973). A developmental study of retention. *Developmental Psychology, 9*, 281.

Horowitz, L.M., & Prytulak, L.S. (1969). Redintegrative memory. *Psychological Review, 76*, 519–531.

Howe, M.L. (1985). Storage and retrieval of associative clusters: A stages-of-learning analysis of associative memory traces. *Canadian Journal of Psychology, 39*, 34–53.

Howe, M.L. (1987). *The development of forgetting in childhood.* Paper presented at the biennial meeting of the Society for Research in Child Development, Baltimore, Maryland.

Howe, M.L. (1991). Misleading children's story recall: Forgetting and reminiscence of the facts. *Developmental Psychology, 27*, 746–762.

Howe, M.L., & Brainerd, C.J. (1989). Development of children's long-term retention. *Developmental Review, 9*, 301–340.

Howe, M.L., Brainerd, C.J., & Kingma, J. (1985). Development of organization in recall: A stages-of-learning analysis. *Journal of Experimental Child Psychology, 39*, 230–251.

Howe, M.L., & Hunter, M.A. (1986). Long-term memory in adulthood: An examination of the development of storage and retrieval processes at acquisition and retention. *Developmental Review, 6*, 334–364.

Kagan, J., Klein, R., & Haith, M., & Morrison, F. (1973). Memory and meaning in two cultures. *Child Development, 44*, 221–223.

Kail, R., & Leonard, L.B. (1986). Sources of word-finding problems in language-impaired children. In S.J.Ceci (Ed.), *Handbook of cognitive, social, and neuropsychological aspects of learning disabilities* (Vol. 1, pp. 185–202). Hillsdale, NJ: Erlbaum.

Lehman, E.B., Mikesell, J.W., & Doherty, S.C. (1985). Long-term retention of information about presentation modality by children and adults. *Memory & Cognition*, *13*, 21–28.

Loftus, E.F. (1983). Misfortunes of memory. *Philosophical Transactions of the Royal Society of London*, *B302*, 413–421.

Loftus, E.F., & Loftus, G.R. (1980). On the permanence of stored information in the human brain. *American Psychologist*, *35*, 409–420.

Madigan, S. (1976). Reminiscence and item recovery in free recall. *Memory & Cognition*, *4*, 233–236.

McClelland, J.L., & Rumelhart, D.E. (1985). *Parallel distributed processing: Explorations in the microstructure of cognition. Vol. II: Psychological and biological models*. Cambridge, MA: Bradford.

McDaniel, M.A., & Masson, M.E.J. (1985). Altering memory representations through retrieval. *Journal of Experimental Psychology: Learning, Memory, and Cognition*, *11*, 371–385.

Morrison, F., Haith, M., & Kagan, J. (1980). Age trends in recognition memory for pictures: The effects of delay and testing procedure. *Bulletin of the Psychonomic Society*, *16*, 480–483.

Murdock, B.B., Jr. (1982). A theory for the storage and retrieval of item and associative information. *Psychological Review*, *89*, 609–626.

Nelson, K. C. (1971). Memory development in children: Evidence from nonverbal tasks. *Psychonomic Science*, *25*, 346–348.

Paris, S.G. (1978). Memory organization during children's repeated recall. *Developmental Psychology*, *14*, 99–106.

Paris, S.G., & Lindauer, B.K. (1977). Constructive aspects of children's comprehension and memory. In R.Kail & J.Hagen (Eds.), *Perspectives on the development of memory and cognition* (pp. 35–60). Hillsdale, NJ: Erlbaum.

Payne, D.G. (1987). Hypermnesia and reminiscence in recall: A historical and empirical review. *Psychological Bulletin*, *101*, 5–27.

Piaget, J., & Inhelder, B. (1973). *Memory and intelligence*. New York: Basic Books.

Raaijmakers, J.G.W., & Shiffrin, R.M. (1981). Search of associative memory. *Psychological Review*, *88*, 93–134.

Richardson, J.T.E. (1985). The effects of retention tests upon human learning and memory: An historical review and an experimental analysis. *Educational Psychology*, *5*, 85–114.

Roediger, H.L., Payne, D.G., Gillespie, G.L., & Lean, D.S. (1982). Hypermnesia as determined by level of recall. *Journal of Verbal Learning and Verbal Behavior*, *21*, 635–655.

Rogoff, B., Newcombe, N., & Kagan, J. (1974). Planfulness and recognition memory. *Child Development*, *45*, 872–877.

Runquist, W.N. (1983). Some effects of remembering on forgetting. *Memory & Cognition*, *11*, 641–650.

Scrivner, E., & Safer, M.A. (1988). Eyewitnesses show hypermnesia for details about a violent event. *Journal of Applied Psychology*, *73*, 371–377.

Shapiro, S.R., & Erdelyi, M. (1974). Hypermnesia for pictures but not words. *Journal of Experimental Psychology*, *103*, 1218–1219.

Shepard, R.N., & Chang, J.-J. (1963). Forced-choice tests of recognition memory under steady-state conditions. *Journal of Verbal Learning and Verbal Behavior*, *2*, 93–101.
Snodgrass, J.G., & Vanderwart, M. (1980). A standardized set of 260 pictures: Norms for name agreement, image agreement, familiarity, and visual complexity. *Journal of Experimental Psychology: Human Learning and Memory*, *6*, 174–215.
Sophian, C., & Perlmutter, M. (1980). Encoding and retention factors in the early development of recall. *Bulletin of the Psychonomic Society*, *15*, 342–344.
Toglia, M.P., & Battig, W.F. (1978). *Handbook of semantic word norms.* Hillsdale, NJ: Erlbaum.
Tulving, E. (1984). Precis of elements of episodic memory. *Behavioral and Brain Sciences*, *7*, 223–238.
Vertes, J.O. (1931/32). Behalten und vergessen des kindes [Retention and forgetting in the child]. *Zeitschrift fur Psychologie*, *122*, 241–354. *Psychological Abstracts*, 1932, *1221*, 145.
Wagner, D.A. (1978). Memories of Morocco: The influence of age, schooling, and environment on memory. *Cognitive Psychology*, *10*, 1–28.
Wickelgren, W.A. (1975). Age and storage dynamics in continuous recognition memory. *Developmental Psychology*, *11*, 165–169.
Wilkinson, A.C., & Koestler, R. (1983). Repeated recall: A new model and tests of its generality from childhood to old age. *Journal of Experimental Psychology: General*, *112*, 423–451.
Yarmey, D. (1976). Hypermnesia for pictures but not for concrete or abstract words. *Bulletin of the Psychonomic Society*, *8*, 115–117.

3
Reasoning, Remembering, and Their Relationship: Social, Cognitive, and Developmental Issues

VALERIE F. REYNA

In this age of specialization, the relationship between memory and reasoning-based judgments is one of the few topics that spans subdisciplines. In cognitive development, for example, much of the post-Piagetian revolution is predicated on explaining reasoning performance (i.e., the accuracy of judgments) in terms of memory constraints (e.g., Bjorklund, 1987, 1989; Brainerd, 1983a, 1983b; Bryant & Trabasso, 1971; Case, 1985; Dempster, 1981, 1985; Trabasso, 1977). At some disciplinary remove from cognitive development, social psychologists have looked to memory-judgment relationships to explain variations in attitudes and attributions (e.g., Cacciopo & Petty, 1985; Hastie & Park, 1986; Higgins & Stangor, 1988; Pratkanis, Greenwald, Leippe, & Baumgardner, 1988). Although there have been some notable exceptions in both fields (e.g., Anderson & Hubert, 1963; Brainerd & Kingma, 1984, 1985), most theorists have assumed a hand-in-glove relationship between memory and reasoning (or reasoning's product, judgment).

Fuzzy-trace theory has been developed with particular attention to the interplay between memory and reasoning (Brainerd & Reyna, 1990b; Reyna & Brainerd, 1990, 1991a). Therefore, I exploit fuzzy-trace theory here in order to discuss some perplexing results regarding reasoning-remembering relationships in the social, cognitive, and developmental literatures. The discussion is divided into two sections, one concerned primarily with short-term retention and the other with long-term retention. The focus is on retention, rather than acquisition, although differences between the two are briefly discussed. In the first section, I emphasize cognition, and illustrate conditions under which fuzzy-trace theory predicts such paradoxical findings as reasoning-remembering independence—that memory for the critical facts of a problem often has no bearing on its solution. In the subsequent section, I address the relationship between memory and social judgment, and the question of bias and suggestibility in long-term retention. Developmental considerations come into play in both sections—in the first, because age determines the nature of remembering, and in the second, through the concept of suggestibility in long-term retention. The discussion is guided by fuzzy-trace theory's fourfold distinction that can be applied to memory performance, whether short- or long-term, namely that it can be based on retrieval of gist or verbatim traces, or on reconstruction of either type of trace.

Short-Term Retention

The Paradox of Reasoning-Remembering Independence

What is the relationship between reasoning and the ability to remember critical informational inputs to reasoning? There are two classic answers to this question, answers that dispute the nature of memory itself. The first and older answer, which has the aura of common sense if not self-evidence, is that retention of decisive information is a necessary precondition for accurate reasoning. In the developmental literature, this position is well illustrated by any number of methodological tracts, some recent ones (e.g., Brainerd, 1983b; Rabinowitz, Howe, & Lawrence, 1989) and some early ones (e.g., Elkind, 1967; Smedslund, 1969) that list as a major source of error children's inability to remember critical background facts long enough to complete a sequence of reasoning operations. In research with adults, the accuracy of reasoning is said to be inherently nonoptimal because it is bound by the limitations of working memory, as well as other cognitive constraints (e.g., Nisbett & Ross, 1980; Simon, 1988). Thus, research with both children and adults assumes that correct reasoning requires, at least, the ability to remember critical information long enough to process it.

Another perspective on the reasoning-remembering relationship grows out of the Bartlett (1932) tradition and was made popular among students of development by Piaget (1968; Piaget & Inhelder, 1973). This constructivist view holds that the nature of reasoning controls what can be remembered about pertinent informational inputs (Bransford & Franks, 1971). Children, for example, can accurately remember certain types of information to the extent that they have developed the reasoning operations that process such information: "The schemata used by the memory are borrowed from the intelligence" (Piaget & Inhelder, 1973, p. 382). Research in this vein with adults is designed to demonstrate that understanding influences memory, for example by determining how information is encoded (Bransford & Johnson, 1973; Kintsch, 1974).

Despite their differences, note that both approaches to the reasoning-remembering relationship imply dependence, in one case because memory requires accurate reasoning and in the other case because reasoning requires accurate memory. In this context, the reasoning/remembering independence effect (or simply *memory independence*) is informative because we must look beyond our usual assumptions in order to explain its existence. The basic datum is simple enough. Solutions to a variety of familiar reasoning problems are independent of short-term memory for background facts that are essential to such solutions (Brainerd, 1985; Brainerd & Kingma, 1985; Brainerd & Reyna, 1988a; Reyna & Brainerd, 1990). Because memory independence occurs across the same age spans in which performance on both reasoning problems and memory measures are steadily improving, it seems that the development of reasoning does not depend in any direct way on the development of memory, even memory for information that is purportedly used in reasoning, and conversely.

The literature on transitivity development is perhaps the best forum in which to illustrate memory independence itself and the challenges it poses for traditional views of reasoning and remembering. The standard problem involves three-term series of the form $A > B > C$. The relationships between the adjacent terms ($A > B$, $B > C$) are presented as background facts, with children then being interrogated about the relationship between the nonadjacent terms. In a recent review of this literature (Reyna & Brainerd, 1990), it was shown that extant studies can be assembled into three historical stages that vary in their assumptions about the role of children's memory for adjacent relationships in transitive inference.

Stage 1 was dominated by Piaget's (e.g., 1970; Piaget & Inhelder, 1969) analysis of transitivity, which claimed that transitive inference consists of deducing the AC relationship from the logical givens that are inherent in the AB and BC relationships. That is, transitivity was treated as a form of deductive logic in which the adjacent relationships play the role of axioms. Children's ability to remember adjacent relationships long enough to effect their deductions was not seriously questioned. So, children who failed transitivity problems were deficient in basic logical competence.

Stage 2 was characterized by an intensive concern with the role of logic versus memory. Certain investigators proposed that children might simply be unable to remember one or both of the adjacent relationships (e.g., Bryant & Trabasso, 1971; Roodin & Gruen, 1970; Trabasso, 1977). It was argued that preschoolers are not logically deficient and, instead, that their reasoning errors were rooted in short-term memory failures. For instance, Bryant and Trabasso (1971) proposed that $p(AC) = p(AB) \times p(BC)$, where $p(AC)$ is the probability of making a transitive inference and $p(AB)$ and $p(BC)$ are the probabilities of correct performance on memory probes for the relevant adjacent relationships. Such arguments were not based on the standard Piagetian transitivity paradigm, however, but on data from an overlearning variant in which children receive extensive training on adjacent relationships and transitivity problems are not posed until memory for these relationships is assured. With this procedure, it was found that inference rates significantly improved for preschoolers and were essentially perfect for older children (Reyna & Brainerd, 1990).

The memory hypothesis proposed by Bryant and Trabasso, that memory for adjacent relationships wholly determined reasoning performance, was soon amended. Investigators who were more sympathetic to logic-based interpretations began exploring the possibility that memory for adjacent relationships is not sufficient for reasoning. Consistent with the insufficiency hypothesis, it was reported that children who are able to retrieve adjacent relationships on memory tests often fail to make the indicated transitive inference (see Grieve & Nesdale, 1979; Halford & Galloway, 1977; Russell, 1981). Although such results indicated that memory was not sufficient for reasoning, nevertheless, it was widely agreed that memory was necessary. Indeed, the overlearning data continued to be interpreted as showing that variations in memory were an important source of variations in reasoning performance. Thus, the essential theme of Stage 2 research was preserved, despite qualifications regarding sufficiency—memory was viewed as a critical factor in transitivity performance.

During Stage 3, the radical hypothesis that memory for adjacent relationships may not be necessary for transitive inference was introduced. The overlearning procedure was replaced because it is subject to a crucial methodological shortcoming, namely that it eliminates the very processes used to solve transitivity problems in the standard procedure (see Brainerd & Kingma, 1984; Reyna & Brainerd, 1990). That is, overlearning not only ensured memory for background facts, but it had the inadvertent effect of changing subjects' reasoning processes as well. Hence, reasoning in the standard task could not be explained by reference to results from the overlearning paradigm (Reyna & Brainerd, 1990). (Data from the overlearning paradigm remain relevant, however, to the question of how linear orderings are constructed solely from pairwise comparisons [see Reyna & Brainerd, in press].)

Therefore, Brainerd and Kingma (1984) developed an elementary modification of the standard transitivity procedure, the probe paradigm. Transitivity problems were administered in the normal way, except that memory probes for adjacent relationships were presented following children's responses to inference questions. In eight experiments with subjects in the 5- to 8-year-old range, Brainerd and Kingma discovered that children's ability to solve transitivity problems involving three-, four-, and five-term series was independent of their memory for adjacent relationships. Previously reported significant correlations between memory and reasoning performance had apparently masked underlying independence that could be detected with more direct tests of memory necessity, such as conditional analysis (Brainerd & Kingma, 1984; Reyna & Brainerd, 1990). This memory independence pattern has been replicated in several subsequent experiments (e.g., Brainerd, 1985; Brainerd &

Kingma, 1985; Chapman, 1989; Chapman & Lindenberger, 1988, in press) and has been found in reanalyses of published data (see Reyna & Brainerd, 1990, 1991a).

Memory independence has also been observed in connection with other familiar reasoning tasks. Examples include class inclusion, probability judgment, conservation, and decisions about text (Brainerd, 1985; Brainerd & Kingma, 1985; Callahan, 1989; Reyna & Brainerd, 1990, 1991a; Swanson, 1990). In each case, memory independence was noted within the age range during which most of the developmental variability in the target form of reasoning occurs. Thus, the nonnecessity of memory seems to be a robust finding, both in the sense that developmental variations in memory do not appear to underlie changes in reasoning, and in the sense that problem solving does not appear to call on memory for problem facts.

Explaining Memory Independence

Fuzzy-trace theory (Brainerd & Reyna, 1988a, 1990b; Reyna & Brainerd, 1990, 1991a) was motivated by the need for a plausible explanation of the fact that reasoning, and memory for information that is critical to reasoning, so often follow independent paths during processing, and developmentally. The explanation that was eventually favored by experimentation is that although reasoning problems and memory probes seem, on first impression, to tap the same memorial substratum, they do not. In the probe paradigm, memory tests typically place a premium on verbatim retention of the background facts (e.g., retention of specific cardinal numbers in probability judgment and class inclusion). At roughly the same time, however, problem information is also mined for senses, patterns, and other cognitive distillates (Brainerd & Reyna, 1990b). Consequently, children's working memories contain an assortment of problem-relevant information that has been extracted in parallel with the encoding of the original background data, information that varies from richly elaborated traces that preserve verbatim details to fuzzy, gist-like traces that preserve only the sense or pattern of the background facts (Reyna & Brainerd, 1991b). These fuzzy-to-verbatim continua are central to understanding cognition because reasoning is predisposed to operate on traces that are as near as possible to the fuzzy extremes of such continua (Brainerd & Reyna, 1988a). One reason for this fuzzy-processing preference is that, because gist is easy to retain but verbatim information decays rapidly, reasoning is naturally engineered to operate on the types of traces that are most likely to be available (Brainerd & Reyna, 1990b). Thus, reasoning performance often develops independently of memory performance in the probe paradigm because memory errors are chiefly due to the loss of verbatim information but reasoning errors are chiefly due to random failures in gist processing (Reyna & Brainerd, 1990).

To flesh out these assumptions, I return to some of the tasks in which reasoning/remembering relationships have been investigated. As noted, the prototypical situation is that memory probes measure verbatim retention of background facts, and reasoning problems measure the processing of gist that was extracted when these facts were encoded. The probe version of probability judgment (e.g., Brainerd, 1981) is illustrative. Subjects are first presented with the cardinal numbers of sets of common objects that comprise a hypothetical sampling space (e.g., Set $A = 7$ red balls, Set $B = 2$ white balls). Experimental evidence indicates that when these numbers are presented, adults and children (as young as age 4) also encode relational gist (e.g., "more *A*s than *B*s") and nominal gist (e.g., "a lot of *A*s"). After presentation, subjects predict a series of random draws from the sampling space (probability judgments) and answer probes for the numerical information. Although the probes query verbatim number memory, results from several experiments suggest that both children and adults base their probability judgments on nominal or relational gist (Brainerd, 1981, 1983a; Brainerd & Kingma, 1985; Callahan, 1989; Estes, 1976; Reyna & Brainerd, 1991b). For example, manipulations that should affect the retention of verbatim numerical information (e.g., increasing the number of values that children must encode; providing an external store of problem information), produce large variations in probe performance but not in probability judgment (Brainerd & Kingma, 1985). The gist on which probability judgments are based is relatively immune to memorial factors. The greater memorial stability of this gist is illustrated by two findings. First, if both verbatim memory probes and probes for relational or nominal gist are administered after a short sequence of probability judgments, the gist is almost invariably present whereas the verbatim numbers have often been lost (Brainerd, 1983a). Second, across such a sequence, the accuracy of probability judgments remains relatively constant, which would not be expected if the relevant memorial substratum is unstable, but performance on verbatim memory probes declines steadily (Brainerd, 1981).

Although it is prototypical for reasoning to be gist-based and for memory probes to tap verbatim information, tasks have been studied in which gist can also be used to answer probes. Transitivity is a case in point. The objects that comprise a target array are normally presented so that their spatial and/or temporal ordering is correlated with the magnitude differences between them. It has been found that, as information about the adjacent relationships is encoded, subjects also store global patterns such as "big things start on the left" and "things get smaller to the right" (for a review, see Reyna & Brainerd, 1990). Even preschoolers encode such patterns (Brainerd & Kingma, 1984), and the patterns are highly resistant to memory failure once they are stored (Reyna &

Brainerd, 1990). Subjects use these patterns both to make transitive inferences and to answer probes about adjacent relationships (Brainerd & Reyna, 1990b; Chapman & Lindenberger, 1988). In other words, they *reconstruct* adjacent relationships from stored *gist* rather than reading out stored verbatim information about those relationships. Consistent with this interpretation, probe performance is unresponsive to manipulations that should affect the availability of the latter information (e.g., varying the number of adjacent relationships that are initially encoded), and it improves across a sequence of repeated memory tests (Brainerd & Kingma, 1984; Chapman & Lindenberger, 1988).

The fact that memory independence has been observed with a paradigm in which reasoning and probe performance involve processing the same gist lends credence to the assumption that gist-processing errors tend to be random in such circumstances (Reyna & Brainerd, 1990). Such a conclusion is corroborated by the beneficial effects of mere practice, and by developmental improvements in performance, the ability to reliably execute operations, developmental constancy in competence, and the nature of processing in the task. Across tasks, the key commonality that seems to be associated with random errors in gist processing is the presence of an external memory support that stores the identity of verbatim elements. Thus, in transitivity, the seriation pattern must be gleaned from the informational inputs because differences in magnitude are not perceptible; however, the individual items need not be memorized, only the direction of "flow," i.e., whether the pattern is a progressively increasing or decreasing one. Problem solution involves reading off elements from the external array and combining the elements with one's memory for the seriation pattern (e.g., "The blue rod must be bigger than the red because I can see that it is on the left"). Thus, subjects apply spatial discrimination operations to the array both to answer transitivity questions (e.g., $A > C$ if A is to the left of C) and to answer memory probes (e.g., $B > C$ if B is to the left of C). Such spatial patterns, once they are extracted, are highly resistant to memory failure. Because memory for gist (the pattern of "flow") and the external array are highly reliable stores, errors are in performance, such as mishearing a question or misidentifying an item in the array. Such performance errors are, of course, random.

By removing such external supports for verbatim elements, it is possible to devise problems that are so constrained that extracted gist is insufficient for solution and, hence, the verbatim background facts must be remembered. Here, mental arithmetic is illustrative. In the mental arithmetic task, children are administered addition and subtraction problems involving small addends, followed by recall probes for the addends (Brainerd, 1983a, 1983b, 1987; Brainerd & Reyna, 1988a). The basic procedure involves presenting children with a linear array of familiar objects (e.g., a row of horses), designating one of the objects in the array as a target, assigning a number to the target, asking children to increment or decrement that target number by small amounts, and finally, following some problems, asking children to recall the number that was originally assigned to the target. Initially, arithmetic performance seemed to depend on children's ability to recall the numbers that were assigned to targets (Brainerd, 1983a, 1983b). However, subsequent research revealed that, surprisingly, recall depended on the accuracy of arithmetical reasoning rather than conversely. Specifically, it was found that children tended to answer recall probes by "working backward" from their solutions to arithmetic problems to the addends that were implied by those solutions. On a problem of the form $m + 2 = k$, for example, children answered m probes not by retrieving the value of m, but by *reconstructing* this *verbatim* value by performing the calculation $k - 2$ (Brainerd & Reyna, 1988a, Exp. 1). When manipulations were imposed that increased children's reliance on verbatim retrieval as opposed to reconstructive memory, the stochastic dependency between performance on arithmetic problems and performance on probes shrank (Brainerd & Reyna, 1988a, Exp. 2).

Therefore, when subjects are presented with problems of the form "if you had 5 cookies and I had 3 cookies, how many cookies would we have altogether," relational gist ("I have more cookies than he does"), nominal gist ("I have a lot of cookies"), and other forms of synoptic information will not support accurate reasoning. If the probe paradigm is employed with mental arithmetic problems, fuzzy-trace theory predicts pronounced reasoning/remembering dependencies because verbatim memory failures contribute to arithmetic performance as well as to probe performance, an outcome that has been consistently obtained (Brainerd, 1983b, 1987; Brainerd & Reyna, 1988a). Similarly, when the external array of verbatim elements is removed in the transitivity task, memory load (the number of premises) then affects reasoning performance (Chapman & Lindenberger, 1988). Note, again, that the external array cannot convey the transitive relationships in the series; differences in magnitude are not detectable by the subject. However, the array does index the verbatim elements (and their locations) so that the reasoner need not remember those particular facts. Everyday reasoning would seem to resemble the verbatim-supported situations, in which gist memory is combined with verbatim prosthetics, such as reference books, lists (e.g., grocery lists), on-line computer "help" options, and so on. Thus, reasoning-remembering independence would seem to be a common state of affairs, with reasoning dependence on verbatim memory requiring situations in which informational patterns and redundancies are impoverished. Whatever the nature of reasoning-remembering relationships in real life, however, it is clear across a wide array of experimental paradigms that subjects avoid reasoning with verbatim details wherever possible, operating instead on gist-like patterns, leaving their reasoning and remembering independent.

Summing up, applications of the probe paradigm have produced three types of relationships between reasoning and remembering: (a) memory independence, because reasoning performance is apparently based on gist, whereas memory performance is based on verbatim traces; (b) memory independence, because both reasoning and memory are based on gist, but errors are random, and therefore independent of one another; and (c) positive memory dependence when reasoning is compelled to tap the same verbatim substratum as memory performance. Standard problem solving paradigms tend to evoke memory independence because the differing specificity of questions allows gist processing to be sufficient for reasoning, whereas retrieval of verbatim background facts is necessary for probe performance (e.g., probability judgment, class inclusion). With such tasks, typical verbatim memory manipulations affect probe performance but not reasoning.[1] Independence is also observed when gist processing governs both reasoning and probe performance (e.g., transitivity) because gist-processing errors in such situations are uncorrelated with each other. In that case, neither reasoning nor probe performance reacts to verbatim memory manipulations. Last, positive dependence is observed in highly constrained situations where the verbatim background facts must be processed because gist will not support accurate reasoning (e.g., mental arithmetic). Research on the probe paradigm, then, argues for memory independence when reasoning involves gist processing, either because, in one class of tasks, reasoning errors are gist-processing failures and probe errors are verbatim memory failures or because, in another class of tasks, errors of both types are random gist-processing failures.

Development of Verbatim and Gist Memory

On the one hand, there is unmistakable evidence of gist extraction in both infrahumans and very young humans (for a review, see Brainerd & Reyna, 1990b). The formation of learning sets (e.g., Harlow, 1949) and cognitive maps (e.g., Tolman, 1948) are hoary illustrations of animal gist extraction. Concerning humans, infants and young children will store cross-modal analogies and other noliteral similarities in which connections between stimuli must exist at some level of abstraction (e.g., Reyna, 1981, 1985; Wagner, Winner, Cicchetti, & Gardner, 1981).

---

[1] Interestingly, such "classic" memory manipulations as load and delay do not necessarily affect memory rather than reasoning (Rabinowitz et al., 1989). When memory is well preserved despite added load or delay, such manipulations can nevertheless affect the complexity of processing (Reyna, 1991). As Rabinowitz et al. have shown, this relationship between "memory" manipulations and reasoning can be unmasked by fitting data with formal models that indicate whether such manipulations affect memory versus reasoning parameters.

On the other hand, there is equally unmistakable evidence that the ability to distill and store gist from the incoming flow of verbatim information develops. Behavioral and neurological evidence favor distinct developmental paths for verbatim memory and gist memory (Brainerd & Reyna, 1990b; Reyna & Brainerd, 1990, 1991a). Fuzzy-trace theory assumes, in connection with such evidence, that early in life human memory is specialized for storing and retrieving verbatim representations of encoded information. (This is not to say that gist is not extracted during early development, as noted above.) Hence, fuzzy-trace theory's basic claims are simply (a) that the memory systems that support retention of verbatim information exhibit rapid maturation and complete their ontogenesis rather early, (b) that the corresponding systems that support retention of senses and patterns exhibit slow maturation and complete their ontogenesis rather late, and (c) that there is a point (probably in early adolescence for most individuals) when verbatim systems begin to deteriorate while gist systems continue to improve.

The behavioral evidence for such claims is broad, but it is especially compelling when it comes to memory for verbal information. Evidence regarding the astonishing verbatim memory of younger children comes from sources ranging from experimental studies of verbal memory to naturalistic observations of children's memory in oral cultures (e.g., Hirsch, 1988). Brainerd and Reyna (1990b) concluded that the literature on first language acquisition supports the contention that such memory systems mature rapidly, and that the literature on second language acquisition supports the related contention that such systems begin to deteriorate rather early. In the former case, the fact that young children acquire a vocabulary comprised of thousands of new words during such a short period of time, roughly 14 new words per day by some estimates (Miller, 1981), attests to their powerful verbatim memory capabilities. In the latter case, the fact that the ability to acquire the vocabulary of a second language decreases steadily after about age 8, and is very limited after early adolescence (see Johnson & Newport, 1989), strongly suggests that verbatim memory systems begin to deteriorate as a consequence of central nervous system maturation (Lenneberg, 1967).

Concerning the development of memory for gist, there is a wealth of studies documenting the increasing tendency of older children to derive gist-like patterns from information, and to utilize those patterns in reasoning (Brainerd & Reyna, 1990b; Reyna & Brainerd, 1991a). For example, a number of studies have addressed developmental trends in the false recognition paradigm developed by Bransford and colleagues (Bransford, Barclay, & Franks, 1972; Bransford & Franks, 1971). In this paradigm, subjects are presented with propositions that can be integrated, for example into a spatial pattern, as in "Three turtles rested on a floating log and a fish swam beneath *it*." The result of principal interest is that adults are unable to distinguish the gist that they have constructed (that the fish swam beneath the *turtles*) from the verbatim sentences. Therefore, subjects falsely recognize story-consistent distractors at high levels of confidence, often at higher levels of confidence than sentences that were actually studied. A variant of this procedure has been used in several developmental studies (e.g., Johnson & Scholnick, 1979; Liben & Posnansky, 1977; Paris & Carter, 1973; Paris & Mahoney, 1974; Prawat & Cancelli, 1976). Like adults, children tend to falsely recognize true inferences that are consistent with the gist of a story. However, this tendency develops, with Weismer (1985), for instance, reporting that kindergarteners and second graders falsely recognized 63% and 75% of the true inferences, respectively. Of course, because younger children are *less* likely to respond on the basis of gist (as opposed to verbatim memory which the task requires), they are *less* prone to err on true inferences. Moreover, by unconfounding certain surface cues, Liben and Posnansky (1977) were able to show that, when younger children did falsely recognize true inferences, they did so based on verbatim cues rather than gist, whereas the reverse was true for older children. This and other research across varied tasks and stimuli suggests that the shift toward gist-based processing begins between kindergarten and second grade (the redoubtable five-to-seven shift, Stevenson, 1972), and predominates by age 9 or 10.

The most incisive evidence about verbatim-gist developmental trends, however, comes from studies in which the two are directly compared. Such studies by Marx (1985, 1986), Schmidt and her associates (e.g., Schmidt & Welch, 1989), Perner and Mansbridge (1983), and others converge on the conclusions that the relevant gist-memory systems evolve slowly and that they are still developing as verbatim systems begin their decline (Reyna & Brainerd, 1991a).

In memory for frequency, for example, Marx (1985, 1986) compared the development of a verbatim strategy (counting) to the development of a gist strategy (forming impressions of strength). He found that use of the verbatim strategy peaked sometime before age 10 and decreased thereafter. Use of the gist strategy continued to increase throughout adolescence and young adulthood. Similarly, Schmidt and her associates devised a technique for classifying children in terms of their ability to retain verbatim details of sentences relative to their ability to retain gist. With kindergartners, a majority of the children retained verbatim information better than gist. With second graders, the reverse was true. Comparing similar age groups, as noted earlier, Liben and Posnansky (1977) demonstrated that older children falsely recognized inferences because they were consistent with the gist of a story, but younger children responded to memory probes on the basis of verbatim similarity to actually presented sentences. Indeed, when verbatim information was a reliable cue, younger children were able to outperform older ones. Last, Perner and Mansbridge (1983) found that retention of verbatim information about ordered pairs peaked by age 7 and declined between early adolescence and young adulthood. However, memory for global magnitude patterns, ordered pairs that formed a series, improved steadily between age 5 and young adulthood. Yet another type of task, quite unlike memory for verbal information or frequency memory, namely face recognition, shows a similar developmental trend through similar age ranges: Memory for piecemeal stimulus characteristics is supplanted by an emphasis on configurational patterns (Carey & Diamond, 1977; Carey, Diamond, & Woods, 1980).

Behavioral evidence suggesting verbatim memory specialization during early development and gist memory specialization later on would make more sense, of course, if it could be demonstrated that the host neurological structures for verbatim and gist representations were different. Preliminary data of this sort are available in the neuropsychological literature (Granger & McNulty, 1986; Staubli, Ivy, & Lynch, 1984). Further, consistent with fuzzy-trace theory, the host structures for verbatim information are developmentally more primitive than those for gist (Brainerd & Reyna, 1990b). One specific type of lesion, of the connection between the dorsomedial nucleus of the thalamus and the frontal cortical system, prevents the acquisition of learning sets in discrimination tasks. According to Granger and McNulty, these rats are "learning specific memories" for correct responses, "but are failing to learn the template information" about the task (p. 42). Disconnection, or lesions, of the hippocampus, on the other hand, produces an apparent inverse of this result. Rats acquire learning sets, but, for a given discrimination, they cannot recall the right specific response if delays of more than 5 min are interposed between trials. Thus, the first group has specific memories, but lacks the gist, and the second group can acquire the gist, but forgets the details after short delays. The ease of acquisition of learning sets, and other kinds of abstract transfer of learning, increases phylogenetically and ontogenetically, that is, from animals to humans, and from younger to older children (Reyna & Brainerd, in press).

Thus, the early elementary years seem to be characterized by a verbatim-to-gist shift across a variety of stimulus domains from memory for faces to memory for stories. Interestingly, increasing gist-based processing does not necessarily lead to deterioration on verbatim tasks, unless tasks are designed so that gist information is orthogonal to verbatim information. In other words, gist memory can facilitate performance on what are ostensibly tests of verbatim memory. For example, recall of nonsense syllables can be vastly improved if they form a meaningful pattern (Glaze, 1928). As pointed out earlier, it is difficult to render a task gist-neutral. Memory probes that seem to tap only verbatim information can often be answered in at least two ways, in principle—simple readout of verbatim traces or reconstruction of information based on remembered gist. Thus, especially with meaningful material, subjects often have the option of verbatim retrieval or (at least some) gist reconstruction in order to correctly answer "verbatim" probes. Therefore, older children are acquiring an approach to thinking with broader utility, compared to a verbatim system, one that can apply to both gist and verbatim memory tasks (see Estes, 1980, for arguments supporting the superiority of fuzzy over precise memory for thinking).

These two claims, that there is a verbatim-to-gist developmental shift and that "verbatim" memory performance can be improved by gist memory, lead to two additional predictions. First and obviously, the tendency to rely on verbatim readout versus reconstruction will depend on the current state of memory specialization, with readout being favored during the years of verbatim specialization and reconstruction being favored thereafter. So, performance on tests that seem, on the surface, to be measuring verbatim retention (e.g., old-new recognition) ultimately come to be governed by reconstruction from gist. Second, relying on readout versus reconstruction when answering probes about verbatim information has consequences for accuracy, and those consequences vary as a function of the state of developmental specialization of memory. At first glance, it would seem natural to suppose that simply reading out verbatim traces would be more accurate than attempting to reconstruct verbatim information from gist. Developmental data suggest otherwise, however.

Here, the studies of Marx (1985, 1986), Perner and Mansbridge (1983), and Schmidt and her associates (e.g., Schmidt & Welch, 1989) are again apropos. As mentioned, Marx found that use of the verbatim strategy peaked and began to decline many years before the gist strategy had finished developing. In addition, however, he found a developmental crossover of the sort that is anticipated by fuzzy-trace theory. Among elementary schoolers, memory for verbatim frequency was in fact better in subjects who relied on the verbatim strategy than among subjects who relied on the gist strategy. Among adolescents and young adults, however, the reverse was true. Schmidt's data provide even broader support for the basic claim. After classifying children in terms of their preference for retaining verbatim information versus gist, the children were administered a series of verbatim memory tests (recalling sentences) and series of reasoning tests (inferences from stories). At both the kindergarten and second grade levels, children who had been classified as having high gist preference performed better on the reasoning tests. On the verbatim memory tests, however, there was a developmental crossover of the type that Marx obtained. Kindergarten children who were classified as having high verbatim preference performed roughly 65% more accurately than kindergarten children who were classified as having high gist preference. But, second grade children who were classified as having high gist preference were roughly 30% more accurate than second grade children who were classified as having high verbatim preference.

The most parsimonious explanation for the difficulty younger children have processing gist is that the presence of verbatim detail in memory interferes with the extraction of gist-like patterns (Brainerd & Reyna, 1990; Reyna & Brainerd, 1991a). To "see" global patterns, one must suppress irrelevant minutiae. Theorists have made a similar point about the relative advantages to cognition of an abstract code such as language, as opposed to pictures that specify irrelevant concrete details (Clark & Clark, 1977). The very superiority of younger children's rote memory, then, might cause them to be bound up in superficial details in ways that interfere with their reasoning (Reyna & Brainerd, 1991a).

In sum, data such as these make a presumptive case for the view that the memorial consequences of relying on verbatim readout versus reconstruction from gist depend on the current state of specialization of memory. Although readout may be more effective in the presence of verbatim specialization, reconstruction may be more effective in the presence of gist specialization. Thus, gist systems eventually become preeminent, even to the extent of controlling performance on what are ostensibly tests of verbatim memory.

Conclusions

In general, the relationship between reasoning and remembering is predicted in fuzzy-trace theory by three assumptions: (a) problem solution must be classified as primarily gist- or verbatim-based, with gist the default option; (b) the nature of retrieval must be determined, whether readout or reconstruction; (c) the extent of environmental support for verbatim information must be known, for example, whether elements are displayed or must be memorized. Table 3.1 shows the four possible combinations of gist versus verbatim bases for memory and reasoning, and the circumstances under which independence and dependence are predicted. Table 3.2 shows the predictions for reasoning-remembering relationships based on whether retrieval is readout or reconstruction. In connection with both Tables 3.1 and 3.2, two crucial assumptions must be underlined for valid prediction. First, the predictions hold only if "all other factors are equal." For example, if the reasoning and memory tasks are given at different delays after the presentation of information, all other factors are not equal, and the stated predictions might not hold. The other caveat is that when matching values in the table are indicated, for example if both memory and reasoning are designated "verbatim," then for the stated relationship to hold, the underlying substratum must be the same. For example, the verbatim information should be the same verbatim information, the reconstructive operations should be the same sort of processes, and so on. (The latter issue will be discussed at greater length in the following section.) A variety of factors have been identified as affecting the probability that gist versus verbatim memory, or re-

TABLE 3.1. The effects of gist versus verbatim memory on the reasoning-remembering relationship.

Reasoning	Remembering	Relationship
Gist	Verbatim	Independence
Verbatim	Gist	Independence
Gist	Gist	Dependence/Independence
Verbatim	Verbatim	Dependence

Note. The predictions regarding relationships assume that all other factors are equal. Where verbatim memory is used for both reasoning and remembering, the same verbatim substrate is assumed for both tasks. Gist-gist relationships turn on whether errors are random.

TABLE 3.2. The effects of readout versus reconstruction on the reasoning-remembering relationship

Reasoning	Remembering	Relationship
Reconstruction	Readout	Independence
Readout	Reconstruction	Independence
Readout	Readout	Independence
Reconstruction	Reconstruction	Dependence

Note. The predictions regarding relationships assume that all other factors are equal. Where reconstruction is used for both reasoning and remembering, the same reconstructive processes are assumed for both tasks. Significant dependence also requires conditions that produce memory (not performance) failures; for example, item displays generally discourage memory failures, but delays encourage memory failures.

construction as opposed to simple readout, will be used in problem solving (Brainerd & Reyna, 1990b; Reyna & Brainerd, 1990). Important among these is age, which plays a significant role in determining the reasoner/rememberer's approach to a task, with a major developmental shift from verbatim to gist processing occurring in the early elementary years. In the next section, I exploit the same assumptions we have used to discuss short-term retention to account for the seemingly complex relationships between thinking and memory over the long term.

Long-Term Retention

Gist versus Verbatim Memory

The memory-judgment relationship may be one of the most theoretically overdetermined relationships in modern psychology. To select but a sample of diverse theories that predict a significant relationship, Bartlett's (1932) view would indicate that memory is at the mercy of efforts to make sense of what is remembered, and, therefore, reasoning would profoundly affect memory. Freudian and cognitive dissonance theories offer multiple means (e.g., motivated forgetting) by which memories and judgments could be distorted in order to be brought in line with one another. Information processing theories have posited such mechanisms as selective encoding, special processing, and selective retrieval in explaining how attitudes (reflected in judgments) might influence memory (e.g., Hastie & Kumar, 1979; Snyder & Uranowitz, 1978). Too, there are a variety of circumstances in which memory is thought to influence judgments, rather than the other way around, for example, via the availability heuristic (Hastie & Park, 1986; Nisbett & Ross, 1980).

Surprisingly, however, empirical evidence paints a different picture. Careful analysis generally reveals that memory and judgment are independent (e.g., Anderson & Hubert, 1963; Brainerd & Kingma, 1984, 1985). As Hastie and Park (1986) note, "In on-line tasks, . . . the memory-judgment relationship is equivocal but usually follows the independence model prediction of zero correlation" (p. 258). Taken together, the hodgepodge of positive, negative, and null relationships between memory and judgment might seem to imply random fluctuation (see Hastie & Park, 1986, for a review). Thus, surveying the empirical and theoretical landscapes provides a stark contrast. An important question for any theory, then, is how to explain the empirical elusiveness of memory-judgment relationships in the face of apparent theoretical overdetermination.

By situating memory with respect to such constructs of fuzzy-trace theory as retrieval versus reconstruction and gist versus verbatim representation, factors that affect the probability of observing memory-reasoning relationships can be identified. Fuzzy-trace theory stipulates conditions under which memory-judgment relationships should (e.g., Brainerd & Reyna, 1988a; Reyna, 1988) and should not (e.g., Reyna & Brainerd, 1990; Reyna, Brainerd, & Woodruff, 1987) be observed (see Tables 3.1 and 3.2). The denouement of the analysis is that undifferentiated outcome measures of reasoning or of memory may not correlate, despite the intuitive appeal of the necessity or dependency hypotheses (Reyna & Brainerd, 1990). Instead, leverage can be gained on the question of dependence by specifying the representations and retrieval operations leading to reasoning and memory performance.

Fuzzy-trace theory assumes that information is redundantly encoded in representations that vary along a fuzzy-to-verbatim continuum (Brainerd & Reyna, 1990b; Granger & McNulty, 1986; Reyna & Brainerd, 1991b; Staubli, Ivy, & Lynch, 1984). Such multiple encoding is globally consistent with the idea of distributed memory, and with notions of redundant representations of memories in the brain dating back to Lashley, although, in fuzzy-trace theory, the multiple versions of remembered information are obviously not taken to be replicas of one another. Behavioral correlates of the verbatim-gist continuum include an effect observed in both animals and humans that memory at one end of the continuum (for gist) is more stable than memory for verbatim detail (Harlow, 1949; Kintsch, 1974). Thus, as retention intervals increase, or other factors that degrade memory are added, memory for gist seems to be relatively more resilient, making it an increasingly likely substrate for memory-based judgments. Ironically, the reliance on gist-based memory in judgments, and more generally the cognitive flexibility afforded by different memory systems, can obscure significant memory-judgment relationships in several ways.

First, delays between measures of memory and measures of judgment can do more than attenuate the memory-judgment relationship. Measurements taken at different times can sample different memory representations. Thus, judgments made immediately after the presentation of evidence, or made on-line using verbatim traces from working memory, might not correlate with later memory measures based on gist. The converse can also be true, namely that later judgments are based on gist, but memory performance draws on verbatim representations. Whenever differential delays produce reliance on different memory systems, independence is predicted (see Table 3.1).

According to fuzzy-trace theory, a major predictor of the kind of memory representation employed in thinking is the goal the subject is attempting to achieve, the overriding consideration being to operate at the lowest possible (most vague) level on a hierarchy of gist (Reyna et al., 1987; Reyna & Brainerd, 1991b). Thus, the nature of the response required in a task, even when it is elicited early after information presentation, significantly determines the nature of the representation used to solve the task. It is often the case that the social judgment task requires only a crude dichotomization (e.g., forced choice) or a global impression (e.g., rated likableness), whereas the memory test queries precise details of presented information. According to fuzzy-trace theory, therefore, such experimental methods favor observing a dissociation between memory and judgment measures.

In both of the scenarios just presented, because different memory systems would underlie memory and judgment, fuzzy-trace theory would predict that there should be no necessary relationship between them. The argument made here is similar to that made by Anderson (e.g., Anderson & Hubert, 1963) in suggesting a two-memories explanation for null or variable results regarding memory-judgment relationships. Fuzzy-trace theory further shares with Anderson's approach the assumption that reproductive memory for arbitrary details is qualitatively different from representations called up because of functional considerations, such as problem solving. (Unlike Anderson's dichotomy, however, fuzzy-trace theory assumes an underlying continuum of representations that vary in fuzziness.) As noted in the discussion of short-term memory, it is difficult to constrain the tasks that subjects perform, and the conditions under which performance occurs, in ways that compel reliance on a verbatim memorial substrate (Brainerd & Reyna, 1988a). Thus, performance in social judgment tasks will typically depend on memory for gist that is independent of memory for the verbatim details of encoded information.

Readout versus Reconstruction

Contrary to traditional theories, fuzzy-trace theory treats both retrieval and storage failure as two thresholds in an underlying continuous process (Brainerd & Reyna, 1990a; Brainerd, Reyna, Howe, & Kingma, 1990; Howe & Brainerd, 1989). Two major findings support such a conception. First, storage failure is more likely than retrieval failure (Brainerd & Reyna, 1988b; Brainerd et al., 1990). This result is at odds with the conventional interpretation of storage and retrieval. If, as the standard view suggests, retrieval requires both availability plus accessibility, but storage implicates only availability, then retrieval failure cannot be less probable than storage failure. The second crucial result is that storage failure can be reversed; traces can be brought back over the zero recall probability barrier (Brainerd et al., 1990; Howe & Brainerd, 1989). The latter finding, replicated repeatedly, challenges the conception of storage failure as the permanent loss of a trace.

These and other results inspired a view of forgetting as a gradual loss of cohesion among bonds that hold features of a trace together (Brainerd & Reyna, 1991; Brainerd, et al., 1990; Howe & Brainerd, 1989; see also Howe, Kelland, Bryant-Brown, & Clark, this volume). As forgetting occurs, the integrity of the trace becomes compromised (it becomes fuzzier), and it cannot be discerned against a background of competing traces. This process of disintegration can sometimes be reversed, however, producing redintegration, because elements are "diffused" rather than lost. Redintegration accounts for the ability of traces to migrate back across the threshold of availability. Thus, memory representations are fuzzy as a result of disintegration of featural bonds, an evolutionary process that affects a trace, or representations can be fuzzy because they were encoded that way to begin with. I have argued elsewhere that this proliferation of fuzzy traces is not coincidentally related to the fuzzy-processing preference in problem solving (e.g., Reyna & Brainerd, 1990).

The idea of forgetting, or memory failure, is typically applied to the memory-judgment relationship by noting that forgotten information cannot figure in memory-based judgments. Thus, the fallibility of memory is thought to provide an inroad for memory-judgment relationships. Such reasoning seems hermetically sealed from possible falsification, a logical necessity. As we have seen, however, one can escape from the circle by acknowledging the existence of more than one type of memory. Memory for gist can compensate for humans' poor verbatim memory, especially because gist suffices in a broad array of circumstances (Estes, 1980). However, the fallibility of verbatim memory can also be circumvented by reconstituting traces.

As noted above, one of the ways memory is reconstituted is through redintegration. Redintegration is item-based, minimally strategic, and developmentally invariant, supplying about 10% recovery across retention tests. As such, redintegration is a basic memory process that is unlikely to be the locus of strong memory-judgment relationships. Memories are also refurbished, however, by reconstructive processes that involve calculation, inference, or other reasoning operations. In contrast to redintegrative processes, reconstruction can involve units larger than a single trace, for example whole episodes, and it can be highly strategic, highly knowledge dependent, and subject to considerable developmental variation. For example, reconstruction can involve using plausibility to infer experienced events, as in "It must have happened in the morning because I was having breakfast at the time." Or, one might work backward in a series of calculations in order to "retrieve" original background facts in problem solving (Brainerd & Reyna, 1988a).

When reconstruction is used, as opposed to simple readout, remembering is essentially a reasoning process, strictly speaking (Kolodner, 1983). Because reasoning processes overlap between memory and judgment, the probability of dependency is increased. Tasks differ in the degree to which they tap reconstruction as opposed to readout. Recall, for example, elicits more reconstruction than recognition does. Because reconstruction is basically a reasoning process, recall tends to elicit gist. Therefore, recall and reasoning with respect to a given stimulus (e.g., a story) may both involve applying information processing operations to gist. (The situation is analogous to the mental arithmetic example of reasoning-remembering dependency, except that gist rather than verbatim memory is involved.) Reconstruction, however, is not inevitable across tasks. Fuzzy-trace theory summarizes the conditions under which one would expect memory to be reconstructive, as opposed to being based on simple readout (see Brainerd & Reyna, 1990b; Reyna & Brainerd, 1990).

Although reconstruction can occur when memory representations are accessible for simple readout, the probability of reconstruction is increased when readout is not an option. Thus, if a task crucially depends on verbatim information that can no longer be recalled, the reasoner may have no choice but to turn to reconstruction. Similarly, we might expect a pattern in which memory-judgment relationships are absent when relevant information is first acquired, but are present after a long interval (Reyna, 1988; Reyna et al., 1987). In other words, after a delay, people are more likely to have to resort to reconstruction, and memory and judgment performance may then share a common denominator of cognitive processes. Such a pattern of acquisition-retention asymmetry is well documented (Brainerd & Reyna, 1990a; Brainerd, et al., 1990), and has been obtained in social judgment tasks (Pratkanis et al., 1988; Reyes, Thompson, & Bower, 1980; Reyna, 1988; Reyna et al., 1987).

The role of reconstruction at acquisition versus long-term retention is illustrated in a series of experiments on memory and attitude change (Reyna, 1988; Reyna et al., 1987). At acquisition, for example, case history information relevant to a social issue was found to be more memorable than comparable statistical information. That is, narrative, anecdotal accounts of juvenile delinquents who did or did not grow up to be criminals as adults were more memorable than statistical reports citing adult outcomes across many juvenile offenders. Of course, case histories were rated as higher in concreteness and imagery value, factors that are well known facilitators of acquisition, but their greater vividness did not translate into greater persuasiveness. Indeed, the acquisition pattern was a crossover type such that the less memorable stimuli, the statistical arguments, were significantly more persuasive than the more memorable arguments. (Taylor and Thompson, 1982, make a similar argument about vividness effects on memory, as opposed to judgment, for case histories versus statistics.) Order effects also displayed a differential pattern for memory and judgment, namely a crossover, with primacy advantages for persuasiveness, but recency advantages for recognition (see also Anderson, 1981; Anderson & Hubert, 1963).

After a delay in which significant forgetting occurred, however, memory-judgment relationships were observed among the same group of subjects that had evinced independence at acquisition. Sleeper effects for judgment occurred; conditions that facilitated retention over the interval were associated with additional opinion change consistent with the better remembered stimulus. Judgment effects on memory were also detected. Memory for opinion-congruent arguments was selectively enhanced, but only when subjects had been asked for their opinions immediately after arguments were presented. Thus, when judgments were not solicited after arguments presentation, memory loss did not fall along the lines of prior opinion. When those opinions were solicited, however, memory for supportive arguments was superior on a subsequent long-term retention test. The latter effects were enhanced if opinions were requested again before, as opposed to after, the retention test.

These and similar results led to the following conclusions: (a) memory changes across a long-term retention interval, 2 weeks in these experiments, did appear to have a reverberative effect on judgments, and (b) solicited opinions seemed to act as retrieval cues around which presented arguments could be reconstructed. Note that the critical opinions were solicited after the arguments were presented, and opinion-change measures obtained at that time showed that the arguments were, in part, the basis for those opinions. Thus, it is not implausible that those opinions, more recent than the arguments, might be used to recover the arguments from which they come. If arguments are reconstructed around opinions, so the reasoning goes, it is no wonder that supportive arguments would be more fully remembered. Initial opinion, however, does not appear to play an ongoing organizing role in memory such that opinion-consistent information is spontaneously favored. This can be inferred because, despite strong initial opinions, opinion biases on memory were absent except when opinions were solicited after argument presentation.

The first phenomenon, that better remembered arguments exert additional effects on opinion, suggests that memory differences continue to coalesce in the long-term retention interval. The second phenomenon, that opinion-consistent arguments are favored in memory when opinions have been solicited, is but one example of retrieval-based distortion in which cues and context at retrieval, for example opinions or leading questions, can determine how memories are reconstructed (Howe & Brainerd, 1989; see also Howe et al., this volume). Retrieval in the absence of reconstruction, however, does not usually lead to memory-judgment correlations. If information for judgments and for memory tests are simply read out, without reconstruction, independence is predicted because retrieval failure is typically stochastic, specifically, a two-stage Markovian process (e.g., Flexser & Tulving, 1978). As in gist-processing failures, random errors do not correlate (Reyna & Brainerd, 1990). Thus, judgments should be independent of memory performance when information for both is simply retrieved rather than reconstructed (Table 3.2).

Despite reconstruction, the results from the experiments on memory-judgment relationships illustrate the pitfalls in demonstrating significant dependencies, although it is simultaneously apparent from these findings that memory and judgment interact (Reyna, 1988; Reyna et al., 1987). One of these pitfalls is the search for dependencies at acquisition, before sufficient forgetting, and consequent restorative processes, have begun to operate. These results are also instructive in showing, consonant with other research, that simply correlating opinion with memory is not apt to reveal significant dependencies. This is because bias does not appear to typically operate at the encoding stage, nor is processing predictably related to opinions or beliefs, but, rather, bias operates on memory through selective retrieval. And, even retrieval is not consistently biased, for example when simple readout occurs. Instead, bias encroaches on memory when the trace must be rebuilt using retrieval cues that, by their nature, are apt to systematically recruit certain kinds of information.

The familiar dichotomy of reconstructive versus reproductive memory, then, does not seem to capture the multifaceted nature of human memory. And, although most theories grudgingly acknowledge the existence of one or the other type of memory, there is an overweaning tendency to emphasize the one at the expense of the other. Rarer still is there an attempt to assign a major role to each, and show how they might operate in tandem. Much predictive power is gained, however, by granting representations that vary in vagueness, along with retrieval operations that vary in their invasiveness with respect to the trace. More importantly, the interplay between availability of alternative levels of representation and task requirements, as well as trade-offs between readout and reconstruction, constrain theoretical explanation (Brainerd & Reyna, 1990b). Thus, despite the fact that fuzzy-trace theory does, in some sense, come down squarely on both sides of the question of whether memory is essentially reproductive or (re)constructive, flexibility is not so great as to obviate prediction under specified conditions.

Still, the inclusion of a concept such as reconstruction, especially as a source of distortion, raises the nettlesome issue of the line between construction and reconstruction in memory. This is a line that is difficult to draw both empirically and theoretically, empirically because people are unable in many cases to differentiate for themselves between mental products and memories of actual experiences (Johnson, 1988). For practical purposes, for example when witnesses to a crime testify as to what they remember, constructive memory is a frightening prospect (Ceci, Ross, & Toglia, 1987a, 1987b). Constructive memory raises the possibility of distorting, or worse, inventing, material facts. The lesson drawn by those interested in maximizing memorial accuracy, then, has been to minimize (re)construction. However, research based on fuzzy-trace theory suggests that reconstruction often enhances accuracy, an enhancement that can be overlooked because successful reconstructions are mistakenly attributed to simple readout (Brainerd, Kingma, & Howe, 1985; Brainerd & Ornstein, 1991; Brainerd & Reyna, 1988b, 1990a; Brainerd, et al., 1990; Howe & Brainerd, 1989).

Also, if the course of remembering naturally turns to reconstruction after an interval, there is no reason to suppose that memory performance will be better if simple readout is used. On the contrary, there is evidence that reconstruction allows us to squeeze additional performance increments from a limited memory system (Brainerd & Ornstein, 1991; Reyna & Brainerd, 1990). Moreover, it is not clear that instructions or limiting the questions asked in memory interviews can diminish the tendency to engage in reconstruction (Kolodner, 1983). The request to remember may unavoidably elicit reconstruction, and it may be impossible for people to separate, and filter out, constructions as opposed to reconstructions.

Therefore, rather than disturbing memories, repeated questioning after a long retention interval can lead to consistent gains in accurate retrieval, including a host of different test-induced enhancement effects (e.g., Brainerd & Ornstein, 1991; Brainerd et al., 1990). Reconstruction in the sense of cautious application of inferences and calculations would be especially warranted where simple readout has failed. Such a reconstructive interview would, ideally, minimize leading or misleading questions, and, more generally, minimize introduction of information, implicitly or explicitly, by the interviewer (Brainerd & Ornstein, 1991; Ceci et al., 1987a, 1987b). Cues and connections employed by the subject should be made explicit so that they can be open to scrutiny, although these are sometimes unavailable to consciousness. Finally, it should be borne in mind that, although people engage in reconstructive processing in order to augment accuracy, and it often does have such an effect, constructions are an inevitable by-product. In some circumstances risking constructions is worthwhile, however, especially if information leads to additional evidence that can corroborate reconstructed memories, for example when vague clues provided by witnesses lead to the apprehension of both a suspect as well as additional incriminating evidence. The decision to encourage reconstructive processing must be weighed against, among other considerations, the need for information and the possibility of corroboration.

When Reconstructive Memory Does Not Lead to Memory-Judgment Dependencies

Reconstructive memory, on the other hand, does not guarantee memory-judgment relationships. It is entirely possible that memory could be reconstructive and unrelated to judgments. First, relevant memories could be reconstructed and judgments retrieved (Table 3.2). The direct retrieval of judgments that were made on-line apparently accounts for the independence of memories for evidence on which the on-line judgment was based, and the judgment itself (Hastie & Park, 1986). Second, both memory and judgments could be based on inferential or computational processes, but they need not be based on the same processes (see the note to Table 3.2). In such cases, the choice of factors to examine can determine whether memory-judgment relationships are observed. For example, large individual differences affecting the efficiency of all information processing might affect both memory and judgment, even though specific processing operations for memory and judgment differed. On the other hand, if measures were sensitive enough to detect subtle differences in processing operations, memory and judgment could be shown to be independent.

Finally, memory-judgment correlations will depend on the nature of measures being related. Brainerd and Kingma (1984, 1985) have found, for example, that representation and processing probably overlap for reasoning and remembering in transitive inference problems, but their measures are stochastically independent. This is because the nature of the representation and the reconstructive heuristic are not significant sources of errors. Instead, errors occur as children's attention wanders, items in questions are misidentified, and the like, and these are random errors. (These performance errors decrease in adults, producing developmental differences in the overall level of performance, but the underlying representation and process does not appear to change in any fundamental way [Reyna & Brainerd, 1990; Trabasso, Riley, & Wilson, 1975].) Thus, paradoxically, stochastic independence can occur when the underlying processes are the same for memory and judgment. The remedy in all three scenarios for detecting the true state of affairs appears to be closer attention to the locus of effects for memory and judgment manipulations, and assessment, or active manipulation, of whether memory and judgment performance are based on readouts or reconstructions.

Summary

Far from being a foregone conclusion, as Tables 3.1 and 3.2 make obvious, a confluence of factors must be in place for reasoning-remembering dependence to be observed. Empirically, independence is the typical finding, both in short- and long-term retention. The door to dependence is opened when, for example, reasoning and remembering must tap a common verbatim substrate in memory, as in experiments involving memory probes for quantities in mental arithmetic problems (Brainerd & Reyna, 1988a). Even in mental arithmetic, however, memory performance depends on reasoning, rather than, as is often assumed, reasoning depending on memory. Moreover, for young children, better verbatim memory may interfere with reasoning, leading to lower performance on tasks that require seeing global patterns.

Like verbatim memory, reconstructive retrieval also increases the probability of reasoning-remembering dependence. Because reconstructive processing can enhance performance, however, insufficient memory failures may occur, and dependencies will not be detected. In transitivity, for example, external arrays store item identities, as well as their locations, in a graded series. Reconstruction of gist in such circumstances generally produces few errors, and the errors that are produced are nonsystematic performance lapses; therefore, reasoning and memory errors are uncorrelated. In contrast, if information must be accessed after an extended delay, in the absence of external memory supports, reconstruction can produce memory-judgment relationships. Again, dependence is far from inevitable, and depends partly on whether judgments are used as cues with which memories are reconstructed.

Acknowledgment. The conduct of some of the research reported herein was supported by a grant from the Spencer Foundation.

References

Anderson, N.H. (1981). *Foundations of information integration theory*. New York: Academic Press.

Anderson, N.H., & Hubert, S. (1963). Effects of concomitant verbal recall on order effects in personality impression formation. *Journal of Verbal Learning and Verbal Behavior, 2*, 379–391.

Bartlett, F.C. (1932). *Thinking*. London: Allen & Unwin.

Bjorklund, D.F. (1987). How age changes in knowledge base contribute to the development of children's memory: An interpretive review. *Developmental Review, 7*, 93–130.

Bjorklund, D.F. (1989). *Children's thinking: Developmental function and individual differences*. Pacific Grove, CA: Brooks Cole.

Brainerd, C.J. (1981). Working memory and the developmental analysis of probability judgment. *Psychological Review, 88*, 463–502.

Brainerd, C.J. (1983a). Young children's mental arithmetic errors: A working memory analysis. *Child Development, 54*, 812–830.

Brainerd, C.J. (1983b). Working memory systems and cognitive development. In C.J. Brainerd (Ed.), *Recent advances in cognitive developmental theory*. New York: Springer-Verlag.

Brainerd, C.J. (1985). Do children have to remember to reason? In C.J.Brainerd & V. F.Reyna (Eds.), *Developmental Psychology* (pp. 143–154). Amsterdam: North Holland.

Brainerd, C.J. (1987). Sources of working-memory error in children's mental arithmetic. In G. Deloche & X. Seron (Eds.), *Mathematical disabilities: A cognitive neuropsychological perspective*. Hillsdale, NJ: Erlbaum.

Brainerd, C.J., & Kingma, J. (1984). Do children have to remember to reason? A fuzzy-trace theory of transitivity development. *Developmental Review, 4*, 311–377.

Brainerd, C.J., & Kingma, J. (1985). On the independence of short-term memory and working memory in cognitive development. *Cognitive Psychology, 17*, 210–247.

Brainerd, C.J., Kingma, J., & Howe, M.L. (1985). On the development of forgetting. *Child Development, 56*, 1103–1119.

Brainerd, C.J., & Ornstein, P.A. (1991). Children's memory for witnessed events: The developmental backdrop. In J.L. Doris (Ed.), *The suggestibility of children's recollections with a view toward children's testimony*. Washington, DC: American Psychological Association.

Brainerd, C.J., & Reyna, V. F. (1988a). Generic resources, reconstructive processing, and children's mental arithmetic. *Developmental Psychology, 24*, 324–334.

Brainerd, C.J., & Reyna, V. F. (1988b). Memory loci of suggestibility development. *Journal of Experimental Psychology: General, 117*, 197–200.

Brainerd, C.J., & Reyna, V. F. (1990a). Can age x learnability interactions explain the development of forgetting? *Developmental Psychology, 26*, 194–203.

Brainerd, C.J., & Reyna, V. F. (1990b). Gist is the grist: Fuzzy-trace theory and the new intuitionism. *Developmental Review, 10*, 3–47.

Brainerd, C.J., & Reyna, V. F. (1990c). Inclusion illusions: Fuzzy-trace theory and perceptual salience effects in cognitive development. *Developmental Review*, *10*, 365–403.

Brainerd, C.J., & Reyna, V. F. (1991). Acquisition and forgetting processes in normal and learning-disabled children: A disdintegration/redintegration theory. In J.E. Obrzut & G.W. Hynd (Eds.), *Neuropsychological foundations of learning disabilities: A handbook of issues, methods, and practice*. New York: Academic Press.

Brainerd, C.J., Reyna, V. F., Howe, M.L., & Kingma, J. (1990). The development of forgetting and reminiscence. *Monographs of the Society for Research in Child Development*, *55*, (3–4, whole No. 222).

Bransford, J.D., Barclay, J.R., & Franks, J.J. (1972). Sentence memory: A constructive versus interpretative approach. *Cognitive Psychology*, *3*, 193–209.

Bransford, J.D., & Franks, J.J. (1971). The abstraction of linguistic ideas. *Cognitive Psychology*, *2*, 331–350.

Bransford, J.D., & Johnson, M.K. (1973). Consideration of some problems of comprehension. In W.G. Chase (Ed.), *Visual information processing*. New York: Academic Press.

Bryant, P.E., & Trabasso, T. (1971). Transitive inference and memory in young children. *Nature*, *232*, 456–458.

Cacciopo, J.T., & Petty, R.E. (1985). Central and peripheral routes to persuasion: The role of message repetition. In L.F. Alwitt & A.A. Mitchell (Eds.), *Psychological processes and advertising effects*. Hillsdale, NJ: Erlbaum.

Callahan, P. (1989). *Learning and development of probability concepts: Effects of computer-assisted instruction and diagnosis*. Unpublished doctoral dissertation, University of Arizona, College of Education, Tucson.

Carey, S., & Diamond, R. (1977). From piecemeal to configurational representation of faces. *Science*, *195*, 312–314.

Carey, S., Diamond, R., & Woods, B. (1980). The development of face recognition—A maturational component? *Developmental Psychology*, *16*, 257–269.

Case, R. (1985). *Intellectual development: Birth to adulthood*. New York: Academic Press.

Ceci, S.J., Ross, D.F., & Toglia, M.P. (1987a). Suggestibility in children's memory: Psycholegal implications. *Journal of Experimental Psychology: General*, *116*, 38–49.

Ceci, S.J., Ross, D.F., & Toglia, M.P. (Eds.). (1987b). *Children's eyewitness testimony*. New York: Springer-Verlag.

Chapman, M. (1989, April). *Cognitive competence and verbal explanations in studies of children's reasoning*. Paper presented at the Biennial Meeting of the Society for Research in Child Development, Kansas City, MO.

Chapman, M., & Lindenberger, U. (1988). Functions, operations, and decalage in the development of transitivity. *Developmental Psychology*, *24*, 542–551.

Chapman, M., & Lindenberger, U. (in press). Transitivity judgments, memory for premises, and models of children's reasoning. *Developmental Review*.

Clark, H., & Clark, E. (1977). *Psychology and language*. New York: Harcourt Brace Jovanovich.

Dempster, F.N. (1981). Memory span: Sources of individual and developmental differences. *Psychological Bulletin*, *89*, 63–100.
Dempster, F.N. (1985). Short-term memory development in childhood and adolescence. In C.J. Brainerd & M. Pressley (Eds.), *Basic processes in memory development: Progress in cognitive development research* (pp. 209–248). New York: Springer-Verlag.
Elkind, D. (1967). Piaget's conservation problems. *Child Development*, *38*, 15–27.
Estes, W.K. (1976). The cognitive side of probability learning. *Psychological Review*, *83*, 37–64.
Estes, W.K. (1980). Is human memory obsolete? *American Scientist*, *68*, 62–69.
Flexser, A.J., & Tulving, E. (1978). Retrieval independence in recognition and recall. *Psychological Review*, *55*, 153–171.
Glaze, J.A. (1928). The association value of nonsense syllables. *Journal of Genetic Psychology*, *35*, 255–267.
Granger, R.H., & McNulty, D.M. (1986). Learning and memory in machines and animals: An AI model that accounts for some neurobiological data. In J.L. Kolodner & C.K. Riesbeck (Eds.), *Experience, memory, and reasoning*. Hillsdale, NJ: Erlbaum.
Grieve, R., & Nesdale, A.R. (1979). Observations on a test of transitive inference in children. *Australian Journal of Psychology*, *31*, 43–48.
Halford, G.S., & Galloway, W. (1977). Children who fail to make transitive inferences can remember comparisons. *Australian Journal of Psychology*, *29*, 1–5.
Harlow, H.F. (1949). The formation of learning sets. *Psychological Review*, *56*, 51–65.
Hastie, R., & Kumar, A.P. (1979). Person memory: Personality traits as organizing principles in memory for behavior. *Journal of Personality and Social Psychology*, *37*, 25–38.
Hastie, R., & Park, B. (1986). The relationship between memory and judgment depends on whether the judgment task is memory-based or on-line. *Psychological Review*, *93*, 258–268.
Higgins, E.T., & Stangor, C. (1988). A "change-of-standard" perspective on the relations among context, judgment, and memory. *Journal of Personality and Social Psychology*, *54*, 181–192.
Hirsch, E.D. (1988). *Cultural literacy*. New York: Vintage.
Howe, M.L., & Brainerd, C.J. (1989). Development of children's long-term retention. *Developmental Review*, *9*, 301–340.
Johnson, J., & Newport, E.L. (1989). Critical period effects in second language learning: The influence of maturational state on the acquisition of English as a second language. *Cognitive Psychology*, *21*, 60–99.
Johnson, J., & Scholnick, E. (1979). Does cognitive development predict semantic integration? *Child Development*, *50*, 73–78.
Johnson, M.K. (1988). Reality monitoring: An experimental phenomenological approach. *Journal of Experimental Psychology: General*, *117*, 390–394.
Kintsch, W. (1974). *The representation of meaning in memory*. Hillsdale, NJ: Erlbaum.
Kolodner, J.L. (1983). Reconstructive memory: A computer model. *Cognitive Science*, *7*, 281–328.

Lenneberg, E.H. (1967). *Biological foundations of language*. New York: Wiley.
Liben, L.S., & Posnansky, C.J. (1977). Inferences on inference. The effects of age, transitive ability, memory load, and lexical factors. *Child Development*, *48*, 490–497.
Marx, M.H. (1985). Retrospective reports on frequency judgments. *Bulletin of the Psychonomic Society*, *23*, 309–310.
Marx, M.H. (1986). More retrospective reports on event-frequency judgments: Shift from multiple traces to strength factor with age. *Bulletin of the Psychonomic Society*, *24*, 183–185.
Miller, G.A. (1981). *Language and speech*. San Francisco: W.H. Freeman.
Nisbett, R., & Ross, L. (1980). *Human inference: Strategies and shortcomings of social judgment*. Englewood Cliffs, NJ: Prentice Hall.
Paris, S.G., & Carter, A.Y. (1973). Semantic and constructive aspects of sentence memory in children. *Developmental Psychology*, *9*, 109–113.
Paris, S.G., & Mahoney, G.J. (1974). Cognitive integration in children's memory for sentences and pictures. *Child Development*, *45*, 633–642.
Perner, J., & Mansbridge, D.G. (1983). Developmental differences in encoding length series. *Child Development*, *54*, 710–719.
Piaget, J. (1968). *On the development of memory and identity*. Worcester, MA: Clark University Press.
Piaget, J. (1970). *Genetic epistemology*. New York: Columbia University Press.
Piaget, J., & Inhelder, B. (1969). *The psychology of the child*. New York: Basic Books.
Piaget, J., & Inhelder, B. (1973). *Memory and intelligence*. New York: Basic Books.
Pratkanis, A.R., Greenwald, A.G., Leippe, M.R., & Baumgardner, M.H. (1988). In search of reliable persuasion effects: III.The sleeper effect is dead. Long live the sleeper effect. *Journal of Personality and Social Psychology*, *54*, 203–218.
Prawat, R., & Cancelli, A. (1976). Constructive memory in conserving and nonconserving first graders. *Developmental Psychology*, *12*, 47–50.
Rabinowitz, F.M., Howe, M.L., & Lawrence, J.A. (1989). Class inclusion and working memory. *Journal of Experimental Child Psychology*, *48*, 379–409.
Reyes, R.M., Thompson, W.C., & Bower, G.H. (1980). Judgmental biases resulting from differing availabilties of arguments. *Journal of Personality and Social Psychology*, *39*, 2–12.
Reyna, V. F. (1981). The animated word: Modification of meaning by context. *Dissertation Abstracts International*, *42*, 3852B, (University Microfilms number 82-03153).
Reyna, V. F. (1985). Figure and fantasy in children's language. In M. Pressley & C.J. Brainerd (Eds.), *Cognitive learning and memory in children: Progress in cognitive development research*. New York: Springer-Verlag.
Reyna, V.F. (1988). *Reiterative versus reconstructive memory in opinion change*. Paper presented at the First Annual Nags Head Conference in Judgment and Decision Making, Kill Devil Hills, NC.
Reyna, V.F. (1991). Class inclusion, the conjunction fallacy, and other cognitive illusions. *Developmental Review*, *11*, 317–336.

Reyna, V.F., & Brainerd, C.J. (1990). Fuzzy processing in transitivity development. *Annals of Operations Research*, *23*, 37–63.
Reyna, V.F., & Brainerd, C.J. (1991a). Fuzzy-trace theory and children's acquisition of mathematical and scientific concepts. *Learning and Individual Differences*, *3*, 27–60.
Reyna, V.F., & Brainerd, C.J. (1991b). Fuzzy-trace theory and framing effects in choice: Gist extraction, truncation, and conversion. *Journal of Behavioral Decision Making*, *4*, 249–262.
Reyna, V.F., & Brainerd, C.J. (in press). A fuzzy-trace theory of reasoning and remembering: Paradoxes, patterns, and parallelism. In A. Healy, S. Kosslyn, & R. Shiffrin (Eds.), *Festschrift for W.K.Estes*. Hillsdale, NJ: Erlbaum.
Reyna, V.F., Brainerd, C.J., & Woodruff, W.J. (1987). *On the relationship between memory and judgment in opinion change*. Paper presented at the 28th Annual Meeting of the Psychonomic Society, Seattle, WA.
Roodin, M.L., & Gruen, G.E. (1970). The role of memory in making transitive judgments. *Journal of Experimental Child Psychology*, *10*, 264–275.
Russell, J. (1981). Children's memory for premises in a transitive measurement task assessed by elicited and spontaneous justifications. *Journal of Experimental Child Psychology*, *31*, 300–309.
Schmidt, C.R., & Welch, M. (1989, April). *The development of rote and gist memory tendencies in young children*. Paper presented at the Biennial Meeting of the Society for Research in Child Development, Kansas City, MO.
Simon, H.A. (1988). Rationality as process and product of thought. In D.E. Bell, H. Raiffa, & A. Tversky (Eds.), *Decision making: Descriptive, normative, and prescriptive interactions*. New York: Cambridge University Press.
Smedslund, J. (1969). Psychological diagnostics. *Psychological Bulletin*, *71*, 237–248.
Snyder, M., & Uranowitz, W. (1978). Reconstructing the past: Some cognitive consequences of person perception. *Journal of Personality and Social Psychology*, *36*, 941–950.
Staubli, U., Ivy, G., & Lynch, G. (1984). Hippocampal denervation causes rapid forgetting of olfactory information in rats. *Proceedings of the National Academy of Sciences*, *81*, 5885–5887.
Stevenson, H.W. (1972). *Children's learning*. New York: Appleton-Century-Crofts.
Swanson, H.L. (1990). *Individual differences in working memory: A model testing and subgroup analysis of learning disabled and skilled readers*. Manuscript submitted for publication.
Taylor, S.E., & Thompson, S.C. (1982). Stalking the elusive "vividness" effect. *Psychological Review*, *89*, 155–181.
Tolman, E.C. (1948). Cognitive maps in rats and men. *Psychological Review*, *55*, 189–208.
Trabasso, T. (1977). The role of memory as a system in making transitive inferences. In R.V. Kail, Jr., & J.W., Hagan (Eds.), *Perspectives on the development of memory and cognition*. Hillsdale, NJ: Erlbaum.
Trabasso, T., Riley, C.A., & Wilson, E.G. (1975). The representation of linear order and spatial strategies in reasoning: A developmental study. In R.J.

Falmagne (Ed.), *Reasoning: Representation and process*. Hillsdale, NJ: Erlbaum.
Wagner, S., Winner, E., Cicchetti, D., & Gardner, H. (1981). "Metaphorical" mapping in human infants. *Child Development*, *52*, 728–731.
Weismer, S.E. (1985). Constructive comprehension abilities exhibited by language-disordered children. *Journal of Speech and Hearing Research*, *28*, 175–184.

Part II
Pragmatic Aspects of Retention

4
Children's Memory for Salient Events: Implications for Testimony

PETER A. ORNSTEIN, BETTY N. GORDON, and
LYNNE E. BAKER-WARD

The alarming increase in reports of the sexual abuse of young children has prompted a growing concern about children's abilities to provide accurate testimony in legal proceedings. Although research in this area is burgeoning (see, e.g., Ceci, Ross, & Toglia, 1987a, 1987b; Ceci, Toglia, & Ross, 1987; Goodman, 1984), much remains to be learned about young children's abilities to provide factual accounts of personally experienced events. Undoubtedly, many factors influence the quality of children's reports, but it is certainly the case that children cannot provide accurate testimony about events that cannot be remembered. Accordingly, the work presented here is based on the fundamental assumption that the accuracy of children's testimony depends to a considerable extent upon their abilities to remember events over time. Indeed, we conceptualize the interview and testimony process as an attempt to help children recall situations in which they were participants or events that they observed (see also Brainerd & Ornstein, 1991; Ornstein, 1991; Ornstein, Larus, & Clubb, in press).

Given the relation between testimony and memory, research on memory development in the early childhood years should be of considerable importance to professionals who work with young children in the legal context. In this chapter, we will first review those segments of the memory literature that seem directly relevant to understanding children's testimony. Then we will present a paradigm that we are exploring for the systematic study of children's memory for salient events, in particular, their retention of the details of a visit to the doctor for a regularly scheduled, well-child physical examination. The results of two studies of children's long-term memory for the doctor visit will be presented and used to illustrate some factors that seem relevant to a consideration of children's testimony. We will close with a discussion of the implications of these studies for the interviewing of young children.

Memory in Young Children

Although much of the literature on memory development has focused on children of elementary school age (see, e.g., Kail, 1989; Schneider & Pressley, 1989; Weinert & Perlmutter, 1988), in the last decade there has been an explosion of interest in preschoolers' memory. Moreover, recent findings have led to fundamental changes in our conceptualization of young children's abilities. For example, preschoolers have been shown to be quite sensitive to regularly occurring events, routinely forming "scripts" or generalized event representations based on prior experience (see, e.g., Nelson, 1986; Nelson, Fivush, Hudson, & Lucariello, 1983). In addition, young children have been shown to have reasonably good retention of individual personally experienced events (e.g., Fivush, Gray, & Fromhoff, 1987; Fivush, Hudson, & Nelson, 1984; Ratner, Smith, & Dion, 1986). And even our earlier views of preschoolers' deficiencies in using strategies are changing (see, e.g., Ornstein, 1978). Thus, research from number of laboratories (e.g., Baker-Ward, Ornstein, & Holden, 1984; DeLoache, Cassidy, & Brown, 1985; Sodian, Schneider, & Perlmutter, 1986; Wellman, 1988) has indicated that preschoolers are indeed capable of strategic activities in the service of a memory goal, at least under certain supportive conditions.

This new view of young children's memory capabilities notwithstanding, there is a real gap in the literature. Specifically, little information is available concerning children's retention of salient autobiographical episodes over delays of varying lengths. This is particularly the case under relatively controlled conditions in which the experimenter can specify the "stimulus event" to which the children were initially exposed. Admittedly, work in this area is beginning, as can be seen in recent studies of children's recall of brief medical procedures such as inoculations and venipuncture, and their recognition of the professionals encountered in dental examinations (see Goodman, Aman, & Hirschman, 1987; Peters, 1987). Nonetheless, to relate work on memory to the issues involved in obtaining accurate testimony, systematic explorations of children's long-term retention of salient experiences are necessary. To examine the importance of this type of research, we turn to a brief treatment of those features of memory that are necessary for an understanding of children's testimony.

Incidental versus Deliberate Memory

Testimony involves memory that is both incidental and deliberate. Typically, a child who experiences a traumatic event is not consciously attempting to remember the details of that experience for future reference. Without the expectation of a subsequent interrogation of memory, as is the case in studies of deliberate memory (see Schneider & Pressley, 1989), it is unlikely that deliberate encoding of the event will take place. Thus, when a child reports or is questioned about a traumatic experience, we are dealing primarily with a case of incidental memory. Of course, as the child is questioned subsequently, and even implored to try to remember, the task becomes one of deliberate recall, and strategies for retrieval may come to be utilized. However, the information that was stored in memory and thus is potentially available for recall was acquired incidentally.

The implications of this distinction between incidental and deliberate memory for an understanding of eyewitness testimony are still unclear. Laboratory studies have shown that age differences in children's incidental recall are typically minimized when simple, highly familiar stimuli are employed and subjects are led to comparable degrees of encoding (see Brown, 1978; Ornstein & Corsale, 1979). But these findings must be generalized with caution to more complex situations in which there are likely to be age differences in knowledge and understanding. Moreover, when the task becomes one of deliberate memory search, older individuals are typically at an advantage, in that they spontaneously utilize effective retrieval strategies (see Kail, 1989; Schneider & Pressley, 1989). However, it is well established that young children who do not spontaneously produce strategies can often benefit from the direction to use them. For this reason, as well as other concerns, the interviewer's skill in structuring and cuing a child's search of memory can be of considerable importance (see, e.g., Brainerd & Ornstein, 1991; Ornstein, 1991).

Memory for Salient Events

Testimony also involves the recall of information about very meaningful and salient events. However, the word lists, sentences, pictures, objects, and even films and stories that are frequently employed in laboratory studies of children's memory (see Kail, 1989; Schneider & Pressley, 1989) would seem to bear little resemblance to these salient events. As such, the ability to generalize from these laboratory studies to situations requiring testimony may be somewhat limited. Further, although testimony sometimes involves memory for events that have been observed, it often calls for recall of experiences in which the child witness was an actual participant. Yet, there have been relatively few investigations of young children's recall of personally experienced events (see, e.g., Goodman et al., 1987; Peters, 1987). It is important to carry out additional research on the memory of personal experiences because recent work suggests that children most likely recall events in which they are participants better than events for which they are bystanders (Baker-Ward, Hess, & Flannagan, 1990; see also Ornstein et al., in press).

Memory over Delays

Testimony also involves memory over very substantial delays. Unfortunately, although psychologists have long been interested in remembering, (e.g., Bartlett, 1932; Ebbinghaus, 1885; Melton & Irwin, 1940; Postman & Underwood, 1973), remarkably little information is available concerning the time course of retention and forgetting. To some extent, this reflects the impact of the cognitive revolution of the 1960s in psychology, with its emphasis on charting the acquisition of information, as opposed to forgetting, but it also stems from the theoretical focus of the majority of the explorations of long-term retention that have been reported. These studies have led to major advances in our understanding of a number of fundamental issues, such as the relations between original learning and forgetting (e.g., Bogartz, 1990; G. R. Loftus, 1985a, 1985b; G. R. Loftus & Bamber, 1990; Slamecka, 1985; Slamecka & McElree, 1983) and between age and forgetting (Brainerd, Kingma, & Howe, 1985; Howe & Brainerd, 1989), as well as the contributions of storage- and retrieval-based mechanisms to both forgetting and reminiscence (Brainerd, Reyna, Howe, & Kingma, 1990). To some extent, of course, these advances have stemmed in part from reports of the recall of children and adults after delays of several weeks (e.g., Howe & Brainerd, 1989; see also Howe, Kelland, Bryant-Brown, & Clark, this volume). Nonetheless, what is lacking is a significant data base concerning what individuals of different ages can remember over extended time intervals.

Systematic and extensive studies of children's long-term retention are clearly necessary because testimony involves recall over intervals that are measured in weeks, months, and often years. Indeed, in some cases, these delays are long enough for the child to undergo significant intellectual development. The consequences of this development are unknown, but one result might be an altered understanding of the event and consequently the memory of it (see Ornstein & Naus, 1985; Piaget & Inhelder, 1973). Moreover, these long delays are often filled with events that can potentially interfere with the later recovery of information. Thus, questions from attorneys, nurses, social workers, and even psychotherapy to help the child overcome a traumatic experience, may serve to alter the basic underlying memory trace and/or the child's subsequent report. The mnemonic consequences of these long delays and intervening events are simply not known.

Framework for Examining Children's Autobiographical Memory

Given the types of memory that are involved in testimony, it is clear that the developmental literature does not provide a great deal of data to guide those who are working with children in the context of the legal system. Nonetheless, the literature on children's cognition does offer some suggestions for conceptualizing the underlying processes. Accordingly, in this section, we outline three critical themes that, taken together, can serve as a framework for understanding children's testimony. An additional treatment of some of these issues is provided by Brainerd and Ornstein (1991) and Ornstein et al. (in press).

The Impact of Knowledge on Remembering

It is well known that what an individual knows can have a profound effect on the processing and retention of information (see, e.g., Bartlett, 1932; Binet & Henri, 1894; Bjorklund, 1985; Chi, 1978; Chi & Ceci, 1987; Ornstein & Naus, 1985). "Prior knowledge" can influence how one monitors the world, codes material for storage, and subsequently retrieves information from memory. For example, memory performance is often enhanced when the task involves remembering material from a well-known domain (e.g., Bjorklund, 1985; Spilich, Vesonder, Chiesi, & Voss, 1979). Further, age differences may be reduced or even reversed when children are particularly knowledgeable about the domain from which the to-be-remembered materials have been selected. Thus, for example, children who are chess experts are better able to remember the positions of chess pieces on the board than are adults who are average players (Chi, 1978). Nonetheless, it must be stated that the field has not progressed much beyond demonstrations of the impact of prior knowledge and that little is known about the mechanisms by which knowledge influences memory performance (Ornstein, 1990; Ornstein & Naus, 1985). In addition, under some conditions, knowledge effects cannot be unambiguously interpreted, particularly when expertise may be confounded with interest and motivation (Ornstein & Naus, 1985; see also Peverly, 1991).

These interpretive concerns notwithstanding, there is a consensus view (see, e.g., Schneider & Pressley, 1989) that what is already known can have a serious impact on the acquisition and retention of information. Moreover, consistent with accounts of the constructive nature of memory performance (e.g., Bartlett, 1932; Bransford & Franks, 1971; Cofer, Chmielewski, & Brockway, 1976), the influence of prior knowledge may be especially pronounced at delayed tests of retention. As the delay interval increases, information stored in memory can be altered and interpreted so as to be more consistent with preexisting knowledge. Indeed, even without changes in the underlying memory trace, constructive activities at retrieval can yield reports that reflect the impact of prior knowledge. Thus, over time, memory may be less reproductive and more reconstructive in character.

These constructive activities may pose a particular problem with young children, who have been shown to effectively construct "scripts" of familiar routines (see, e.g., Fivush, 1984; Nelson, 1986; Nelson & Gruendel, 1981) and whose delayed reports may be influenced considerably by this knowledge. Thus, with increasing delay intervals, it is possible that a young child may quite unconsciously use this generic knowledge to supplement a report about an event that is partially forgotten. For example, as memory for the details of a particular school day fades, young children's recollections of that day may come to be influenced considerably by general knowledge of school routines (see, e.g., Myles-Worsley, Cromer, & Dodd, 1986). Of course, reliance on scripts and expectations carries with it the distinct possibility of errors of commission, as children's reports may include "intrusions" of plausible details that were not component features of the specific event to be remembered.

An implication of research demonstrating the linkage between knowledge and memory is that our understanding of children's abilities to provide evidence in legal settings would be increased if information were available about children's knowledge about salient domains in their experience (see Brainerd & Ornstein, 1991; Ornstein & Naus, 1985). Unfortunately, despite the emphasis placed on prior knowledge in current accounts of memory and cognition, relatively little is known about what children know and how this knowledge may change with experience and age (see Ornstein, 1990). Because of the frequency with which children are being called to provide evidence in cases of alleged sexual abuse, it is particularly important to learn just what it is that children of different ages know about anatomy and sexual behavior. Gordon, Schroeder, and Abrams (1990) recently provided an initial description of the sexual knowledge of children between the ages of 2 and 7, but additional research is clearly necessary.

Effects of Experiences in the Delay Period

As suggested above, testimony typically involves the provision of information about an event after a considerable amount of time has elapsed. As such, children's reports about their experiences may be influenced greatly by the events that occur during the delay interval. Indeed, this period is not neutral, and events that take place during the delay interval can have both positive and negative effects upon memory traces as well as subsequent reports. Thus, intervening events, including contacts with experimenters and/or interviewers, can serve both to facilitate and to distort memory performance.

Events That Maintain Memory

One of the classic principles of memory is that repetition facilitates performance. It is well known that exposure to an event or a set of materials after its initial presentation serves to increase the probability of later recall (see, e.g., Crowder, 1976). However, partial "reinstatement" of the initial stimulus situation can also have beneficial effects on subsequent retention. Thus, for example, a certain amount of experience between initial exposure to an event and a subsequent test can function as a "booster shot" in maintaining memory over an extended delay (e.g., Campbell & Jaynes, 1966; Rovee-Collier & Hayne, 1987; see also Rovee-Collier & Shyi, this volume). Most critically, this level of experience, in and of itself, is insufficient to promote new learning, but it can serve as a type of inoculation against later forgetting. With children, repeated discussion of an earlier experience and partial repetitions of that event (e.g., return visits to the situation, etc.) can likely serve to maintain it. Moreover, under some conditions, substantial inoculation effects on later recall can be produced by simply testing memory for an event in close proximity to that event (e.g., Howe & Brainerd, 1989; see also Slamecka & Katsaiti, 1988).

Events That Distort Memory

In contrast to the facilitative effects of repetition and reinstatement, another classical principle of memory is that of retroactive interference (see Melton & Irwin, 1940; Postman & Underwood, 1973): subsequent events can interfere with the recall of earlier experiences. Thus, although some intervening experiences serve to facilitate memory, many events that take place in a delay interval can have a negative impact on subsequent retention. Consider, for example, the mnemonic consequences of children being repeatedly interviewed by police officers, social workers, psychologists, lawyers, judges, etc., in the interval before an appearance in court. It is quite likely that the perspectives of these various interviewers will become intertwined with the children's own reports. Moreover, it might be expected that such interference would be especially great when children are exposed to complex events about which there is a lack of complete understanding, exactly the situations they are most often asked to discuss in the context of legal proceedings.

Given some measure of uncertainty about the details of an episode, exposure to other (often divergent) accounts of what happened can lead to an alteration of memory for the event. Similarly, changes in what is remembered may be prompted by the form of the questions that are directed to individuals attempting to remember. Indeed, the literature on the effects of exposure to misleading postevent information (e.g., Ceci, et al., 1987a, 1987b; Zaragoza, 1987; Zaragoza & Wilson, 1989; see also Toglia, Ross, & Ceci, and Zaragoza, Dahlgren, & Muench, this volume) attests to the suggestibility of children's memory. Thus, misleading postevent questions can easily distort children's reports, and there is evidence that preschoolers are more susceptible to suggestion than are older children (see Ceci, et al., 1987a, 1987b; Toglia, Ceci, & Ross, 1989).

Interestingly, there is considerable debate as to the mechanisms that underlie such suggestibility effects in both adults and children. For example, some researchers claim that the initial memory trace is altered (e.g., E. F. Loftus, 1979; E. F. Loftus, Miller, & Burns, 1978) or made less accessible (e.g., Bekerian & Bowers, 1983; Christiaansen & Ochalek, 1983) by exposure to misleading information, whereas others (e.g., McCloskey & Zaragoza, 1985a, 1985b) suggest that memory is not involved and that social pressure causes some misled subjects to report misleading information (see Ornstein et al., in press, for a more complete discussion of these issues). At present, the literature on children's suggestibility is somewhat confusing because of conflicting findings regarding the factors responsible for their responses to misleading information. Ceci and his colleagues (Ceci, et al., 1987a, 1987b; Toglia, et al., 1989; see also Toglia, Ross, & Ceci, this volume) report evidence for both memory impairment and the acceptance of misinformation, whereas Zaragoza (1987; Zaragoza & Wilson, 1989; see also Zaragoza, Dahlgren, & Muench, this volume) has not been able to find evidence of memory impairment. The reasons for this discrepancy are not clear, but it should be emphasized that there is no disagreement with regard to the fundamental demonstration of suggestibility in children.

Context Specificity and Issues of Cognitive Diagnosis

A third feature of children's memory that has serious implications for understanding testimony reflects the fundamental difficulty of making firm "diagnoses" or assessments of underlying cognitive competence (see Flavell, 1985; Ornstein, 1991; Ornstein et al., in press). A basic finding in the cognitive development literature is that children's performance varies markedly from setting to setting. For example, although young children tend not to use strategies spontaneously in the service of memory goals, they may in fact do so when the information processing demands of the task are reduced, when more meaningful stimuli are provided, or when the task context is altered in some other way (Folds, Footo, Guttentag, & Ornstein, 1990; Ornstein, Baker-Ward, & Naus, 1988). This pervasive context specificity is only now coming to be examined seriously by researchers concerned with memory development, but it has profound implications for assessments of whether a particular child does or does not have a certain ability. Among other things, it suggests that children's reports of personally experienced events may be imperfect indicators of what has been stored in long-term memory. Thus, although demonstrations of context specificity do not rule out storage-based accounts of forgetting, they do focus attention on possible retrieval problems in the interview situation.

Recognizing that children's reports may vary across different assessment contexts, interviewers must be concerned about the extent to which slight changes in the mode of inquiry may yield different estimates of competency. Among other things, it is important to consider the form of the questions addressed to children. For example, consistent with repeated demonstrations of age-related changes in performance on tasks such as free recall that provide minimal prompts (see, e.g., Bjorklund & Muir, 1988), older children are better than younger children in the effective utilization of open-ended questions (e.g., "Tell me everything that you can remember about what happened"). Younger children, in contrast, tend to require more specific (e.g., yes-no) types of probes to support their recall (e.g., Dent & Stephenson, 1979). Nonetheless, the ability of young children to respond to simple objective questions about experienced events is remarkably good, despite their need for more cues to prompt their responses (see, e.g., Goodman & Reed, 1986). However, it should be noted that these two general forms of inquiry differ in terms of the amount and accuracy of the information produced. In general, open-ended queries elicit incomplete but quite accurate responses, whereas specific questions prompt the recollection of additional information, albeit with an increased risk of error, particularly if misleading questions are included (Dent & Stephenson, 1979; Goodman et al., 1987). Moreover, the use of leading as opposed to neutrally toned questions has the potential to turn an interview into an interrogation, thereby increasing the likelihood that children's responses may be governed less by what they can remember than by what is suggested by the interviewer (Clarke-Stewart, Thompson, & Lepore, 1989).

Other features of the interview context can also have an impact on children's reports. The actual location of the interview may be quite important, because the features of the context may make some settings more facilitative of recall than others. Thus, for example, returning to the scene of an earlier encounter may have positive effects on children's recollections of the experience (Ornstein, 1991; Ornstein et al., in press). On the other hand, it is possible that the emotional distress triggered in some settings may interfere with retrieval. In general, stress experienced by children as they are being questioned can have a negative impact on their recall. Although work in this area is only beginning, Peters (1989) suggests children's performance will be especially impaired if they are questioned about a stressful event by an interviewer who employs a stressful, confrontational style. Further, the very language used in an interview can have a clear impact on what is reported, and interviewers must be particularly sensitive to match their questions to the child's level of language competence (Ornstein et al., in press).

Finally, as implied above, certain characteristics of the interviewer's style can have a substantial impact on children's reports. Not only are some interviewers more skillful than others in establishing rapport and putting children at ease, but there are also differences in the extent to which young children are led to understand the interview process

(Ornstein, 1991; Ornstein et al., in press). Good interviews depend upon the examiner and the child sharing certain assumptions about the nature and objectives of the task. For example, in some situations it seems likely that a child may report relatively little information because he or she assumes that the examiner already has the relevant knowledge (Best & Ornstein, 1986; Ornstein, 1991). Moreover, when subjected to repeated questioning, some children may change their responses because they assume that the interviewer was dissatisfied with their reports (see, e.g., Ornstein et al., in press; Siegal, Waters, & Dinwiddy, 1988), although under some conditions, repeated testing can facilitate children's performance (e.g., Howe & Brainerd, 1989).

Overview

Other cognitive skills no doubt play a role in children's performance in testimony-like situations. For example, abilities to differentiate between experienced and imagined events (e.g., Jens, Gordon, & Shaddock, 1990; Johnson, Foley, Suengas, & Raye, 1988) and to take the perspective of another individual (e.g., Selman, Schorin, Stone, & Phelps, 1983) must be considered in any assessment of the child as a potential witness. Nonetheless, the three broad themes outlined here—the role of prior knowledge, the nature of intervening experiences, and the characteristics of the interview context—represent an effective starting point for conceptualizing the memory processes involved in children's testimony. Moreover, given the great gaps in the research literature, this informal framework may serve as a guide to the generation of studies that can truly increase our understanding of the testimony of children.

In the next section, we present an overview of two of our experiments that were influenced by the perspective presented here. These studies reflect the collaborative efforts of developmental psychologists interested in children's memory and clinical child psychologists who have worked extensively with victims of child sexual abuse, including the preparation of these children for appearances in court. A fundamental assumption underlying the work that we report is that of the importance of gathering systematic data on young children's long-term retention of the details of salient, personally meaningful events.

Explorations of Children's Memory for Visits to the Doctor

As indicated above, we are in the midst of a programmatic series of studies concerning young children's memory for visits to the doctor for a well-child physical examination. Several factors influenced our choice of the doctor visit as a "stimulus event" in studies of young children's long-term retention. First, it is naturally occurring, salient event in the lives of all children. It is also a situation that in some respects is similar to instances of sexual abuse: an adult has bodily contact with a child who is in varying states of undress. Moreover, not all aspects of the experience are pleasant, and the child may be anxious or stressed. Most importantly, with the cooperation of the pediatricians who carry out the checkups, we have been able to determine the features of the examination that is given to each individual child. In general, by studying children's recall in this context, we are able to maintain a level of control that is typically obtained only in the laboratory.

Our research strategy is first to determine baseline information concerning what children of different ages are able to remember about a visit to the pediatrician for a physical examination. Once children's retention over varying intervals is known, it will be possible to examine systematically the influence of the critical variables mentioned above—e.g., children's knowledge, intervening events, etc.—that should affect children's retention and testimony. In this section, we describe two initial studies that were designed to obtain baseline data on retention. In these studies (Baker-Ward, Gordon, Ornstein, Larus, & Clubb, 1991; Ornstein, Gordon, & Larus, 1992), the memory performance of children between 3 and 7 years of age was assessed immediately after the physical examination and at delays extending to 6 weeks. We also discuss ongoing extensions of this work.

Basic Procedures

The Samples

Similar procedures were employed in both investigations. The samples were drawn from the patient rolls of children seen at two private pediatric practices. Parents of children who were scheduled for normal (i.e., well-child) checkups were contacted just prior to their scheduled appointments. Sick children, or those who came to the practices with injuries, were not included in these studies.

The Physical Examinations

Each checkup was divided into two parts, with the child first being seen by the nurse and then by the doctor. The nurse's segment of the examination included the usual weighing and measuring, checking hearing and vision and blood pressure, drawing blood, obtaining a urine specimen, and so on. The doctor's segment of the examination included looking in the child's mouth, eyes, and ears, checking the genitals, listening to heart and lungs, etc. Because examinations could vary as a function of the age and behavior of the child, the nurses and physicians filled out checklists indicating which particular features were included in the examination of each individual child. The nurses also took a Polaroid photo of each child, in an attempt to determine if the child was remembering this particular examination or was recalling from some script for a visit to the doctor's office. Moreover, it turns out that the overwhelming majority of the children remembered the picture taking.

The Interviews

The initial and delayed interviews followed a structured format that involved a general-to-specific mode of questioning. The children were initially asked a very open-ended question: "Tell me what happened during your checkup." After prompting for additional information, a less general open-ended question was asked: "Tell me what the doctor (or nurse) did to you." After prompting, the questioning became more specific concerning those features of the physical examination that were not spontaneously mentioned. For all features remembered, the children were asked to elaborate on their responses. For example, if a child said "The doctor checked my eyes," the interviewer probed with: "How did she/he check your eyes?"

Coding

The interviews were audiotaped in the initial study and videotaped in the second experiment. In each investigation, the tapes were then transcribed and coded according to a system that focused on the particular features of the physical examination (i.e., procedures carried out in the checkup) that were recovered and the level of specificity of the probes that was required to retrieve the information. Moreover, because the number of examination features varied from child to child, typically ranging between 15 and 25, the basic data are in percentage terms. For each individual child, the "items" that were both "presented" by the office staff and probed by the experimenter were determined. We then calculated the proportion of the features that were recalled during the interviews in response to the different types of questions.

The Initial Investigation

Method

In this study, Ornstein et al. (1992) worked with 26 3-year-olds and 25 6-year-olds. Immediately after the physical examination, all of the children were interviewed by an experimenter. One half of the subjects were then retested 1 week later in their homes, whereas the others were seen at their homes after a delay interval of 3 weeks. All interviews involved the use of a common protocol that was designed to probe for the children's retention of the standard features of the physical examination. However,

TABLE 4.1. Percentage of correct recall by type of question at each interview.

	Initial	1 week	3 weeks
3-year-olds			
Open-ended	19.4	23.0	15.9
Yes-no	62.4	50.0	51.0
Total	81.8	73.0	66.9
6-year-olds			
Open-ended	41.2	36.9	45.8
Yes-no	50.4	52.8	46.5
Total	91.7	89.7	92.3

Adapted from "Children's Memory for a Personally Experienced Event: Implications for Testimony" by P.A. Ornstein, B.N. Gordon, and D.M. Larus, 1992, *Applied Cognitive Psychology*, *6*, 49–60.

because the checkups differed somewhat from child to child, the use of this protocol typically involved questioning each subject about some features of a physical examination that had not been experienced.

Results

As might be expected, on the initial test of memory, the 6-year-olds remembered more than the 3-year-olds. These older children recovered 91.7% of the examination features, whereas the younger children recalled 81.8% of the components of the office visit. Thus, recall was very good, but the performance of the older children was nonetheless superior. Moreover, the children also differed in the extent to which their recall was prompted by general versus more specific yes/no questions. Indeed, as can be seen in Table 4.1, the older children were better able to produce information in response to general, open-ended probes, whereas the younger children tended to require more specific prompts. Among the 3-year-olds, only 19.4% of the features were recalled in response to open-ended questions, whereas 62.4% were generated when specific yes-no questions were used as probes.

Consistent with performance at the immediate test, the 6-year-olds remembered more features of the physical examination than the 3-year-olds at both the 1-week and 3-week delay intervals. Nonetheless, as can be seen in Table 4.1, performance is still quite good. The 3-year-olds dropped from 81.8% to 73% at 1 week, and then to 66.9% at 3 weeks. In contrast, the performance of the 6-year-olds is remarkable in that these children did not seem to forget over the 3-week interval. These subjects still correctly recalled approximately 90% of the features of the examination. Inspection of Table 4.1 also indicates that the 6-year-olds recalled more aspects of the physical examination in response to general questions than did the younger children, paralleling performance at the initial test.

To understand further the children's recall at these delay intervals, we divided their recall into two components. For each subject, we first calculated the percentage of initially correct items that were included in recall at the two delayed tests. It turns out that the 3-year-olds were able to report in excess of 70% of the examination features that they remembered initially, and that the 6-year-olds remembered more than 90% of these "old" features. Thus, even the older children showed some forgetting when measured in terms of their initial recall performance. We also looked at delayed recall in terms of features of the physical examination that were recalled for the first time at 1 or 3 weeks. The mean numbers of such "new" features generated ranged between 1.5 and 2.0, and these values did not vary systematically with age. Thus, at the delays, children at both age levels produced items that they had not initially recalled.

Further consideration of the data revealed that the children provided very little false information. For example, when questioned about features of a medical examination that had not been part of their checkups, the subjects made very few intrusions (i.e., false positive errors). That is, they did not claim that items that were not part of the physical examination had in fact been "presented" by the nurses and the doctors. At the initial interview, the 3-year-olds made an average of 0.5 intrusions, and the 6-year-olds produced 0.4 intrusions. In addition, the children were reasonably efficient in their generation of correct denials. The 3-year-olds produced 3.4 correct denials, whereas the older children generated 3.8, corresponding to 63.9% and 85.8%, respectively, of the correct denials that were possible.

Errors increased somewhat over the delay intervals, but nonetheless there were still relatively few intrusions. The analysis of the correct denials indicated that although the percentage of correct denials decreased over time (to 59.8% and 65.2% at 3 weeks for 3- and 6-year-olds, respectively), the children continued to be reasonably effective in their ability to reject, that is, say "no" to, features of the examination that had not been included.

Interpretation

The data presented here indicate that young children's recall of the details of an office visit can be quite impressive, even after a 3-week delay. Given the salience of the "stimulus," we expected that performance would be good. Nonetheless, we were surprised both by the remarkable levels of initial recall and by the high degree of retention over time, especially among the 6-year-olds. To chart the course of forgetting, it seems clear that we must extend the delay intervals considerably. We also must examine some of the factors that may contribute to the elevated levels of retention that were observed here, one of which may be the initial testing that was given to all children after the physical examination. To explore these issues, a second study was designed in which the delay was extended to 6 weeks and controls for the initial interview were introduced.

Replication and Extension

Method

In this experiment, Baker-Ward et al. (1991) established a sample of 187 children, with approximately equal representation from 3-, 5-, and 7-year-olds. At each age level, three groups of children were interviewed twice, once immediately after the physical examination and a second time in a university laboratory at one of three delay intervals: 1, 3, or 6 weeks. In addition, to examine in a preliminary fashion whether the initial interview could facilitate subsequent retention, a fourth group of children at each age level was interviewed only once, after a delay of 3 weeks. As in the first investigation, a standard interview protocol was employed, with the result being that each child was asked some questions about components of a physical examination that were not included in his or her checkup. The protocol also included two other types of misleading questions: probes about activities that might be expected to occur in interaction with nonmedical professionals (e.g., "Did the nurse cut your hair?") and questions about actions that would not be included in such activities (e.g., "Did the doctor lick your knee?").

Results

In general, the findings were similar to those obtained by Ornstein et al. (1992). As can be seen in Table 4.2, recall was again quite good, although there was a clear age-related progression in performance. At the initial interview, the 3-year-olds recalled a total of 75.4% of the features, compared with 82.2% and 92.2% by the 5- and 7-year-olds, respectively. Again, the 3-year-olds evidenced some loss over the 1- and 3-week delays, and the older subjects showed relatively little forgetting. Indeed, even at 6 weeks, the 5-year-olds recalled 76.4% of the examination features, and the 7-year-olds, 89.8%. Only the 3-year-olds showed clear forgetting over time, and even among these children the drop in performance was not great. The data shown in Table 4.2 also replicate the earlier finding of an age-related progression in the ability to provide information about the examination features in response to open-ended, general questions.

As was found in the initial study, the children in the Baker-Ward et al. (1991) experiment were skilled at being able to differentiate between

TABLE 4.2. Percentage of correct recall by type of question at each interview.

	Initial	1 week	3 weeks	3 weeks control	6 weeks
3-year-olds					
Open-ended	26.4	14.0	17.2	15.4	20.1
Yes-no	49.0	50.0	39.8	46.2	45.6
Total	75.4	64.0	57.0	61.6	65.7
5-year-olds					
Open-ended	42.4	30.6	30.3	37.6	34.2
Yes-no	39.8	46.7	44.3	44.8	42.2
Total	82.2	77.3	74.6	82.4	76.4
7-year-olds					
Open-ended	61.1	59.9	51.3	47.1	55.1
Yes-no	31.1	33.3	35.7	32.9	34.7
Total	92.2	93.2	87.0	80.0	89.8

Adapted from "Young Children's Long-term Retention of a Pediatric Examination" by L. Baker-Ward, B.N. Gordon, P.A. Ornstein, D.M. Larus, and P.A. Clubb.

activities that were and were not part of the physical examination. In general, in response to these misleading questions, the frequencies of correct denials were high and those of intrusions were low, although the performance of the 3-year-olds was poorer than that of the older children. For example, when questioned at the initial interview about components of a normal physical examination that had not been included in their checkups, the correct denial scores of the 3-, 5-, and 7-year-olds were 71.4%, 92.7%, and, 88.3%, respectively. Most interestingly, the performance of the children was outstanding when they were questioned about activities that would not be expected to take place in a physical examination. In response to these misleading questions, the correct denial scores at the initial interview were 83.8%, 95.2%, and 97.4% for the 3-, 5-, and 7-year-olds, respectively.

Finally, this study resulted in one surprise, namely, the performance of the control groups. Inspection of Table 4.2 suggests that the initial interview after the physical examination had remarkably little impact upon subsequent retention. In general, the performance of the control subjects who were interviewed for the first time after 3 weeks is quite comparable to that of their age-mates who were tested initially and then at the 3-week delay. Only among the 7-year-olds was there a hint that the control group might perform below the level of the children who were interviewed twice, and this difference was not statistically significant. Indeed, among the 3- and 5-year-olds, the control groups actually tended to outperform the children who were tested initially and after 3 weeks.

Interpretation

These data reinforce our initial impressions of young children's abilities to remember the details of a visit to the doctor for a physical examination.

Again, these children demonstrated impressive recall of the component features of their checkups, coupled with clear evidence of being able to respond negatively to questions about events that were not part of their physical examinations. Moreover, the high levels of recall after 6 weeks, especially for the 5- and 7-year-olds indicate that our efforts to obtain baseline information concerning the course of forgetting must be continued with longer delay intervals. Further, given that performance of control subjects who were interviewed only at 3 weeks was comparable to that of children tested twice, immediately and at 6 weeks, it is unlikely that the initial interview contributed to the high levels of recall observed at the delays. It thus is important to continue to explore factors that may be responsible for the elevated levels of retention.

General Discussion

The two experiments outlined here represent the initial stages in our exploration of young children's long-term retention of salient events. The doctor-visit paradigm has been selected for study because it represents a memory situation that is similar in some respects to events about which children are called upon to provide testimony. The office visit is clearly a meaningful event in the lives of the children, and their incidental memory was tested after substantial delays. It was thought that these experiments would provide baseline data concerning performance in this situation that would serve as a foundation for an examination of variables expected to be important in the legal context. Although a number of such studies are now being conducted—e.g., explorations of the effects of repeated questioning and the use dolls as props for the recall of 3-year-olds—it is also apparent that the high levels of performance observed in these two experiments require that additional baseline data be gathered at longer delays. A 12-week delay interval is being examined in a study that is currently underway.

As we continue to extend this research program in these directions, it is also necessary to ask why the children's performance was so good. As indicated above, our first thought was that the initial interview after the physical examination might have facilitated their later recall. The data do not seem to support this hypothesis, at least in terms of recall at 3 weeks, but additional control conditions at other delays are needed. Moreover, we do not know whether interviews repeated several times over the course of weeks or months and that involve different interviewers each time (common in cases of child abuse) would have a greater impact on delayed recall. We are currently examining this issue.

It is also important to determine if factors not under the researchers' control could have facilitated the children's recall. For example, to what extent might the parents have primed or reinstated the children's memory by reminding them of the impending (follow-up) visit with the experimenter? Moreover, other experiences that occur in the delay interval have the potential to affect the children's subsequent reports. A return visit to the pediatrician, reading a book about going to the doctor, and telling Grandma about what happened at the doctor's office are just a few of many possibilities that need to be investigated systematically.

Another potential contributor to the children's recall is their general knowledge about doctors and medical procedures. Given that young children readily form scripts for regularly occurring events (Fivush, 1984; Nelson, 1986), they may well have formed such event representations for visits to the doctor. Thus, their reports at extended delays may reflect reliance on this generalized knowledge to some extent, as opposed to their memory for the details of the particular office visit in question (see Myles-Worsley et al., 1986).

That prior knowledge may have an impact on recall of the physical examination is suggested by a recent study carried out by Clubb, Nida, Merritt, and Ornstein (1991) in which a sample of 5-year-olds who did not have a checkup was asked to describe what typically goes on in a visit to the doctor. When the information provided by this normative sample about individual features of the physical examination was related to the recall of these features by the 5-year-olds in the Baker-Ward et al. (1991) study, correlations in excess of .60 were obtained, and these correlations increased as a function of delay. Nonetheless, these correlations are not inconsistent with the view that the children could also be remembering details of their recently experienced physical examinations. Evidence consistent with this perspective is seen in the children's retention of the picture-taking episode that was added to the checkup and in their ability to respond well to the misleading questions. However, additional attention must be devoted to this issue.

Implications for Interviewing

A number of features of our doctor-visit studies have implications for thinking about the interviewing of children in the context of the legal system (see also Ornstein, 1991; Ornstein et al., in press). For example, both experiments discussed above provide evidence that estimates of children's recall (or, in general, competence) might depend upon the form of the questions addressed to them. Consistent with other studies (e.g., Dent & Stephenson, 1979), an age-related progression in the ability to make use of open-ended questions was found. Indeed, our interviewers needed to work harder to obtain information from 3- and 5-year-olds than from 6- and 7-year-olds. Thus, when talking with the younger children, these interviewers had to rely more completely on specific yes-no forms of questioning than was the case with the older children. The memoral competence of the younger children would have been underestimated considerably if the interviewers' assessments were based solely on responses made to the open-ended questions. However, in the legal system, there may be drawbacks associated with the use of specific questions, and interviewers must be careful to avoid introducing information into the interview and thus potentially biasing the child's report. Further work to develop interview procedures to facilitate accuracy in the reports of young children is clearly needed.

In addition, consistent with the theme of context specificity developed above, it is important to note that the context in which our subjects were asked to remember what had happened to them was a relatively optimal one. This is true both with regard to the emotional climate created by the skilled interviewers and the voluntary nature of the children's participation, as well as with respect to the information processing support that was available in the form of specific probes. Each of these features may be missing in legal situations, where children must discuss unpleasant events in a possibly foreboding context, and where the interviewer does not have complete knowledge of the child's experience. These findings indicate that children's retention of a salient personally experienced event can be remarkably good under close to ideal situations. However, care should be taking in generalizing these findings. It cannot be assumed that children's performance will approach this level of competence in all settings.

Finally, even though a great deal remains to be done to clearly understand the children's performance in this situation, the doctor visit paradigm appears to be a useful vehicle for exploring the long-term retention of autobiographical information and for providing—eventually—some assistance to those who are primarily concerned with the testimony of children. A long-term goal of ours is the development of interview guidelines for professionals who interact with child victims prior to court appearance, guidelines that may serve to maintain but not distort memory (see also Brainerd & Ornstein, 1991; Ornstein, 1991; Ornstein et al., in press).

Acknowledgment. Preparation of this report was supported in part by grant MH 43904 from the United States Public Health Service.

References

Baker-Ward, L., Gordon, B.N., Ornstein, P.A., Larus, D.M., & Clubb, P.A. (1991). *Young children's long-term retention of a pediatric examination.* Manuscript submitted for publication.

Baker-Ward, L.E., Hess, T.M., & Flannagan, D.A. (1990). The effects of involvement on children's memory for events. *Cognitive Development, 5*, 55–70.

Baker-Ward, L., Ornstein, P.A., & Holden, D.J. (1984). The expression of memorization in early childhood. *Journal of Experimental Child Psychology*, *37*, 555–575.

Bartlett, F.C. (1932). *Remembering*. London: Cambridge University Press.

Bekerian, D.A., & Bowers, J.M. (1983). Eyewitness testimony: Were we misled? *Journal of Experimental Psychology: Learning, Memory, and Cognition*, *9*, 139–145.

Best, D.L., & Ornstein, P.A. (1986). Children's generation and communication of mnemonic organizational strategies. *Developmental Psychology*, *22*, 845–853.

Binet, A., & Henri, V. (1894). La memoire des phrases (memoire des idees). *L'Annee Psychologique*, *1*, 24–59.

Bjorklund, D.F. (1985). The role of conceptual knowledge in the development of organization in children's memory. In C.J. Brainerd & M. Pressley (Eds.), *Basic processes in memory development: Progress in cognitive development research* (pp. 103–142). New York: Springer-Verlag.

Bjorklund, D.F., & Muir, J.E. (1988). Children's development of free recall memory: Remembering on their own. In R. Vasta (Ed.), *Annals of child development* (Vol. 5, pp. 79–123). Greenwich, CN: JAI Press.

Bogartz, R.S. (1990). Evaluating forgetting curves psychologically. *Journal of Experimental Psychology: Learning, Memory, and Cognition*, *16*, 138–148.

Brainerd, C.J., Kingma, J., & Howe, M.L. (1985). On the development of forgetting. *Child Development*, *56*, 1103–1119.

Brainerd, C.J., & Ornstein, P.A. (1991). Children's memory for witnessed events: The developmental backdrop. In. J. Doris (Ed.), *The suggestibility of children's memory* (pp. 10–20). Washington, DC: American Psychological Association.

Brainerd, C.J., Reyna, V.F., Howe, M.L., & Kingma, J. (1990). The development of forgetting and reminiscence. *Monographs of the Society for Research in Child Development*, *55*(3–4, Serial No. 222).

Bransford, J.D., & Franks, J.J. (1971). Abstraction of linguistic ideas. *Cognitive Psychology*, *2*, 331–350.

Brown, A.L. (1978). Knowing when, where, and how to remember: A problem of metacognition. In R. Glaser (Ed.), *Advances in instructional psychology* (Vol. 1, pp. 77–165). Hillsdale, NJ: Erlbaum.

Campbell, B.A., & Jaynes, J. (1966). Reinstatement. *Psychological Review*, *73*, 478–480.

Ceci, S.J., Ross, D.F., & Toglia, M.P. (1987a). Suggestibility of children's memory: Psycholegal implications. *Journal of Experimental Psychology: General*, *116*, 38–49.

Ceci, S.J., Ross, D.F., & Toglia, M.P. (1987b). Age differences in suggestibility: Narrowing the uncertainties. In S.J. Ceci, M.P. Toglia, & D.F. Ross (Eds.), *Children's eyewitness testimony* (pp. 79–91). New York: Springer-Verlag.

Ceci, S.J., Toglia, M.P., & Ross, D.F. (Eds.). (1987). *Children's eyewitness testimony*. New York: Springer-Verlag.

Chi, M.T.H. (1978). Knowledge structures and memory development. In R.S. Siegler (Ed.), *Children's thinking: What develops?* (pp. 73–96). Hillsdale, NJ: Erlbaum.

Chi, M.T.H., & Ceci, S.J. (1987). Content knowledge: Its role, representation, and restructuring in memory development. In H.W. Reese (Ed.), *Advances in*

child development and behavior (Vol. 20, pp. 91–142). New York: Academic Press.
Christiaansen, R.E., & Ochalek, K. (1983). Editing the fleeting information from memory: Evidence for the coexistence of original and post-event information. *Memory and Cognition*, *11*, 467–475.
Clarke-Stewart, A., Thompson, W., & Lepore, S. (1989). *Manipulating children's interpretations through interrogation*. Paper presented at biennial meeting of Society for Research in Child Development, Kansas City.
Clubb, P.A., Nida, R., Merritt, K., & Ornstein, P.A. (1991). *Visiting the doctor: Children's knowledge and memory*. Poster presented at the biennial meeting of the International Society for the Study of Behavioural Development, Minneapolis.
Cofer, C.N., Chmielewski, D.L., & Brockway, J.P. (1976). Constructive processes and the structure of human memory. In C.N. Cofer (Ed.), *The structure of human memory* (pp. 190–203). San Francisco: Freeman.
Crowder, R.G. (1976). *Principles of learning and memory*. Hillsdale, NJ: Erlbaum.
DeLoache, J.S., Cassidy, D.J., & Brown, A.L. (1985). Precursors of mnemonic strategies in very young children's memory. *Child Development*, *56*, 125–137.
Dent, H.R., & Stephenson, G.M. (1979). An experimental study of the effectiveness of different techniques of questioning child witnesses. *British Journal of Social and Clinical Psychology*, *18*, 41–51.
Ebbinghaus, H. (1885). *Uber das Gedachtnis*. Leibzig: Duncker. [Reprinted as *Memory* (H.A. Ruger & C.E. Busenius, Trans.). New York: Teachers College, 1913].
Fivush, R. (1984). Learning about school: The development of kindergarteners' school scripts. *Child Development*, *55*, 1697–1709.
Fivush, R., Gray, J.T., & Fromhoff, F.A. (1987). Two year olds talk about the past. *Cognitive Development*, *2*, 393–409.
Fivush, R., Hudson, J., & Nelson, K. (1984). Children's long-term memory for a novel event: An exploratory study. *Merrill-Palmer Quarterly*, *30*, 303–316.
Flavell, J.H. (1985). *Cognitive development* (2nd ed.). Englewood Cliffs, NJ: Prentice-Hall.
Folds, T.H., Footo, M., Guttentag, R.E., & Ornstein, P.A. (1990). When children mean to remember: Issues of context specificity, strategy effectiveness, and intentionality in the development of memory. In D.F. Bjorklund (Ed.), *Children's strategies: Contemporary views of cognitive development* (pp. 67–91). Hillsdale, NJ: Erlbaum.
Goodman, G.S. (1984). Children's testimony in historical perspective. *Journal of Social, Issues*, *40*, 9–32.
Goodman, G.S., Aman, C., & Hirshman, J. (1987). Child sexual and physical abuse: Children's testimony. In S.J. Ceci, M.P. Toglia, & D.F. Ross (Eds.), *Children's eyewitness memory*. New York: Springer-Verlag.
Goodman, G.S., & Reed, R.S. (1986). Age differences in eyewitness testimony. *Law and Human Behavior*, *10*, 317–332.
Gordon, B.N., Schroeder, C.S., & Abrams, J.M. (1990). Age and social-class differences in children's knowledge of sexuality. *Journal of Clinical Child Psychology*, *19*, 33–43.
Howe, M.L., & Brainerd, C.J. (1989). Development of children's long-term retention. *Developmental Review*, *9*, 301–340.

Jens, K. G., Gordon, B.N., & Shaddock, A.J. (1990). Remembering activities performed versus imagined: A comparison of children with mental retardation and children with normal intelligence. *International Journal of Disability, Development, and Education*, *37*, 201–213.

Johnson, M.K., Foley, M.A., Suengas, A.G., & Raye, C.L. (1988). Phenomenal characteristics of perceived and imagined autobiographical events. *Journal of Experimental Psychology: General*, *117*, 371–376.

Kail, R. (1989). *The development of memory in children* (3rd ed.). New York: Freeman.

Loftus, E.F. (1979). *Eyewitness testimony*. Cambridge: Harvard University Press.

Loftus, E.F., Miller, D.G., & Burns, H.J. (1978). Semantic integration of verbal information into visual memory. *Journal of Experimental Psychology: Human Learning and Memory*, *4*, 19–31.

Loftus, G.R. (1985a). Consistency and confoundings: Reply to Slamecka. *Journal of Experimental Psychology: Learning, Memory, and Cognition*, *11*, 817–820.

Loftus, G.R. (1985b). Evaluating forgetting curves. *Journal of Experimental Psychology: Learning, Memory, and Cognition*, *11*, 396–405.

Loftus, G.R., & Bamber, D. (1990). Learning-forgetting independence: Unidimensional memory models and feature models: Comment on Bogartz (1990). *Journal of Experimental Psychology: Learning, Memory, and Cognition*, *16*, 916–926.

McCloskey, M., & Zaragoza, M.S. (1985a). Misleading postevent information and memory for events: Arguments and evidence against memory impairment hypotheses. *Journal of Experimental Psychology: General*, *114*, 1–16.

McCloskey, M., & Zaragoza, M.S. (1985b). Postevent information and memory: Reply to Loftus, Schooler, and Waganaar. *Journal of Experimental Psychology: General*, *114*, 383–387.

Melton, A.W., & Irwin, J. McD. (1940). The influence of interpolated learning on retroactive inhibition and the overt transfer of specific responses. *American Journal of Psychology*, *53*, 175–203.

Myles-Worsley, M., Cromer, C.C., & Dodd, D.H. (1986). Children's preschool script reconstruction: Reliance on general knowledge as memory fades. *Developmental Psychology*, *22*, 22–30.

Nelson, K. (1986). *Event knowledge: Structure and function in development*. Hillsdale, NJ: Erlbaum.

Nelson, K., Fivush, R., Hudson, J., & Lucariello, J. (1983). Scripts and the development of memory. In M.T.H. Chi (Ed.), *Trends in memory development research* (pp. 52–70). New York: Karger.

Nelson, K., & Gruendel, J. (1981). Generalized event representations: Basic building blocks of cognitive development. In M.E. Lamb & A.L. Brown (Eds.), *Advances in developmental psychology* (Vol. 1, pp. 131–158). Hillsdale, NJ: Erlbaum.

Ornstein, P.A. (Ed.). (1978). *Memory development in children*. Hillsdale, NJ: Erlbaum.

Ornstein, P.A. (1990). Knowledge and strategies: A discussion. In W. Schneider & F.E. Weinert (Eds.), *Interactions among aptitudes, strategies, and knowledge in cognitive performance* (pp. 147–156). New York: Springer-Verlag.

Ornstein, P.A. (1991). Putting interviewing in context: Commentary on Dent's "Experimental studies of interviewing child witnesses." In J. Doris (Ed.), *The suggestibility of children's memory* (pp. 147–152). Washington, DC: American Psychological Association.

Ornstein, P.A., Baker-Ward, L.E., & Naus, M.J. (1988). The development of mnemonic skill. In F.E. Weinert & M. Perlmutter (Eds.), *Memory development: Universal changes in individual differences* (pp. 31–50). Hillsdale, NJ: Erlbaum.

Ornstein, P.A., & Corsale, K. (1979). Process and structure in children's memory. In G. Whitehurst & B.J. Zimmerman (Eds.), *The functions of language and cognition* (pp. 199–228). New York: Academic Press.

Ornstein, P.A., Gordon, B.N., & Larus, D.M. (1992). Children's memory for a personally experienced event: Implications for testimony. *Applied Cognitive Psychology*, *6*, 49–60.

Ornstein, P.A., Larus, D.M., & Clubb, P.A. (in press). Understanding children's testimony: Implications of research on the development of memory. In R. Vasta (Ed.), *Annals of Child Development* (Vol. 8). London: Jessica Kingsley.

Ornstein, P.A., & Naus, M.J. (1985). Effects of the knowledge base on children's memory strategies. In H.W. Reese (Ed.), *Advances in child development and behavior* (Vol. 19, pp. 113–148). Orlando: Academic Press.

Peters, D.P. (1987). The impact of naturally occurring stress on children's memory. In S.J. Ceci, M.P. Toglia, & D.F. Ross (Eds.), *Children's eyewitness memory* (pp. 122–141). New York: Springer-Verlag.

Peters, D.P. (1989). *The influence of stress and arousal on the child witness*. Paper presented at biennial meeting of the Society for Research in Child Development, Kansas City.

Peverly, S.T. (1991). Problems with the knowledge-based explanation of memory and development. *Review of Educational Research*, *61*, 71–93.

Piaget, J., & Inhelder, B. (1973). *Memory and intelligence*. New York: Basic Books.

Postman, L., & Underwood, B.J. (1973). Critical issues in interference theory. *Memory & Cognition*, *1*, 19–40.

Ratner, H.H., Smith, B.S., & Dion, S.A. (1986). Development of memory for events. *Journal of Experimental Child Psychology*, *41*, 411–428.

Rovee-Collier, C., & Hayne, H. (1987). Reactivation of infant memory: Implications for cognitive development. In H.W. Reese (Ed.), *Advances in child development and behavior* (Vol. 20, pp. 185–238). New York: Academic Press.

Schneider, W., & Pressley, M. (1989). *Memory development between 2 and 20*. New York: Springer-Verlag.

Selman, R.L., Schorin, M.Z., Stone, C.R., & Phelps, E. (1983). A naturalistic study of children's social understanding. *Developmental Psychology*, *19*, 82–102.

Siegal, M., Waters, L.J., & Dinwiddy, L.S. (1988). Misleading children: Causal attributions for inconsistency under repeated questioning. *Journal of Experimental Child Psychology*, *45*, 438–456.

Slamecka, N.J. (1985). On comparing rates of forgetting. *Journal of Experimental Psychology: Learning, Memory, and Cognition*, *11*, 812–816.

Slamecka, N.J., & Katsaiti, L.T. (1988). Normal forgetting of verbal lists as a function of prior testing. *Journal of Experimental Psychology: Learning, Memory, and Cognition*, *14*, 716–727.

Slamecka, N.J., & McElree, B. (1983). Normal forgetting of verbal lists as a function of their degree of learning. *Journal of Experimental Psychology: Learning, Memory, and Cognition*, *9*, 384–397.
Sodian, B., Schneider, W., & Perlmutter, M. (1986). Recall, clustering, and metamemory in young children. *Journal of Experimental Child Psychology*, *41*, 395–410.
Spilich, G.J., Vesonder, G.T., Chiesi, H.L., & Voss, J.F. (1979). Text processing of domain-related information for individuals with high and low domain knowledge. *Journal of Verbal Learning and Verbal Behavior*, *18*, 275–290.
Toglia, M.P., Ceci, S.J., & Ross, D.F. (1989). *Prestige vs. source monitoring in children's suggestibility*. Paper presented at the biennial meeting of the Society for Research in Child Development, Kansas City.
Weinert, F.E., & Perlmutter, M. (Eds.). (1988). *Memory development: Universal changes and individual differences*. Hillsdale, NJ: Erlbaum.
Wellman, H.M. (1988). The early development of memory strategies. In F.E. Weinert & M. Perlmutter (Eds.), *Memory development: Universal changes and individual differences* (pp. 3–29). Hillsdale, NJ: Erlbaum.
Zaragoza, M. (1987). Memory, suggestibility, and eyewitness testimony in children and adults. In S.J. Ceci, M.P. Toglia, & D.F. Ross (Eds.), *Children's eyewitness memory* (pp. 53–78). New York: Springer-Verlag.
Zaragoza, M., & Wilson, D. (1989). *Suggestibility in the child witness*. Paper presented at the biennial meeting of the Society for Research in Child Development, Kansas City.

5
The Misinformation Effect: Transformations in Memory Induced by Postevent Information

ELIZABETH F. LOFTUS, HUNTER G. HOFFMAN, and
WILLEM A. WAGENAAR

When people encounter misleading information after they view an event, their recollection of the event is often affected (see Loftus, Miller, & Burns, 1978; Bekerian & Bowers, 1983; for examples). We refer to the change in report arising from postevent misinformation as the *misinformation effect.* In thinking about the impact of misinformation, it is useful to distinguish between a memory report (or what people claim to remember), and a memory trace (or what memory information is stored in the brain). Because the memory traces themselves are, obviously, never directly accessible to researchers, we must rely on memory reports to give us clues about the nature of the underlying trace.

In the typical misinformation study, a three-stage paradigm is used. Subjects first view a complex event, such as a simulated crime or accident. Next they encounter new information about the event. The new information might include exposure to another witness's version of the event, or to an interrogation about the event that contains within it new details. Finally, subjects are tested on their memory for the original event to assess whether the postevent information produces changes in recollection. Unquestionably, new information, when it is misleading, can produce errors in what subjects report they have seen. Stop signs are recalled as yield signs, and hammers are recalled as screwdrivers. Why?

When a person erroneously claims she saw a yield sign, it may appear as if the original stop sign was "forgotten." The phenomenon of forgetting has a long history in psychology; the fundamental issues are quite straightforward. Is the forgotten stop sign due to a loss of information from the person's memory? Or are we seeing merely a loss of access to that information? Put another way, does the erroneous report reflect storage failure or retrieval failure (Crowder, 1976)?

One specific "retrieval failure" interpretation of the effect of misinformation on memory reports is that postevent information coexists with event information and that these two traces compete with each other at the time of retrieval. According to this coexistence view, the memory trace most consistent with the cues available at retrieval will be the trace that is accessed and reported (Bekerian & Bowers, 1983; Christiaansen & Ochalek, 1983; Morton, Hammersley, & Bekerian, 1985).

A different interpretation of the erroneous reports of misinformation is that they reflect storage changes in memory. The idea here is that memory may be updated as a consequence of postevent information (Loftus, 1979; Loftus & Loftus, 1980; Loftus, Schooler, & Wagenaar, 1985). According to the strong version of the updating hypothesis, misinformation replaces or overwrites event information. Once this occurs, the event information is no longer available. A weaker version of this interpretation suggests that the event trace is altered rather than replaced. The final recollection might be for the event item, but the memory for that item might contain some features from the postevent source.

In misinformation studies people report that they have seen objects as part of an event when in fact those objects came from other sources. The idea that people can and do combine information from a variety of sources is not novel. Such a notion is easily seen in theories about the nature of remembering advocated by Bartlett (1932), Neisser (1967), Bransford and Franks (1971) and others. The notion of memory that underlies all of this work is that when we remember our past we do not simply activate or locate a memory trace and then produce this exact trace. Rather the process involves a highly constructive activity that gathers bits and pieces from different sources and "constructs" a memory. The current experiments provide new information on the nature of this constructive memory process.

The idea that new information can affect old memories is also not novel. Such a notion is seen in the prototypical interference tasks of the past, in which the learning of a new connection ($A-C$) influences the retention of the earlier learned connection ($A-B$) (Adams, 1967). Controversies that abounded in the $A-B$, $A-C$ literature resurface today. However, the modern instantiation of these issues is important to explore because the modern experiments make much greater strides toward capturing some of the important social dynamics of memory experiences (Wells & Turtle, 1987). The current experiments provide valuable data bearing on how and when new information combines with earlier information, in settings that are closer to naturalistic.

The extensive interest today in the misinformation effect concerns in part an effort to identify the factors that lead people to be susceptible to postevent information and the factors that lead to resistance. Along with an interest in these factors, researchers have raised questions about the fate of the memory underlying the overt report. Was Freud correct when he said "in mental life nothing which has once been formed can perish"? (Freud, 1930, p. 69). Or, when misinformation is encountered does it alter the underlying memory that was stored? Exactly how does misinformation affect overt performance? Some biologically oriented psychologists have suggested that additional neurobiological facts will be required before we can settle the issue of whether impaired performance reflects an actual loss of information from storage and a corresponding regression of some of the synaptic changes that originally represented that stored information (Squire, 1987), but others disagree. The writings of Tulving (1983, 1984) suggest that underlying memories can actually be modified by postevent information. In his landmark book, *Elements of Episodic Memory*, Tulving (1983) noted that one of the most pervasive facts about episodic memory has to do with changes, over time, in recollective experience and memory performance pertaining to a given event. Some changes in memory performance, he argued, can be attributed to changes in retrieval factors, whereas others come about because of changes in "engrams" (p. 164). He gave the name "recoding" to the class of processes that take place after an event is encoded that cause changes in the engram associated with that event. A strong implication of the "recoding" notion (that is an integral part of his general abstract processing system [GAPS] theory) is that utilization of certain information contained in an original engram should not be possible after recoding has taken place, depending upon the nature of the modification of that engram (p. 168). The notion of recoding is one to which many modern-day connectionists are sympathetic. In the distributed, superpositional conceptualization of McClelland and Rumelhart (1985), for example, there is the explicit suggestion that we do not keep each memory in a separate place, but rather we superimpose them so that what the memory contains is a composite from various inputs.

Tulving himself directly acknowledged that some theorists might wish to argue that engrams, once formed, are never changed, and the recoding phenomena are simply the result of additional memory traces being formed from new inputs. Indeed, as far as the misinformation effect is concerned, some theorists have claimed that the idea of recoding is not needed as an explanation. Changes in memory performance could involve the simultaneous activation of original and postevent traces, with the stronger of the two "winning" out (Ceci, Toglia, & Ross, 1988). Changes in memory performance could come about because of an enhancement in memory for control subjects rather than a reduction in memory for misled subjects (Brainerd & Reyna, 1988). Morton et al. (1985) argued that changes in memory performance in misled subjects are due to a reduced accessibility of the original trace caused by new inputs, rather than a recoding of the trace. Tulving's partial answer to those who would doubt the existence of recoding is to deny that memory traces have independent existence, and to emphasize the point that memory performance depends heavily on not only what information is available when inputs are stored but what information is available at retrieval. This theoretical backdrop sets the stage for discussing the importance in the misinformation paradigm of the specific testing conditions that are employed. The deter-

TABLE 5.1. Testing procedures.

Condition	Slides	Narrative	Test
		Standard test procedure	
Control	Hammer	—	Hammer vs. screwdriver
Misled	Hammer	Screwdriver	Hammer vs. screwdriver
		Modified test procedure	
Control	Hammer	—	Hammer vs. wrench
Misled	Hammer	Screwdriver	Hammer vs. wrench

mination of circumstances under which the various processes operate, given certain testing conditions, is critical not only for theoretical models of forgetting, but also for applied questions (Johnson & Hasher, 1987).

A major empirical demonstration of the importance of the information (cues) available at retrieval is that of McCloskey and Zaragoza (1985; Zaragoza, McCloskey, & Jamis, 1987). McCloskey and Zaragoza disagreed with the idea that the misinformation effect was due to recoding processes or updating of previously stored memories (Loftus et al., 1985), and also with the idea that the effect was due to the older memory being rendered less accessible through a mechanism of inhibition or suppression (Morton et al., 1985). These authors argued that the misinformation does not affect memory at all. Misinformation merely influences the reports of subjects who never encoded (or do not recall) the original event. Instead of guessing at the time of test, these subjects would be lured into "guessing" the misinformation item. Misinformation effects could also be obtained if subjects remember both sources of information but select the misleading information because they conclude it must be correct. To test their hypothesis that misinformation does not impair earlier memories, they used a procedure that differs from previous examinations of the misinformation effect (Table 5.1). The traditional procedure permits subject to respond to a test item with the misinformation. If the subject originally saw a burglar place a stolen object under a hammer and later received misinformation that it was placed under a screwdriver, the traditional two alternative forced choice test is between hammer and screwdriver. McCloskey and Zaragoza's modified test, on the other hand, does not permit the subject to give the misinformation response, screwdriver. If the subject originally saw a hammer and later received misinformation about a screwdriver, the modified test might be between hammer and wrench. Using the modified test, they observed no effect of misinformation on performance and consequently concluded that the original memory trace was not affected by exposure to misinformation.

The research of these authors with the modified test (and their newer work with a variation in which subjects try to recall the original information while simultaneously being prevented from recalling the misinformation [Zaragoza et al., 1987]) has provoked considerable interest. We now describe some reactions to that research.

Performance on the Modified Test

McCloskey and Zaragoza (1985) argued that unlike the standard test procedure (event versus postevent item), the modified test procedure (event versus novel item) "can be used to determine whether misleading information affects subjects' memory for what they initially saw" (p. 4). If misinformation impairs ability to remember the original information, then misled subjects should perform more poorly than control subjects on the modified test. On the other hand, if misinformation does not affect ability to remember the original information, then control and misled conditions should not differ. McCloskey and Zaragoza found, as discussed above, that control and misled conditions did not differ, constituting evidence for them against the impairment hypothesis.

To complicate matters, other investigators have used a modified test and have found different results. Using different materials, at least two other laboratories (Ceci, Ross, & Toglia, 1987; Chandler, 1989) have used a version of the modified test and found decrements in performance due to misinformation. Chandler argued that she found decrements whereas McCloskey and Zaragoza (1985) did not because she used a more sensitive experimental design. After conducting experiments that used a test that was sufficiently sensitive to capture a loss of accessibility of information due to misleading inputs, Chandler concluded that new inputs can make original item information less accessible to cues that would have otherwise been effective.

Because it can be argued that Chandler's (1989) materials are somewhat peculiar, and that Ceci et al. (1987) obtained an impairment with children as opposed to adults as subjects, it is worth presenting an additional demonstration of the impairing effect of misinformation on a modified test. Such a demonstration can be found in the honors thesis research of Benzing (1985), who used a more sensitive test involving "betting forms." In the betting-form test, a subject distributes probability points among, say, four alternatives. For example, if a subject was reasonably confident of seeing a hammer, then on the betting form he or she might assign 70 probability points to hammer and 10 points each to wrench, pliers, and crowbar. On the other hand, if the subject was simply guessing, the response might be 25, 25, 25, and 25. The betting-form test has several advantages over the simple modified test used by McCloskey and Zaragoza (1985). First, because it allows subjects to weight their responses according to how confident they are, it discriminates between subjects who are guessing and those who truly believe they are correct. Second, by offering subjects more than two alternatives, it reduces the

TABLE 5.2. Percentage of correct items given a clear majority of probability points.

	Misled	Control
Standard	18.8%	27.8%
Modified	22.6%	33.3%

number of subjects who make a correct response simply by guessing. As a result, the betting form procedure is better able to identify subjects who truly recall the event information.

These ideas motivated a replication of McCloskey and Zaragoza's (1985) procedure with one change, namely the betting-form test. In Benzing's replication, the burglary slides were shown followed by a narrative. The procedures used by McCloskey and Zaragoza were followed as closely as possible, using their materials and their design and procedure, until the time of the final test. The experiment involved over 140 subjects who saw the slide series at a 5-sec rate of presentation. The final test required subjects to distribute 100 probability points among four alternatives according to how confident they were that each particular item appeared in the slides. Some subjects received a betting-form test that mirrored the standard test in which the suggested alternative is a possible choice. That is, the four alternatives from which subjects could choose included the original correct detail, the suggested detail, and two neutral distractors. Other subjects received a betting-form test that mirrored the modified test in which the suggested alternative was not a possible choice. That is, the four alternatives from which subjects could choose included the original correct detail and three neutral distractors.

To reduce the influence of subjects who were simply guessing, Benzing tabulated the percentage of people who gave a clear majority of probability points to the correct alternative. A clear majority was defined as any response in which the correct alternative was assigned at least 40 probability points more than any other alternative. For example, a distribution of 55, 15, 10, and 10 would represent a clear majority. The percentage of correct items that were given a clear majority of probability points can be found in Table 5.2.

Both the standard and the modified betting-form tests revealed an effect of postevent information. Subjects who received postevent information were less likely to assign a clear majority of points to the correct alternative (standard test: $z = 1.82$, $p<.05$, one-tailed; modified test: $z = 2.01$, $p<.05$).

These results are consistent with McCloskey and Zaragoza's (1985) interpretations in one respect. By identifying which subjects were simply guessing, the betting-form test produced a substantially smaller misinformation effect than that observed using the more traditional two-alternative forced choice tests. The relatively smaller misinformation effect here could mean that under the more traditional testing circumstances, a substantial proportion of the misinformation effect is likely due to subjects who, not having encoded the original information in the first place, are simply biased toward guessing the suggested item. However, not all of the misinformation effect is due to a bias of guessing. Using the more sensitive betting-form test, postevent information can be seen to affect test performance even when the suggested item is not provided as an option. Apparently, postevent information not only increases bias toward the suggested item, it lures one away from the event item, suggesting that postevent information can affect the recollections of subjects who did indeed initially encode the event item.

Are Memories Ever "Destroyed"?

McCloskey and Zaragoza (1985) assumed, perhaps erroneously, that the modified test would reveal the destruction of memory if such destruction ever occurred. In fact, a careful analysis of their design and data suggest that the modified test cannot distinguish between models that do and do not assume destructive updating. To see this, we must briefly reiterate the procedure they used. Using their example, recall that subjects first saw a man with a hammer. Then they received misleading information about a screwdriver or neutral information about a tool. Finally, they took a modified test, choosing between hammer and wrench. If any misled subjects had their memories for hammer destroyed by screwdriver, they would be forced to guess when they had to choose between two tools of which they had no recollection. McCloskey and Zaragoza claim that if any memories were destroyed, there would be fewer correct responses in the modified misled condition than in the modified control condition. Their actual results contradicted this prediction, as the observed percentages were 72% and 75%, respectively. With the standard test, they obtained the usual effect of misleading information (37% vs. 72% correct).

McCloskey and Zaragoza (1985) assume that if memories were destroyed, it should be evident on the modified test, and the misinformation effect should be of considerable size, just as it is with the standard test. Actually, a careful examination of their hypothetical model for the modified test reveals that even if some memories are destroyed by misinformation, the misinformation effect would be rather small. To see this, we must take a brief trip through the original hypothetical models proposed by McCloskey and Zaragoza, and then consider what would happen if we added parameters that reflected some destruction of memory.

TABLE 5.3. Expected test performance in a hypothetical situation.

Memory state for original information	Percent of subjects in memory state	Expected performance on test
	1. Control condition	
Remember	40	100%
Do not remember	60	50% correct
Total % correct		70% (40% + 30%)
	2. Misled condition (standard test)	
Remember	40	100%
Do not remember	60	25% correct
Total % correct		55% (40% + 15%)
	3. Misled condition (modified test)	
Remember	40	100%
Do not remember	60	50% correct
Total % correct		70% (40% + 30%)
Expected test performance assuming some memories are destroyed		
	4. Misled condition (standard test)	
Remember		
No destruction	30	100% correct
Destruction	10	0% correct
Do not remember	60	25% correct
Total % correct		45% (30% + 15%)
	5. Misled condition (modified test)	
Remember		
No destruction	30	100% correct
Destruction	10	50% correct
Do not remember	60	50% correct
Total % correct		65% (30% + 5% + 30%)

Note. Modeled after format used in "Misleading Postevent Information and Memory for Events: Arguments and Evidence Against Memory Impairment Hypotheses" by M. McCloskey and M. Zaragoza, 1985, *Journal of Experimental Psychology: General*, *114*, pp. 1–16.

The hypothetical situation these authors posed assumes that 40% of control subjects remember the event information (e.g., hammer) after exposure and 60% do not (Table 5.3, Condition 1). The overall percent correct for the control group is expected to be 40% (all subjects who remember the hammer) plus 30% (half of the subjects who do not remember the hammer) for a total of 70%. Control performance is assumed to be the same, no matter whether the standard or modified test is given.

Consider now performance for the misled group who take the standard test. We know performance is routinely much worse, and McCloskey and Zaragoza (1985) claim that this performance deficit could be achieved without assuming any memory impairment whatsoever. To continue with their hypothetical example, assume no impairment in the memories of the

40% of subjects who remember the event information (hammer) (Table 5.3, Condition 2). Assume that the only people who are affected by misinformation are the 60% who would not have remembered the hammer anyhow. These subjects are not simply going to guess between a hammer and a screwdriver. Rather, many of them may recall reading about a screwdriver, and may systematically choose screwdriver on the standard test. This would cause the overall level of performance for misled subjects who do not remember hammer to be lower than the corresponding control level of 50%. As a consequence, performance would be worse. Let's say half of the misled subjects who do not remember the hammer to remember the screwdriver. These subjects will choose the screwdriver. The other half will simply guess, and some (25% of those who do not remember hammer) will choose hammer correctly. Overall performance for the misled condition, then, would be 55% (Condition 2). This is 40% (all of the subjects who remember the hammer) plus 15% (a quarter of the subjects who do not remember the hammer) or 55%, considerably below the control level of 70%. Their argument has thus shown that even if misinformation has no effect on subjects' ability to remember the event information, performance will be worse in the misled condition than in the control condition. This occurs because misinformation biases the responses of subjects who fail to remember the event information. Adding the assumption that some subjects who actually do remember the event information, hammer, might deliberately choose screwdriver because they remember reading about it, further impairs misled performance—again without impairing any event memories.

They extended this hypothetical example to include expectations for performance with the modified test (Table 5.3, Condition 3). Misled subjects who remember the original information should, like the controls, uniformly be correct on the modified test. Even if subjects remember reading about a screwdriver, the absence of this option on the test between hammer and wrench means subjects will invariably choose hammer. However, misled subjects who do not remember the event information should also perform like controls. Misled subjects when faced with the choices of hammer and wrench must guess, and half will be correct. Expected performance is 40% (all subjects who remember the hammer) plus 30% (half of the subjects who do not remember the hammer), or 70%, the same as in the control condition.

In sum, McCloskey and Zaragoza (1985) claimed that performance on the standard test would be worse if subjects were misled compared to controls, but performance on the modified test would not. This occurred in their hypothetical model without assuming any destruction of event memories whatsoever. Now consider what happens if we add parameters to their hypothetical model that reflect some destruction of memory. Adding such parameters, it turns out, produces predictions that fit well with existing data.

To demonstrate the fit, we begin with the same assumptions for control subjects, namely that 40% remember the event information and 60% do not. Expected performance is 70% overall. Consider now performance for the misled groups who take the standard test (Table 3, Condition 4). Assume that only one fourth of the people who remembered the event detail, hammer, had their memories destroyed by the misleading screwdriver. They would consequently be wrong on the test. The 30% who remembered hammer without further destruction would be correct on the standard test. The 60% who do not remember hammer will not simply guess between a hammer and as crewdriver. Rather many of them, say half, would recall the misinformation screwdriver and systematically choose it on the standard test. The others will simply guess and some will choose hammer correctly. Overall performance for the misled condition, then, would be 45%. This is 30% (all subjects who remember the hammer and experienced to destruction) plus 15% (a quarter of the subjects who do not remember the hammer), or 45%, a dramatic drop in performance, comparable to that observed in many experiments using the standard test.

Now consider the predictions for the modified test under the assumption that misinformation destroys some original memories (Table 3, Condition 5). Misled subjects would be expected to perform less well than controls, but only slightly so. If we assume that 40% of the subjects remember the event detail, but one fourth of these experience some destruction of memory, then 30% would actually recall the event item on the modified test. Everyone else would simply have to guess. Put another way, the 10% who had memories destroyed plus the 60% who never encoded the event information would be forced to guess. If half of these subjects guess correctly, then the performance expected in the group as a whole is 65% (the 30% who recalled the event item plus the 35% who guessed correctly). Thus, by adding the assumption to McCloskey and Zaragoza's (1985) hypothetical model that some destruction of memories occurs in misled subjects (in this example, one fourth), we observe that the accuracy prediction for misled subjects on the modified test is only 5% less than that predicted for controls. Based upon this reasoning the modified test is a rather weak measure of whether any original memories are destroyed as a consequence of misinformation.

To reiterate, McCloskey and Zaragoza (1985) assume that if memories are destroyed, the misinformation effect on the modified test should be of a size comparable to that found using the standard test. Yet at least one model assumes that some memories are destroyed by misinformation, and makes the prediction that the misinformation effect can be quite large with the standard test, but quite small with the modified test. The model is quite consistent with data reported by Ceci et al. (1987) who found a misinformation effect on the modified test. In their Experiment 3, the level of correct recognition was 87% for the control group, and 52% for misled subjects given the standard test, a difference of 35%. The level of correct recognition was 72% for misled subjects given the modified test, a difference of only 15%. In their Experiment 4, a similar pattern emerged; there was a large misinformation effect on the standard test (42% worse performance for misled subjects) but a much smaller misinformation effect on the modified test (16% worse performance for misled subjects).[1]

A more formal way to demonstrate the viability of the assumption that some memories are destroyed by misinformation is to analyze its predictions by means of event trees (Wagenaar & Boer, 1987). The analysis involves four event trees, corresponding to the four conditions in the McCloskey and Zaragoza (1985) experiments: standard versus modified test, and nested within these, misleading versus neutral information. These four event trees are presented in Figure 5.1, and each is read from left to right. Each time a node is encountered, subjects are split into two groups, depending on whether they are successful in performing a critical act (or critical event). Successful subjects are placed in the upper branch following the node; unsuccessful subjects are placed in the lower branch.

Consider the event tree for the modified misled condition (Figure 5.1a). It contains four events, the first of which occurs when hammer is presented during the slide sequence. In Phase 1, we divide the subjects into two groups: those who encoded hammer in such a way that it can later be recalled during the test (proportion p) and those who did not ($1 - p$). The second critical event occurs when screwdriver is presented during the postevent narrative. In Phase 2, we divide the subjects into two groups: those who encoded screwdriver in such a way that it could be recalled during the test (if the test had permitted this), producing an incorrect response (proportion q) and those who did not (proportion $1 - q$). Also in this phase, another critical event is the destruction of the memory trace of hammer. This event can take place only in those subjects who succeeded in both previous events, that is, in those cases in which both hammer and screwdriver are encoded. Of those subjects, a proportion, d, will destroy hammer and replace it with screwdriver. The remaining subjects will not be misled and hence they retain hammer. A fourth critical event is to simply guess between hammer and wrench, but guessing can take place only in those subjects who have no memory representation of hammer.

The proportion of all subjects who follow a particular branch of the tree is obtained by simple multiplication of the proportions encountered along the branch. For example, the uppermost branch will contain a proportion of $p \times q \times d \times \frac{1}{2}$ subjects; the lowermost branch for the

[1] Ceci et al. (1987) got a misinformation effect on the modified test using young children as subjects. McCloskey and Zaragoza (1985) used adults. Later in this chapter we discuss developmental differences in susceptibility that relate to this apparent discrepancy.

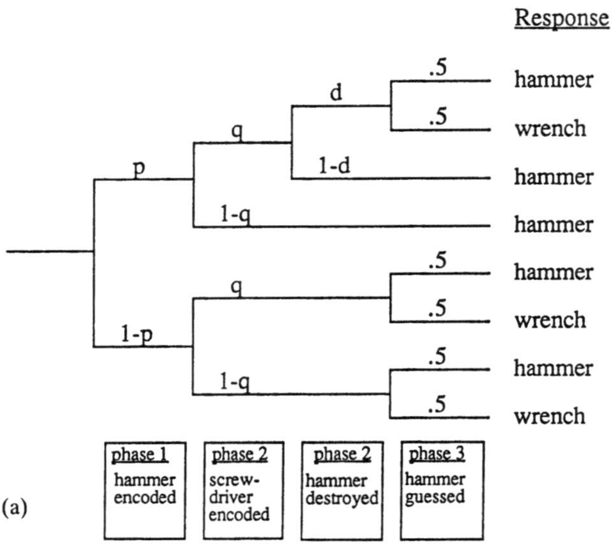

(a)

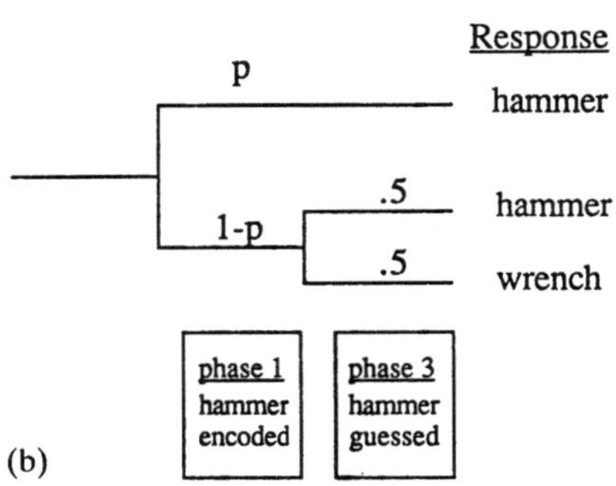

(b)

FIGURE 5.1. Event trees for the various conditions of the McCloskey and Zaragoza (1985) experiment: (a) modified misled; (b) modified control; (c) standard misled; (d) standard control.

modified, misled event tree contains $(1 - p) \times (1 - q) \times \frac{1}{2}$ subjects. The proportion of subjects giving the correct response, hammer, is obtained by adding across all branches showing "hammer" in the final column. In the modified misled condition, the predicted proportion of subjects producing the correct response is

$$pqd/2 + pq(1 - d) + p(1 - q) + (1 - p)q/2 + (1 - p)(1 - q)/2$$

which, after some rearrangement of terms, reduces to

$$(p - pqd + 1)/2. \tag{1}$$

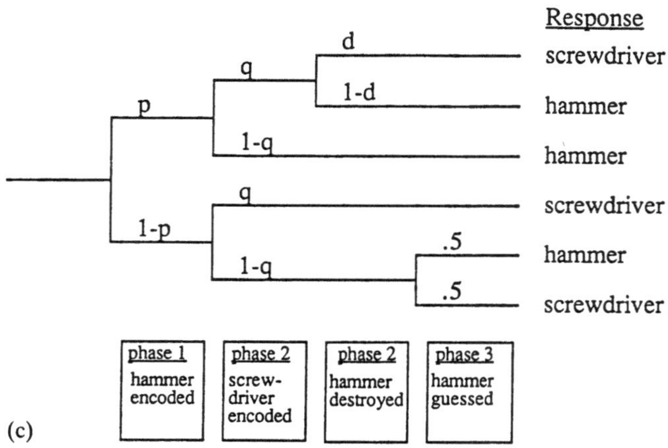

(c)

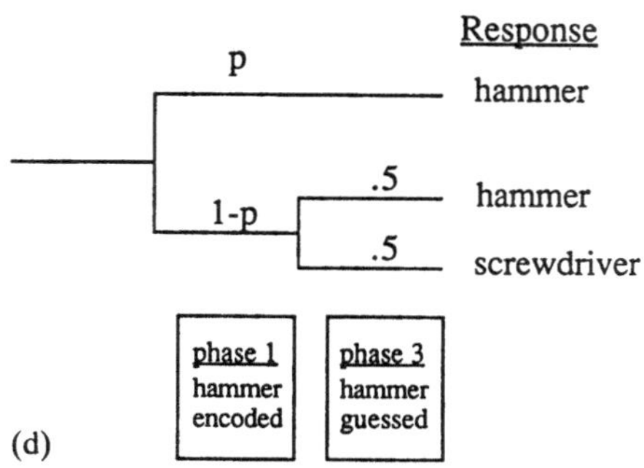

(d)

FIGURE 5.1 (Continued)

Note that Figure 5.1a includes includes two important groups of subjects represented by the third and fourth branches of the tree. The third branch contains those subjects who encoded both hammer and screwdriver, but did not destroy hammer. The fourth branch contains the subjects who encoded only hammer. In all other branches of this condition, hammer is either encoded and destroyed, or not encoded at all. Therefore, subjects end up guessing in these branches.

In the modified control condition (Figure 5.1b), the predicted proportion of correct "hammer" responses is

$$(p + 1)/2. \quad (2)$$

The difference between the misled and control conditions amounts to Equation 2 − 1 or $pqd/2$. It is not a priori clear that this proportion should constitute a significant difference, even when as many as 200

TABLE 5.4. Fitting of the destructive updating model to the data collected by McCloskey and Zaragoza (1985).

		Proportions		Raw scores	
Conditions	Model prediction	Data	Fitted model	Data	Fitted model
Standard control	$(p + 1)/2$	0.72	0.735	144	147
Standard misled	$((p - q + pq + 1)/2) - pqd$	0.37	0.390	74	78
Modified control	$(p + 1)/2$	0.75	0.735	150	147
Modified misled	$(p - pqd + 1)/2$	0.72	0.700	144	140

Note. Fitted parameter values: $p = 0.47$; $q = 1.0$; $d = 0.17$.

subjects per condition are used. With proportions hovering around .70, the .05 level of significance is reached at $pqd/2 = .09$. Put another way, at around .7, two sample proportions must differ by .09 to reach significance (assuming 200 subjects). If p, q, and d are all around .5, the product of proportions $pqd/2$ is not more than a significance level of .063. This means that there may exist a wide variety of parameter values that fail to produce the difference intuitively assumed by McCloskey and Zaragoza (1985).

The event trees for the remaining conditions are also shown in Figure 5.1. The predictions of the destructive updating model are presented in Table 5.4. The model contains three parameters: p, q, and d. Because four empirically obtained accuracy values are available, a least-squares approximation produces the needed parameter estimations. This solution is degenerate, however, because it yields $q > 1$. As q is a proportion of subjects, it can never be above 1. Setting q at 1.0, we obtain the best-fitting solution for $p + .47$ and $d + .17$. The resulting model predictions, also shown in Table 5.4, closely resemble McCloskey and Zaragoza's (1985) results. The difference between the empirical data and the predictions is not significant ($\chi^2 = 1.18$, df $= 3$, ns).

A destruction probability of .17 is of course not very large; one could even argue that such a low value would for all practical purposes refute the destructive updating position. However, it should be realized that all sets of parameter fittings in which $pqd/2$ is less than .09 produce solutions that are in agreement with the notion of destructive updating. The only reason that the data yield such a low estimate of d is that the effect of misleading information is so excessively large in the standard test. In related work that obtained performance values of .6 in this condition (Wagenaar & Boer, 1987), values for p and q were about .5, and d was estimated to be below .66. In fact, the arbitrary parameter values of $p = q = d = .50$ yield a perfectly acceptable solution for the McCloskey and

Zaragoza (1985) modified test. Because these values also produce an insignificant value for the proportion $pqd/2$, we infer that the attempt to refute the assumption that some memories are destroyed by misinformation was doomed even before it began. In sum, we have used event trees to more closely inspect the data of McCloskey and Zaragoza and found that those data cannot distinguish between a model that assumes some memories are destroyed (i.e., that some destructive updating does occur) and models that do not make this assumption.[2] Within a reasonably wide range of parameter values, such a model predicts outcomes that are compatible with McCloskey and Zaragoza's results in the modified test.

The weakness of the above argument is that the experiment yielded in fact only four data points. Hence, a model with three free parameters is almost certain to yield a good fit. There is information in the obtained parameter values, but not in the goodness of fit. A better test is provided when the experiment is designed such that more data points are obtained.

Here is an example of such a design (cf. Wagenaar, 1989). The experiment used as the original information a rather amusing written story called "Prince." The story tells about a woman who loses her slipper while boarding a streetcar. The narrator of the story chases the streetcar with the slipper in his hands, but at the next stop it appears that the woman has already boarded a streetcar in the opposite direction in order to retrieve her slipper. After some adventure, the narrator decides that he does not want to be the prince with the glass slipper anymore. A total of 12 one- to three-word text clauses were chosen as critical events. Postevent information was presented in the traditional way by means of questions. All items were equally often supplied with neutral and misleading information. In Stage 3, a free recall test was administered, which consisted of a sentence completion test in which the critical clauses were replaced by ellipses. Then, in Stage 4, a forced-choice test was presented, which was either in the form of a standard test, or in the form of a modified test. In this manner there were four groups, resulting from the factorial combination of neutral/misleading information in Stage 2, and

[2] Event trees naturally are not models of the processes that occur in individual subjects, although they are based upon some simplifying assumptions about those processes. One assumption is that the successive events are independent of one another, an assumption that some might find questionable. However, a model that did not include this assumption would have many more parameters because of the introduction of transition probabilities. Another assumption of the event tree approach is that the outcome of each critical event is described in an all-or-none fashion, rather than as being continuous. This assumption, too, could be dropped in favor of a continuous variable, but this, too, would lead to an enormous increase in parameters. It is well known that as the number of free parameters approaches the number of data points, the testing of mathematical models becomes futile (Wagenaar & Boer, 1987). For the moment, the data do not force us to introduce these further complications into the event tree model.

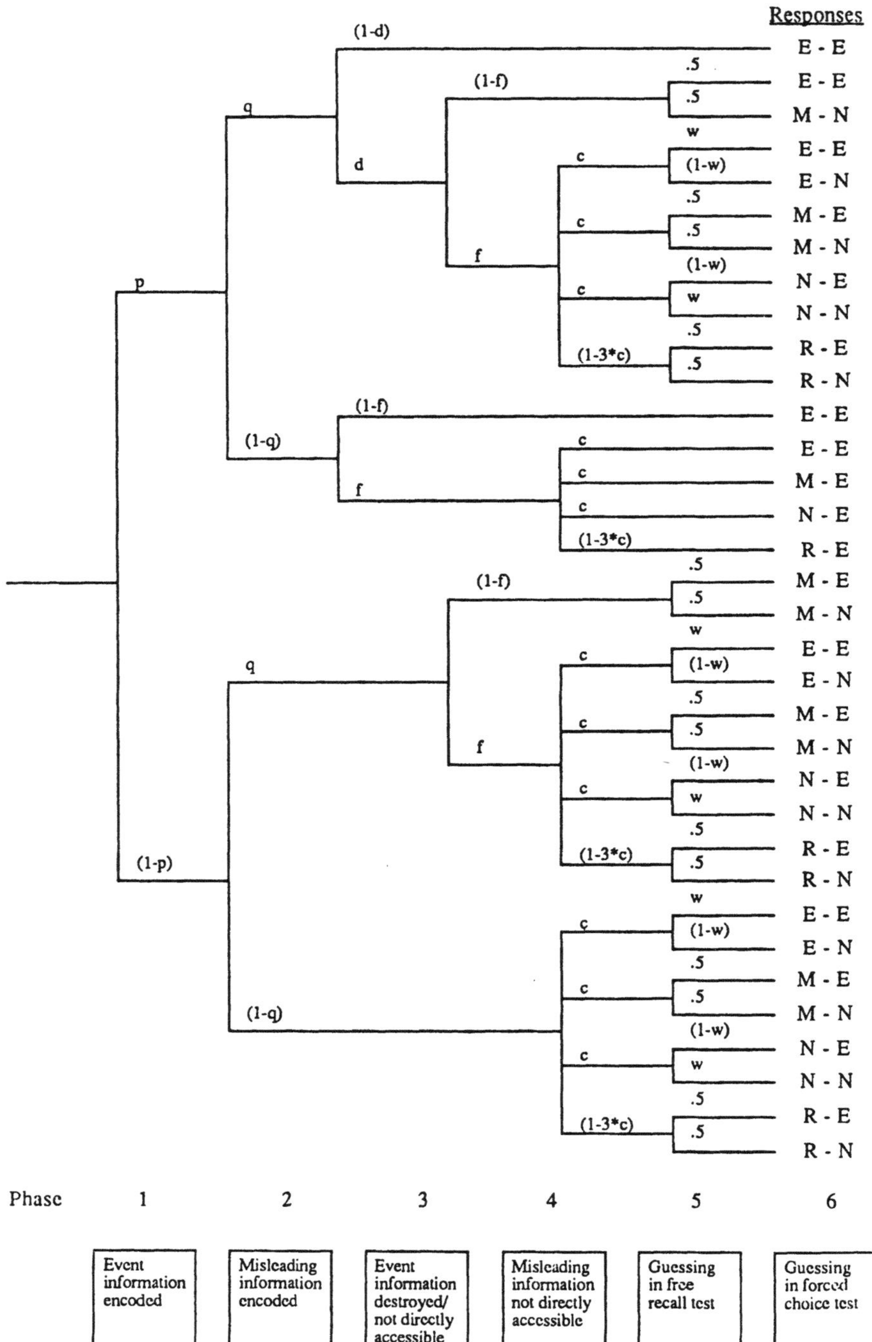

FIGURE 5.2. Event trees for the modified misled condition, assuming some destructive updating.

TABLE 5.5. Raw results of "Prince" study.

	Standard test			Modified test	
	Control	Misled		Control	Misled
E–E	24%	18%	E–E	25%	19%
E–M	4%	5%	E–N	2%	2%
M–E	2%	7%	M–E	4%	15%
M–M	5%	22%	M–N	3%	13%
N–E	7%	4%	N–E	4%	3%
N–M	3%	2%	N–N	5%	5%
R–E	38%	19%	R–E	37%	30%
R–M	18%	23%	R–N	20%	13%

Note. N = 576 in each group. E = event item; M = misinformation item; N = novel item; R = random item.

standard/modified test in Stage 4. Within each group there were eight possible response combinations. In the free recall test one could produce the event item (E), the misinformation item (M), the novel item that was used in the modified test (N), or another item (R, for random) as an answer. In the forced-choice test there were always two choices, E or M in the standard test, E or N in the modified test. Thus each subject produced, for each critical item, one out of eight possible response sequences. The whole experiment produced 32 data points, with 28 degrees of freedom. Each data point is a percentage, based on 576 observations.

This significant increase of data points allows us to introduce a few more parameters, which makes the model a little more realistic. The event trees are exemplified by Figure 5.2, which shows the destructive updating model for the misleading-modified condition. The successive processing stages are (a) encoding of event information; (b) encoding of misleading information; (c) destruction of event information in case of a conflict, or rendering event information inaccessible to free recall; (d) rendering misleading information inaccessible to free recall; (e) guessing in the free recall task, with equal probabilities for guessing E, M, and N; (f) guessing in the forced-choice task, with, where applicable, an extra parameter (w) for persisting on the item guessed in the free recall task.

The results are presented in Table 5.5. These results are evidence that memory distortion occurred in the free recall test: the misinformation item was produced 28% of the time for subjects in the misled condition whereas only 7% in the control condition produced the misinformation item. In the standard forced-choice test there was only evidence of memory distortion: the misinformation item was chosen 52% of the time in the misleading condition, versus 30% in the control condition.

The parameter fitting was obtained through the EUREKA program (1986) and yielded, for the destructive updating model, p = 0.46, q =

TABLE 5.6. Forced-choice responses in the misleading condition of the "Prince" study, and corresponding model outcomes of the fitted model allowing for destructive updating.

		Data	Model
Standard test	Event	0.48	0.43
	Misled	0.52	0.57
Modified test	Event	0.67	0.63
	Novel	0.33	0.37

0.46, $d = 0.82, f = 0.48, c = 0.10, w = 0.61$. The model fitted to the data quite well: the mean absolute error across 32 cells was 1.9%. The comparison between observed values and model predictions by means of chi-square is not so meaningful because, with a total of 2,304 observations, even small deviations tend to result in high chi-squares. Moreover, the real point of the parameterization is to demonstrate that a model assuming destruction in case of a conflict between original and misleading information predicts the kind of results obtained by McCloskey and Zaragoza (1985). This is demonstrated in Table 5.6, which shows that the results obtained in the modified test, which replicate the McCloskey and Zaragoza results discussed above, and which are taken by these investigators as a disproof of destructive updating, are in fact in full agreement with a model in which destructive updating occurs in 82% of the cases where there is a conflict between event and misleading information. Hence, the real discussion should concentrate, not so much on whether the data are in agreement with predictions from one or another theory, but rather on which predictions follow from the theories. For the relatively simple paradigms discussed thus far, our analyses indicate that the differences among these predictions are too small to be tested empirically.

The Yes/No Test

One criticism of the modified testing procedure used by McCloskey and Zaragoza (1985) is that it is insensitive to detecting memory impairment (Belli, 1989). If the postevent item had not been excluded, perhaps there would be preferential access to it, rendering the event item less accessible. The modified test does not allow us to see whether this is the case.

Another problem with the modified test is that its exclusion of the postevent item as a response alternative prevents detection of other possible influences of postevent misinformation. The notion of "source misattribution" (Lindsay & Johnson, 1987) is relevant here. Source misattribution, in this context, refers to the remembering of the postevent item and mistakenly accepting it as the item originally seen. The modified test does not allow us to see whether this occurs. The modified test essentially communicates to the subject that the postevent item is wrong.

With these considerations in mind, Belli (1989) devised a new way of testing, involving the use of a yes/no test. Subjects saw a simulated burglary involving several critical details (e.g., a hammer in a toolbox). Afterward, subjects read a narrative that contained misleading information (e.g., referring to the hammer as a screwdriver) or neutral information regarding the critical details. Finally, subjects took a yes/no test in which they reported if certain details had appeared in the original event. They responded either to the event item (e.g., hammer) or to a novel item (e.g., wrench). Thus, although the postevent item was not explicitly presented, Belli's yes/no test permitted misled subjects to select "no" as a response alternative to either the event or the novel item if they believed that the postevent item was originally shown.

It was very important for Belli (1989) to ask not just about the event item, but also about the novel item. Suppose Belli had asked only about the event item, hammer. Fewer "yes" responses to the event item in misled subjects compared to controls could mean that misinformation impaired ability to remember what was originally seen. But it could also occur for reasons having nothing to do with impairment. Misinformation could bias the responses of subjects who, for reasons unrelated to any presentation of misinformation, do not remember the event item. Control subjects who do not remember the hammer must guess when asked if hammer appeared. Misled subjects who do not remember the hammer, but do remember reading about a screwdriver might be less likely to say "yes" to hammer. In other words, if misled subjects accept the misinformation, they may be biased away from producing a "yes" response to the event item, hammer. This is what Belli refers to as "misinformation acceptance."

The inclusion of a yes/no test concerning the novel item helps to disentangle these interpretations. Suppose that misinformation acceptance is all that is going on when misled subjects shy away from the event item (that is, say "no" to the event item). Then, they should also shy away from a novel item, to the same extent. In doing so they would improve their performance relative to controls, because, of course, the "no" response is the correct response to the novel item. Put another way, misleading information should hurt performance in the event item, but help performance on the novel item. When the two are collapsed, the effects should cancel each other, and misled and control performance would be equivalent. On the other hand, Belli reasoned, a reduction in performance on the event item that exceeded an enhancement of performance on the novel item, would constitute evidence for memory interference.

Belli (1989) found that misinformation reduced the likelihood of saying "yes" to the event item. Misinformation also helped performance on the novel item (that is, by reducing the incorrect "yes" responses) but not to as great a degree. So, in Experiment 2, for example, control subjects said "yes" to the event item 63% of the time compared to misled subjects who said yes 36% of the time—a difference of 27%. For the novel item, misled subjects performed better than control (83% vs. 70% correct "no" responses—a difference of 13%). Based upon the extra large decreased recognition of the event item, Belli argued that there is more going on than misinformation acceptance.

What else is going on? Belli (1989) argued that misinformation interference is also going on. More specifically, he proposed that memory impairment or source misattribution or some combination could be responsible for the observed interference. Memory impairment could refer to a weakening of memory traces, or an impoverishment of memory. It has something in common with source misattribution in that both embrace the notion that misleading information interferes with the ability to remember an original item. Belli declines to commit to deciding whether impairment, or source misattibution, or both are responsible for the misinformation effect.

Naturally, Zaragoza and McCloskey (1989) disagreed with Belli's (1989) conclusions that some form of memory interference is necessarily occurring. Perhaps misinformation produces some form of conscious deliberation at the time the subject is tested. Subjects may say to themselves, something like: "I thought I saw a hammer, but the narrative said screwdriver. The narrative is probably right, and I am probably wrong." Misinformation could shake confidence in the event item and lower the likelihood of responding "yes" to that item. To his credit, Belli considered this type of deliberation mechanism, but rejected it. He felt that the usual two-alternative forced choice test might encourage deliberation because both items are immediately present. But the yes/no test on the event item does not promote such deliberation because the postevent item is not immediately present. Zaragoza and McCloskey agree that the event item is probably less likely to be rejected through deliberation on the yes/no test than the standard forced choice test.

We have argued elsewhere that deliberation is not a common mechanism on the forced choice test (Loftus, Donders, Hoffman, & Schooler, 1989). We based this conclusion on the finding that misled subjects who took a standard forced choice test in which the misinformation item was a possible response option, responded very quickly and confidently when making this incorrect choice. Misled subjects responded as quickly and confidently to the misinformation option as control subjects did to their genuine memories. If deliberation is even less likely on the yes/no test, then it does not stand as a viable mechanism for the misinformation effects we are discussing here.

Another recent use of the yes/no test is in the work of Tversky and Tuchin (1989). These investigators commented on the modified test by noting that there are two ways that a person can succeed on such a test. Either the new alternative can be correctly rejected or the original item can be correctly accepted. If subjects are relatively good at knowing what they have not been exposed to, they do not have to remember what they have actually seen in order to succeed on the modified test. A yes/no recognition procedure circumvents this difficulty of interpretation.

The study of Tversky and Tuchin (1989) differed from Belli's (1989) in terms of the number of tests concerning a critical category item (e.g., the number of tests about various tools) that any individual subject received. Belli's subjects were tested either on the event item or the novel item, but not both. Tversky and Tuchin's subjects were tested on both the event and novel items, and on the postevent item. The three test items within a category were worded slightly differently and scattered throughout the questionnaire. The example provided in the manuscript concerned the critical category of magazines. Subjects were asked about three different magazines: one event item, one postevent item (for misled subjects), one novel item. "Below the magazine rack there was a copy of *Vogue* magazine." "On the table was a copy of *Glamour* magazine." "There was a copy of *Mademoiselle* magazine on the table." Given this methodology, conceivably subjects could claim they saw more than one magazine, and not be aware of any contradiction.

Tversky and Tuchin (1989) found, like Belli (1989), that fewer subjects claimed to have seen the event item if they were misled rather than controls (43% vs. 65%). This impairment in performance exceeded any improvement for misled subjects on the novel item. Misled subjects embraced the postevent item more than they embraced the event item (62% incorrect "yes" responses on the postevent item vs. 43% correct "yes" responses on the event item). Interestingly, a number of subjects claimed to see more than one item. Specifically, close to half of the misled subjects who said "yes" to the event item also said "yes" to the postevent item. This suggests that in some instances the effect of postevent misinformation may be to add something to a subject's recollection rather than to alter the recollection.

Tversky and Tuchin (1989) use their data to argue against the proposition that postevent information has no effect on event information in memory. The data also speak, they claim, for the proposition that both the event and postevent information can coexist as evidenced by those subjects who said "yes" more than once.

To reiterate, both Belli (1989) and Tversky and Tuchin (1989) found performance decrements due to misinformation with the yes/no testing procedure. Subjects who saw a hammer, and were misled with screwdriver, were subsequently less likely to say they saw a hammer. They said "no" when it was explicitly presented on the test. The relatively large decrement in performance stands in contrast to the smaller or null decrements obtained with the modified forced choice test. Subjects clearly chose hammer over wrench. Perhaps the testing procedures invoke very different mechanisms. Given the hammer/wrench choice, subjects can perform accurately by rejecting the wrench as being "new." Given the single item, hammer, with the requirement of a yes or no response, a misinformed subject might feel that hammer is "not old." Deciding that an item is "not old" is not the same thing as deciding that an item is "new" (Brainerd & Reyna, 1988). Moreover, the capacity to recognize that a new item is in fact new increases as young children get older, which has implications for potential developmental trends in susceptibility to misinformation, a topic we consider later.

In addition, both Belli (1989) and Tversky and Tuchin (1989) appear to believe that misleading information can lead to "misinformation acceptance," on the part of some subjects. McCloskey and Zaragoza (1985) act as if this is not particularly interesting. We have argued elsewhere (Loftus & Hoffman, 1989) that misinformation acceptance that occurs in the absence of previous storage into memory may not tell us anything about impairment of original memories. However, it does tell us something about the creation of new memories. If a memory that arose from misinformation were to be subjectively vivid and real to a subject, as vivid and real as memories that arise from perception, this fact would be of the utmost significance. We thus argued that researchers should be more interested in misinformation acceptance, particularly when the acceptance of those new memories is associated with a high degree of conviction that they actually were perceived.

The challenge for future researchers in the misinformation paradigm is to devise new techniques capable of differentiating responses reflecting misinformation acceptance from those indicative of memory impairment. It should be kept in mind that even if memory impairment is shown to occur, further steps will be needed to discriminate between impairment that arises from storage failure and impairment that arises from retrieval failure.

Developmental Issues

A question has arisen repeatedly about developmental changes in the susceptibility to misinformation. For example, are children more susceptible than adults? The question does not have quite as straightforward an answer as one might suppose. If children form a relatively impoverished initial representation of an event, they might be more susceptible to postevent suggestions. This greater susceptibility would be expected because they would be less likely to detect a discrepancy between their original memory and the postevent input.

Another potential mechanism by which children could be more susceptible than adults is via forgetting rates. If the memory of a child fades more quickly than an adults (for some types of information), the weakened memory might be more susceptible to postevent contamination. Apart from actual memory loss, a child's differential ability to retrieve information could also lead to greater apparent susceptibility to misinformation. Failures to retrieve original memories could be associated with greater reliance on suggestive questioning.

There are other considerations, however, that lead to the prediction that children might occasionally be less susceptible to misinformation. Sometimes misinformation contaminates a report by leading to the generation of inferences that are then integrated into a prior memory. If children are less efficient at generating inferences, then they may also be less influenced by them. Sometimes misinformation involves complex sentences or subtle manipulations of meaning to which a young child may be oblivious. When suggestion occurs through the use of certain words (e.g., the cars smashed vs. the cars hit) it is conceivable that a child's relatively short experience with language is associated with lack of realization of the subtle differences and thus lack of influence by them. Thus, a young child might fail to show influence by misinformation because he or she failed to comprehend the language nuance.

Research in which misinformation has been presented to children has produced mixed results. Ceci et al. (1987) showed that children are susceptible to misleading information, and ages 3 to 4 were particularly vulnerable. These performance decrements due to misinformation occurred on both the standard and the modified tests. Zaragoza (1987), on the other hand, found children were susceptible only if tested with the standard test. At present, we do not know whether the differences obtained in these two laboratories are due to materials or procedures. Moreover, whether children's susceptibility is primarily due to misinformation acceptance, or whether it is a reflection of true memory impairment also remains a problem to be solved by future empiricists. One promising approach to clarifying these issues is that suggested by Howe and Brainerd (1989), namely the use of multiple testing opportunities and the application of a mathematical model to retention performance, one that factors storage and retrieval processes. This approach has been used successfully to disentangle whether variables have their influence at storage, at retrieval, or both (see Howe, Kelland, Bryant-Brown, & Clark, this volume). In fact, Howe (1991) has recently shown that providing children with misinformation affects both their ability to maintain information in storage as well as their ability to retrieve it.

Acknowledgment. The underlying research in this chapter was supported by a grant from the National Institutes of Mental Health.

References

Adams, J.A. (1967). *Human memory*. New York: McGraw-Hill.

Bartlett, F.C. (1932). *Remembering: A study in experimental and social psychology*. New York: Macmillan.

Bekerian, D.A., & Bowers, J.M. (1983). Eyewitness testimony: Were we misled? *Journal of Experimental Psychology: Learning, Memory, & Cognition*, *9*, 139–145.

Belli, R.F. (1989). Influences of misleading postevent information: Misinformation interference and acceptance. *Journal of Experimental Psychology: General*, *118*, 72–85.

Benzing, W. (1985). *Betting forms: A more sensitive measure of the impact of postevent information*. Honors thesis, University of Washington.

Brainerd, C.J., & Reyna, V. F. (1988). Memory loci of suggestibility development: Comment on Ceci, Ross, and Toglia (1987). *Journal of Experimental Psychology: General*, *117*, 197–200.

Bransford, J.D., & Franks, J.J. (1971). Abstraction of linguistic ideas. *Cognitive Psychology*, *2*, 331–350.

Ceci, S.J., Ross, D.F., & Toglia, M.P. (1987). Suggestibility of children's memory: Psycholegal implications. *Journal of Experimental Psychology: General*, *116*, 38–49.

Ceci, S.J., Toglia, M.P., & Ross, D.F. (1988). On remembering . . . more or less: A trace strength interpretation of developmental differences in suggestibility. *Journal of Experimental Psychology: General*, *117*, 201–203.

Chandler, C.C. (1989). Specific retroactive interference in modified recognition tests: Evidence for an unknown cause of interference. *Journal of Experimental Psychology: Learning, Memory, & Cognition*, *15*, 256–265.

Christiaansen, R.E., & Ochalek, K. (1983). Editing misleading information from memory: Evidence for the coexistence of original and postevent information. *Memory and Cognition*, *11*, 73–86.

Crowder, R.F. (1976). *Principles of learning and memory*. Hillsdale, NJ: Erlbaum.

EUREKA (1986). The solver, MacIntosh, Borland International.

Freud, S.S. (1930). *Civilization and its discontents* (standard edition XXI). London: Hargrath Press.

Howe, M.L. (1991). Misleading children's story recall: Forgetting and reminiscence of the facts. *Developmental Psychology*, *27*, 746–762.

Howe, M.L., & Brainerd, C.J. (1989). Development of children's long-term retention. *Developmental Review*, *9*, 301–340.

Johnson, M.K., & Hasher, L. (1987). Human learning and memory. *Annual Review of Psychology*, *38*, 631–668.

Lindsay, D.W., & Johnson, M.K. (1987). Reality monitoring and suggestibility: Children's ability to discriminate among memories from different sources. In S.J. Ceci, M.P. Toglia, & D.F. Ross (Eds.), *Children's eyewitness memory* (pp. 92–121). New York: Springer-Verlag.

Loftus, E.F. (1979). *Eyewitness testimony*. Cambridge: Harvard University Press.

Loftus, E.F., Donders, K., Hoffman, H.G., & Schooler, J.W. (1989). Creating new memories that are quickly accessed and confidently held. *Memory and Cognition*, *17*, 607–616.

Loftus, E.F., & Hoffman, H.G. (1989). Misinformation and memory: The creation of memory. *Journal of Experimental Psychology; General, 118*, 100–104.

Loftus, E.F., & Loftus, G.R. (1980). On the permanence of stored information in the human brain. *American Psychologist, 35*, 409–420.

Loftus, E.F., Miller, D.G., & Burns, H.J. (1978). Semantic integration of verbal information into a visual memory. *Journal of Experimental Psychology: Human Learning and Memory, 4*, 19–31.

Loftus, E.F., Schooler, J.W., & Wagenaar, W.A. (1985). The fate of memory: Comment on McCloskey and Zaragoza. *Journal of Experimental Psychology: General, 114*, 375–380.

McClelland, J.L., & Rumelhart, D.E. (1985). Distributed memory and the representation of general and specific information. *Journal of Experimental Psychology: General, 114*, 159–188.

McCloskey, M., & Zaragoza, M. (1985). Misleading postevent information and memory for events: Arguments and evidence against memory impairment hypotheses. *Journal of Experimental Psychology: General, 114*, 1–16.

Morton, J., Hammersley, R.H., & Bekerian, D.A. (1985). Headed records: A model for memory and its failures. *Cognition, 20*, 1–23.

Neisser, U. (1967). *Cognitive psychology*. New York: Appleton-Century Crofts.

Squire, L.R. (1987). *Memory and brain*. New York: Oxford University Press.

Tulving, E. (1983). *Elements of episodic memory*. New York: Oxford University Press.

Tulving, E. (1984). Precise of elements of episodic memory. *Behavioral & Brain Sciences, 7*, 223–238.

Tversky, B., & Tuchin, M. (1989). A reconciliation of the evidence on eyewitness testimony: Comments on McCloskey and Zaragoza. *Journal of Experimental Psychology: General, 118*, 86–91.

Wagenaar, W. (1989). *The misinformation feud: Parameterized models and undeterminate differences*. Unpublished manuscript, Leiden University.

Wagenaar, W., & Boer, H. (1987). Misleading postevent information: Testing parameterized models of integration in memory. *Acta Psychologica, 66*, 291–306.

Wells, G.L., & Turtle, J.W. (1987). Eyewitness testimony research: Current knowledge and emergent controversies. *Canadian Journal of Behavioral Science, 19*, 363–388.

Zaragoza, M.S. (1987). Memory, suggestibility, and eyewitness testimony in children and adults. In S.J. Ceci, M.P. Toglia, & D.F. Ross (Eds.) *Children's eyewitness memory* (pp. 53–78). New York: Springer-Verlag.

Zaragoza, M.S., & McCloskey, M. (1989). Misleading postevent information and the memory impairment hypothesis: Comment on Belli (1989) and reply to Tversky and Tuchin (1989). *Journal of Experimental Psychology: General, 118*, 92–99.

Zaragoza, M.S., McCloskey, M., & Jamis, M. (1987). Misleading postevent information and recall of the original event: Further evidence against the memory impairment hypothesis. *Journal of Experimental Psychology: Learning, Memory, & Cognition, 13*, 36–44.

6
The Role of Memory Impairment in Children's Suggestibility

MARIA S. ZARAGOZA, DONNA DAHLGREN, and JEAN MUENCH

A central issue in the study of children's long-term retention is an understanding of children's susceptibility to memory failures. It has long been recognized that an important cause of memory failures is interference caused by new learning. Recently, interest in memory failures caused by subsequent learning has been revived in the context of studies on suggestibility and eyewitness memory. These studies have shown that, for subjects of all ages, exposure to misinformation (i.e., false information presented as truth) after viewing an event can lead to profound decrements in performance on later tests of memory for the originally seen event.

These *misinformation effects* have received a great deal of attention in both the adult and developmental literatures. Misinformation phenomena have been widely interpreted as having implications for theories of forgetting and event representation, and, because they illustrate people's tendency to put together separately acquired facts, provide an opportunity to study integrative and constructive memory processes. These effects have also generated widespread interest because of their implications for the reliability of eyewitness memory and testimony in real-world situations involving eyewitnesses to a crime. In short, by documenting the effects of misleading suggestions on later reports, these studies provide a laboratory analogue of "suggestibility effects" that could be brought about in the court situation by questions, conversations, or other new information a witness may be exposed to after viewing an event.

Although the effects of misinformation on memory performance are well-documented, the theoretical interpretation of these effects is still far from resolved. In this chapter we review the available evidence on the effects of misinformation on young children's memory in an attempt to shed some light on the implications of misinformation phenomena for understanding children's memory. A central goal will be to characterize the nature of the memory failures caused by misleading suggestions. Much of the discussion will focus on the *memory impairment hypothesis* that has dominated research and theory on this topic. We begin by describing the misinformation effect.

TABLE 6.1. Examples of the original-test and modified-test procedures.

Condition	Original (saw)	Misinformation (heard twice)	Test
	Original-test procedure		
Misled	Rabbit	Dog	Rabbit or dog?
Control	Rabbit	—	Rabbit or dog?
	Modified-test procedure		
Misled	Rabbit	Dog	Rabbit or bear?
Control	Rabbit	—	Rabbit or bear?

The Misinformation Effect

Most studies of the misinformation effect have employed a three-phase procedure where children first view some event, are later asked leading or misleading questions about some aspects of the original event, and finally are tested on their memory for the originally seen details. One widely used version of this three-phase procedure is the original-test procedure (also known as the standard test) developed by Loftus, Miller, and Burns (1978). The original-test procedure is illustrated in the top half of Table 6.1. In this example, all subjects first view a series of slides that depict a little girl playing with a toy rabbit. Later, children in the *misled* group are told incorrectly that the girl had been playing with a toy dog, whereas children in the *control* group are not given any misinformation about the stuffed animal. Finally, when tested on their memory for the stuffed animal they saw in the slides, subjects in both groups are given a forced choice between the original item (e.g., rabbit) and the item provided as misinformation for subjects in the misled group (e.g., dog). The typical finding is that subjects in the misled group perform more poorly than subjects in the control group, because misled subjects are more likely to report the misinformation "dog." For example, in a study we conducted with preschoolers who were given the original test, 71% of the children in the control condition (who had not been misled) correctly chose the originally seen item (e.g., "rabbit") on the test, but only 54% of the children in the misled condition did so (Zaragoza, 1987).

It has now been established that misinformation effects occur in children from 3 years of age to college age (e.g., Ceci, Ross, & Toglia, 1987; Cohen & Harnick, 1980; Duncan, Whitney, & Kunen, 1982; Goodman & Reed, 1986; Marin, Holmes, Guth, & Kovak, 1979). However, it is well documented that the testimony of adults can be heavily influenced by misleading suggestions as well (Bekerian & Bowers, 1983; Christiaansen & Ochalek, 1983; Loftus, 1975, 1977, 1979a, 1979b; Loftus & Loftus, 1980; Loftus et al., 1978; Loftus & Palmer, 1974; McCloskey & Zaragoza,

1985a; Weinberg, Wadsworth, & Baron, 1983; Zaragoza, McCloskey, & Jamis, 1987). Attempts to identify developmental differences in misinformation effects have failed to reveal consistent age-related trends (cf., Loftus & Davies, 1984), although there is some evidence that preschool children may be more heavily influenced by misinformation than older children and adults (Ceci et al., 1987). More recently, researchers have turned to studying the psychological mechanisms that underlie misinformation effects in an attempt to better understand children's susceptibility to misleading suggestion.

What Factors Contribute to Misinformation Phenomena?

To briefly summarize, the specific phenomenon we will focus on in this chapter concerns the memory performance of children who have been exposed to misleading information that contradicts some aspect of a previously witnessed event. The finding of interest is that misled subjects are more likely than children who have not been misled to report the suggested (misleading) item, rather than the item they saw, on tests of memory for the original event. Thus, there are two aspects of this finding that require explanation: (a) subjects' failure to report the originally seen item following exposure to misinformation, and (b) subjects' tendency to incorrectly report the misleading item following exposure to misinformation. As we shall see, the various proposals that have been put forward to explain this phenomenon have differed in the extent to which they emphasize one or the other of these aspects of the phenomenon.

The Role of Nonmnemonic Factors

A notorious interpretive problem with studies of misinformation phenomena is disentangling the contribution of mnemonic and nonmnemonic factors to memory performance. Because the misinformation is provided by someone (e.g., the experimenter) who is likely to be perceived as a knowledgeable authority figure, subjects may report the misinformation for reasons that are unrelated to their memory of the originally witnessed event. In particular, it is always possible that subjects who report the misinformation are merely conforming to the suggestion provided by the interviewer. A subject may conform to suggestion because they trust the information provided by the experimenter more than their own memory, or because they feel some social pressure to go along. For example, there is evidence from studies with adults that subjects are much less likely to incorporate misleading suggestions into their reports if they suspect that the person providing the misinformation has intentions to mislead (e.g., Dodd & Bradshaw, 1980). With children, the influence of such social pressures are likely to be greater in light of the greater difference in social status between a young child and an adult authority figure. Consistent with this hypothesis, Ceci et al. (1987, Exp. 2; see also Toglia, Ross, and Ceci, this volume) demonstrated that when the misinformation was presented to preschool children by a child (a 7-year-old boy) rather than an adult, the magnitude of the misinformation effect was reduced. That is, when misinformation had been provided by a peer, children were less likely to later report the misinformation on the test. In a more recent study (Toglia et al., this volume) these same investigators report evidence that preschool children will be more heavily influenced by misinformation that is provided by a credible adult than a noncredible adult. Taken together, these results suggest that non-mnemonic factors play an important role in misinformation phenomena. This fact has often been overlooked in much of the theorizing about misinformation phenomena, which has tended to interpret these effects exclusively in memorial terms (e.g., see Metcalfe, 1990, for a recently proposed memory model of misinformation phenomena). Hence, in assessing the implications of misinformation phenomena for theories of memory it is important to keep in mind that the observed effects are likely due, at least in part, to factors other than memory. Of course, it is possible, if not likely, that these social and memorial factors interact in important ways. Unfortunately, however, relatively little is known about the specific ways in which these social factors contribute to misinformation effects (cf. Toglia et al., this volume). Thus, teasing apart the contribution of social and memorial factors to misinformation effects, and understanding how they interact, are important theoretical and methodological concerns.

The Role of Constructive Memory Processes in Misinformation Phenomena

The act of incorporating subsequently learned misinformation into one's report of a witnessed event is essentially a *constructive* memory process. By constructive process we mean a process whereby two or more pieces of information acquired at separate points in time are (a) recognized as related to each other and (b) put together in a coherent way. Although the ability to integrate knowledge across separate episodes is useful and even necessary in many circumstances (e.g., for comprehension of prose), it can lead to errors in the eyewitness situation where verbatim memory of an originally witnessed episode is required. One interesting finding from the developmental literature is that the tendency to engage in integrative processing appears to increase with age (e.g., Liben & Posnansky, 1977; Paris & Lindauer, 1976; Paris, Lindauer, & Cox, 1977). Nevertheless, research with misinformation phenomena suggests that the memory performance of even very young children can be influenced by postevent misinformation, suggesting not only the ability, but the tendency, to relate these separate events.

Surprisingly, the role of inferential and integrative memory processes in misinformation phenomena is an issue that has received virtually no attention. It is nonetheless clear that constructive processes play an important role in misinformation effects. Hence, a complete understanding of these effects, and of children's susceptibility to them, will require further study of the circumstances under which witnesses tend to relate information acquired from separate sources and the circumstances under which they tend to keep them separate.

The Role of Memory Impairment (Forgetting) in Misinformation Phenomena

A review of the developmental and adult literatures on misinformation phenomena reveals that one issue has dominated interest and research on this topic: the "fate" of the original memory following exposure to misinformation (i.e., the fate of the memory for the originally seen event). Initially, misinformation effects were widely interpreted as evidence that misleading suggestions impaired subjects' ability to remember originally seen details. In other words, it was taken for granted that because misled subjects failed to report the originally seen details on tests of their memory for the original event, the misleading suggestions must have caused *forgetting* of the originally seen details. Although there was widespread consensus that misinformation phenomena reflected forgetting of originally seen details, researchers debated whether this presumed forgetting was due to *storage failure* or to *retrieval failure*. For example, Loftus and colleagues (Loftus, 1979a, 1979b; Loftus & Loftus, 1980; see also Ceci et al., 1987, for a similar proposal about children's memory) strongly endorsed the position that the misinformation alters the original memory trace such that the original item contradicted by the misinformation is partially or completely lost from storage. Other investigators (e.g., Bekerian & Bowers, 1983; Christiaansen & Ochalek, 1983) have posited that misinformation does not alter or erase the original memory trace, but merely renders the original memory trace difficult or impossible to retrieve.

To differentiate forgetting caused by exposure to misinformation from other sorts of forgetting that may go on in the eyewitness situation, we hereafter employ the term *memory impairment* to refer specifically to forgetting of originally seen details that is caused by exposure to contradictory misleading suggestions. Note that in using the term *memory impairment* we refer to forgetting that is restricted both in terms of the cause of the forgetting (the misinformation) and the target that is forgotten (the original detail contradicted by misinformation). In addition, our use of the term *memory impairment* subsumes *both* storage failures and retrieval failures caused by exposure to misinformation. In other words, the term *memory impairment* does not distinguish between these two possible forms of forgetting of the originally seen details.

The assumption that misinformation phenomena reflect memory impairment has recently been called into question by McCloskey and Zaragoza (1985a, 1985b). The crux of their argument is that misinformation can lead to inaccurate memory performance for reasons entirely unrelated to forgetting of originally seen details. They discuss two reasons why misled subjects can be expected to perform more poorly than control subjects even if misinformation has not caused forgetting of originally seen details.

The assumption that misinformation causes forgetting of originally seen details presumes that the original event is stored in memory. However, because levels of control performance in these experiments are typically well below ceiling, it is obvious that some of subjects do not remember[1] the original details even before they are misled, perhaps because they failed to encode them or because they have forgotten the original details in the interval between the original and misleading presentations. The problem is that among subjects who fail to remember the original detail, those who are later exposed to misinformation are likely to perform more poorly on the memory test than control subjects who are not. When faced with a choice between the original and misleading items on the test, the control subjects for whom neither of the items are familiar can be expected to guess and select the correct alternative at a probability equal to chance. In contrast, the corresponding subjects in the misled group can be expected to perform more poorly than chance. This is because some of the misled subjects who fail to remember the original detail will nonetheless remember the more recently presented misleading item. These subjects are likely to select the incorrect misleading alternative on the test because it is the only one of the two alternatives that is familiar to them. Note that in this case, the tendency for misled subjects to select the misleading alternative more often than control subjects (although an important error in its own right) cannot be attributed to memory impairment. This is because exposure to misinformation is causing decrements in performance among subjects who never encoded (or have forgotten)

---

[1] When we say that a subject has forgotten, or cannot remember, some piece of information, we mean that under the conditions of the test the subject cannot access the information in memory. This is not meant to imply an "all-or-none" conception of memory. We assume that there is a strength threshold for recognition such that strengths above the threshold are sufficient to permit a correct response on a recognition test and strengths below the threshold are not. We also assume that across subjects the initial strength of the original information is distributed along a strength continuum, such that some items fall above the recognition threshold and some items fall below. Those items that fall above the threshold are remembered and those items that fall below are not.

the original detail, even before they were misled. Thus, for these subjects, the misleading information is more accurately described as "filling a gap" in memory.

McCloskey and Zaragoza (1985a) also pointed out a second class of reasons why misled subjects may perform more poorly than control subjects even if their ability to remember the original details has not been impaired. This has to do with the fact that subjects may choose to report the misleading items even if they can remember the original details. They may do so, for example, because they feel pressure to conform to the misleading suggestion, because they trust the information provided by the experimenter more than their own memory, or because they confuse which of the items came from the original event and which one was presented later in the context of the postevent questioning.

For the reasons described by McCloskey and Zaragoza (1985a) it is clear that the widespread assumption that misinformation effects reflect forgetting of original details is unfounded. Although it is certainly possible that misinformation causes forgetting of originally seen details, evidence of forgetting cannot be inferred from the finding that misled subjects report the misleading items on memory tests. In other words, although the finding of misinformation effects is certainly consistent with the memory impairment idea, these effects are not diagnostic with regard to memory impairment because of the other factors that can be expected to contribute to performance in ways that mimic a memory impairment effect. Hence, on the basis of these misinformation phenomena alone, it remains an open question whether misinformation leads to memory impairment.

This analysis of the factors that can influence performance in misinformation experiments reveals that the basic question, Does misinformation impair children's ability to remember originally seen details?, cannot be answered on the basis of the available studies documenting misinformation effects in children. Nevertheless, an answer to this question is important for several reasons. First, a resolution of the memory impairment issue is important for understanding the mechanisms that give rise to misinformation phenomena in children, and more generally, to their suggestibility. In other words, it is important to understand the contribution of memory impairment to the inaccuracies observed in misinformation effects. Second, misinformation phenomena have been widely regarded as a vehicle for studying forgetting in a naturalistic context. Before we can assess what implications misinformation effects might have for theories of forgetting and its development, it is necessary to first establish that misinformation causes forgetting of originally stored memories. Third, studies with adults have consistently failed to find evidence of memory impairment caused by misinformation (Bowman & Zaragoza, 1989; McCloskey & Zaragoza, 1985a; Zaragoza et al., 1987) even though they consistently find evidence of misinformation effects.

Hence, knowing whether children are similarly resistant to memory impairment is important from both a theoretical and practical point of view.

Preschool Children's Susceptibility to Memory Impairment

Are young children particularly susceptible to forgetting caused by subsequent information? The literature on the development of forgetting does not provide a very clear answer to this question. Chief among the problems is the dearth of available research on this topic (see Brainerd, Reyna, Howe, & Kingma, 1990, for a recent review and discussion of this problem). Of the studies on developmental differences in forgetting that do exist, several (e.g., Hasher & Thomas, 1973; Merriman, Azmita, & Perlmutter, 1988; Rogoff, Newcombe, & Kagan, 1974) have shown that young children do not forget faster than older children. However, a recent series of studies by Brainerd and colleagues (see, e.g., Brainerd et al., 1990) reveal evidence of age-related changes in forgetting in the direction of more forgetting among children than young adults. Although these latter findings suggest that young children might be more susceptible to memory impairment than older children or adults, the extent to which these developmental trends in forgetting reflect heightened susceptibility to interference (as opposed to, for example, decay) is unclear.

Perhaps more relevant to the issue of children's susceptibility to memory impairment are the classic list-learning studies of retroactive interference (RI). The $A-B$, $A-C$ paradigm employed in studies of RI is similar to the misinformation paradigm in that (a) subjects learn new information that contradicts a specific item from the original learning episode, and (b) subjects are later tested on their memory for the originally learned item. Interestingly, the evidence from the RI literature, although very scant, suggests that very young children are *less* susceptible to memory impairment effects than older children and adults. In fact, several studies have shown that children 4 to 5 years of age show no evidence of retroactive interference under conditions that produce significant interference effects in older children (e.g., Koppenaal, Krull, & Katz, 1964; Loomis & Hall, 1968). Although one cannot be certain that the results of RI studies, which involve paired associates learned to criterion, should generalize to misinformation studies, the RI literature provides no support for the claim that young children's memories are especially vulnerable to forgetting.

We turn now to a review of the available evidence bearing directly on children's susceptibility to memory impairment caused by misinformation.

Although many studies have examined misinformation effects in young children, very few of these studies can be used to evaluate the memory impairment claim directly, because of the reasons given by McCloskey and Zaragoza (1985a) as described above. In other words, to assess memory impairment caused by misinformation it is necessary to employ test procedures that control for the influence of "gap-filling," demand characteristics, and other factors unrelated to memory impairment that can lead to differences in misled and control performance.

Assessment of Memory Impairment with the Modified Test Procedure

In the foregoing discussion we pointed out that factors other than memory impairment can lead misled subjects to perform more poorly than control subjects on the original test typically employed in studies of misinformation phenomena. For these reasons, to assess memory impairment caused by misinformation, a test other than the original-test procedure is needed. The modified-test procedure illustrated in the bottom half of Table 6.1 is one procedure that has been developed for this purpose (McCloskey & Zaragoza, 1985a). The advantage of the modified test is that it ensures that misled and control performance will differ if, and only if, there is a difference in the proportion of misled and control subjects who can remember the original detail at the time of test. This modified-test procedure is identical to the original-test procedure with the exception that the misleading item is not a choice on the test. Instead, subjects are asked to choose between the original item (e.g., rabbit) and a new item (e.g., bear). Because the misinformation is not a choice on the test, it eliminates the social pressure to agree with the experimenter's suggestion. In addition, because the misleading alternative is not an option on the test, it eliminates the bias toward the misleading response among misled subjects who fail to remember the original detail. On the other hand, if fewer misled than control subjects can remember the original detail (i.e., if misinformation impairs memory) misled subjects will perform more poorly on this test. Thus, with this procedure, misled subjects will perform more poorly than control subjects if, and only if, their ability to remember original details is impaired (see McCloskey & Zaragoza 1985a, 1985b, for a more detailed analysis and discussion of this procedure).

To date, only a few studies have attempted to assess children's susceptibility to memory impairment with the modified test, and these studies have produced contradictory results (Ceci et al., 1987; Zaragoza, 1987, 1991). In the next section we review the limited available research conducted with the modified test, and present some new results.

Evidence in Favor of the Memory Impairment Claim

Ceci et al. (1987; Exp. 4) employed the modified test in a study that provides the first direct evidence that preschool children are susceptible to memory impairment[2] (see also Toglia et al., this volume, for a replication of this finding.) In their study, 3- to 4-year-old preschoolers listened to a story about a family that attends a school carnival. The story was accompanied by 12 black and white illustrations that depicted scenes involving clowns and animals. One day after presentation of the original story, the children were interviewed by a 7-year-old boy. For subjects in the misled group the boy provided misinformation about two aspects of the original story: the color of a clown's balloon and the type of fruit eaten by the children in the story. For children in the control group, the boy did not provide misinformation about either of these items. Two days later all subjects were given a memory test on the original story. Half the subjects were tested with the original test and the other half were given the modified test. The results obtained with the original test evidenced a substantial misinformation effect, with control performance at 88% correct and misled performance at 46% correct. Of course, the results

[2] Ceci et al. (1987) actually reported the results of two experiments with the modified test (Exps. 3 and 4), and in both experiments they observed a significant misled/control difference. However, it is not clear that the decrement in misled performance reported in Experiment 3 can be attributed to memory impairment. This is because in Experiment 3 the items used as original, misleading, and new items were not counterbalanced across subjects. Asymmetries in similarity among the three items can cause response biases that ultimately result in misled/control performance differences unrelated to memory impairment. For example, children in Ceci et al.'s Experiment 3 saw pictures of a boy wearing a *red* hat, and were later exposed to misinformation that the hat was *green*. (Children in the control group were not exposed to any postevent information about the color of the hat.) On the modified test, both groups of children were asked to choose between the correct red hat and a new blue hat. The problem here is the expected performance of misled subjects who remember only the misinformation "green" because they had forgotten the color of the original hat even before they were misled. When faced with a choice between red and blue, these children may be biased toward the incorrect response "blue" because it is the response that is more similar to the color they remember, green. In contrast, control subjects who fail to remember the red hat will not be biased toward the incorrect response the same way, because they were never exposed to the misinformation about a green hat. Such a bias in misled subjects' responses may have been sufficient to produce the moderate misled/control performance difference Ceci et al. observed. The possibility of such response biases contaminating performance can be controlled for by ensuring that each version of the critical item (red, blue, and green) serves equally often as the correct and incorrect response. Ceci et al. employed such counterbalancing procedures in Experiment 4 of their study and nonetheless obtained a significant memory impairment effect. For all of the above reasons, only the results of Experiment 4 can be marshaled in favor of the memory impairment claim.

obtained with the original test cannot be attributed to memory impairment, for all of the reasons we have outlined above. However, Ceci et al. found that for subjects given the modified test, performance in the misled group (72% correct) was significantly lower than performance in the control group (88% correct), thus providing evidence that the children's ability to remember the original event was indeed impaired. On the other hand, the difference in misled performance on the original and modified tests (46% correct vs. 72% correct) shows quite clearly that original-test performance is influenced by factors other than memory impairment.

Ceci et al.'s (1987) finding that preschool children are susceptible to memory impairment is particularly important in light of the fact that similar studies conducted with adults have uniformly failed to find evidence of memory impairment when the modified test is used (e.g., Bowman & Zaragoza, 1989; McCloskey & Zaragoza, 1985a). Although direct comparisons across studies cannot be made, the Ceci et al. results suggest that preschoolers' memories may be more vulnerable to memory impairment than those of older children and adults. Before exploring the implications of this finding, we review the evidence against the claim that preschool children are susceptible to memory impairment.

Evidence against the Memory Impairment Claim

In contrast to the findings of Ceci et al. (1987), several studies we have conducted with the modified test have consistently failed to reveal evidence of memory impairment in preschool children (Zaragoza, 1987, 1991). In each of these studies we have nevertheless obtained substantial misinformation effects when the original-test procedure was used. In this section we briefly review these studies and present some new results that converge on the earlier findings.

Unless otherwise noted, all of the studies to be discussed employed the same experimental procedure: Subjects viewed a slide sequence depicting an event that was accompanied by a story narrated by the experimenter. The slide sequence contained four *critical details* that subjects would later be tested on, and across the experiment there were three versions of each critical detail. After a 10-min filler task, the experimenter provided subjects with a synopsis of the event that provided misleading information about two of the critical details they had seen (misled condition), and neutral information about the remaining two critical details (control condition). Immediately following the misleading manipulation, subjects were tested on their memory for the original slides. In each experiment one group of subjects was tested with the modified test to assess potential memory impairment caused by misinformation. In addition, in all but one of the experiments a second group of subjects was tested with the original-test procedure to ensure that we could replicate the misinformation effect.

Memory Impairment and Multiple Exposures to Misinformation

Zaragoza (1987) conducted two experiments where preschoolers 3 to 6 years of age viewed a series of slides depicting a girl in a city park. The slide sequence contained four critical details that subjects would later be tested on: the type of item held by an old man in the park (a cane, umbrella, or broom), the type of ball a boy was playing with (baseball, basketball, or football), a toy on the playground (a train, airplane, or boat), and the type of tool a construction worker was holding (a hammer, screwdriver, or saw). The two experiments were identical to each other with the exception that in the first experiment subjects were exposed to the misinformation once, and in the second experiment subjects were exposed to the misinformation twice. The two misleading presentations were accomplished by presenting the synopsis of the event twice in immediate succession.

The modified-test results revealed no evidence of memory impairment in either experiment. Following one exposure to misinformation, performance in the misled condition (74% correct) was as accurate as performance in the control condition (71% correct), $p > .05$. When the children were misled twice, the same result was obtained; misled performance (69% correct) was as accurate as control performance (70% correct), $p > .05$. In contrast, a second group of subjects tested with the original test (following one exposure to misinformation) showed marked decrements in misled performance (54% correct) when compared with control performance (77% correct).

The next three studies to be discussed are reported in Zaragoza (1991). In contrast to both the Ceci et al. (1987) and Zaragoza (1987) studies described above, in these experiments children viewed a series of slides depicting a live event (as opposed to illustrations). The slides depicted a young girl spending a typical day at home (e.g., eating, picking up toys, playing with a friend, etc.). The sequence contained four critical slides that subjects would later be tested on: a fruit (apple, orange, or banana), a stuffed animal (rabbit, dog, or bear) a toy musical instrument (piano, drum, guitar), and a toy vehicle (airplane, truck, or boat). In each of the three experiments the experimenter went over the postevent synopsis twice in immediate succession, so that in effect all subjects were misled twice. Finally, all three experiments were conducted with children between the ages of 3 and 5.

Is Memory Impairment Age Dependent?

Zaragoza (1991) conducted an experiment designed to investigate the possibility that young preschoolers are more susceptible to memory impairment than older preschoolers. Because subjects in Zaragoza's (1987) study were approximately 1 year older (M = 4 years 11 months) than subjects in Ceci et al.'s (1987) study (M = 3 years 8 months), a possible explanation for the discrepancy in their results is the difference in the age of the subjects tested. To test this hypothesis, Zaragoza (1991) employed the modified-test procedure to compare the performance of 60 3-year-olds with that of 36 5-year-olds.

The modified-test results provided no evidence that 3-year-olds are more susceptible to memory impairment than 5-year-olds; in fact, there was no evidence of memory impairment in either age group. In the 3-year-old group, performance was 71% correct in the misled condition and 73% correct in the control condition, and in the 5-year-old group, performance was 94% correct in the misled condition and 97% correct in the control condition (both *ps* $>.05$).

In addition to the subjects tested with the modified test, a separate group of 36 3-year-olds and 24 4-year-olds were tested with the original-test procedure. In both groups a significant misinformation effect was observed. For the 3-year-olds performance was 65% correct in the misled condition and 82% in the control condition, and for the 5-year-olds performance was 79% correct in the misled condition and 95% correct in the control condition (both *ps* $<.05$).

These results show that even very young preschoolers, 3 years of age, can be resistant to memory impairment following exposure to misleading suggestions. It should be noted, however, that Ceci et al. (1987) did not evaluate the memory impairment hypothesis in children older than approximately 3 years of age. Hence, it is an open question whether they would have observed memory impairment in older children as well. Toglia et al. (this volume) attempted to assess memory impairment in children 8 years of age, but were unable to do so because of ceiling effects.

Memory Impairment and Strength of Original Memory

Zaragoza (1991) reports the results of an experiment that was designed to investigate if there is a relationship between memory impairment and strength of the original memory. Many researchers have assumed, either explicitly or implicitly, that there is a relationship between the strength of the original memory and its susceptibility to memory impairment (Brainerd & Reyna, 1988; Ceci et al., 1987). Some investigators have put forward the hypothesis that a weak memory for the original detail should be more susceptible to memory impairment than a strong trace, a claim that has some basis in the retroactive interference literature (see Crowder, 1976; Postman & Underwood, 1973, for reviews). Given the assumption that control performance is an index of the "strength" of the original memory, this hypothesis would predict an inverse relationship between levels of control performance and susceptibility to memory impairment. That is, all other things being equal, large memory impairment effects should be observed at low levels of control performance and small memory impairment effects should be observed at high levels of control performance.

However, several researchers have made the opposite prediction (cf. Chandler, 1989), that is, that memory impairment effects should get larger the higher the level of control performance. The basis for the latter prediction is a focus on the factors that enhance and/or diminish the chances of detecting memory impairment effects. Under conditions that produce weak traces of the original event control performance will be low. If few subjects can retrieve the original information even before they are exposed to the misleading information, there are few subjects whose memories can be potentially impaired by the misinformation, thus making it difficult to detect memory impairment effects. With high levels of control performance, there are more subjects who can retrieve the original information, and hence more subjects whose memories can potentially be impaired. Hence, from this point of view, memory impairment effects are more likely to be observed at higher levels of control performance.

In light of the above discussion, it is interesting to note that in the initial studies we conducted with the modified test (Zaragoza, 1987), control performance was between 70% and 73%, approximately halfway between ceiling (100%) and guessing (50%). Although this intermediate level of memory would seem to be ideal for assessing potential memory impairing effects of misinformation, it is possible that higher levels of memory would be more likely to reveal a memory impairment effect. With regard to this latter point it is important to note that the level of control performance in Ceci et al.'s (1987) study was 88%, even though subjects were tested 3 days after viewing the original event. One possibility, then, is that moderately high levels of control performance are necessary for memory impairment effects to be observed.

To investigate this hypothesis, Zaragoza (1991) tested a group of 48 3-year-olds and a group of 24 4-year-olds in experiments identical to those described above with the exception that two changes were made in an attempt to improve subjects' memory for the original slides. First, the number of filler slides in the sequence was reduced from 45 to 12 and, second, the exposure duration of the slides was increased from 4 sec to 8 sec.

The results provided no support for the hypothesis that memory impairment is more likely to be observed at high levels of control performance. Although the manipulations were effective in raising levels of control performance, there was no evidence of memory impairment in either age group. In both age groups misled and control performance on the modified test did not differ significantly. In the 3-year-old group performance was 76% correct in the misled condition and 82% correct in the control condition, and in the 4-year-old group performance was 96% correct in the misled condition and 98% correct in the control condition (both *p*s $>.05$).

Once again, the results obtained with the original test were quite different; in both age groups a significant misinformation effect was observed. For the 3-year-olds, performance was 69% correct in the misled condition and 86% correct in the control condition, and for the 4-year-olds, performance was 74% correct in the misled condition and 94% correct in the control condition (both *ps* $<.05$).

Memory Impairment and Retention Interval

A third potentially important difference between the Ceci et al. (1987) and Zaragoza (1987) studies was the retention interval involved. In the Ceci et al. study subjects were misled 1 day after the original story, and were tested 2 days after presentation of the misinformation. In contrast, in the Zaragoza study (1987), the entire experiment was conducted in a single 20-min session. One possibility is that misinformation has a greater impact on memory if it is presented after a lag of a few days instead of a short retention interval. This is likely to come about for two reasons: (a) the original memory representation may have decayed somewhat, perhaps rendering it more susceptible to impairment, and (b) subjects are likely to devote more attention to the misinformation after a delay. To test this idea, Zaragoza (1991) conducted an experiment with 48 4-year-olds in which presentation of the misinformation occurred 2 days after the original event, and testing occurred shortly after presentation of the misinformation.

The results provided no support for the hypothesis that subjects would be more susceptible to memory impairment if misinformation were presented after a delay of a few days. Performance in the misled condition (69% correct) did not differ from performance in the control condition (73%), $p > .05$.

In summary, in five experiments involving over 250 subjects (Zaragoza, 1987, 1991) we found no evidence that misinformation leads to memory impairment in preschool children. Attempts to identify any factors or circumstances that contributed to the memory impairment effect observed by Ceci et al. (1987) have not been successful. However, one variable that has not been examined is the possible contribution of stimulus materials to memory impairment effects. Hence, it is possible that our failures to replicate the results of the Ceci et al. study are tied to differences in the experimental materials employed. For this reason we have recently conducted a fourth study, reported in the next section, that was primarily a replication of the fourth experiment in the Ceci et al. study.

A Failure to Replicate

In this study we used the stimulus materials and experimental procedures used by Ceci et al. in Experiment 4 of their 1987 study (with a few minor modifications to be described below).[3] Two groups of subjects were tested: the replication group and the misled-twice group. As the name implies, the purpose of the replication group was to replicate the results obtained in Ceci et al. The misled-twice group was treated the same as the replication group with the exception that they were misled on each of two days. We hypothesized that two presentations of the misinformation, especially if spread out over time, would have a greater impairing effect on original memories than one presentation. Once more, this latter prediction is consistent with the finding in studies of retroactive interference that interference increases with increasing trials on the interpolated list.

In the experiment reported by Ceci et al. (1987), the original story contained two *critical items* that the children were tested on: (a) the color of the clown's balloons (either blue, green, or orange), and (b) the type of fruit eaten by the girl (either apple, banana, or grapes). One day after presentation of the story, the subjects were questioned individually by a 7-year-old boy. For children in the misled conditions, the 7-year-old boy provided misinformation about the color of the balloon and the type of fruit. For children in the control condition, the 7-year-old omitted these two sources of misinformation from the interview. Three days after the story was presented (2 days after the children were interviewed) all children were tested individually by one of the experimenters. Of the children who were misled, 36 were assigned to the original-test condition where they were given a recognition test that involved choosing between the critical item originally seen and the item presented as misinformation. The remaining 36 children who had been misled were given the modified test, which provided a choice between the originally seen picture and a new version of the critical item. Finally, the 36 subjects in the control condition (who had not been misled) were given a choice between the original picture and a distractor that had not been seen or suggested.

The study we conducted was identical to that described above with the following exceptions. We increased the number of critical items from two to four. This change allowed us to increase the amount of information gleaned from each subject while still permitting us to examine performance on the two items used in the original Ceci et al. (1987) study. To accomplish this, we created three versions of two of the pictures from the original story. For example, the fifth picture in the original story showed a boy flying a kite. For this picture we created two additional versions that were nearly identical except the same boy was either jumping rope or kicking a soccer ball. Second, we took two pictures from the original story (one showing rabbits and a second showing goats) and converted them into a single critical item such that the subjects saw only one type of

[3] We thank Steve Ceci, David Ross, and Michael Toglia for providing us copies of their stimulus materials and experimental protocol.

animal (rabbits, goats, or pigs). Thus, the four critical items in the experiment we conducted were (a) the color of the balloons held by the clown, (b) the type of fruit eaten by the protagonist, (c) the activity of the boy, and (d) the type of farm animal.

A second difference was that we employed a within-subjects misled/control comparison. That is, each subject received misinformation about two of the critical details and no information about the other two. We used a within-subjects comparison for several reasons. First, because we have employed within-subjects comparisons in all our previous studies, it was important to maintain this procedure in order to facilitate comparisons between the present study and our previous studies. Second, a within-subjects manipulation provides greater power than a between-subjects comparison, and should therefore be better able to detect any differences in misled and control performance.

A third difference was that for each child tested, the same person (an adult experimenter) interacted with the child in each phase of the experiment (i.e., read the story, provided the misinformation, gave the test). Because Ceci et al. (1987) showed that children were less influenced by the misnformation when it was presented by a child than an adult, we employed the stronger manipulation.

Subjects in the misled-twice group were treated identically to subjects in the replication group with the exception that they were misled for a second time on Day 3 of the experiment. In this way, the delay between the original story and the test was the same for both groups. Although in previous studies we have found no evidence of memory impairment after subjects were misled twice, the two presentations of the misinformation have always been presented in immediate succession. Given the evidence that memory improves the greater the lag between successive presentation (e.g., Madigan, 1969) we reasoned that presenting the misinformation on separate days would lead to better memory for the misinformation and hence maximize its interfering effect.

At this time, we have tested 68 3- and 4-year-olds with the modified test. Of these subjects, 36 were in the replication group (i.e., the replication of Ceci et al., 1987) and 32 were in the misled-twice group. The discussion that follows focuses on the results when the analysis is restricted to the two critical items Ceci et al. employed in their original study (i.e., the color of the balloons and the type of fruit) in order to facilitate comparisons between the two studies. The results do not differ when the two additional critical items we added are included in the analysis.

Overall, the results revealed no evidence of memory impairment in either group. The replication and misled-twice groups did not differ from each other, nor did group (the number of times subjects were misled) interact with the misled/control manipulation (both *p*s $>.05$). When the results are collapsed across the two groups, performance in the misled and control conditions are identical, at 81% correct. Considered individually, performance in the replication condition was 80% correct in the misled condition and 77% correct in the control condition, ($p > .05$), and in the misled-twice condition, mean performance was 83% correct in the misled condition and 86% correct in the control condition. Subsequent analyses revealed that the size of the misled/control difference did not vary as a function of critical item (balloons vs. fruit), or age (3 years old vs. 4 years old), both $ps > .05$.

In contrast to the results obtained with the modified test, subjects tested with the original test ($n = 24$) showed impaired performance following exposure to misinformation (presented once). Mean performance in the original-test condition was 63% correct in the misled condition and 78% correct in the control condition, ($p < .05$). Hence, the failure to observe a memory impairment effect cannot be attributed to the fact that the children failed to attend to and encode the misinformation.

In summary, the major finding of this study is that we failed to replicate the memory impairment effect reported by Ceci et al. (1987) even when subjects were misled twice instead of once. A close comparison of our results with those of Ceci et al. reveal several differences that are difficult to explain. First, in spite of the fact that we used Ceci et al.'s materials, control performance in our study was 81% correct, a level that is not as high as the 88% correct obtained by Ceci et al. This difference in control performance, although not very large, is surprising for several reasons. First, the mean age of the subjects in our study was 4.6 years, approximately 1 year older than the mean age of subjects in the Ceci et al. study. In addition, two thirds of the children in our sample were from an exclusive private school in a large metropolitan area, and therefore most likely from a much higher socioeconomic status bracket than Ceci et al.'s subjects, whom they describe as primarily from "agricultural and blue-collar families" (p. 42). Given the differences in the two samples of subjects employed, one would expect much higher levels of control performance in our study than in Ceci et al.'s study.

This focus on levels of control performance is potentially important for several reasons. First, because in the Ceci et al. (1987) study the misled-control manipulation was conducted between subjects (that is, half the subjects were misled about two items and the other half were not misled at all) spuriously high control performance could have led to a significant misled-control difference. On the other hand, the failure to achieve the same level of control performance as Ceci et al. in spite of the fact that our subjects were in general older and from a higher social class, suggests the possibility that there may be something about our experimental procedure that systematically lowered control performance. One potentially important difference between the two studies is that in our study the misled/control manipulation was manipulated within-subjects and in Ceci et al. it was manipulated between-subjects. Thus, in our study all subjects were exposed to misinformation about two items, whereas in the Ceci et al. study subjects in the control group were not exposed to misinformation at all. One possibility is that exposure to misinformation has a "dampening" effect on memory for all aspects of the original event. From this view, the level of control performance observed in our experiment was lower than it would have been if subjects in the control condition had not been misled at all. Of course, this dampening effect, if it exists, need not be a memory effect at all. It is possible that exposure to misinformation has other effects, such as shaking the child's confidence or confusing the child, which could disrupt the child's performance on the test. In any event, determining whether the between versus within subjects misled/control manipulation has a systematic effect on observed memory impairment effects cannot be determined without conducting a study that manipulates this variable within the same experiment.

In discussing the discrepancy in control performance between the two studies, we do not mean to imply that our failure to replicate Ceci et al.'s (1987) results is limited to performance on control items. A more important difference between the two studies is the fact that misled performance (on the modified test) in our study was 81% correct, much higher than the 72% correct obtained by Ceci et al. Hence, even if the levels of control performance in our study had reached those observed by Ceci et al., it is unlikely that a significant memory impairment effect would have emerged.

Another salient difference between the results obtained by Ceci et al. (1987) and those we obtained is in the magnitude of the misinformation effect obtained when the original-test procedure is used. Misled performance in the Ceci et al. study was 46% correct, and in our study it was 63%. Thus, even though we observed a significant misinformation effect in our study, the effect was smaller than that obtained in the Ceci et al. study. This is particularly surprising in light of the fact that in the Ceci et al. study a 7-year-old presented the misinformation, whereas in our study the misinformation was presented by an adult. As already mentioned above, there is evidence that preschool children are less influenced by misinformation when it is provided by a child than when it is provided by an adult, presumably because they view the child as less credible (cf. Ceci et al., 1987, Exp. 2; see also Toglia et al., this volume). (It is worthwhile noting, however, that all of the children who participated in the original-test condition in this experiment were exposed to the misinformation only once. In contrast, approximately half the children tested with the modified test were misled twice. We have good reason to believe, based on studies we have conducted with adults, that the observed misinformation effects would have been much greater for children who were misled twice.)

Given that we employed the same materials and procedures as Ceci et al. (1987) when misleading the subjects, it is clear that the differences in the results of the two studies must be due to factors other than what the experimenter said during the misleading episode. In particular, the characteristics of the children, the characteristics of the interviewer, and characteristics of the interaction between the child and interviewer could all effect the extent to which children accept and ultimately report the misinformation. At this time, research on the interaction between interviewer characteristics and suggestibility is virtually nonexistent. Nevertheless, it appears that this variable can substantially influence the extent to which children will conform to misleading suggestion.

It is not clear, however, whether the factors that are responsible for the larger misled/control difference observed in original-test condition of Ceci et al.'s (1987) study are the same factors that led to the memory impairment effect they observed. Although both effects require that subjects encode the misinformation, relate it to the original episode, and remember it at the time of test, there are a number of factors that can influence the subjects tendency to report the misinformation that may or may not be related to the memory impairment effect. For example, Toglia et al. this volume, report the results of a study where they obtain a memory impairment effect comparable in size to that reported by Ceci et al. (a 20% misled-control performance difference on the modified test), even though the magnitude of the misinformation effect (i.e., a 20% misled-control performance difference on the original test) was much smaller than the effect reported in the original Ceci et al. (1987) paper (i.e., a 42% misled-control performance difference). Hence, it cannot be assumed that the size of the misinformation effect will predict the size of the memory impairment effect.

Assessment of Memory Impairment with Recall Procedures

The studies bearing on the memory impairment issue that have been discussed thus far have all employed the modified recognition test procedure. However, procedures have also been developed for assessing memory impairment in recall situations. Unfortunately, when used to assess memory impairment, most recall tests suffer from the same interpretive problems as the original recognition test. To see why this is the case, consider the situation where a child sees a toy rabbit in the slides and is later exposed to misinformation about a dog. (Control subjects, of course, see the rabbit but receive no misleading information.) At the time of test the children are asked to name the type of stuffed animal they saw in the slides. The problem here is that children in the misled group may report the suggested item "dog", even if they can remember the originally seen item, for all of the reasons we discussed earlier (e.g., perceived social pressure to conform). Furthermore, recall procedures also have the problem that subjects in the misled and control groups who fail to encode the original detail may not perform the same way on the test. In particular, to the extent that control subjects who cannot remember the original item are likely to recall the correct answer by chance, corresponding subjects in the misled condition are likely to perform more poorly because they are likely to report the misinformation rather than guess (see Zaragoza et al., 1987, for a more extensive discussion of this issue). Below we describe the results of a study that assesses memory impairment in a recall situation.

Zaragoza (1991) reports the results of an experiment designed to investigate the possibility that memory impairment in preschoolers would be more readily observed when children are tested with a recall rather than a recognition test procedure. A recall procedure has the advantage of providing fewer retrieval cues and therefore being a more sensitive measure of possible memory impairment. In addition, a recall procedure is more likely to detect small memory impairment effects than the modified test because the probability of guessing correctly on a recall test is much lower. Because subjects who cannot remember the original information have a 50% probability of responding correctly on the modified test (a two-alternative forced choice), half the subjects whose memories are impaired can be expected to respond correctly by chance (cf., Loftus, Schooler, & Wagenaar, 1985). With a recall procedure the probability of guessing correctly is likely to be much lower, and larger differences between misled and control performance can therefore be expected.

A group of 48 children 4 to 5 years of age was tested with a cued recall procedure analogous to one that has been developed for use in studies with adults (see Zaragoza et al., 1987). Briefly, with this procedure the items employed as original and misleading information were chosen such that the misleading item was an inappropriate response on the recall test. For example, subjects who saw a child holding a stuffed dog in the slides were exposed to misinformation suggesting it was a pillow, and were later asked to recall the stuffed animal they had seen in the slides.

The results of this experiment showed that even with a test procedure that was better able to detect memory impairment, there was no evidence of memory impairment in children 4 to 5 years of age. In fact, misled subjects performed slightly better than control subjects, though not significantly so. Performance in the misled condition was 32% correct, and performance in the control condition was 30% correct ($p > .05$).

In addition to the children tested with the recall test, a second group of 24 subjects was tested with the original recognition test procedure. Once more, the results revealed a significant decrement in misled performance when this test is used. Misled performance was 49% correct and control performance was 78% correct, $p < .05$. Thus, we can be assured that even with this change in the items employed as misinformation, the children were in fact misled.

Current Status of the Memory Impairment Claim

What can be concluded about the memory-impairing effects of misinformation on preschool children's memories? It is always difficult to argue in favor of the null hypothesis—that preschool children are not susceptible to memory impairment—and we do not aim to do so here. However, the research we have reviewed raises questions about the magnitude and reliability of the memory impairment effect Ceci et al. (1987) observed (see also Toglia et al., this volume). Several attempts to replicate the effect have failed, even when studies were conducted under nearly identical conditions. Resistance to memory impairment has been observed for preschool children across a 3-year age range (from 3 to 6 years of age), across various retention intervals, across three sets of stimulus materials, after single and multiple presentations of misinformation, at various levels of memory for the original information, and on tests of both recognition and recall. In short, we have not been able to identify any variables or conditions that are related to memory impairment effects in young children.

In attempting to come to some conclusions about the status of the memory impairment claim, it is prudent to keep in mind some of the limitations of the existing research. The available evidence is still relatively sparse, and the available studies have employed a restricted set of stimulus materials. In addition, it is important to note that the typical misinformation study tests subjects' memory for only two to four items. This imposes two limitations on the results from these studies. First, the conclusions that can be drawn are restricted to a rather small set of items, leaving it unclear whether the results are likely to generalize to other sorts of items. Second, because every subject contributes very few data points, large numbers of subjects are required in order to obtain reliable results. For example, in comparable studies we have conducted with adults, we have typically tested between 60 and 100 subjects per group. In contrast, most of the studies conducted with preschool children have tested between 30 and 40 children per group (although see Experiment 1 of Zaragoza, 1991, for an exception). Hence, one needs to exercise caution in interpreting the results of studies with small numbers of subjects that have not been replicated.

For all of these reasons, we would not be surprised to find that there are some circumstances, that have yet to be identified, under which misinformation does reliably impair children's memory. Nevertheless, the ephemeral character of the memory impairment effect stands in marked contrast to the consistency and reliability of the misinformation effect observed when standard testing procedures are used. This dissociation between memory impairment and misinformation effects would seem to imply that memory impairment does not play a necessary role in misinformation phenomena.

Misinformation Phenomena, Memory Impairment, and the Development of Forgetting

Much of the developmental and adult research on misinformation phenomena has been interpreted as having strong implications for theories of forgetting. However, as McCloskey and Zaragoza's (1985a) analysis suggests, the tendency for misled subjects to report the suggested items on memory tests cannot be taken as a direct index of forgetting caused by misinformation. This is because there are a variety of other factors, such as "gap-filling," demand characteristics, source confusion, and conforming to perceived social pressure that can lead to inaccuracies in misled performance, even in the absence of memory impairment caused by exposure to misinformation.

The program of research we have described was our attempt to isolate memory impairment and assess its contribution to misinformation effects. To do so, we employed special test procedures designed to control for factors unrelated to memory impairment that may contribute to misled/control performance differences. As evident from the studies reviewed here, we have consistently failed to find convincing evidence that misleading information causes forgetting of previously stored original memories. Given that there is at least one study to find evidence to the contrary (Ceci et al., 1987) it would certainly be rash to conclude that misinformation never causes forgetting of original details. Nevertheless, when one compares the very weak and nonexistent evidence for memory impairment (forgetting) with the consistently reliable and robust misinformation effects observed in these very same studies, it becomes clear that defining the misinformation effect as a "forgetting" or "interference" phenomenon is inappropriate.

Research on the memory impairment hypothesis has generated a great deal of controversy and debate, both at the level of theory and at the level of its implications for assessing children's competence as witnesses. It is our impression that much of the controversy surrounding this issue stems from a misinterpretation of the memory impairment claim, its implications, and the implications of the available research on this topic. In an attempt to ameliorate this situation, we delineate, in what follows, the implications of the existing research on memory impairment for broader theoretical and practical issues in memory and memory development. In so doing, we also provide some suggestions for future research.

As evidenced by the title of this book, one of the larger issues driving research on children's susceptibility to memory impairment is a concern with understanding the development of retention and forgetting. Certainly, studying children's susceptibility to memory impairment provides a unique opportunity for studying retention and forgetting in a naturalistic context. However, in attempting to extract the broader implications of the existing research for theories of development, it is important to recognize the limitations of the data base that is currently available. The first point has to do with our inability at the present time to draw firm conclusions about developmental issues. As our review of the available research shows, all of the available memory impairment studies have been conducted with either preschoolers or adults. Hence, no truly developmental studies of memory impairment exist. Although it is true that we have examined memory impairment for children across the preschool years, the age range we examined (3-year-olds vs. 5-year-olds) was severely restricted. At least one study has attempted to include both preschoolers and adults in the same study (Ceci et al., 1987, Exp. 4), and a second study included both preschoolers and 8-year-olds (Toglia et al., this volume). However, because these researchers did not attempt to equate initial levels of learning, performance in the adult and 8-year-old groups was at ceiling. Thus, in order to assess potential age differences in susceptibility to memory impairment studies are needed that both sample from a variety of age groups and control for confounds resulting from age differences in acquisition.

It is worth pointing out that although no developmental studies of memory impairment have been conducted, several studies have shown developmental trends in performance when the original test (or variants of this test) are used. Although it is reasonable to assume that developmental differences in susceptibility to memory impairment will produce corresponding developmental trends on the original test, it is important to keep in mind that one cannot infer developmental differences in memory impairment from developmental trends on the original test. This is because of the many factors other than memory impairment, some of which may be correlated with age, that can influence performance on this test (see also Brainerd & Reyna, 1988). To assess developmental differences in memory impairment it is necessary to test subjects of different age groups with test procedures that can assess memory impairment directly.

A knotty methodological issue with regard to assessing developmental differences in susceptibility to memory impairment has to do with the difficulty of interpreting null effects. The only way to draw confident conclusions about developmental differences in memory impairment would be to demonstrate an effect that varies in size with age. Given that the memory impairment effect has been difficult to obtain, it may be difficult to come to firm conclusions about developmental differences (or lack thereof) in susceptibility to memory impairment.

Another issue that has not received any attention in the literature is the relationship between susceptibility to memory impairment and susceptibility to other forms of forgetting. Hence, caution must be exercised in extrapolating from studies of memory impairment to conclusions about forgetting in general. For example, even if one were to establish with certainty that young children are not more susceptible to memory impairment than older children and adults, this would not rule out the possibility that, in general, young children forget more, or faster, than older children and adults.

In addition to a concern with issues of development, researchers have also turned to studies on misinformation phenomena for insights into classic theoretical issues in the study of forgetting such as whether or not forgetting is due to storage failures (changes or loss in the original memory trace) or retrieval failure (the inability to retrieve an intact trace). The problem here is that in order to ask whether forgetting is due to storage or retrieval failure, it is first necessary to establish that some forgetting caused by misinformation has occurred. As we have seen, the evidence that misinformation causes forgetting of originally encoded details is far from substantial. Furthermore, the extensive literature documenting misinformation effects cannot be brought to bear on issues concerning forgetting for all of the reasons we have discussed before. Given this state of affairs, the existing research on misinformation effects and memory impairment cannot be used to resolve debates about whether or not forgetting is storage or retrieval based.

A third general set of issues for which research on memory impairment has some relevance are questions about the completeness, accuracy, and reliability of young children's memory. If one were to demonstrate that young children's memories are highly susceptible to memory impairment, this would certainly imply that children's memories are highly susceptible to failure (in the sense of being impoverished or incomplete). However, the opposite finding, that young children are not susceptible to memory impairment, cannot be taken as evidence that children have very good memory for the originally seen details. Nevertheless, our conclusion that misinformation does not cause memory impairment in young children has been misinterpreted by some researchers as a claim that an accurate, original memory trace is completely intact (see, for example, Toglia et al., this volume). This interpretation is incorrect for several reasons. First, it is clear (e.g., from examinations of control performance) that a substantial proportion of subjects who participate in these experiments fail to remember the original details even before they are misled, and in fact we have argued that these subjects are the ones who are primarily responsible for the misinformation effects that are observed. Hence, the finding that misinformation does not cause memory impairment in no way implies that subjects remember the original event perfectly. It merely implies that misled subjects remember the original detail as well as they would have had they not been misled. An assessment of the completeness of young children's memory therefore depends on studies that examine this issue directly.

A related point is the relation between the memory impairment hypothesis and the accuracy of children's memory for originally witnessed events. Although it is probably reasonable to assume that heightened susceptibility to memory impairment might leave a child more prone to inaccuracies in memory (e.g., because of a greater tendency to commit reconstructive errors, etc.), the finding that young children are not susceptible to memory impairment does not necessarily imply that their memory will be accurate, not does it imply that what they remember about the event will be uninfluenced by the misinformation. As we have pointed out, subjects who fail to remember the original detail may very well have an inaccurate memory of the original event if they have accepted the misleading suggestion because it fills a gap in their memory (although, as we discuss in the next section, this is still an open question). Such potential inaccuracies in memory, although brought on by the misinformation, are theoretically and conceptually distinct from claims about misinformation causing forgetting of some preexisting item in memory. This failure to distinguish between *inaccurate* recall and *failure* to recall has often led to confusion in theoretical discussions of misinformation phenomena and suggestibility. We explore this issue more fully in the next section.

Memory Impairment and the Suggestibility of Children's Memory

Much of the work on misinformation phenomena, in general, and the memory impairment hypothesis, in particular, has been motivated by a concern with the suggestibility of children's memories. Thus, it is important to consider the implications of memory impairment for the suggestibility of children's memory. For example, if young children are susceptible to memory impairment, as Ceci et al.'s (1987) results suggest, what can be concluded about their suggestibility? Alternatively, if preschool children are not susceptible to memory impairment, as our data suggest, what does this imply about their suggestibility? An answer to these questions requires that we first consider how the "suggestibility of memory" might be defined.

What does it mean to say that a child's memory is suggestible? At a general level, for memory to be suggestible means that children can be led to remember events as being different from those they actually witnessed. In the context of misinformation phenomena, the assumption has been that children's memories are suggestible because they remember the suggested items rather than the events they saw. Consideration of this definition leads quickly to the realization that the relationship between memory impairment and suggestibility is not at all clear. This is because memory impairment (as operationalized by the modified test) focuses exclusively on *failures* to remember originally seen events, whereas suggestibility is concerned with *inaccuracies* in memory for originally seen events. In other words, memory impairment refers to errors of omission and suggestibility refers to errors of commission.

Thus, memory impairment and suggestibility are logically independent of each other. Susceptibility to memory impairment does not imply that memory is inaccurate, nor does resistance to memory impairment imply that memory will be accurate. For example, it is entirely possible that a child whose memory has been impaired by misinformation may nevertheless have an accurate (albeit incomplete) memory for the original event. By the same token, a child whose memory has not been impaired by misinformation may nonetheless remember the event inaccurately as a consequence of exposure to misinformation. For example, inaccurate memory in the absence of memory impairment could come about in those cases where a child fails to remember the original detail even before he or she is misled. In this case, misinformation might fill a gap in the child's memory rather than impairing a child's ability to retrieve an originally stored detail. Alternatively, inaccurate memory in the absence of memory impairment could come about if the child can retrieve both the original and misleading items (i.e., the child's memory for the original item is not impaired), but the child confuses the source of these two items in memory. Thus, the child could misremember seeing the misleading item, while still having access to the original item in memory.

The argument that memory impairment and suggestibility are logically independent does not preclude the possibility that they interact in important ways. For example, it is possible that children's memories are most suggestible when memory for the original details is weak or nonexistent. If this is the case, then susceptibility to memory impairment might be associated with increased suggestibility. Nevertheless, it is important to recognize that whether memory impairment and suggestibility interact is still an open question.

Our evaluation of the role of memory impairment in suggestibility reveals that many of the key questions about children's suggestibility remain unresolved and even unasked. In particular, there is a large gap in our knowledge of children's susceptibility to inaccuracies in remembering as a consequence of exposure to suggestion. Although numerous studies have shown that children will report misleading suggestions when tested on their memory for the original event, it is not known to what extent children experience these as true distortions in remembering. There are a variety of reasons why children may report suggested items even if they do not remember the original event inaccurately. For example, children may report the suggested items because (a) they feel pressure to conform to the suggestion, (b) they want to please an adult authority figure, (c) they trust the information provided by the interviewer more than their own memory, or (d) the information provided by the interviewer seems plausible and they have no memory of their own to contradict it. In summary, it cannot be taken for granted that children who report the suggested items remember the original event inaccurately.

Thus, one important remaining question with regard to children's suggestibility is determining to what extent children confuse misleading suggestions for their "real memories" of a witnessed event (cf. Lindsay & Johnson, 1987). That is, to what extent do children come to believe they actually remember *seeing* details that were merely suggested to them? Although no studies have addressed this question directly, this issue has begun to receive some attention in the adult literature. The evidence suggests that adults do, under some conditions, come to believe they remember seeing the suggested items they report (Lindsay, 1990; Zaragoza & Muench, 1989). Nevertheless, it is also clear that, for adults, source misattribution errors are not an inevitable consequence of exposure to misinformation (Lindsay & Johnson, 1989; Zaragoza & Koshmider, 1989). Hence, a critically important question for future research is evaluating whether children are more susceptible to these sorts of source misattribution errors.

Determining the extent to which children misremember seeing suggested items is in essence a question about children's ability to monitor the *source* of their memories: To what extent are children likely to take memories derived from one source (e.g., leading questions provided by an experimenter) and misattribute them to another source (e.g., the witnessed event)? Although no studies have examined children's tendency to misattribute the source of suggested items, we do know a fair amount about children's ability to make other sorts of source monitoring decisions (Johnson & Foley, 1984). In fact, research has shown that in many instances children are as good as older subjects at discriminating between the sources of their memories (e.g., Foley, Aman, & Gutch, 1987; Foley, Johnson, & Raye, 1983; Foley & Johnson, 1985; Johnson, Raye, Hasher, & Chromiak, 1979). For example, 6- and 7-year-olds are just as good as adults at distinguishing what they said from what they heard someone else say, at remembering which of two people said what, and at distinguishing words they actually heard from those they only imagined hearing. Nevertheless, young children are more likely than adults to confuse what they said and what they imagined others saying (Foley et al., 1983), what they did and what they imagined doing (Foley & Johnson, 1985) and what they watched others do and imagined others doing (Nigro & Dyk, 1989). In summary, the literature suggests that in some, but certainly not all, circumstances children are more likely than adults to confuse the origin of their memories. Thus, it may be the case that young children will be more likely than older children to confuse items that were suggested to them for those they actually saw. We are currently investigating this question.

To date, research on developmental differences in source monitoring has not sampled children of preschool age. However, there is reason to believe that children of preschool age may be especially deficient in their ability to discriminate the origin of their memories. This is because children in the early preschool years may lack the metacognitive skills that source monitoring requires. In particular, there is evidence to suggest that children up to the age of 4 have no idea where their knowledge comes from, and hence do not understand the role that perception, communication, imagination, and thought processes play as sources of knowledge (Wimmer, Hogrefe, & Sodian, 1988). Without an explicit awareness of the origins of their knowledge, children in the early preschool years may be incapable of distinguishing between different sources of information in memory, thus rendering their memories highly suggestible. Hence, extending the study of source monitoring to children in the preschool years would seem to be of vital importance in assessing age-related differences in the suggestibility of memory.

One advantage of studying the suggestibility of children's memory from a source monitoring perspective is that the source monitoring process has been extensively researched and is well understood (e.g., Foley & Johnson, 1985; Foley et al., 1983; Hashtroudi, Johnson, & Chrosniak, 1989; Lindsay & Johnson, 1987). As summarized in the reality monitoring model of Johnson and Raye (1981), source monitoring is a decision process that involves evaluating the characteristics of memories. From this perspective, source misattribution in the misinformation paradigm will be a function of the overlap in the memory characteristics of the originally perceived and suggested details. To the extent that the memory representation of misleading suggestions contain characteristics that are typical of memory for witnessed events (e.g., visual details) source misattributions will be likely. On the other hand, to the extent that the memory representations of the original and suggested items contain characteristics that uniquely specify their origin, source monitoring is likely to be accurate. The reality monitoring model also posits that the decision processes and reasoning processes that subjects engage in at the time of test can also influence the source monitoring judgment. An important aspect of the reality monitoring framework is that it shows how one might confuse the origin of some item in memory even if memory for the item itself is very good (i.e., it has high strength).

The reality monitoring model underscores the important role that the *qualitative* characteristics of memories play in determining whether or not events will be remembered accurately. In particular, the evidence suggests that it is the qualitative characteristics of memories, rather than their strength, that form the basis for attributions witnesses make about the origins of memories. Hence, a complete understanding of inaccuracies in children's memories will likely require an assessment of the nature of children's recollections of witnessed events. Because children's reports of witnessed events may include information they know they have learned from other sources, assessing what children remember about a witnessed event requires asking them specific questions about the origin of the information they report. The research on source monitoring conducted to date shows that it is possible to ask children questions about the sources of their memories and obtain meaningful results.

Summary and Conclusions

One potentially important consequence of exposure to misinformation is an impaired ability to remember originally witnessed events. At this time, however, questions about preschool children's susceptibility to memory impairment are far from resolved. More research is clearly needed to determine the extent to which preschool children's memories are susceptible to memory impairment, and to determine if resistance to memory impairment develops with age.

As evidenced by the studies reviewed here, much of the research conducted to date has been concerned with losses in the original memory representation (or its accessibility) that result from exposure to misleading suggestions. Consequently, relatively little attention has been paid to investigating the nature of children's memories for the suggested items they report. Although many studies have shown that children incorporate misleading suggestions in their reports, no studies have attempted to determine whether these inaccurate accounts reflect children's true memory for what they saw or children's tendency to conform to misleading suggestion. Nevertheless, investigating possible inaccuracies in children's memories is essential to understanding the suggestibility of their memories. In the long run, it is not what children fail to remember, but what they remember inaccurately, that poses the greater threat to justice.

Acknowledgments. We would like to thank Diana Wilson, Renee Bruckner, Ann Louis, and the director and staff of Laurel School for their generous assistance and support. This work was supported in part by NIMH grant MH43581.

References

Bekerian, D.A., & Bowers, J.M. (1983). Eyewitness testimony: Were we misled? *Journal of Experimental Psychology: Learning, Memory, and Cognition*, *9*, 139–145.

Bowman, L.L., & Zaragoza, M.S. (1989). Similarity of encoding context does not influence resistance to memory impairment following misinformation. *American Journal of Psychology*, *102*, 249–264.

Brainerd, C.J., & Reyna, V.F. (1988). Memory loci of suggestibility development: Comment on Ceci, Ross, and Toglia. *Journal of Experimental Psychology: General*, *117*, 197–200.

Brainerd, C.J., Reyna, V.F., Howe, M.L., & Kingma, J. (1990). The development of forgetting and reminiscence. *Monographs of the Society for Research in Child Development*, *55*(3–4, Serial No. 222).

Ceci, S.J., Ross, D.F., & Toglia, M.P. (1987). Suggestibility of children's memory: Psycholegal implications. *Journal of Experimental Psychology: General*, *116*, 38–49.

Chandler, C.C. (1989). Specific retroactive interference in Modified Recognition Tests: Evidence for an unknown cause of interference. *Journal of Experimental Psychology: Learning, Memory, and Cognition*, *15*, 256–265.

Christiaansen, R.E., & Ochalek, K. (1983). Editing misleading information from memory: Evidence for the coexistence of original and postevent information. *Memory & Cognition*, *11*, 467–475.

Cohen, R.L., & Harnick, M.A. (1980). The susceptibility of child witnesses to suggestion. *Law and Human Behavior*, *4*, 201–210.

Crowder, R.G. (1976). *Principles of learning and memory*. Hillsdale, NJ: Erlbaum.

Dodd, D.H., & Bradshaw, J.M. (1980). Leading questions and memory: Pragmatic constraints. *Journal of Verbal Learning and Verbal Behavior*, *21*, 207–219.

Duncan, E.M., Whitney, P., & Kunen, S. (1982). Integration of visual and verbal information in children's memory. *Child Development*, *83*, 1215–1223.

Foley, M.A., Aman, C., & Gutch, D. (1987). Discriminating between action memories: Children's use of kinesthetic cues and visible consequences. *Journal of Experimental Child Psychology*, *44*, 335–347.

Foley, M.A., & Johnson, M.K. (1985). Confusions between memories for performed and imagined actions: A developmental comparison. *Child Development*, *56*, 1145–1155.

Foley, M.A., Johnson, M.K., & Raye, C.L. (1983). Age-related changes in confusion between memories for thoughts and memories for speech. *Child Development*, *54*, 51–60.

Goodman, G.S., & Reed, R.S. (1986). Age differences in eyewitness testimony. *Law and Human Behavior*, *10*, 317–332.

Hasher, L., & Thomas, H. (1973). A developmental study of retention. *Developmental Psychology*, *9*, 281.

Hashtroudi, S., Johnson, M., & Chrosniak, L. (1989). Aging and source monitoring. *Psychology and Aging*, *4*, 106–112.

Johnson, M.K., & Foley, M.A. (1984). Differentiating fact from fantasy: The reliability of children's memory. *Journal of Social Issues*, *40*, 33–50.

Johnson, M.K., & Raye, C.L. (1981). Reality monitoring. *Psychological Review*, *88*, 67–85.

Johnson, M.K., Raye, C.L., Hasher, L., & Chromiak, W. (1979). Are there developmental differences in reality-monitoring? *Journal of Experimental Child Psychology*, *27*, 120–128.

Koppenaal, R.J., Krull, A., & Katz, H. (1964). Age, interference, and forgetting. *Journal of Experimental Child Psychology*, *1*, 360–375.

Liben, L.S., & Posnansky, C.J. (1977). Inferences on inferences: The effects of age, transitive ability, memory load, and lexical factors. *Child Development, 48*, 1490–1497.
Lindsay, D.S. (1990). Misleading suggestions can impair eyewitness's ability to remember event details. *Journal of Experimental Psychology: Learning, Memory, and Cognition, 16*, 1077–1083.
Lindsay, D.S., & Johnson, M.K. (1987). Reality monitoring and suggestibility: Children's ability to discriminate among memories from different sources. In S.J. Ceci, M.P. Toglia, & D.F, Ross (Eds.) *Children's eyewitness memory* (pp. 92–121). New York: Springer-Verlag.
Lindsay, D.S., & Johnson, M.K. (1989). The eyewitness suggestibility effect and memory for source. *Memory & Cognition, 17*, 349–358.
Loomis, D., & Hall, V. (1968). The effects of age and overlearning in an A-B, A-C design using high and low H value. *Journal of Verbal Learning and Verbal Behavior, 7*, 182–188.
Loftus, E.F. (1975). Leading questions and the eyewitness report. *Cognitive Psychology, 7*, 560–572.
Loftus, E.F. (1977). Shifting human color memory. *Memory and Cognition, 5*, 696–699.
Loftus, E.F. (1979a). *Eyewitness testimony*. Cambridge, MA: Harvard University Press.
Loftus, E.F. (1979b). The malleability of human memory. *American Scientist, 67*, 312–320.
Loftus, E.F., & Davies, G.M. (1984). Distortions in the memory of children. *Journal of Social Issues, 40*, 51–67.
Loftus, E.F., & Loftus, G.R. (1980). On the permanence of stored information in the human brain. *American Psychologist, 35*, 409–420.
Loftus, E.F., Miller, D.G., & Burns, H.J. (1978). Semantic integration of verbal information into a visual memory. *Journal of Experimental Psychology: Human Learning and Memory, 4*, 19–31.
Loftus, E.F., & Palmer, J.E. (1974). Reconstruction of automobile destruction: An example of the interaction between language and memory. *Journal of Verbal Learning and Verbal Behavior, 13*, 585–589.
Loftus, E.F., Schooler, J.W., & Wagenaar, W. (1985). The fate of memory: Comment on McCloskey and Zaragoza. *Journal of Experimental Psychology: General, 114*, 375–380.
Madigan, S.A. (1969). Intraserial repetition and coding processes in free recall. *Journal of Verbal Learning and Verbal Behavior, 8*, 828–835.
Marin, B.V., Holmes, D.L., Guth, M., & Kovak, P. (1979). The potential of children as eyewitnesses. *Law and Human Behavior, 3*, 295–305.
McCloskey, M., & Zaragoza, M. (1985a). Misleading postevent information and memory for events: Arguments and evidence against memory impairment hypotheses. *Journal of Experimental Psychology: General, 114*, 3–18.
McCloskey, M., & Zaragoza, M. (1985b). Postevent information and memory: Reply to Loftus, Schooler, and Wagenaar. *Journal of Experimental Psychology: General, 114*, 381–387.
Merriman, W.E., Azmita, M., & Perlmutter, M. (1988). Rate of forgetting in early childhood. *International Journal of Behavioral Development, 11*, 467–474.

Metcalfe, J. (1990). Composite holographic associative recall model (CHARM) and blended memories in eyewitness testimony. *Journal of Experimental Psychology: General, 119*, 145–160.
Nigro, G., & Dyk, C. (1989). *Who done it? A developmental study of confusions between memories for performed and imagined actions*. Poster presented at the biennial meetings of the Society for Research in Child Developmental, Kansas City, MO.
Paris, S.G., & Lindauer, B.K. (1976). The role of inference in children's comprehension and memory for sentences. *Cognitive Psychology, 8*, 217–227.
Paris, S.G., Lindauer, B.K., & Cox, G.L. (1977). The development of inferential comprehension. *Child Development, 48*, 1728–1733.
Postman, L., & Underwood, B.J. (1973). Critical issues in interference theory. *Memory & Cognition, 11*, 101–104.
Rogoff, B., Newcombe, N., & Kagan, J. (1974). Planfulness and recognition memory. *Child Development, 45*, 972–977.
Weinberg, H.I., Wadsworth, J., & Baron, R.S. (1983). Demand and the impact of leading questions on eyewitness testimony. *Memory & Cognition, 11*, 101–104.
Wimmer, H., Hogrefe, J., & Sodian, B. (1988). A second stage in children's conception of mental life: Understanding informational access as origins of knowledge and belief. In J.W. Astington, P.L. Harris, & D.R. Olson (Eds.), *Developing theories of mind* (pp. 173–192). Cambridge: Cambridge University Press.
Zaragoza, M.S. (1987). Memory, suggestibility, and eyewitness testimony in children and adults. In S.J. Ceci, M.P. Toglia, & D.F. Ross (Eds.), *Children's eyewitness memory* (pp. 53–78). New York: Springer-Verlag.
Zaragoza, M.S. (1991). Preschool children's susceptibility to memory impairment. In J. Doris (Ed.), *The suggestibility of children's memory (with special reference to the child witness)* (pp. 27–39). Washington, DC: American Psychological Association.
Zaragoza, M.S., & Koshmider, J.W. (1989). Misled subjects may know more than their performance implies. *Journal of Experimental Psychology: Learning, Memory, and Cognition, 15*, 246–255.
Zaragoza, M.S., McCloskey, M., & Jamis, M. (1987). Misleading postevent information and recall of the original event: Further evidence against the memory impairment hypothesis. *Journal of Experimental Psychology: Learning, Memory, and Cognition, 13*, 36–44.
Zaragoza, M.S., & Muench, J. (1989, November). *Source confusion following exposure to misleading postevent information*. Paper presented at the annual meeting of the Psychonomic Society, Atlanta, GA.

7
The Suggestibility of Children's Memory: A Social-Psychological and Cognitive Interpretation

MICHAEL P. TOGLIA, DAVID F. ROSS, STEPHEN J. CECI, and HELENE HEMBROOKE

The suggestibility of the child witness has been a concern of the American judicial system since the turn of the century. At that time, a number of studies (e.g., Binet, 1900; Marple, 1933; Pear & Wyatt, 1914; Stern, 1910; Varendonck, 1911; Whipple, 1909, 1911, 1912) were reported indicating that young children were quite susceptible to suggestive or leading questions. For example, Whipple (1909) wrote that "the one factor that more than any other is responsible for the poor reports of children is their suggestibility, especially in the years before puberty" (p. 162). Much of this early research, however, was methodologically flawed (Goodman, 1984a). Only recently has there been a resurgence of research on this topic. These newer studies have produced conflicting results as young children are not always more likely to succumb to suggestion than are older children or adults. Such complexities have raised questions about the nature and bases of the suggestibility of children's memory (as well as adults' suggestibility). Therefore, the major goals of this chapter are (a) to briefly review research on children's suggestibility, (b) to describe social and cognitive factors that influence children's susceptibility to suggestion, and (c) to address the theoretical significance of these factors.

Setting the Stage: A Brief Note on Adult Suggestibility

To place the current research on the child witness in perspective, it is important to note that studying the effects of misleading postevent information on the eyewitness accounts of adults has been a primary issue in psycholegal research over the last 15 years and a source of considerable debate (Belli, 1989; Bowers & Bekerian, 1984; Lindsay & Johnson, 1989; Loftus, 1975, 1979; Loftus, Miller & Burns, 1978; Loftus, Schooler & Wagenaar, 1985; McCloskey & Zaragoza, 1985a, 1985b; Tversky & Tuchin, 1989; Weinberg, Wadsworth, & Baron, 1983; Zaragoza &

McCloskey, 1989; Zaragoza, McCloskey, & Jamis, 1987). The typical paradigm employed in this research involves three stages. First, there is an acquisition phase in which witnesses/subjects view and/or hear an event. Second, the subjects are exposed to new information at some point after the original event. For some subjects this postevent information contains erroneous or misleading suggestions about a few details of the witnessed episode. Finally, there is a retrieval/testing phase in which memory is assessed for the original event.

The results of a variety of studies have generally revealed that adult subjects who have received misleading postevent information do not perform as well on a subsequent memory test as control subjects who were not misled. Consider, for example, a study by Loftus et al. (1978). Their subjects viewed a slide series depicting an automobile-pedestrian accident. In one condition, a car was shown stopped at a stop sign. During postevent questioning, it was suggested to some observers that the car had been stopped at a yield sign. In a recognition test that followed, these subjects were more likely to erroneously identify the yield sign as having been in the slide series than were control subjects who had not been misled in this fashion.

Based on a variety of studies with similar findings, Loftus and her colleagues have argued that postevent information competes with the original information in such a manner that it alters or transforms underlying memory traces producing changes in recollection of the event (also see Loftus, Hoffman, & Wagenaar, this volume). Thus, the original memory is said to be "erased," at least partially so, through a destructive updating process. This position implies true forgetting and has been referred to as "storage-based forgetting" (Howe & Brainerd, 1989). Another interpretation of the influence of misleading postevent information has been termed the "coexistence hypothesis." According to a weak version of this hypothesis, several investigators have contended that memory traces for the original information and the biased information coexist in memory and the existence of the biased information simply makes the process of retrieving the original information more difficult (e.g., Bowers & Bekerian, 1983; Christiaansen & Ochalek, 1983; Tversky & Tuchin, 1989). In the terminology of Howe and Brainerd (1989), memory accessibility problems reflect "retrieval-based forgetting." However, McCloskey and Zaragoza (1985a, 1985b) in arguing for a strong version of coexistence have claimed that misleading postevent information has no effect at all on memory for the original episode, neither erasing it nor competing with it during retrieval. Thus, memory traces remain intact and accessible, but other factors such as demand characteristics and source misattribution errors produce performance deficits (Zaragoza & McCloskey, 1989).

If one assumes that adult memories are truly impaired by suggestive questions, then it is relevant to ask if children are as susceptible as adults.

But even if distortions are not characteristic of adults' memories, it may be that children are vulnerable to suggestions.

Current Trends in Children's Suggestibility Research

As noted above, recent research regarding children's memory in forensically relevant settings has produced conflicting findings. Some investigators have found that, compared to adults, children under the age of 10 possess poorer eyewitness memory abilities (e.g., Brigham, VanVerst, & Bothwell, 1986; Saywitz, 1987; Yarmey, 1984). In a similar vein, developmental differences in susceptibility to suggestion have been reported in a variety of studies (Ceci, Ross & Toglia, 1987a; Cohen & Harnick, 1980; Dale, Loftus & Rathbun, 1978; Goodman & Reed, 1986; King & Yuille, 1987). For instance, Cohen and Harnick showed a film of a purse snatching incident to 9-year-olds, 12-year-olds, and adults followed immediately by a questionnaire containing both leading and nonleading questions. Developmental differences in suggestibility were observed as the older groups were influenced less by the leading questions than were the 9-year-olds. A follow-up test given a week later revealed that to some degree all subjects incorporated erroneous information from the questionnaire, but this tendency was more marked among the 9-year-olds. Similar findings were reported in a related study by Goodman and Reed (1986) in which 3-year-olds, 6-year-olds, and adults met with an unfamiliar adult for 5 min to engage in a brief conversation and play a game. Four or five days later subjects were asked both objective and subjective questions, were required to free-recall the interaction, and were administered a photo identification task. The 3-year-olds recalled fewer details, performed more poorly in identifying the adult, and were found to be more suggestible than the other two groups. Six-year-olds were also more suggestible than the adults, but the effect was small.

Importantly, Goodman and Reed (1986) noted that although the 3-year-olds found it difficult to resist false information present in the suggestive questions, the suggested information rarely appeared in their free-recall protocols. That is, young children did not necessarily accept misleading ideas and later report them as true. They did, in fact, remember some information that would have been useful if real consequences had been involved, and they actually produced fewer errors in recall than adults, though this may have been due in part to floor effects in total recall.

Therefore, children may not always be more suggestible than adults. Consistent with this notion are several studies that have failed to demonstrate any developmental differences in suggestibility or have even found younger children to be less suggestible than older persons. For example, under realistic conditions Marin, Holmes, Guth, and Kovac (1979) had subjects from 5 to 25 years of age witness a live incident involving an angry confrontation between two experimenters and a confederate. Shortly after this altercation, subjects were asked to provide a narrative account of the event, answer both leading and nonleading questions, and identify the confederate (assailant) from a photo lineup. Although recall improved with age, there were no age differences in performance on the leading questions (even though they did produce sizable suggestibility effects) and the identification task. Some caution, however, is advised in interpreting the lack of developmental trends in suggestibility due to the use of a single within-subject misleading question.

Duncan, Whitney, and Kunen (1982) had 6-, 8-, and 10-year olds, as well as college students, view a slide presentation of cartoons. Subjects were then asked informational, factual, and suggestive questions about the slides. After controlling for level of information remembered, Duncan et al. reported that younger children's visual memories were *less* vulnerable to distortion by misleading verbal cues.

Clearly, the results of studies examining the influence of age on suggestibility are mixed. Loftus and Davies (1984) concluded that the recent literature on this topic does not warrant, "... the simple notion that children are always more suggestible than adults" (p. 62). This belief has been echoed by other researchers as well (e.g., Goodman, Aman & Hirschman, 1987). A variety of factors have been offered to account for the discrepant results. These include differences in the type of witnessed episode, the exposure duration of the event, and the length of the retention interval (Loftus & Davies, 1984). Nevertheless, perhaps the most compelling and fundamental difference between the various studies on susceptibility to suggestion is the age of the participants (Hall, Loftus, & Tousignant, 1984). This presents problems in making comparisons among experiments that have tested different age groups because the groups are known to differ in memory abilities (e.g., Chi & Ceci, 1987), and/or learning abilities (e.g., Brainerd & Howe, 1982; Howe & Brainerd, 1989). Furthermore, in the research where developmental differences in suggestibility were not found many of the studies did not test *very* young children (i.e., 3- and 4-year olds). This was a major impetus for the program of research we embarked on several years ago. As will be seen, apparently children in this age range are among the most likely to succumb to the influence of misleading information with both social and cognitive factors responsible.[1]

---

[1] In recent years Carolyn Rovee-Collier and her colleagues (see Rovee-Collier & Shyi, this volume) have used the mobile conjugate reinforcement procedure and demonstrated with infants as young as 3 to 6 months of age that new (postevent) information can modify or become integrated with old memories. On the basis of a series of such studies, Rovee-Collier and Shyi concluded that results on infant memory modification are (a) consistent with the position that memory traces can be impaired and (b) indicate that storage and retrieval factors must be part of the equation in understanding infant long-term retention.

To examine the conditions under which children succumb to the influence of misleading postevent information, Ceci et al. (1987a) conducted a series of four experiments in which the events were short picture stories. That is, the events consisted of a narrative accompanied by pictures such that they were not unlike slide, film, or videotape presentations frequently employed in eyewitness studies. To test the notion that preschoolers might be influenced to a greater extent than older children, age trends in suggestibility were addressed in the first experiment. There were four age groups: 3 to 4, 5 to 6, 7 to 9, and 10 to 12. Each child was tested with a three-session, 4-day, procedure that was also employed in subsequent experiments. On Day 1 a story, accompanied by pictures, was read to each child by an adult. Briefly, this story involved a little girl named Loren getting ready for her first day at school. It describes and shows her waking up and taking a bath before getting dressed for school. She spends too much time in the tub daydreaming and her mother tells her to hurry or she'll miss the bus. She quickly finishes, dresses herself, runs downstairs, and eats her breakfast (*eggs*) too fast and gets a *stomachache*. The event continues with her catching the bus, seeing a friend, and then forgetting about feeling sick.

The next day the children were briefly interviewed by another adult experimenter and received either biased or unbiased information about the story. Subjects in the biased conditions were asked, "Do you remember the story about Loren who had a *headache* because she ate her *cereal* too fast?" The control (unbiased) groups heard, "Do you remember the story about Loren, who was sick?"

Then two days following the biasing manipulation the children were given a two-alternative, forced-choice recognition test concerning critical items. The test involved choices between original pictures paired with pictures depicting information that had been suggested to those children in the biased conditions. For example, the children were shown a picture of Loren eating eggs and one of Loren eating cereal and asked to identify which was in the story. Because this testing procedure is the one that has traditionally been employed in suggestibility studies, those receiving biased information are said to be participating in the so-called standard condition (also known as the original-test condition).

Mean proportion correct recognition two days later in the control conditions was .84, .87, .95, and .95 for the four age groups in ascending order. The corresponding percentages in the biased (standard) conditions were .37, .58, .67, and .84. Although the effects for age and condition (biased/unbiased) were both reliable, there was also a significant Age × Condition interaction. Post-hoc tests indicated that the 3 to 4-year-old children's memories were disproportionately distorted by the misleading information (i.e., control: .84 vs. biased: .37 correct).

Social Influences on Children's Suggestibility

Although we were intrigued by the demonstration of developmental differences in suggestibility, the question of why preschoolers were more suggestible than older children remained to be answered. That is, although there are a number of cognitive reasons why young children should be more suggestible, the results of Experiment 1 did not allow us to determine whether or not the effects could be attributed to memorial phenomena such as alterations in memory as described by Loftus and her colleagues. This concern was specifically addressed in Experiments 3 and 4 which will be described later in this chapter. Another issue, namely source credibility, was examined in Experiment 2. In addition to memorial factors, the notion that *social factors* (e.g., Dodd & Bradshaw, 1980; Toglia, Ceci, & Ross, 1988) and *demand characteristics* (e.g., Weinberg et al., 1983) may be important contributors to suggestibility led us to wonder if young children might be responding to please an adult authority figure. If such a prestige effect was operating, then one would expect suggestibility to be reduced if the interviewer was of a similar social status to the subjects. Accordingly, a child biaser was employed in the second study (and subsequent experiments as well). Because the youngest children were most vulnerable to the effects of misinformation, each of the remaining experiments was designed to explore the basis of young (3 to 5 years old) children's susceptibility to postevent suggestions.

In Experiment 2 the same story and general procedure from the first study was employed with the following exceptions: (a) only young children were included, (b) stimulus counterbalancing was used (combinations of *eggs/cereal*, *headache/stomachache*), and (c) another child (age 7) provided the biased/unbiased information on Day 2. This last modification was motivated by the belief that some of the "distortions" in the first study may have reflected a prestige effect wherein children relinquished accurate memories about the story. That is, the preschoolers may have remembered the original fact that Loren ate eggs, but did not have confidence it was correct given they also recalled the adult interviewer suggesting something different. Or the children were simply trying to please the tester by reporting the adult's version of the story.

The results showed, as suspected, that when the interviewer is also a child, the misinformation effect, though still reliable, was substantially reduced (control: .72 correct; biased: .53 correct). Stimulus counterbalancing was not significant as either a main effect or in the interaction with the other conditions.

The data from Experiments 1 and 2 for children of the same age range were compared in an analysis of Condition × Age of Interviewer (7-year-old vs. adult). Although both main effects were present, the important finding was the interaction. The difference in recognition performance between the biased and unbiased conditions for the 7-year-old interviewer was only .19, whereas a substantially greater difference (.40) was observed in the corresponding adult conditions. Thus, when we compared these findings with the results of Experiment 1, we found that preschoolers were far more susceptible to misleading questions when an adult, as opposed to a young child, asked the misleading questions. Thus some portion of children's suggestibility is due to social-psychological factors.

Our most recent work has focused on social factors and can be viewed as extensions of the just-described second study of Ceci et al. (1987a). Because the biasing manipulation was less powerful with a child compared to an adult questioner, Ceci et al. interpreted this result in terms of a "prestige effect" wherein children may have felt pressured to conform to the demands of an adult authority figure whom they may have perceived as highly credible.

An alternative explanation, however, has been raised by the work of Lindsay and Johnson (1987, 1989). They discussed an external-source monitoring interpretation of suggestibility effects, arguing that misleading information may lead some subjects to mistakenly believe that the source of the misinformation was the original event. As applied to the findings of Ceci et al. (1987a) it could be argued that test discriminations are more difficult when both the presenter and interviewer are adults (Experiment 1) than when widely different sources, an adult and a child, serve as presenter and interviewer, respectively (Experiment 2).

Study 1

Accordingly, we empirically compared the source monitoring and prestige explanations in a study with preschoolers that conformed to a 2 × 2 × 3 between-subjects factorial. The Presenter (adult, child) of the original event (the Loren story) was varied and so was the Interviewer (adult, child) on Day 2. The third factor was Condition for which there were three levels (control, standard, and modified[2]). As in our previous research, recognition testing occurred two days after the second session, three days after the initial story was presented.

---

[2]The modified condition was developed by McCloskey and Zaragoza (1985a). Subjects assigned to this condition, like the standard group, are biased with misleading postevent information. However, unlike standard subjects, they receive a recognition memory test that excludes the biased items as testing choices. That is, they are administered a "modified" recognition test in which each forced choice contains the original information (e.g., Loren eating *eggs*) and a new item (e.g., Loren eating *pancakes*) introduced for the first time at the retrieval stage. If control performance reliably exceeds performance by the modified group, then memory impairment is said to be operative. The logic of the modified test procedure will be more fully described in the section on cognitive factors and suggestibility.

The data analysis indicated a significant main effect of condition as control performance (.78) was the best, followed by the modified (.64), and then standard (.52) groups. Post-hoc tests confirmed that the control group performed better than both the modified and standard groups, and the modified condition was superior to the standard condition. Thus suggestibility was reduced, but not eliminated, in the modified condition. This replicated, as will be seen later, the findings of Experiments 3 and 4 of Ceci et al. (1987a).

Turning to the focus of this study, although there was no effect of Presenter, there was a main effect of Interviewer showing better performance with a child interviewer (.70) than an adult interviewer (.60). None of the interactions were reliable, a curious outcome given that based on our earlier work one might have expected an Interviewer × Condition interaction. Though not reliable, the pattern of means for this interaction was entirely consistent with our previous research. That is, the levels of performance were greater when the interviewer was a 7-year-old child as opposed to an adult in both the modified (.68 vs. .60) and standard (.64 vs. .39) conditions. As anticipated, performance was essentially identical for control subjects who were interviewed by a child (.80) or by an adult (.77).

If external source confusions were causing subjects to misattribute biased information to the original event, then one would have expected recognition to suffer when the presenter and interviewer were congruent, compared to when they were incongruent. This did not happen. Instead, suggestibility was reduced when a child presented the misinformation. This is consistent with the notion that another child would not be viewed as an authority figure—i.e., a prestige effect. Several other investigators have reached similar conclusions. For example, Smith and Ellsworth (1987) demonstrated, with adult subjects, that misleading questions reduced witness accuracy on a questionnaire only when the interrogator was assumed to be knowledgeable about the crime.

Study 2

The results of Smith and Ellsworth's study with adults in part prompted us to conduct the second recent study to be reported in this chapter. Specifically, an experiment was designed that investigated the impact of interrogator knowledge on children's suggestibility. Having found that children viewed adults as authority figures, although not startling, raised the question of whether it was simply the older the biaser, the greater the likelihood of suggestibility. Perhaps some adults are perceived as more "authoritative" or "credible" than others. To examine this possibility in this experiment we varied the prestige of adult biasers. This was accomplished by having children greeted on Day 2 by *both* a credible and noncredible interviewer. The manipulation of interviewer credibility was achieved by what each interviewer said regarding his familiarity with the Loren story presented the day before. For example, after saying hello and introducing himself, in control conditions the credible interviewer said,

> Do you remember the story you heard yesterday? The one about Loren who was sick on the first day of school. I really like this story, I know it *real well* and it is one of my *favorite* stories. I read it to children *all* the time. (Child's name), did you like the story?

For the biased conditions he said,

> Do you remember the story you heard yesterday? The one about Loren who got a headache after eating her cereal on the first day at school. I really like this story, I know it *real well* and it is one of my *favorite* stories. I read it to children *all* the time. (Child's name), did you like the story?

Similarly, the noncredible interviewer told control subjects,

> Do you remember the story you heard yesterday? The one about . . . about Loren wasn't it? Who was sick on her first day at school. I do not *remember very much* about the story because I have not read it in a *long* time. (Child's name), do you think other children will like the story?

In the biased groups subjects were asked,

> Do you remember the story you heard yesterday? The one about . . . about Loren wasn't it? Who got a headache after eating her cereal on the first day at school. I do not *remember very much* about the story because I have not read it in a *long* time. (Child's name), do you think other children will like the story?

Condition (control, modified, standard) was also a factor, as control groups were not misled by either interviewer, whereas the other groups received misleading postevent information about certain details from both interviewers who each biased two critical items. The order of appearance of the interviewers was counterbalanced and the four critical items were biased equally often by each interviewer. A third variable was age (4-year-olds vs. 8-year-olds/second graders). If prestige is assumed to be a critical factor, then less suggestibility could be expected in the noncredible interviewer conditions because this person should be accorded less prestige. However, we reasoned such an effect may very well be qualified by age because making credibility distinctions might be more difficult for 4-year-olds than second graders who are more cognitively sophisticated.

An initial 2 × 3 analysis of variance (ANOVA) was computed to examine just the age and condition variables on proportion correct recognition for the critical items. This analysis revealed no effect of condition primarily because performance was nearly at ceiling for the older subjects. There was, however, a main effect of age as 8-year-olds (.89) outperformed the 4-year-olds (.67), and a reliable interaction. Accordingly, we examined just the data for the 4-year-olds. A one-way ANOVA indicated a significant difference among conditions. Follow-up tests demonstrated that recognition performance in the control group (.80) was more accurate than both the modified (.62) and standard (.60) conditions, and that the latter groups did not differ.

Because Credibility (credible vs. noncredible) was a pseudo manipulation for control subjects, this factor was included in an analysis (2 × 2 × 2 ANOVA) with age (still referring to 4- vs. 8-year-olds) and condition (involving only two levels, modified vs. standard). The results indicated, as before, a main effect of age with recognition accuracy for the older children (.90) exceeding that for the preschoolers (.61). There was also an effect of credibility as overall subjects were much more likely to be correct when biased by the noncredible interviewer (.82) than by the credible interviewer (.67). Only one interaction, Age by Credibility, approached significance, as there was a tendency for the credibility effect to be larger for the 4-year-olds as compared with the 8-year-olds.

Discussion of Studies 1 and 2

The results of the first study, pitting source monitoring against prestige, indicated that the age of the biaser/interviewer was a key factor in determining young children's suggestibility. Our subjects were more susceptible to misinformation when they were confronted on Day 2 by an adult interviewer, rather than another child interviewer, regardless of the age of the story presenter. The pattern of findings is consistent with the notion that adults apparently are inherently perceived as authority figures by children. However, Study 2 revealed that this notion is too simplistic and requires qualification. In particular, 4-year-olds and 8-year-olds discriminated between the credible and noncredible providers of information they met on Day 2. Their ability to make such distinctions is impressive; when given the opportunity to make direct comparisons (as credibility was manipulated within-subjects) between interviewers the children were able to do so. Thus, preschoolers and second graders were less likely under the conditions of our experiment to succumb to misleading suggestions when someone's knowledge of an event was in question. The conclusion that a noncredible interviewer is accorded less prestige than a credible source seems inescapable. Therefore, adults are not inevitably viewed as authority figures.

Although we believe that our research is the first to directly show the importance of an interviewer's credibility on children's reports, it has long been assumed that children typically perceive parents, police, social workers, and the like as authority figures who are credible. Research (e.g., Ceci et al., 1987a; Raskin & Yuille, 1989) has generally supported this view, although children, particularly preschoolers, may not be able to articulate why someone is or is not credible (cf. Saywitz, 1989).

Certainly credibility is in part determined by the perceived knowledge of an interviewer. At a general level children realize that adults are more knowledgeable than themselves. This becomes problematic if a child believes, compared to himself, that the adult interviewer has as much or more knowledge about the specific event in question (i.e., the one witnessed by the child). For this reason, and others, the interview process itself may be suggestive for children. That is, the wording of questions and a child's assumptions about the purpose of the interview are among the factors that can influence how a child performs (King & Yuille, 1987). Children may think that the interviewer knows the correct answer or expects them to have an answer. A dramatic demonstration of the latter notion was reported by Hughes and Grieve (1980). They posed nonsensical questions to 5- and 7-year-old children apparently in a manner that would not challenge their credibility and found that their subjects attempted to make sense of the queries in order to provide an answer. For example, when asked "Is milk bigger than water" most of the children gave answers like "Milk is bigger because it has more color." It would seem then, especially in an interview context, that what a credible adult says and asks is taken seriously by young children. Based on our results with a 7-year-old questioner one would predict that another child would be less successful in eliciting responses to questions of the type employed by Hughes and Grieve.

Not surprisingly, interviewer knowledge is a factor to which adults are sensitive. As alluded to earlier, in research similar to ours, Smith and Ellsworth (1987) had college students watch a videotape of a bank robbery followed by a series of questions about the crime. The questioner was introduced to subjects as either highly knowledgeable or totally naive about the crime the subjects had witnessed. In addition, in half of the conditions the series contained several misleading questions. Smith and Ellsworth found that misinformation reduced witness accuracy on questionnaires only when the interrogator was assumed to be knowledgeable about the events in the videotape.

A related literature has examined the influence that a communicator has on individuals or an audience as a function of perceived prestige. If a message is attributed to a credible source, subjects are more likely to agree to it than if the communicator is viewed as not credible (Hovland, Janis, & Kelley, 1953; Hovland & Weiss, 1951; Ward & McGuinnes, 1974). From the perspective of memory, there have been several studies that indicate that subjects can resist reporting misinformation at the time of testing, if there are reasons to suspect the intentions and/or credibility of the person asking the leading questions. Perhaps the best example of this was reported in an investigation by Dodd and Bradshaw (1980). They showed subjects slides depicting an automobile accident followed by a series of initial questions. In two conditions the questions, including some that were misleading, were attributed to either an unspecified source or a source identified as a lawyer for one of the drivers. Compared to a control group, a misinformation effect was observed in the no-source condition but not the lawyer condition. Similar results were found in a second study. After seeing the event, subjects read an eyewitness account of the car accident that contained some misleading information. The accounts were attributed to either a neutral bystander or the driver who caused the mishap. Misleading information influenced memory performance only in the bystander condition. In general, then, subjects did not claim to remember presuppositions attributed to a source who could be assumed to be biased. Such sources may serve as a "warning," alerting subjects to the possibility of being misled (Greene, Flynn, & Loftus, 1982).

Although the role of memorial factors in susceptibility to postevent misleading information continues to be an area of dispute since it was raised by McCloskey and Zaragoza (1985a, 1985b), there seems to be substantial agreement that social factors such as demand characteristics are, or can be, responsible for suggestibility. In recent writings Zaragoza and her colleagues (e.g., Zaragoza, 1991; Zaragoza & McCloskey, 1989; see also Zaragoza, Dahlgren, & Muench, this volume) have noted that the effects of misleading questions need not reflect memory impairment, but rather may indicate the operation of source misattribution, misinformation acceptance, and whether or not the person providing suggestive information is perceived as an authority. Regarding the latter factor, we have shown that the gate swings both ways. Credible sources can increase suggestibility, but sources that are suspect may actually reduce the likelihood of succumbing to misinformation. If a child or adult challenges the credibility of the questioner it is likely that a misinformation effect will not be observed.

Credibility is a factor worthy of attention when considering a recent series of experiments reported by Zaragoza (1991). In these studies she examined young children's (ages 3 to 5) memory for an event, involving a young girl spending a typical day at home, that was presented in a series of color slides. The critical items were the fruit the girl ate and three toys she played with during the day. The event was followed by a summary (presented twice) that contained misleading information about two of the critical details. In each study recognition memory performance did not differ between the control group and the group administered the modified test. The fact that each critical item was prominently displayed in the slides and were usually toys that are particularly important in the life of a preschooler, strongly indicates that the critical information was highly salient for Zaragoza's subjects. It is not surprising, then, that it would be difficult to bias a child's memory about such items. It is likely, similar to a study reported by Loftus (1979), that many children may have viewed one or more of the pieces of misinformation as blatantly false. Loftus demonstrated that subjects who were confronted with blatant postevent information were more adept in resisting suggestions for other critical items than subjects who did not receive a blatant suggestion.

This issue of saliency is relevant to the current discussion for another reason. That is, when children were confronted, especially on *two* occasions, with misleading suggestions about highly salient details they may very well have challenged the credibility of the questioner. This would of course undermine the biasing manipulation. Thus an important social factor, the reverse of what Zaragoza might have expected, may have accounted for her null effects. In a preliminary check on this hypothesis, we have attempted to replicate her findings, using her own script but altering her slides in order to make the target stimuli somewhat less salient (Toglia, Hembrooke, & Ceci, 1990). Although we have yet to finish the complete counterbalancing for this study (this is necessary because we altered Zaragoza's slides in ways that could have produced stimulus and/or order effects), we have some indication that the misinformation effect is present for some stimuli but not for others. Clearly, this is a very tentative report of work in progress, but it does serve to highlight a caveat we made in our original report in 1987, namely that researchers should be careful not to make sweeping generalizations about the existence or nonexistence of age differences in suggestibility because many of the factors that are potentially causative remain unexplored:

> It is clear that not all attempts at postevent suggestion are successful. Specific conditions may tilt the odds either in favor of distortion or against it, and it is the specification of these conditions that is presently lacking. Our own data indicate that very young children's memories *can be* distorted through postevent suggestions, not that they inevitably will be. Our suspicion is that conditions other than those used in these experiments may lead to different outcomes. (Ceci, et al., 1987a, p. 47)

Cognitive Influences on Children's Suggestibility

Social factors are, however, only partly responsible for suggestibility stemming from misleading postevent information. Our work also indicates that memorial factors play a role in vulnerability to suggestion.

In this vein, several other researchers, for example, Goodman and Reed (1986) and King and Yuille (1987), using much different paradigms than ours, adopted, though not exclusively, a cognitive approach to explaining their results. In both studies evidence of age differences in suggestibility was found with the younger groups being quite susceptible to misinformation as shown in the children's answers to questions about an event. However, Zaragoza (1987) did not find evidence of suggestibility in young children. It should be noted that Zaragoza did not report age comparisons, and in light of the Ceci et al. (1987a, Exp. 1) results, her averaging the memory performances of 3- to 6-year-olds may have obscured suggestibility for the youngest subjects (Cole & Loftus, 1987). More recently, Zaragoza (1991) examined 3- and 4-year-olds in the typical eyewitness memory paradigm and again concluded they were not suggestible. She has also noted on several occasions that suggestibility in *reports* may not imply suggestibility in *memory*. Thus, the original memory trace may not be impaired. This distinction is said to be a problem when using the traditional or standard recognition paradigm (e.g., Loftus et al., 1978) that Ceci et al. (1987a) employed in Experiments 1 and 2.

Accordingly, Experiments 3 and 4 conducted by Ceci et al. (1987a) included the modified recognition testing condition, described earlier, which was developed by McCloskey and Zaragoza (1985a). The focus of these experiments was to examine the "cognitive" basis for preschoolers' suggestibility.

McCloskey and Zaragoza (1985a) argued that traditional tests are slanted in favor of demonstrating memory distortion (also see discussion in Loftus et al., this volume). For example, consider a story in which *apples* are mentioned, and some subjects are biased with *bananas*. On a subsequent recognition memory test, for those who do not remember the original information (apples) one would expect control subjects to guess and be correct 50% of the time. However, biased subjects would perform with less than 50% accuracy because the only item that could possibly be familiar to them is the biased information (bananas). Hence, McCloskey and Zaragoza (1985a) designed studies that included an additional biased group (e.g., the original event includes *apples*, but the interviewer/questioner suggests it was *bananas*). Then subjects receive a modified recognition test involving, for example, a choice between *apples* and *grapes*. Therefore, the modified test excludes the biased items as test choices, avoiding the baseline problem above. In a series of six experiments, McCloskey and Zaragoza found no difference between the performance of adult subjects in the control and modified conditions. On the basis of these results, they argued that the presentation of misleading postevent information does not produce memory impairment (such as "erasure") of the original information.

Thus, like the second study in Ceci et al. (1987a), only young children served as subjects, and we continued to use the child interviewer. A new story was used in Experiment 3 and still another story was presented in Experiment 4 in which the stimuli were counterbalanced.

The experimental condition factor continued to be manipulated between subjects.[3]

Counterbalancing had no effect in Experiment 4 and the results were virtually identical to those of Experiment 3 so only the findings of the fourth study will be described here. Performance in the control group (.88) was better than *both* the modified condition (.72) and the standard condition (.46). And the modified group performed reliably better than the standard group. So the modified procedure reduced suggestibility in comparison to the standard condition. However, in sharp contrast to McCloskey and Zaragoza (1985a) and Zaragoza (1987), we found (and replicated in Study 1 and Study 2) that suggestibility was not eliminated by the modified test. This finding is impressive given that it occurred with two *different stories* and with a *child interviewer*—who dilutes the effect. A theoretical position that may explain why our results differ from Zaragoza's, based on memory trace strength, will be elucidated now.

In our previous work (Ceci, et al., 1987a, Exps. 3 & 4) and in the two studies reported in this chapter recognition performance in control conditions reliably exceeded that in the modified groups. These results indicate that memory impairment in some form is implicated in children's susceptibility to misinformation. Of course as Zaragoza (1987, 1991) has shown there are conditions in which apparently memory impairment does not operate. To understand these discrepancies we have argued that it is fruitful to examine the suggestibility of children's memory from the

---

[3] Zaragoza Dahlgren, and Muench (this volume) report a replication of Ceci et al. (1987, Exp. 4). The replication study differs, we believe, in several important ways. As Zaragoza et al. explained, and we agree, they chose to employ an adult rather than a child interviewer because this should enhance the chances of finding a misinformation effect. Thus, it is not who does the biasing that is problematic, but rather that in the replication the *same* adult presented the story, interviewed the child, and administered the test. In our 1987 study (and other studies) three *different* people performed these roles. We have adopted this procedure because of concerns regarding the believability of the interviewer and demand characteristics of the testing environment. When the same person is involved in each phase, a child is given the opportunity to challenge the credibility of the experimenter and/or to be warned about possible misinformation, both of which as described earlier undermine the misinformation manipulation. The fact that Zaragoza's misled-twice group showed no evidence of memory impairment is consistent with our earlier argument concerning reduced credibility with multiple presentations of misleading information. Finally, we think that the within-subjects/between-subjects difference of manipulating the conditions variable is probably critical. We have argued elsewhere (i.e., Toglia, 1991) that when misled subjects serve as their own controls, misinformation may have a "spreading effect" that serves to lower control performance and therefore militates against observing memory impairment. Indeed, as suggested by a metaanalysis of investigations in which the modified recognition test has been employed, Toglia (1991) concluded that it is at moderately high levels of control performance that one is most likely to find evidence of memory impairment.

perspective of a trace-strength model (Ceci et al., 1987b; Ceci, Toglia, & Ross, 1988). Other theorists have also taken this perspective (e.g., Brainerd & Reyna, 1988; Chandler 1989). Below we provide an in-depth treatment of this theoretical position.

Trace strength models hold that the presentation of an event results in a memory trace with an abrupt increase in strength. The strength of a given trace is said to decay over time with a constant forgetting slope (cf. Crowder, 1976). Clearly then, trace strength is not constant and varies with retention interval. It is well known that a variety of other factors affect the durability of memory. These include elaboration of encoding/ level of original learning, number of study trials, interference, and contextual considerations such as those dictated by the encoding specificity hypothesis (see for example Crowder, 1976; Johnson & Hasher, 1987; Kintsch, 1977). Thus, both storage and retrieval factors may promote forgetting. Although clearly not startling, this logic extends to suggestibility experiments. For example, Brainerd and Reyna (1988) proposed a forgetting explanation that assumes that misleading information does degrade memory by either distorting the trace, interfering with retrieval, or both. They also suggested that the degree of degradation is a monotonic function of the current strength of memory for the original event.

In spite of evidence implicating both storage and accessibility mechanisms as responsible for forgetting, memory theorists have tended to favor retrieval accounts of forgetting (see Loftus & Loftus, 1980). The argument is that memory failures are actually retrieval failures that result from impoverished retrieval conditions, caused for example by retroactive interference, changes in context and so forth. As applied to suggestibility studies, retrieval theories posit that the introduction of new (postevent) information does not modify previously stored events; rather the new information is stored in a separate trace. As alluded to earlier, this situation is captured by the "coexistence" hypothesis, which implies that all traces survive, though at different strengths (Howe & Brainerd, 1989). Postevent suggestions may therefore make original memories less accessible, though still potentially retrievable at some time. Recent theories regarding memory have included the idea that all memories are potentially recoverable. The "headed-records" proposal of Morton, Hammersley, and Bekerian (1983) is a case in point.

The view that memory traces are permanent has not, however, gone unchallenged. Long ago Bartlett (1932) claimed that memories were susceptible to distortion when he outlined a reconstructive approach to memory. Modern-day advocates of Bartlett's position have proposed "schema" theories of memory. These models suggest that what is stored in memory is influenced by previous knowledge schemata that choose and actively change experience so as to arrive at a coherent, unified representation of an experience (Alba & Hasher, 1983). Reconstruction, therefore, emphasizes that forgetting results from some kind of alteration in what is stored. As alluded to earlier, alteration characterizes what can be called storage accounts of forgetting, and necessarily implies an actual loss of information from memory.

Evidence of reconstructive changes in memory with adults and children abound as exemplified by studies of semantic integration (Bransford & Franks, 1971; Johnson & Scholnick, 1979), story comprehension (Paris & Upton, 1976; Spiro, 1980), prior knowledge (Ceci, Caves, & Howe, 1981; Dooling & Christiaansen, 1977) and memory blending (Belli, 1988; McClelland & Nystrom, 1988). Alterations in memory may also be reflected by "erasure" (substitution) and/or destructive updating due to new inputs. Most students of memory believe that the processes involved in encoding and storage are dynamic and that new information is integrated with current knowledge structures (e.g., Chi & Ceci, 1987). In this vein, Howe and Brainerd (1989) noted that "because memory is updated by new information and is being restructured to accommodate more sophisticated knowledge, it would be farfetched to claim that traces are immutable" (p. 314). Similarly, with regard to suggestibility, Tversky and Tuchin (1989) presented data in a yes/no recognition paradigm that led them to conclude that it is inappropriate to "claim that nothing happens to the memory of the original event as a consequence of misleading information" (p. 89). Also, in a recent free recall investigation, Howe (1991) examined children's recollections of a scripted story event and concluded "... it is clear that misinformation can affect the originally stored information by altering the contents of the trace itself" (p. 760).

In two experiments Howe had kindergartners and second graders read a story about a birthday party at McDonald's, followed shortly by an unpaced free recall test. Half the subjects continued with study-test trials until they achieved a criterion of two perfect protocols in succession. Following the encoding phase, the children received information (Exp. 1) or were asked a question (Exp. 2) that for half of them was consistent with the birthday episode, and for the other half was inconsistent (misleading) with the episode. After a delay of 2 or 9 days, all subjects received a series of four recall trials. Although age, degree of initial encoding, and retention interval produced predictable main effects, the consistency/inconsistency factor did not influence recall nor did it enter into any interactions of interest. However, analyses based on the trace-integrity model revealed there were some instances in which memory was better if consistent, rather than inconsistent or misleading, information had been presented following acquisition. Importantly, these cases were attributed to storage-based forgetting, which was greater in the particular misled than control conditions.

From the foregoing pages, it should be clear that there are memory impairments of various kinds that may be attributed to storage or retrieval. It is likely, however, that both storage and retrieval factors interact to produce memory failures. Certainly, to the extent that some aspects of memory have been distorted, trace accessibility will be difficult because one is attempting to search for traces that no longer match the originally encoded event. And, retrieval itself may alter the existing contents of storage. Although it may not always be feasible to disentangle storage and retrieval effects (but see Howe, 1991 for an approach that evaluates these effects with the mathematically based trace-integrity model), factors that influence access and storage also modify trace strength. For this reason, it is believed that a trace strength model goes a long way in understanding forgetting phenomena associated with suggestibility. The importance of a trace strength model is clear when one examines the restrictive nature of how McCloskey and Zaragoza (1985a) and later Zaragoza (1987) conceptualized memory impairment hypotheses. They reasoned in studies involving postevent misleading information that memory problems could be the result of three mechanisms. One mechamism is erasure, posited by the "alteration" hypothesis, such that the original memory trace is distorted beyond recognition and, consequently, cannot be retrieved. The other mechanisms that create memorial problems are retrieval difficulty (noted earlier as the "coexistence" hypothesis) and demand characteristics. However, these sources of memory difficulties are not exhaustive, as a variety of other factors that were detailed above, in conjunction with trace strength, may contribute to memory impairment.

As first noted by Ceci et al. (1987b), the failure to acknowledge other mechanisms in explaining the potential negative influence of misleading questions, is critical when one considers the "all-or-none" manner in which McCloskey and Zaragoza conceptualized memory states (McCloskey & Zaragoza, 1985a, p. 4). That is, in using their modified procedure they assumed that memory is either clear and intact (strong trace strength) or it is nonexistent (no trace strength). Implicit in such reasoning is the assumption that postevent suggestions either have no effect on subsequent efforts to retrieve the original memory trace or that any observed effects are the result of demand characteristics. Yet, it is more realistic to conceptualize the recognition memory performance of subjects in suggestibility experiments in terms of a continuous "trace strength" model rather than an "all-or-none" approach, a position recently acknowledged by them (Zaragoza & McCloskey, 1989). According to the former model, subjects may have strong, weak (and likely fragmented), or nonexistent memory traces for an original event as well as strong, weak, or nonexistent traces for the postevent suggestion.

Consider the following examples. If one's memory is equally strong for the original event and the postevent information, this could create a suggestibility effect in the standard (biased) condition because a pair of equally strong traces may compete to create a retrieval decision problem. That is, subjects *may* face the prospect of not being able to discern the trace for the original event, and hence guess between the original and the suggested information with 50% accuracy. If, however, the postevent trace is weaker than the original trace, then the rate of choosing the original trace would be greater than chance. Finally, if the trace for the postevent information is nonexistent and the original trace is strong, then subjects always would be expected to recognize the original item. The same rationale can be applied to other combinations of trace strength for original and postevent information (e.g., weak-strong, weak-weak, etc.).

The first example (both traces are strong) represents a situation in which memory impairment in the form of retrieval difficulty could be operative. That is, young children could experience difficulties on a recognition memory test because the presentation of misleading postevent information diminishes their ability to discriminate between the original episode and the suggested one. As we have seen, a trace strength position argues that accurate recognition depends on both the trace strength of the original stimulus event and the strength of the postevent trace, but also upon the availability of temporal and contextual tags associated with the two events. These latter factors and those that affect trace strength noted earlier, allow for the possibility that misleading information may completely distort an original trace. However, less than total memory impairment can occur if the original event trace is only weakened by misleading postevent information. If a recognition choice is between a weak original trace and a completely new trace (with *no* preexisting postevent strength—as in McCloskey and Zaragoza's (1985a) modified testing condition), then correct selection of the original event is quite likely with performance approximately equal to control conditions in which no postevent suggestion occurred. Under these circumstances one would erroneously conclude there was no memory impairment. It is only with the standard (original) test, when there is choice between a weak original trace and a postevent trace that may be *stronger* than the original trace, that less than complete memory impairment can be assessed. It is assumed in this situation that subjects would frequently incorrectly choose the postevent item.

Thus, memory distortion need not be due to total erasure of the original trace, but only to a weakening of it or to the creation of response competition. When performance in the modified condition was equivalent to that found in the control group and exceeded that found in the standard/biased testing condition, McCloskey and Zaragoza (1985a) argued that the modified procedure was a more sensitive indication of the degree to which postevent suggestions distorted memory for the original stimulus (and that no impairment occurred). As just seen, however, the logic of this argument is not compelling because recognition selections on the standard/biased test are the only ones that allow an examination of two competing memory traces. A postevent trace may be stronger because of its recency, its saliency due to subjects' attention being drawn to it by the experimenter, or because the presentation of the postevent information has weakened the original trace. (Note that in situations where only a weak trace of the original information exists *prior* to the introduction of misleading information, postevent suggestions may serve to further reduce its trace strength [Ceci et al., 1988]).

In the Ceci et al. (1987a) experiments as well as in the two recent studies that we have reported, the misleading information was presented the day after the original event, making it likely that postevent traces were somewhat stronger than their corresponding original traces at the time of testing (three days after the original event).[4] This state of affairs should promote susceptibility to misinformation. In fact, control performance exceeded recognition accuracy in the standard condition in both the prestige versus source monitoring study (.78 vs. .52) and the credibility study (.80 vs. .60). Following the logic of McCloskey and Zaragoza (1985a) one cannot assume that these differences reflect memory impairment. However, because control subjects also outperformed children in the modified groups (.78 vs. .64, and .80 vs. .62), impairment of some form is present. Thus, biased information can even exert a detrimental impact on test decisions between an original event and a similar, though never experienced, event. Such decrements were predicted in a "model" outlined by Ceci et al. (1987b). Then, as now, most trace strength predictions must be treated as "guestimates" because memory performance levels remain largely uncharted for most combinations of strength for original and postevent traces. Thus, although a trace strength interpretation of suggestibility holds considerable promise, its true explanatory "strength" awaits empirical confirmation.

Conclusion

Taken together, the experiments discussed in this chapter clearly demonstrate that both social and memorial factors may be responsible for children succumbing to misleading postevent information. Having said that, we end with some words of caution prompted by the fact that many laymen, attorneys, and even members of the scientific community have woefully misinterpreted the thrust of our work. Perhaps most disturbing is the all-too-frequently drawn conclusion, despite caveats to the contrary, that our findings represent an indictment against children's ability to give reliable testimony. This conclusion is not supported by the data. For example, we have repeatedly found very high (near ceiling) levels of

[4] If, however, as in Zaragoza (1991) misinformation is delayed but the test is administered shortly after its introduction, then one is likely not to observe memory impairment. This is because such a procedure clearly should greatly reduce the likelihood of source misattribution errors (a social factor) as well as influence the degree of trace consolidation for the postevent information (a cognitive factor).

accuracy in control conditions. And a close examination of Experiment 4 in Ceci et al. (1987a) reveals that preschoolers were quite capable of correctly *recalling* information they received during the first experimental session. In fact, young children's free reports typically contain little if any erroneous information (Goodman et al., 1987). Thus we believe that children can provide accurate testimony. The challenge, of course, is to elicit information in ways that are not likely to taint it. A skillful forensic interviewer must guard against suggestive statements and/or questions that might impair memory and attempt to minimize the influence of demand characteristics. If left unbridled, powerful social forces are likely to cause children to report details that are discordant with their underlying recollections.

References

Alba, J.W., & Hasher, L. (1983). Is memory schematic? *Psychological Review*, *93*, 203–231.

Bartlett, F.C. (1932). *Remembering: A study in experimental and social psychology*. Cambridge: University Press.

Belli, R.F. (1988). Color blend retrievals: Compromise memories or deliberate compromise responses? *Memory & Cognition*, *16*, 314–326.

Belli, R.F. (1989). Influence of misleading postevent information: Misinformation interference and acceptance. *Journal of Experimental Psychology: General*, *118*, 72–85.

Binet, A. (1900). *La suggestibilite*. Paris: Schleicher Freres.

Bowers, J.M., & Bekerian, D.A. (1984). When will postevent information distort eyewitness testimony? *Journal of Applied Psychology*, *69*, 466–472.

Brainerd, C.J., & Howe, M.L. (1982). Stages-of-learning analysis of developmental interactions in memory, with illustrations from developmental interactions in picture-word effects. *Developmental Review*, *2*, 251–273.

Brainerd, C.J., & Reyna, V.F. (1988). Memory loci of suggestibility development: Comment on Ceci, Ross, and Toglia (1987). *Journal of Experimental Psychology: General*, *117*, 208–211.

Bransford, J.D., & Franks, J.J. (1971). The abstraction of linguistic ideas. *Cognitive Psychology*, *2*, 331–350.

Brigham, J.C., VanVerst, M., & Bothwell, R.K. (1986). Accuracy of children's eyewitness identifications in a field setting. *Basic and Applied Social Psychology*, *7*, 295–306.

Ceci, S.J., Caves, R., & Howe, M.J.A. (1981). Children's retention of information that is incongruous with their long-term knowledge. *British Journal of Psychology*, *72*, 443–450.

Ceci, S.J., Ross, D.F., & Toglia, M.P. (1987a). Suggestibility of children's memory: Psycholegal implications. *Journal of Experimental Psychology: General*, *116*, 38–49.

Ceci, S.J., Ross, D.F., & Toglia, M.P. (1987b). Age differences in suggestibility: Narrowing the uncertainties. In S.J. Ceci, M.P. Toglia, & D.F. Ross (Eds.), *Children's eyewitness memory* (pp. 79–91). New York: Springer-Verlag.

Ceci, S.J., Toglia, M.P., & Ross, D.F. (1988). On remembering . . . more or less: A trace strength interpretation of developmental differences in suggestibility. *Journal of Experimental Psychology: General*, *117*, 201–203.
Chandler, C.C. (1989). Specific retroactive interference in modified recognition tests: Evidence for an unknown cause of interference. *Journal of Experimental Psychology: Learning, Memory, and Cognition*, *11*, 467–475.
Chi, M.T.H., & Ceci, S.J. (1987). Content knowledge and the reorganization of memory. *Advances in Child Development and Behavior*, *20*, 1–37.
Christiaansen, R.E., & Ochalek, K. (1983). Editing misleading information from memory: Evidence for the coexistence of original and postevent information. *Memory & Cognition*, *11*, 467–475.
Cohen, R.L., & Harnick, M.A. (1980). The susceptibility of child witnesses to suggestion. *Law and Human Behavior*, *4*, 201–210.
Cole, C.B., & Loftus, E.F. (1987). The memory of children. In S.J. Ceci, M.P. Toglia, & D.F. Ross (Eds.), *Children's eyewitness memory* (pp. 178–208). New York: Springer-Verlag.
Crowder, R.G. (1976). *Principles of learning and memory*. Hillsdale, NJ: Erlbaum.
Dale, P. S., Loftus, E.F., & Rathbun, L. (1978). The influence of the form of the question on the eyewitness testimony of preschool children. *Journal of Psycholinguistic Research*, *7*, 269–277.
Dodd, D.H., & Bradshaw, J.M. (1980). Leading questions and memory: Pragmatic constraints. *Journal of Verbal Learning and Verbal Behavior*, *19*, 695–704.
Dooling, D.J., & Christiaansen, R.E. (1977). Levels of encoding and retention of prose. In G.H. Bower (Ed.), *The psychology of learning and motivation* (Vol. 11). New York: Academic Press.
Duncan, E.M., Whitney, P., & Kunen, S. (1982). Integration of visual and verbal information in children's memory. *Child Development*, *53*, 1215–1223.
Goodman, G. (1984). Children's testimony in historical perspective. *Journal of Social Issues*, *40*(2), 9–32.
Goodman, G.S., Aman, C., & Hirschman, J. (1987). Child sexual and physical abuse: Children's testimony. In S.J. Ceci, M.P. Toglia, & D.F. Ross (Eds.), *Children's eyewitness memory* (pp. 1–23). New York: Springer-Verlag.
Goodman, G.S., & Reed, R.S. (1986). Age differences in eyewitness testimony. *Law and Human Behavior*, *10*, 317–332.
Greene, E., Flynn, M.S., & Loftus, E.F. (1982). Inducing resistance to misleading information. *Journal of Verbal Learning and Verbal Behavior*, *21*, 207–219.
Hall, D.F., Loftus, E.F., & Tousignant, J.P. (1984). Postevent information and changes in recollection for a natural event. In G.L. Wells & E.F. Loftus (Eds.), *Eyewitness testimony: Psychological perspectives* (pp. 124–141). New York: Cambridge University Press.
Hovland, C.I., Janis, I.L., & Kelley, H.H. (1953). *Communication and persuasion*. New Haven, CT: Yale University Press.
Hovland, C.I., & Weiss, W. (1951). The influence of source credibility on communication effectiveness. *Public Opinion Quarterly*, *51*, 635–650.
Howe, M.L. (1991). Misleading children's story recall: Forgetting and reminiscence of the facts. *Developmental Psychology*, *27*, 746–762.

Howe, M.L., & Brainerd, C.J. (1989). Development of children's long-term retention. *Developmental Review*, *9*, 301–340.

Hughes, M., & Grieve, R. (1980). On asking children bizarre questions. In M. Donaldson, R. Grieve, & C. Pratt (Eds.), *Early childhood development and education*. Oxford: Basil Blackwell.

Johnson, J.W., & Scholnick, E.K. (1979). Does cognitive development predict semantic integration? *Child Development*, *50*, 73–78.

Johnson, M.J., & Hasher, L. (1987). Human learning and memory. *Annual Review of Psychology*, *38*, 631–668.

King, M., & Yuille, J.C. (1987). Suggestibility and the child witness. In S.J. Ceci, M.P. Toglia, & D.F. Ross (Eds.), *Children's eyewitness memory* (pp. 24–35). New York: Springer-Verlag.

Kintsch, W. (1977). *Memory and cognition*. New York: Wiley.

Lindsay, D.S., & Johnson, M.K. (1987). Reality monitoring and suggestibility: Children's ability to discriminate among memories from different sources. In S.J. Ceci, M.P. Toglia, & D.F. Ross (Eds.), *Children's eyewitness memory* (pp. 92–121). New York: Springer-Verlag.

Lindsay, D.S., & Johnson, M.K. (1989). The eyewitness suggestibility effect and memory for source. *Memory & Cognition*, *17*, 349–357.

Loftus, E.F. (1975). Leading questions and the eyewitness report. *Cognitive Psychology*, *7*, 560–572.

Loftus, E.F. (1979). *Eyewitness testimony*. Cambridge, MA: Harvard University Press.

Loftus, E.F., & Davies, G.M. (1984). Distortions in the memory of children. *Journal of Social Issues*, *40*, 51–67.

Loftus, E.F., & Loftus, G.R. (1980). On the permanence of stored information in the human brain. *American Psychologist*, *35*, 409–420.

Loftus, E.F., Miller, D.G., & Burns, H.J. (1978). Semantic integration of verbal information into a visual memory. *Journal of Experimental Psychology: Human Learning and Memory*, *4*, 19–31.

Loftus, E.F., Schooler, J., & Wagenaar, W. (1985). The fate of memory: Comment on McCloskey and Zaragoza. *Journal of Experimental Psychology: General*, *114*, 375–380.

Marin, B.V., Holmes, D.L., Guth, M., & Kovac, P. (1979). The potential of children as eyewitnesses. *Law and Human Behavior*, *3*, 295–306.

Marple, C.H. (1933). Comparative susceptibility of three age levels to suggestion. *Journal of Social Psychology*, *4*, 176–184.

McClelland, J.L., & Nystrom, L.E. (1988, November). *Trace synthesis in memory: Blend errors in cued recall*. Paper presented at the meeting of the Psychonomic Society, Chicago, IL.

McCloskey, M., & Zaragoza, M. (1985a). Misleading postevent information and memory for events: Arguments and evidence against memory impairment hypotheses. *Journal of Experimental Psychology: General*, *114*, 1–16.

McCloskey, M., & Zaragoza, M. (1985b). Postevent information and memory: Reply to Loftus, Schooler, and Wagenaar. *Journal of Experimental Psychology: General*, *114*, 381–387.

Morton, J., Hammersley, R., & Bekerian, D.A. (1983). *Headed records: Framework for remembering and its failures*. Unpublished manuscript, M.R.C. Applied Psychology Unit, Cambridge, England.

Paris, S.G., & Upton, L. (1976). Children's memory for inferential comprehension. *Child Development*, *47*, 660–668.

Pear, T., & Wyatt, S. (1914). The testimony of normal and mentally defective children. *British Journal of Psychology*, *3*, 388–419.

Raskin, D.C., & Yuille, J.C. (1989). Problems in evaluating interviews of children in sexual abuse cases. In S.J. Ceci, D.F. Ross, & M.P. Toglia (Eds.), *Perspectives on children's testimony* (pp. 184–207). New York: Springer-Verlag.

Saywitz, K. J. (1987). Children's testimony: Age related patterns of memory errors. In S.J. Ceci, M.P. Toglia, & D.F. Ross (Eds.), *Children's eyewitness memory* (pp. 36–52). New York: Springer-Verlag.

Saywitz, K. J. (1989). Children's conception of the legal system: "Court is a place to play basketball." In S.J. Ceci, D.F. Ross, & M.P. Toglia (Eds.), *Perspectives on children's testimony* (pp. 131–157). New York: Springer-Verlag.

Smith, V.C., & Ellsworth, P. C. (1987). The social psychology of eyewitness accuracy: Misleading questions and communicator expertise. *Journal of Applied Psychology*, *72*, 294–300.

Spiro, R.J. (1980). Accommodative reconstruction in prose recall. *Journal of Verbal Learning and Verbal Behavior*, *19*, 84–95.

Stern, W. (1910). Abstracts of lectures on the psychology of testimony and on the study of individuality. *American Journal of Psychology*, *21*, 270–282.

Toglia, M.P. (1991). Memory impairment: It is more common than you think. In J. Doris (Ed.), *The suggestibility of children's recollections: Implications for eyewitness testimony* (pp. 40–46). Washington, DC: American Psychological Association.

Toglia, M.P., Ceci, S.J., & Ross, D.F. (1988, November). *The prestige effect in children's susceptibility to suggestion*. Paper presented at the meeting of the Psychonomic Society, Chicago, IL.

Toglia, M.P., Hembrooke, H., & Ceci, S.J. (1990). [Evaluating failures to find memory impairment in children's eyewitness recollections: A replication.] Unpublished raw data.

Tversky, B., & Tuchin, M. (1989). A reconciliation of the evidence on eyewitness testimony: Comments on McCloskey and Zaragoza. *Journal of Experimental Psychology: General*, *118*, 86–91.

Varendonck, J. (1911). Les temoignages d'enfants dans un proces retentissant. *Archives de Psychologie*, *11*, 129–171.

Ward, C.D., & McGuinnes, E. (1974). Persuasive effects of early and late mention of credible and noncredible sources. *Journal of Psychology*, *86*, 17–23.

Weinberg, H., Wadsworth, J., & Baron, R. (1983). Demand and the impact of leading questions on eyewitness testimony. *Memory & Cognition*, *11*, 101–104.

Whipple, G.M. (1909). The observer as reporter: A survey of the psychology of testimony. *Psychological Bulletin*, *6*, 153–170.

Whipple, G.M. (1911). The psychology of testimony. *Psychological Bulletin*, *8*, 307–309.

Whipple, G.M. (1912). Psychology of testimony and report. *Psychological Bulletin*, *9*, 264–269.

Yarmey, A.D. (1984). Age as a factor in eyewitness memory. In G.L. Wells & E.F. Loftus (Eds.), *Eyewitness testimony: Psychological perspectives* (pp. 142–154). New York: Cambridge University Press.

Zaragoza, M.S. (1987). Memory, suggestibility and eyewitness testimony in children and adults. In S.J. Ceci, M.P. Toglia, & D.F. Ross (Eds.), *Children's eyewitness memory* (pp. 53–78). New York: Springer-Verlag.

Zaragoza, M.S. (1991). Preschool children's susceptibility to memory impairment. In J. Doris (Ed.), *The suggestibility of children's recollections: Implications for eyewitness testimony* (pp. 27–39). Washington, DC: American Psychological Association.

Zaragoza, M.S., & McCloskey, M. (1989). Misleading postevent information and the memory impairment hypothesis: Comment on Belli and reply to Tversky and Tuchin. *Journal of Experimental Psychology: General*, *118*, 92–99.

Zaragoza, M.S., McCloskey, M., & Jamis, M. (1987). Misleading postevent information and recall of the original event: Further evidence against the memory impairment hypothesis. *Journal of Experimental Psychology: Learning, Memory & Cognition*, *13*, 36–44.

Part III
Current Issues and Future Directions

8
Toward a Theory of the Development of Long-Term Retention

MARK L. HOWE, JULIA T. O'SULLIVAN, and TAMMY A. MARCHE

Around the beginning of this century, a time that loosely marks the dawn of scientific inquiry into child development, the factors that controlled forgetting and reminiscence from infants' and children's long-term memory were a source of considerable debate (see discussions in Ballard, 1913; Freud, 1914/1938; Vertes, 1931/1932). Historically, speculation concerning the ontogenesis of long-term retention has ranged from hypotheses in which forgetting was said to increase with age (e.g., critical periods in early experience that were deemed essential to development and, hence, were believed to be preferentially preserved [Bowlby, 1960; Tinbergen, 1951]) to those in which forgetting was said to decrease with age (e.g., Ballard, 1913; Vertes, 1931/1932). A similar range of hypotheses has been entertained concerning the locus of forgetting, extending from pure retrieval positions in which, barring head trauma, information was thought to remain forever intact in storage, simply fluctuating in accessibility (e.g., Freud, 1914/1938; Hoffding, 1891) to positions in which changes occur in the information that was stored (e.g., Kohler, 1929, 1941; Wulf, 1922).

Given the historical preeminence of studying the ontogenesis of long-term retention, it is curious that with only a handful of exceptions (see Howe & Brainerd, 1989), the developmental analysis of memory has been confined to processes involved in the initial acquisition of information. This modern-day anachronism is reflected in contemporary undergraduate (e.g., Bjorklund, 1989) and graduate (e.g., Schneider & Pressley, 1989) textbooks on memory development, neither of which contain discussions of research on children's long-term retention. Perhaps interest has waned because age trends in retention have been notoriously difficult to produce in memory laboratories (e.g., see studies by Fajnsztejn-Pollack, 1973; Hasher & Thomas, 1973; Lehman, Mikesell, & Doherty, 1985; Merriman, Azmita, & Perlmutter, 1988). Only recently, under rigorous measurement and methodological circumstances, have age differences in retention been uncovered (e.g., Brainerd, Kingma, & Howe, 1985; Brainerd, Reyna, Howe, & Kingma, 1990; Howe, 1987,

1991). More than a "rediscovery" of ontogenetic trends in retention, a number of recent findings illustrate that developmental differences in forgetting and reminiscence obey different rules than those that govern acquisition. Because age trends at retention are not simply mirror images of age trends in acquisition, it is time to rekindle our commitment to the study of the ontogenesis of forgetting and reminiscence.

More importantly, the issues of whether forgetting increases or decreases with age, and whether changes in retention occur because of alterations in the retrieval of permanently stored information, changes in the nature of stored information, or both, which led to such a vibrant debate at the beginning of this century, still need to be resolved. Perhaps this need is even more pressing today in light of the very real problems involved in evaluating age trends in the reliability of children's eyewitness memory and testimony. Given the growing number of reported cases of physical and sexual abuse of children (e.g., Archdiocesan Commission, 1990; Roarke, 1990; Russell, 1983; Yuille, 1988), there is a concomitant need to apprise the legal community as to the nature of children's memory. Theoretically, because acquisition development is at most half of the memory development picture, it is imperative that we resuscitate interest in the retention half of the memory development picture.

The chapters in this volume represent a major step forward in that direction, with each of the authors addressing key issues critical to the elucidation of a complete theory of long-term retention and its development. In what follows, we draw together the various perspectives presented and attempt to provide modern-day answers to the questions that have sparked vigorous debate since the beginning of this century. In particular, we focus our discussion on what is now known about the direction of forgetting and reminiscence development and on the contributions of storage and retrieval factors to these age trends. In a subsequent section, we confront questions concerning the reliability of children's long-term retention, a problem that has an equally long and hoary tradition in the historical annals of children's memory development (e.g., see Ceci, Ross, & Toglia, 1987).

Although considerable progress has been made toward solving each of these problems outlined above (as witnessed by the contributions to this volume), research tends to beget as many questions as it answers. In the final section of this chapter we outline a number of those questions that remain to be answered, ones that we hope will serve as the focus of future research efforts. Although such an agenda is only a beginning, if implemented, sufficient information may be garnered so that a more comprehensive theory of children's retention, and, thus, children's memory development, will be forthcoming.

Age Trends in Forgetting and Reminiscence

As mentioned at the outset of this chapter, two classes of speculation existed earlier this century concerning the direction of age trends in forgetting and reminiscence. We discuss forgetting first. On the one hand, early experiences were said to be primary, serving to "fix" the foundation of psychological development (e.g., Freud, 1914/1938; Tinbergen, 1951). Although conscious recollection of such experiences was not a requisite for their existence (e.g., as witnessed in Freud's notion of motivated forgetting or repression of painful experiences), memories of early experiences were said to exert their influence on behavior throughout a lifetime (e.g., the redoubtable "Freudian slips"). As these early experiences were said to be preferentially preserved relative to later experiences, the logical inference is that forgetting rates should accelerate as development proceeds. On the other hand, given the familiar tenet that forgetting varies inversely with the amount or speed of initial learning (e.g., Underwood, 1954, 1964), rate of forgetting should decelerate with age because older children learn almost any information more completely and faster than younger children. Consistent with this prediction, Vertes (1931/1932) found that older children tended to forget less than younger children following a 24-hr retention interval.

Next, consider reminiscence. In perhaps the first study of its type, Ballard (1913) found that, contrary to what intuition might dictate, younger children exhibited greater reminiscence than older children. Contrariwise, Vertes (1931/1932) found that older children's reminiscence exceeded that of younger children's, although, like Ballard's (1913) study, all children evidenced reminiscence. Unfortunately, however, a number of problems existed with both of these studies (see Ammons & Irion, 1954), with attempts to replicate even the simplest finding of reminiscence in children usually failing (see review in Howe & Brainerd, 1989).

The evidence from this volume is consistent with the idea that *forgetting decreases with age* and that there are *few age trends in reminiscence*. For example, Rovee-Collier and Shyi (this volume) demonstrated that younger infants (e.g., 3-month-olds) retained less information than older infants (e.g., 6-month-olds) over a constant retention interval. In addition, regardless of age, reactivation reinstates performance to levels akin to those found at the end of acquisition. Reactivation is associated with age inasmuch as the amount of reactivation is correlated with trace content (i.e., what remains of the originally encoded event at the time of reactivation) which, in turn, is correlated with time since acquisition (or last reactivation), which, in turn, is correlated with age. However, this is clearly a by-product of age trends in forgetting rates, not reactivation rates. Although other variables associated with reactivation may be correlated with age (e.g., the nature of the reactivation cues varies with age), the fact remains that trace reinstatement per se is an age-invariant characteristic of long-term retention.

Similarly, Howe, Kelland, Bryant-Brown, and Clark (this volume), using a mathematical model to separate forgetting and reminiscence, found that although forgetting rates decreased with age (from grade 2 to college), age trends were negligible in reminiscence. Although subjects did reminisce across trials, age differences were largely confined to forgetting processes. These findings are consistent with other recent studies (e.g., Brainerd et al., 1990; Howe, 1991).

It would appear, then, that whereas forgetting tends to decrease with development, there are few developmental changes in rates of reminiscence. Although it is clear that considerably more research is required in order to understand the conditions that lead to ontogenetic changes in forgetting rates, it is equally imperative that we examine conditions that confer immunity to forgetting and that serve to reinstate traces in memory. Although the nature of the features or cues that help to trigger trace reinstatement may change with age (or with correlates of age such as knowledge), the fact is that simply reencountering cues in the environment serves to inoculate memory against forgetting at all ages. Whether such reinstatement occurs as a function of externally provided cues (as in cued recall [Howe et al., this volume] and reactivation [Rovee-Collier & Shyi, this volume]) or internally generated cues (e.g., as in free recall [Brainerd et al., 1990; Howe, 1991]), the memory-preserving characteristics of this phenomenon are both powerful and incontrovertible. Although reinstatement and reminiscence figure prominently in recent theories of children's long-term retention (e.g., Howe & Brainerd, 1989; Reyna, this volume), more work, like the programmatic studies by Rovee-Collier and her associates (Rovee-Collier & Shyi, this volume), is needed with children of all ages in order to map the domain of variables affecting this trace-preserving function. In particular, because there is some evidence that reminiscence plays an important role in children's eyewitness recollections (Dent & Stevenson, 1979), knowledge of those variables affecting trace reinstatement would be invaluable in assessing the reliability of ostensibly reminisced eyewitness memories.

Contributions of Storage and Retrieval Factors to Long-Term Retention Development

Throughout the history of research on long-term retention, the question of whether long-term memory is a permanent storehouse of information, one where knowledge is immutably deposited, has remained an enigma. On the one side, there are those who believe that memory is an unalterable reservoir of originally encoded information and that forgetting represents a problem with retrieval (e.g., Freud, 1914/1938). In contrast to this *retrieval-failure hypothesis* stands the *storage-failure hypothesis* in which long-term memory is viewed as dynamic rather than static, with forgetting of originally encoded information being possible through modifications of information in storage (e.g., Kohler, 1929, 1941). (For a more detailed treatise, see Brainerd et al., 1990; Howe & Brainerd, 1989.)

In the modern day, many have taken the position that forgetting is more a matter of trace accessibility than trace availability. For example, Loftus and Loftus (1980) reported that 84% of respondents to a survey on forgetting (laypersons and those who had taken psychology courses) believed that the retrieval-failure explanation of forgetting was correct. Recently, however, the trace accessibility versus trace availability debate has resurfaced in both the memory development literature (e.g., Howe & Brainerd, 1989; Howe et al., this volume; Rovee-Collier & Shyi, this volume) and in the context of eyewitness memory (e.g., Loftus, 1983; Loftus, Hoffman, & Wagenaar, this volume). Indeed, the renewal of interest in this storage-retrieval debate is amply represented in the chapters of the present volume. In fact, many of the authors have confronted the complexity of these issues directly, acknowledging that forgetting (as well as reminiscence) can originate in changes in stored information, changes in the retrievability of information, or both. Indeed, the positions espoused by the authors in this volume reflect the growing recognition that long-term memory is a dynamic medium, one that is the product of a conspiracy between storage and retrieval processes. Given the overwhelming acceptance of this interactive stance today, perhaps the proper question no longer concerns the locus of forgetting and reminiscence, for the answer is that it lies both in storage and retrieval. Rather, the question should be under which circumstance(s) does one type of alteration (storage or retrieval) dominate the other in changes in long-term retention performance and to what extent are such alterations reversible?

Equally important is the need to chart the nature of storage and retrieval modifications in memory. Although there is not space to elaborate here, two points need to be emphasized. First, as it turns out, there are many instances in which what was thought to be a pure retrieval effect at retention was, in fact, produced by changes in storage (see Howe & Brainerd, 1989). For example, if items from a categorized list cannot be freely recalled, but can be subsequently remembered when a category cue is presented, this is interpreted as evidence that initial forgetting was a pure retrieval phenomenon. However, this conclusion is *not* ineluctable as it is equally probable that the presentation of the category cue served to reinstate traces (a change in storage) through processes such as redintegration (e.g., Horowitz & Prytulak, 1969). This brings us to the second and related point, which is that because alterations in memory reflect the conjoint influence of changes in storage and retrieval, it is counterproductive to insist on a strong dichotomy between these components of long-term retention. More likely, these represent extreme points at different ends of a single continuum such as memory strength or featural integrity (e.g., see Howe et al., this volume; Reyna, this volume; Rovee-Collier & Shyi, this volume).

Reliability of Children's Long-Term Retention

All of the issues raised so far in this chapter are being similarly debated with equal vigor in the psycholegal literature. The primary question here concerns the reliability of children's long-term recollections, especially when it comes to testifying about events they have witnessed. Several specific issues have arisen in this forum, ones that focus on the nature of the questioner, the type of question being asked, and the potential influence of misinformation on the accuracy of children's remembrances. Clearly, what is recovered from children's memory depends in large measure on who does the questioning (Toglia, Ross, Ceci, & Hembrooke, this volume) as well as on how the question is framed (Ornstein, Gordon, & Baker-Ward, this volume). What is most striking is that in most studies (presented here and elsewhere), young children's recollections of personally experienced events are remarkably accurate (in particular, see Ornstein et al., this volume).

Although children's retention of these events can be very reliable, the question that still haunts us is whether they can be made fallible by the presence of misinformation. Specifically, does misinformation actually impair memory (i.e., alter the original memory trace in storage) or simply coexist as a separate trace that may or may not impede retrieval (depending on a number of factors including the test situation, the nature of the cues/questions, and questioner) of the original information? Although this issue has not been resolved, both sides are well represented in this volume. For example, although preschool children may report misleading information when tested on their memory for an event, this does not necessarily imply that their memories of the original experience are actually altered (Zaragoza, Dahlgren, & Muench, this volume). Indeed, the reporting of misinformation may be an artifact of social pressures rather than a reflection of changes in memory per se (Zaragoza et al., this volume).

Although there is no doubt that social pressures influence what children report in their long-term recollections, there are indications that children's memories are potentially alterable (Loftus et al., this volume; Toglia et al., this volume). Unfortunately, the nature of these alterations, as well as their extent, is still a matter of debate (e.g., see Howe, 1991). However, because there is no reason to suspect that the long-term retention of memories of events behave in a substantially different manner than other long-term memories, it is probable that both storage and retrieval factors contribute to eyewitness memory reports as they do to other long-term recollections. What is required is a litmus test that differentiates those circumstances in which the memory itself has been discernibly altered from those in which misinformation merely coexists with the original event. Clearly, the chapters in this volume have helped considerably in that search.

An Agenda for Research on Children's Long-Term Retention

The overview of research on the development of children's long-term retention presented here reflects an optimistic picture of children's ability to remember a variety of types of information over rather extended intervals. Indeed, in aggregate, the knowledge base fashioned from the chapters in this volume reveals a number of general properties of children's long-term retention skills: (a) forgetting rates tend to decline with age; (b) regardless of age, memory traces can be reinstated (reactivated); (c) reminiscence rates tend to be developmentally constant; and (d) forgetting, reinstatement, and reactivation all result from a harmony of changes in both storage and retrieval processes. In addition, we have amassed considerable knowledge about children's retention of everyday events and the potential interfering influence of misleading information. Although the nature of misinformation effects may still represent a somewhat contentious issue, it is clear that children's memories are neither as indelible nor as malleable as previously portrayed.

Although we have provided answers to a number of the questions initially posed at the beginning of this century, and have achieved considerable theoretical progress (e.g., the trace-integrity [Howe et al., this volume] and fuzzy-trace [Reyna, this volume] proposals), there remain a number of issues that need to be resolved prior to assembling a complete theory of children's long-term memory. As we cannot possibly cover all of the topics that need programmatic research in one chapter, we focus on what we believe to be three core issues, namely, the dual nature of reinstatement effects, the development of the relationship between memory strength and interference/misinformation effects, and the development and influence of children's knowledge of retention processes on forgetting and reminiscence. As mentioned earlier, because memory represents a dynamic synthesis of storage and retrieval, it is critical that all future efforts to understand long-term retention and its development ensure that the relative contribution of each of these processes to forgetting and reminiscence is measured precisely (also see Howe et al., this volume).

First, further research is needed to explore the boundary conditions of reinstatement effects in children of all ages. If we let the term *reinstatement* stand for any circumstance in which some aspect of the originally presented context or material is re-presented, then understanding age trends in reinstatement is paramount to any theory of retention that seeks to explain interference, redintegration, and reminiscence effects in memory. Indeed, in traditional laboratory studies, different reinstatement conditions can lead to either positive (e.g., reactivation [Rovee-Collier & Shyi, this volume] and reminiscence [Howe et al., this volume]) or negative (e.g., interference [Koppenaal, Krull, & Katz, 1964)] effects on the memory trace (also see Howe, Courage, & Bryant-Brown, 1991). Importantly, similar effects have been observed in studies of children's memory for everyday events. For example, both memory improvements (e.g., Dent & Stevenson, 1979) and decrements (e.g., Loftus et al., this volume; Toglia et al., this volume) have been observed in children's eyewitness memory. Although it appears that reinstatement and reminiscence are developmentally invariant characteristics of children's retention, it is not clear whether age trends exist in conditions that affect the presence and strength of these effects in memory. It is apparent, however, that regardless of whether one is interested in laboratory or everyday memory paradigms, it is imperative that we map developmental changes in those conditions where reinstatement leads to enhanced, as opposed to diminished, levels of retention.

Second, considerable work is needed to sketch the role of memory strength in long-term retention, particularly in terms of its memory-preserving properties. Specifically, are better encoded (stronger) traces more resistant to memory distortions due to postevent suggestion than more poorly encoded (weaker) traces? To answer this question, however, it is necessary to provide a more precise characterization of the nature of trace composition. Although most authors agree that traces are probably comprised of features, or some featural analogue, it must be clear which properties of featural cohesion are critical to trace survival (for discussions on this topic, see Howe et al., this volume; Reyna, this volume). It is only when measures of trace durability are in place that we may begin to properly understand those conditions that make traces immune to forgetting or mutation and those that effectively promote changes in trace structure or content (also see Howe, 1991). Knowledge of the developmental course of such factors will be critical when articulating the nature of changes in children's susceptibility to the memory-impairing effects of postevent information.

Finally, a third area, one that has received little attention to date, concerns children's theories of forgetting (or "metaforgetting"). Although a considerable amount is known about children's metamemory and the role it plays in memory development (e.g., see Howe & O'Sullivan, 1990), it should not be assumed that metaforgetting is simply the opposite side of the metamemorial coin. Some preliminary studies in this area have provided evidence that children do understand some properties of long-term retention and forgetting (e.g., Howe, O'Sullivan, & Marche, 1991; Wellman & Johnson, 1979) and have some conscious control over some aspects of forgetting (see Lehman & Bovasso, in press). Clearly, however, more information on what children know about potential sources of interference in memory (e.g., postevent suggestions and misleading information), including what they believe can be done to forestall or prevent forgetting, will be important in understanding how children try to maintain information in long-term memory.

As already noted, there are a number of other important aspects of the development of children's long-term retention that deserve to be the focus of programmatic research efforts. What we hope is that this volume has awakened sufficient interest in these problems that efforts in this direction will continue to expand. The chapters that comprise this volume attest to the considerable progress that has already been made, especially recently, in our understanding of children's long-term retention. More importantly, each of these chapters provides a rich theoretical and empirical base from which subsequent investigations can arise. Given the tremendous growth of research and theory in this area, we expect that it should not be long until a more complete theory of the development of long-term memory, one that incorporates the processes involved in the development of children's long-term retention, will be forthcoming.

Acknowledgments. Preparation of this chapter was supported by grants OGP0003334 to Mark L. Howe and OGP0046514 to Julia T. O'Sullivan from the Natural Sciences and Engineering Research Council of Canada.

References

Ammons, H., & Irion, A.L. (1954). A note on the Ballard reminiscence phenomenon. *Journal of Experimental Psychology*, *48*, 184–186.

Archdiocesan Commission (1990). *The report of the archdiocesan commission of enquiry into the sexual abuse of children by members of the clergy*. St. John's, Newfoundland, Canada: Archdiocese of St. John's.

Ballard, P.B. (1913). Obliviscence and reminiscence. *British Journal of Psychology Monograph Supplements*, *1*, 1–82.

Bjorklund, D.F. (1989). *Children's thinking: Developmental function and individual differences*. Pacific Grove, CA: Brooks/Cole.

Bowlby, J. (1960). Grief and mourning in infancy and early childhood. *Psychoanalytic Study of the Child*, *15*, 9–52.

Brainerd, C.J., Kingma, J., & Howe, M.L. (1985). On the development of forgetting. *Child Development*, *56*, 1103–1119.

Brainerd, C.J., Reyna, V.F., Howe, M.L., & Kingma, J. (1990). The development of forgetting and reminiscence. *Monographs of the Society for Research in Child Development*, *55*(3–4, Serial No. 222).

Ceci, S.J., Ross, D.F., & Toglia, M.P. (1987). Suggestibility in children's memory: Psycholegal implications. *Journal of Experimental Psychology: General, 116*, 38–49.

Dent, H.R., & Stevenson, G.M. (1979). An experimental study of the effectiveness of different techniques of questioning child witnesses. *British Journal of Social and Clinical Psychology, 18*, 41–51.

Fajnsztejn-Pollack, G. (1973). A developmental study of decay rate in long-term memory. *Journal of Experimental Child Psychology, 16*, 225–235.

Freud, S. (1914/1938). *The psychopathology of everyday life*. In A.A. Brill (Ed.), *The writings of Sigmund Freud*. New York: Modern Library. (Original work published 1914.)

Hasher, L., & Thomas, H. (1973). A developmental study of retention. *Developmental Psychology, 9*, 281.

Hoffding, H. (1891). *Outlines of psychology*. New York: Macmillan.

Horowitz, L.M., & Prytulak, L.S. (1969). Redintegrative memory. *Psychological Review, 76*, 519–531.

Howe, M.L. (1987). *The development of forgetting in childhood*. Paper presented at the biennial meeting of the Society for Research in Child Development, Baltimore, MD.

Howe, M.L. (1991). Misleading children's story recall: Forgetting and reminiscence of the facts. *Developmental Psychology, 27*, 746–762.

Howe, M.L., & Brainerd, C.J. (1989). Development of children's long-term retention. *Developmental Review, 9*, 301–340.

Howe, M.L., Courage, M.L., & Bryant-Brown, L. (1991). *Reinstating preschoolers' memories*. Manuscript submitted for publication.

Howe, M.L., & O'Sullivan, J.T. (1990). The development of strategic memory: Coordinating knowledge, metamemory, and resources. In D.F. Bjorklund (Ed.), *Children's strategies: Contemporary views of cognitive development* (pp. 129–155). Hillsdale, NJ: Erlbaum.

Howe, M.L., O'Sullivan, J.T., & Marche, T. (1991). *The development of children's understanding of forgetting*. Manuscript submitted for publication.

Kohler, W. (1929). *Gestalt psychology*. New York: Liveright.

Kohler, W. (1941). On the nature of associations. *Proceedings of the American Philosophical Society, 84*, 489–502.

Koppenaal, R.J., Krull, A., & Katz, H. (1964). Age, interference, and forgetting. *Journal of Experimental Child Psychology, 1*, 360–375.

Lehman, E., & Bovasso, M. (in press). Development of intentional forgetting in children. In M.L. Howe & R. Pasnak (Eds.), *Emerging themes in cognitive development. Vol. I: Foundations*. New York: Springer-Verlag.

Lehman, E., Mikesell, J.W., & Doherty, S.C. (1985). Long-term retention of information about presentation modality by children and adults. *Memory & Cognition, 13*, 21–28.

Loftus, E.F. (1983). Misfortunes of memory. *Philosophical Transactions of the Royal Society of London, B302*, 413–421.

Loftus, E.F., & Loftus, G.R. (1980). On the permanence of stored information in the human brain. *American Psychologist, 35*, 409–420.

Merriman, W.E., Azmita, M., & Perlmutter, M. (1988). Rate of forgetting in early childhood. *International Journal of Behavioral Development, 11*, 467–474.

Roarke, A.C. (1990, January 25). Experts fault McMartin child interview methods. *Los Angeles Times*, pp. A1, A26.

Russell, D.E.H. (1983). The incidence and prevalence of intrafamilial and extrafamilial sexual abuse of female children. *Child Abuse and Neglect*, *7*, 133–146.

Schneider, W., & Pressley, M. (1989). *Memory development from 2 to 20*. New York: Springer-Verlag.

Tinbergen, N. (1951). *The study of instinct*. London: Oxford University Press.

Underwood, B.J. (1954). Speed of learning and amount retained: A consideration of methodology. *Psychological Bulletin*, *51*, 276–282.

Underwood, B.J. (1964). Degree of learning and the measurement of forgetting. *Journal of Verbal Learning and Verbal Behavior*, *3*, 112–129.

Vertes, J.O. (1931/1932). Behalten und vergessen des kindes [Retention and forgetting in the child]. *Zeitschrift fur Psychologie*, *122*, 241–354. (*Psychological Abstracts*, 1932, *1221*, 145.)

Wellman, H.M., & Johnson, C.N. (1979). Understanding of mental processes: A developmental study of "remember" and "forget." *Child Development*, *50*, 79–88.

Wulf, F. (1922). Uber die veranderung von vorstellungen. *Psychologisch Forschung*, *1*, 333–373.

Yuille, J.C. (1988). The systematic assessment of children's testimony. *Canadian Psychology*, *29*, 247–262.

Author Index

(Italicized entries refer to reference list citations)

Subject Index

MIX
Papier aus verantwortungsvollen Quellen
Paper from responsible sources
FSC® C105338

If you have any concerns about our products,
you can contact us on
ProductSafety@springernature.com

In case Publisher is established outside the EU,
the EU authorized representative is:
Springer Nature Customer Service Center GmbH
Europaplatz 3, 69115 Heidelberg, Germany

Printed by Libri Plureos GmbH
in Hamburg, Germany

Development of Long-Term Retention